## Also by David Pierce

*Attitudes to Class in the English Novel* (with Mary Eagleton) (London: Thames and Hudson, 1979).

*W. B. Yeats: A Guide Through the Critical Maze* (Bristol: Bristol Classical Press, 1989).

*James Joyce's Ireland* (London and New Haven: Yale University Press, 1992).

*James Joyces Irland* (trans Jörg Rademacher and Cristoforo Sweeger) (Köln and Basel: Bruckner and Thünker, 1996).

*Yeats's Worlds: Ireland, England and the Poetic Imagination* (London and New Haven: Yale University Press, 1995).

*Sterne in Modernism/Postmodernism* (co-editor with Peter de Voogd) (Amsterdam: Rodopi, 1996).

*W.B.Yeats: Critical Assessments* 4 Vols (Robertsbridge: Helm Information, 2000).

*The House of Music and the Cupboard Under the Stairs* (Privately Printed, 2000).

*Irish Writing in the Twentieth Century: A Reader* (Cork: Cork University Press, 2001).

*Light, Freedom and Song: A Cultural History of Modern Irish Writing* (London and New Haven: Yale University Press, 2005).

*Joyce and Company* (London: Continuum, 2006).

*Reading Joyce* (Harlow: Pearson Longman, 2007).

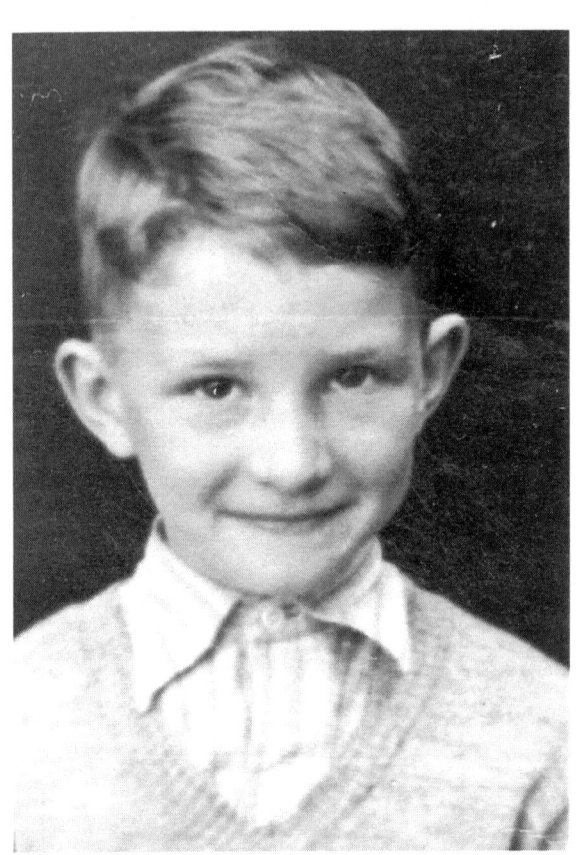

# The Long Apprenticeship

## A Writer's Memoir

### David Pierce

Matador
9 Priory Business Park,
Wistow Road, Kibworth Beauchamp,
Leicestershire. LE8 0RX
Tel: (+44) 116 279 2299
Fax: (+44) 116 279 2277
Email: books@troubador.co.uk
Web: www.troubador.co.uk/matador

ISBN 978 1780881 027

British Library Cataloguing in Publication Data.
A catalogue record for this book is available from the British Library.

Typeset in 11pt Aldine401 BT Roman by Troubador Publishing Ltd, Leicester, UK
Printed and bound in the UK by TJ International, Padstow, Cornwall

**Matador** is an imprint of Troubador Publishing Ltd

# Contents

# Prologue

And would it have mattered if I had remembered who else was in that room the afternoon she first entered my life? Or recalled the names of the writers who that week occupied centre stage? Was it Ibsen or Brecht, Lawrence or Joyce? I can't recall now which writers were on that university postgraduate programme. They are nothing now but names from the past on a list of names about the past. I must have been then elsewhere, just as I am now elsewhere. As I slipped into that room filled with a weak drizzle of afternoon sunlight, I was expecting little, except not to be unduly noticed. After all, I was late, I hadn't done the reading, and I had stepped uninvited into a room where a new cohort of expectant MA students, who had been together for some weeks before I had tagged along to join them, had already gathered round a nest of tables in the centre. On a chair by a long dark wall I sat awkwardly, looking intent and at the same time vacant. No, I couldn't say who else was in that room at Lancaster University that autumn afternoon. No characters, no memories, no authors come back to me now.

It's reassuring to realise that something else plays havoc with our memories. Or is it that context has no part to play in some memories? A professed literary critic and cultural historian should remember what author was under discussion that afternoon. Apart from David Craig, the open-necked, Scottish tutor leading the seminar, only one person stood out, a young woman across from me, who had a delightfully sunny head full of gently folding hair and who was confidently addressing the point under discussion. Was it that that first drew me to her? Not so much fate, as the ancients would have it, but initially something less defined – the sense of drama and occasion in the voice, the power of articulation, and the reasoning mind in full flow. Across a crowded room – isn't that the most romantic way for things to get started for all of us whether yesterday or today, whether as poets or dreamers, teachers or bankers, poseurs or innocents? From a jack to a king in one hand of cards. Forty years later, I can still recall feeling a certain suppressed agitation, the ear and the eye suddenly awake, and me so full of unease, and she so justified, gloriously confident, and primed to advance some heretical line of argument.

Over the following few weeks our relationship developed. Every morrow thereafter, as John Donne's poetic persona also gleaned from the front-line of experience, was good, and I was never the same again. Internment in Northern Ireland had been introduced three months before, and in those days my head was full of Ireland and causes. She was everything, complete; I was nothing, confused, a work in progress. It was a moment in time that time knows nothing about. Forty years on I anticipate her every mood, register her every sigh, feel her every disappointment, her every wish for the future. What an odd autumn to usher in so much of a spring for me! So much strangeness to end in so much familiarity. Or, alternatively, so much familiarity which began in so much strangeness and awkwardness. One minute you're strangers, the next you're talking about everything under the sun.

Imagine if I hadn't returned to Britain after my year abroad teaching in Spain. There would have been no life-long encounter with her, no one to set me straight, something else. 'By my troth,' as the youthful Donne in his now old-fashioned, declamatory style puts it, 'thou and I'. What did we do before we met? 'Were we not wean'd till then?' There couldn't be, I know that, and yet there was no sign of welcome to begin with, no guardian angel to whisper in my ear, 'Take note. Here in this room is your life-long partner.' It was just a cheerless room echoing to the sound of scraping chairs on grey vinyl, an hour from the tranquillity of the Lake District, in a newly chartered university, surrounded by a group of people I had little in common with, each protective, on edge, in pursuit of something beyond us all.

In retrospect, it was as if the group had come together just for us, which of course only happens in exaggeratedly pointed accounts such as you might encounter in school assemblies, or in classical myths or fictions of improbable encounters. Looked at from a sociological point of view, it wasn't a case of the self in identity with the group, but of the self in identity with just the one individual, a necessary pairing off from the flock or tribe. Thou and I. That's the proper way round, with the other encouraging or bringing out the self. Not Martin Buber's 'I and Thou', *Ich und Du*, which frequently, and perhaps inevitably, leads to a discussion about the self's relation with It. Thou and I, on the other hand, has no need for It – at least at first.

As ever, I was in flight from a group identity. Whatever adversity, whatever It, against which we were to struggle in life, it was not against the group where the weaning started. It – that word again - goes without saying that the real text that afternoon in that autumn-facing classroom was a light-bringer from Salford in Lancashire, a child of light, a bright-eyed reasoner who stood out from the group and who refused to accept no for an answer. I wasn't going to be on my own for ever. My 'I' would now have a heaven-sent Lucifer for company. I didn't know how lucky I was.

*The tiny back yard on Newland Road, Worthing, Sussex, with my younger brother,
Stephen, in a highchair, and my sister, Christine, and my older brother, John. Taken in
1950. I must have been looking at my mother, who must have been telling me to look at
the person taking the photo. 'Yard' is not to be confused with American usage. We had a
back yard, and it was not somewhere you could sit out in or invite friends. Behind the
person taking the photograph was the outside toilet and the place where we stored the
coal.*

Chapter One

# The Cupboard Under the Stairs

## The marble clock and the open fire

I enjoy nothing more than returning in my mind to first moments and to a phrase that underpins part of the inspiration for this book – the hinterland of consciousness. The first moment when you set eyes on your life-long partner, the first time you left home to go to boarding school in my case, the first European city to make an impression on you, the first time in adulthood you entered the house that was to become your home. I hardly ever return in my mind to lost or what-if moments, to past girlfriends, to what it's now like in that room where I once lived or slept. Perhaps I should, for these lost moments are also, like forgotten or abandoned dreams, part of me. I often imagine if I delayed too much on such moments I would encounter an overpowering sense of loss or guilt, just as today I'm occasionally unsure how to respond when asked how I am. 'Much the same,' I normally reply. In my mind I deflect the question. 'Do you really want to know?' And then add if that doesn't do the trick, 'I doubt it'.

I wonder what cobwebs now occupy that cupboard under the stairs in the house of my childhood which we boarded up and papered over as we decanted to another home north of the railway tracks in 1962? Is the big, heavy, marble clock that didn't ever keep time still there, sealed behind the tongue-in-groove panelling, Buddha-like, staring out, in grand isolation on the floor, minus a congregation? Or did the new occupants of 79 Newland Road, Worthing, Sussex ever discover it under the stairs and find a key for it in the process? Or did it ever start up again by itself when the household ghost periodically stirred to walk abroad? How many people coming down those stairs did that clock bother to recognise thereafter? Did it miss the personal signature of our own individual creaks and pressure points on the steep, narrow treads, the soles of our childish feet, our dare-devil leaps, the sound of our frequent sulks on the way up, our sudden, impetuous shrieks and mawkish cries of the heart? Or is it always dark and unresponsive in that boarded-up cupboard under the stairs?

As I look back, my thoughts seek out that clock under the stairs. Locked away, through time, unknown possibly even today to the present occupants, a half a century and more later. The storehouse of memory. Recollection. In retrospect. Rediscovery. Retrieval. Recuperation. The passage from here to there, present to past, past to present. I wonder how we might conceive such 'transitional arrangements'. Not I suspect if we're honest with the confidence of a biographer, for anything prefaced by 'auto' must be more tentative and less available to an objective reading. It was a marble clock, heavy, ornate, with pillars, more like an object on an altar than a homely timepiece. I never recall it working. But why did we lock it away? Was it our way of stating: here in this house in the post-war years was spent the childhood of four children, born to an Irish mother and English father? Or was it something else? Was it a burial notice, an entombment? Or was it a refusal to draw a line with the past? A memory of the time when we lived on top of each other, our destiny obscure, but the time still ticking, a point of return, a symbol in the making, a gesture or fling against necessity?

There is a book or thesis to be written on the hierarchy of furniture and fittings in two-up two-down terraced houses. That unloved cupboard, which was just too small to play in, constituted one of a series of three in a room that also sported on an adjacent wall three ornamental birds ascending in determined flight toward heaven. Next to it was the cupboard for hanging up coats, and it was here that the electricity meter, like a miserly god in our midst, silently continued spinning without care or sympathy for the financially strapped denizens. Then came the tallest and most appreciated cupboard of them all, the larder where we kept the crockery, tins of baked beans and Argentine corned beef, and where we nibbled the crusts of stale bread until our mother, rushed off her feet, arrived home for dinner, our midday meal, with fresh supplies. Time, light, and food, parcelled out and costed, the trefoil of our lives downstairs. A space for everything in a room where space was at a premium. I come back to it. Did time stop for ever on the face of that clock? Or was there nothing symbolic in that papered-over cupboard under the stairs? Nothing but a memory of childhood?

Such intensity is impossible to recover later in life, and the reason for this is in part a question of space. Six people in a house with four rooms plus a scullery and an outside toilet ironically leaves plenty of room for the imagination. The most utilised room was the living room where there was a fire, a table, which occupied centre stage with four, sturdy, wooden chairs, a sideboard with two drawers and two cupboards which were always in need of sorting, a central light over the table, a window overlooking the back yard, a side-table for the bulky, brown *Pye* wireless positioned near the window, and two upright armchairs with wooden arms. In summer, with the help of sturdy drawing pins, we would hang from the ceiling, somewhere close to the central light, brown tapers of sticky flycatcher. The mantelpiece collected letters and bills; the fire was lit with old newspapers; the chimney sometimes caught fire and on one occasion the fire brigade was called.

It was a small room measuring 14 x 10 feet, which, translated into terms for a child to understand, was barely enough room for a game of Blind Man's Buff. Around 1956 we got a budgerigar and called it Joey. We must have been enchanted by an Australian film called *Smiley* then showing at the cinema, a film with a flaxen-haired boy called Smiley, who had a friend called Joey. Smiley and Joey and all their adventures outdoors came into the small room of our lives indoors. Every night we would drape a curtain over Joey's cage and every morning we would wake him up as Smiley. In the evenings we would put the cat out, shut the doors and the window, and let Joey come out to play. He would fly round the room at first, banging his wings against the walls and whatever he seemed incapable of avoiding. Our new-found friend had some learning to do, we surmised. We liked nothing better than having him perch on our heads and letting him hop from one of us to the other and back again. And we in turn reciprocated. For fear the slightest movement might upset him, we stayed very still. Then, once he settled, stiffly, but as sedately as we could, we would begin parading up and down the room with Joey perched on our heads, all the time quietly hoping that he wouldn't drop anything on us. 'Has he?'

As with all good things it came to an end, in this case when my mother took a swipe at my brother, John, who had been misbehaving or acting up. Unfortunately for Joey, he was perched on the wrong head, for John ducked and the poor thing received the full force of the palm of my mother's broad hand, and he met a sudden and an untimely death. It was unwarranted, we could discern that, but we weren't sure who to blame, John or my mother. The jurors eventually decided that it was shared. That night we placed Joey carefully back in his cage on his hurt side, shut the cage door, carefully draped the cover over him, took one last peep, and prayed that he might be mercifully resurrected in the morning as Smiley. No smiles, however, were forthcoming from Joey and no transfiguration had occurred, for the following morning there was nothing stirring in the cage. He was beyond recall, as dead as the droppings which surrounded him. He had given up the ghost or the will to live. That morning before setting out for school we buried poor Joey with full honours in the little patch of earth we had in the back yard and shed some sentimental but genuine tears. That marked the end of our venture into the outback and thereafter we returned to looking after the grumpy cat. I don't remember what we did with the cage.

The room where Joey met his untimely end was the room where for me the world took shape. It was a room where the tragi-comic mingled with the prosaic and the poetic. Whatever I am as a person has its origins and takes its bearing from what took place between those four walls. And yet now I struggle to recreate in words what it was like beating my way to consciousness in that room from 1947 until 1962, to capture some of the moments when the iron of the world entered my lyrical soul. If someone were to ask me for one word to describe that room and that home I suppose I would resort to something in the atmosphere. It was intense. Small, yes, and frequently untidy, but intense is the word I would now settle on, and of all English writers Charles Dickens is the one who best understood what I'm getting at.

Anything coming into that room risked being subjected to the same process of intense scrutiny, and only occasionally did something escape the time-frame of those years. When we got a television, our heads filled up with jingles such as the one with a Mexican flavour 'theeeesosighmeanzappymotorin', which took some time to decipher as 'The *Esso* sign means happy motoring'. One of the oddest things we did was to take a photograph of the coronation of Pope John XXIII in November 1958. Without realising how significant it was to become, we somehow felt such a moment should not go unnoticed, but in turn that fuzzy photograph of the new Pope with his huge tiara and prominent, Roncalli nose monopolising the screen, the Pope that is who sought to modernise the Church, has become in its own way a personal and historical document of the time we spent in that intense small room before all our yesterdays were changed for ever. The clock on the television says nearly twelve.

Even the act of lighting the fire proved intense in my childhood home for there was always the risk of setting the chimney on fire. We never bothered with the luxury of newly available firelighters, preferring instead to employ traditional, scrunched-up newspaper and bundles of firewood, and when that method didn't work we resorted to holding a spread newspaper over the opening to the fireplace to create a wind tunnel and then waiting until the fire scorched the paper we were holding and trying to read. Then came the panic, singeing hair, and shouts of 'Put the damn thing on the fire' and 'Jesus, where are the tongs?' Sometimes, the chimney did indeed catch fire or at least bits of soot fell down alight, which reminded us all of the danger we faced daily during the winter months or during most of the year for we were seldom without a fire in the living room. Everything costs, only death is for free, as Brecht wittily observed. It was probably the extra expense that meant we never bothered with firelighters or with regular visits by chimney sweeps. I sometimes wonder what would have happened if the house did indeed burn down for I'm sure my parents had little or no property insurance.

Whether in the west of Ireland or the south of England, an open fire, one looking west, the other east, dominated proceedings. Of course the fire heated only one room in the house, but if there was nothing to fill the fireplace and hearth we would have been bereft of a focus in the evening. 'Move up from the fire' was a remark often heard as we sought to maximise warmth for ourselves. Everything seemed to involve sharing or dividing in our family. 'Shut that door' kept up the hectoring, followed by 'Were you born in a barn or what?' One minute you were basking in the warmth of a blazing hearth, the next you were cast into outer darkness. One minute scalded, the next scolded. We imagined chilblains, which are an abnormal response to cold, were but part of growing up. Didn't everyone, arriving home on a cold winter's day, leave off their wet, outdoor shoes and holey socks for the warmth of the fender and grate? You, we, I, everyone – I notice I'm using all these personal pronouns interchangeably, for we all come together at this point as if what was personal was indeed shared by other members of the family and indeed shared by ordinary people everywhere in Britain in the 1950s. It's what an obscure destiny gives us, not so much upper-class 'good behaviour' as something less refined, more common and down-to-earth, in this case a shared past of cold houses and chilblains.

The single source of warmth in the house was from that one fire. All the other rooms were cold. Only rarely was the fire in our bedroom lit and that tended to be when one of us was ill and confined to bed. What this meant was that the living room became the room where we did, indeed, do most of our living. It was not a house for exploration – even the grumpy cat somehow knew that as it hunkered down in front of the fire. With central heating, people today have funnelled out into different rooms in a house, but in the 1950s we were confined to just the one room. The bedroom, which was just large enough for three beds side by side, was a retreat into a cold universe, the scullery was always cold especially when taking a bath in the tub, the outside toilet, which had no electricity, had nothing to protect it from the cold outside. Cold provided a kind of ironic leitmotif in 'sunny Worthing' as it advertises itself to the world. From morning to night, we were all thrown together, never on our own, registering every mood change in each other and throughout the house. Think of that. Where could you go to sulk or listen to music or do some quiet reading or take up a hobby or lay out an electric train-set? No wonder the English travel the world in search of something called space.

I recall being curled up in bed and pushing my feet gingerly down into the dark extremities and my sister observing I would grow up crooked or bent over like our grandmother in Ireland if I didn't stretch my legs. I recall my brother, John, reading by the landing light when the central light had been switched off by my mother. I recall my younger brother, Stephen, rocking his head from side to side as he fell asleep counting. I recall petitioning God to ensure I didn't die in the night and to grant me, if at all possible and within His gift, another day to enjoy on His good earth. I recall being enchanted by images of centaurs, which trespassed on my consciousness altering how I perceived the two halves of my body. In summers, I recall seeing the blood-red sunsets through the thin cotton curtains and listening to my mother recite:

Red sky at night, shepherds' delight.
Red sky in the morning, shepherds' warning.

I recall Christmas mornings and waking to presents on the end of my bed. Those mornings were as intense and as cold as it gets. 'Hey, look what I've got,' which was soon followed by 'Look what he's got'. From excitement to resentment was just one intense glance away.

To allay the cold, coal was delivered once a week by our coalman, who carried his once-white sack on his bent back though the house to the back yard. With a deft little movement of his shoulder, he deposited the hundredweight contents in the space provided next to the outside toilet. Then he folded up his sack before stepping through the house again back to his lorry where he threw his sack over the side before fastening the tailgate. I remember nothing distinctive about his features except that his cap was to one side of his head and that he was covered in coal dust. He had a knack of skirting round the furniture and not depositing too much soot and dust round the house. I don't recall how he was paid, but it must have been cash in hand for I don't remember him knocking at the door later in the week as our milkman Don, with his fingerless mitts, did. It couldn't be otherwise but we gave no thought to our own carbon footprint as we filled up the scuttle in readiness for the next evening's fun by the open fire, fun which was sometimes augmented by our own pantomime version of toast and crumpet on a fork in front of the open fire.

We could have spent more time in the front room if we were more rational. Soon after my younger brother, Stephen, was born, my sister slept in that room on a brown put-u-up, which was easy enough to pull down at night. During the day it was effectively a spare room. We could have kept the net curtains but assigned that room to say 'light entertainment'. Just inside the door of that front room there was a floor-standing, antiquated, wind-up gramophone, complete with spare, stainless-steel needles and fifty and more 78s, some of which were cracked and beyond use but were never discarded. The 78s weren't exactly dance records but we did enjoy following His Master's Voice round and round to the visual accompaniment of a large speaker and a fine-looking dog sitting on its hind legs. Round and round the dog of His Master went. The thing we enjoyed the most was when His Voice began to slur and we would rush over to wind Him up until He was running faster than He should. In our scoffing household, where nothing quite functioned as it should have done, that was considered fun.

The front room, measuring 10 x 11 feet, also played host to rarely seen important visitors such as Fr Faussett, a priest from my boarding school who came down to see me when I was twelve. Local priests such as the unbelievably untamed Fr Jeremiah Corcoran, who insisted on throwing plastic footballs at us inside the house as if we were in training for a Gaelic Athletic Association football team, or the more formal Fr 'Dicky' Veal, who enjoyed a cup of tea and sitting down with us to watch *Yogi Bear* or *Popeye the Sailorman*, had to make do with the living room. High-class or posh visitors were so rare as to make the room's special status somewhat redundant. It would have been better to have turned it into another living room, but that would have sinned against the tribe and the belief that we should live all together as a unit. There was also a question of keeping up with appearances. Even though it was hidden behind a net curtain, neighbours would know that you had a 'front room' and that you were therefore slightly posher than those who didn't. In addition it was useful to have a room that was managed, for in spite of living from hand to mouth the possession of a front room gave you a certain comfort, even if it had been bought at the cost of space. Visitors wouldn't be treated to bottles of milk on the table or disarranged furniture or sagging cushions. The situation was full of irony, for if the lack of space in the house didn't get you, class habits would.

In the 1911 Census for England and Wales, people were asked for the number of the rooms in their house and to exclude the water closet and the scullery. The scullery, therefore, was not dignified as a room and so went unrecorded. In our house, as I suspect in that of most people, the scullery was the ugliest room in the house. Put a 'k' in the spelling and you have 'skullery', a much more appropriate spelling for an anteroom, for what was it but an addition to the main structure of the house, a non-room, tacked on like an afterthought or a question-mark? You stepped down into the scullery onto an uneven and uncertain brick floor. It was both literally and metaphorically one step away from living outdoors. 'Skullduggery' would be a better word, somewhere where you dug down into the loose earth and uncovered the skulls of the departed. Scullery was a word which somehow was always etched into our minds and at the same time to be avoided when speaking to those outside the family. 'Say kitchen can't you?' my mother would say. 'No, I can't. We lived in a house with a scullery.'

The scullery, which measured 7½ x 6½ feet, was about half the size of the living room. Against the outside wall there was a sink and along the party wall with our next door neighbour, Mrs Long, a fairly intimidating gas cooker. Facing you was a blank wall, which in time we pushed through to make a bathroom and inside toilet. However, for most of my childhood the scullery was a reminder of worse times now, worse times ahead, and worse times in the past. I always associate it with a story about a boy at school with us, who was scalded by boiling water in his scullery, for they were dangerous places. Poor Hoey only just managed to survive after passing out in a sealed room with steam all around him. He must have pulled down on his head a saucepan of boiling water which was going to fill his bath. Half his face was scarred for life.

The scullery was not a place to spend too much time in, and even today I avoid it in my mind. In that tiny, ugly, dark room my mother performed a range of tasks including the cooking, the washing up, washing all our clothes and handkerchiefs, washing and bathing us. Hanging on the wall in the back yard was the metal tub for taking a bath, and next to it was the mangle which my mother used to wring water from washed clothes. From scullery to outdoors was a short step. We passed through the scullery's portals on the way to the even less salubrious outside toilet, which was fine except at night, when we had to face the ghosts and monsters who came out in the dark. So, with lighted, flickering candles in hand, we always accompanied each other when making a visit at night. 'Hurry up, can't you.'

There's nothing like doing without or deploying ugly words such as 'scullery' and 'mangle' to remind you of identity. When we visited our grandmother in the west of Ireland for summer holidays, there was no toilet, only a cow cabin or a neighbour's field. Equally, I didn't need to grow up in a highly political household to know how absurd it was for Harold Macmillan, the Conservative Prime Minister at the time, to claim in 1957 that we'd never had it so good (and that workers and trade unionists should exercise pay restraint). Nobody teaches it, but those of us brought up in houses with sculleries and outside toilets (and indeed no toilets) learn the lesson early on, that we not only know our place but that we also owe the world everything and at the same time nothing.

## Neighbours

The elderly Mrs Long, whose son had died on board HMS Hood when it was torpedoed during the war, lived next door. Until we got our own rented television in 1956 she would let us watch afternoon children's hour from five to six on her set. Her house was neat, quiet and also cold. We would sit cross-legged in our socks on a rough mat until the white light disappeared into the back of the screen. When the masked Lone Ranger, with the help of Tonto, had dealt with another batch of dusty miscreants, and Eamonn Andrews had lit another *Crackerjack* and left us all jumpy and on edge, it was time, according to the BBC, for children to adjourn to bed, so we respectfully thanked our elderly neighbour, put on our shoes, and disappeared next door, wondering all the time whether or not she could hear us through the wafer-thin dividing walls. Only occasionally would she hammer on the wall when the noise we made got too much for her. *Crackerjack*, I am sure, was nothing but a racket disturbing the quiet of her house. If he had ever had the good fortune of meeting her, the American author, Raymond Carver, would have made Mrs

Long the subject or the occasion for one of his brief but intense stories, and he might have called it 'The disappearing white dot'.

Whether it is on account of the limits of space or of the limits of language, the world never stops rebounding on us. That's another lesson I learnt early on. Our neighbours on the other side were the friendly Ronson family. On account of his size, we speculated that Raymond, who was the eldest, would become a jockey but he never did. Mrs Ronson, who deserved a long life, was always cheerful and pleasant with us, even when I accidentally smashed a tennis ball into her living room where she was breastfeeding her baby daughter, Carole. Every day her front doorstep was cleaned and polished and came up shining red, the colour on my face when I went round to apologise for shaking the peace of her house. I don't know why we never mixed more with the children. Maybe it was because we were too loud for them.

Before the fresh-faced Ronson family arrived next door, there lived an older, grey-haired woman, Mrs Orme, but I don't remember much about her, nor Paddy, her lodger, unless he was the one who caught me with my pants down running indoors from the outside toilet shouting for more toilet paper. I think Mrs Orme reminded me of someone out of a fairy tale, but whose side she was on I couldn't quite decide. One of my earliest memories is watching the ambulance transport her to hospital and thinking we would never see her again. Me so young and she so old. Memories are such strange things, at times like torn-off bits of paper blowing in the wind waiting for some hedge or mind to collect them. Standing watching the ambulance pull out into the road has unaccountably stayed with me as an early memory. Did one part of me stumble upon the contrast between the permanence of a house and the temporariness of a home? Was that it, that the world was intent on teaching me a lesson about life's temporary arrangements? If so, it was a rivet being driven in before I could discern its meaning or effect. From the protection of our small sunny forecourt, next to the patch where grew purple, delicate lilacs and yellow roses fortified by horse dung, we waved goodbye, and the ambulance disappeared up Park Road a short distance to the hospital. We then went indoors. How soon afterward she passed away I never asked and my mother never told us.

Just recently a woman knocked at my front door in York seeking support for a local charity. She lives several doors down on the other side of a busy street which acts as a rat-run for drivers through the city. 'I haven't seen you before,' she volunteered. 'Have you lived long down here?' 'Since 1978,' I replied. That was a rare moment, for my present neighbours are the friendliest imaginable, but in my working-class, childhood home you would never hear such a conversation. That didn't mean you spoke to everybody; you knew for example the people you didn't mix with and you always distinguished yourself from neighbours, often through forms of put-down humour about them. We played in each other's homes, but not as much as you might imagine, and we never held back from inviting each other to play out in the street or the park. 'June'll be out soon,' was more often than not the response from June Smith's overly-protective, elderly mother, and we could never quite work out why June couldn't just appear on the doorstep and tell us this herself.

The Laughter brothers, Michael and Christopher, whose father was in the Royal Navy and therefore away most of the time, were not that good at sport or games but they always came out to be vanquished when invited. In one area of life, though, Christopher excelled, for he happened to be in possession of the most extraordinary belch of any of us. His prowess was by any standards exceptional, and it amounted to what I can only describe as a vocal declaration of independence, though against whom or what was never that clear. Simultaneously, to accompany the explosion, he would manage somehow to dredge up the word 'Gob'. To help him out with the completion of the compound word, we would then add 'shite', or if we thought we were being summoned to participate in a form of repartee or responsorial chant we would reply not with some weak excuse on his behalf such as 'I beg your pardon' but with the down-to-earth expletive 'Your mug', which was a common catch-phrase at the time, occasionally used as a matey, in-your-face way of greeting or hailing contemporaries.

I'm pretty certain 'Gobby', the neighbourhood's own Monsieur Le Pétomane, never erupted like that inside his home, or if he did I am sure he apologised for his bad manners in front of his mother, his absent father on the high seas, and his quieter and more scholarly, elder brother, Michael. He was delightfully crude in his boyish way, and he had a ready audience in the 'pissy Pierces' as we were sometimes called by older, rougher playmates in Homefield Park. But he was not foul like the members of another family who took to urinating against the innocent plane trees that graced Newland Road. It goes without saying that the sounds 'Gobby' made were not to be confused with performance poetry; they were more like the grunts of creatures given to phatic communion but to little else by way of language. Belch, gob, shite, your mug. To be called 'deaf-lugs' in my childhood was one thing, but the mouth seemed to attract the worst forms of abuse, ranging from the simple adjective 'lippy' to the

11

speaker's triumph in the phrase 'Put that in your pipe and smoke it' to the raised anger in the forthright command 'Shut your trap' or, worse, 'Shut your hole'.

In any working-class area there are gradations in status and poshness, and these are not only externally visible but also psychologically internalised almost from the outset. I don't know why but the Laughters seemed a little above us. Perhaps it was the status of their father in the Royal Navy, perhaps the way their mother bawled at the boys in the street, or maybe it was their huge collection of *Commando* and cowboy comics, which we occasionally managed to borrow or read on the forecourt under their possessive eyes after they had been beaten at jacks or beggar thy neighbour. It must have been the comics which attested to a greater spending power and which thus gave them the edge.

Early on, I began to discern the internal dynamics of social relationships within the class I came from. In *Landscape for a Good Woman* (1986), a thoughtful inquiry into 1950s working-class life, Carolyn Steedman mentions in passing that seven is the age when children become conscious of social detail and social distinction. If my memory serves me right, I was absorbing class distinctions before that. In fact I can't recall a time when distinctions weren't part of me or my view of the world. After all, my mother cleaned other people's houses and we would sometimes accompany her. In spite of Christopher's crudeness, we felt the Laughters were perhaps a half-rung above us, that Mrs Long's quietness was a class marker, and that Mrs Ronson's front step was a little too clean, as if she was trying too hard to be respectable. At the entrance to Homefield Park was a detached house where we would occasionally be let in to play. The boy I was let in to play with, whose name I have now forgotten, seemed quite cosseted by his parents, and, while I didn't articulate it at the time in these terms, what I was perceiving was the distinct presence or aroma of class. I believe the boy's father held an important position with Worthing Borough Council.

Whenever it is learned, a subtle, internal history informs most working-class life, and its best aspects, which are not to be confused with envy or resentment, are cherished by those brought up within its confines. In due course, after passing the 11+, Michael went on to the newly established Technical High School, the equivalent of a grammar school for technically gifted children and long since abandoned as an idea. I don't know if Christopher followed him there or if he made better use of his vocal talents.

## Neighbourhood

I like to imagine my neighbourhood as a place of experiment, where some early lessons about the world were learned. I say 'experiment' because, in retrospect, it felt more like this than 'experience'. My family was intense experience, but the neighbourhood was a detached experiment. Historically, the two words overlapped, but today we distinguish them. The neighbourhood was like a field laboratory where you discovered things by trial and error and by repetition. This was especially true of the plan of the neighbourhood, for there was no natural centre and it lay at the intersection of three or four quite busy minor roads. As you stepped down from the forecourt of home into the street, you had to have your wits about you. You only played marbles in the gutter if you were sure there was no traffic around and it was a quiet part of the day.

I didn't need to be taught the contrast between experience and experiment. You can't change your family, so those relationships tend to be well-established and follow an order or pattern, but in childhood you can and do change your friends or those you choose to invite out to play. Equally, while my neighbourhood was generally quite friendly, you couldn't take that for granted. Not every shopkeeper was particularly welcoming, and, with some, you were chivvied along if on a Saturday evening you couldn't make up your mind how to spend your little bit of pocket-money. When queing, my eye would be drawn to the notice prominently displayed behind the counter about not asking for credit SINCE REFUSAL MAY OFFEND, and I would wonder about its tone, its use of capitals, and who was speaking and who was being addressed.

As for the extent of the neighbourhood, today I recognise this stretched no more than about a hundred metres in any direction from our house on Newland Road, but as a child it felt like the world. Opposite us was Homefield Park, a few doors along was the Forester's Hall, then the beautifully named Globe, a public house; across the road were a number of shops including a newsagents, a greengrocers, a bakers, and a grocers. A little further up High Street was a shop selling wet fish, where we would wander along at an opportune moment at the end of the day when the fishmonger was hosing down to ask for scraps for the cat. Beyond that on North Street was Worleys fish-and-chip shop, where we would queue for the individually wrapped fish-and-chips and then hurry home to keep the catch warm. On Chapel Road, a busy main road and on the edge of our neighbourhood, was Searles, a bicycle shop, and Bidgood the butchers we occasionally patronised. Several shops and businesses in the neighbourhood we never bothered with including a laundry opposite and a grocers and a hairdressers along the road toward Chesswood Road. By the bridge leading round to Worthing Station on what was Railway Approach was a row of shops which I seem to remember visiting. One was a sports shop, another a vegetarian cafe, and one was Greens the butchers, where we would buy our Christmas turkey. It was pulled down to make way for a car-park, but it was a very popular row of shops, and with its destruction went a little of my past.

In terms of people, the neighbourhood must have been constantly changing. If you compare the 1912 with the 1962 Directories for Worthing, only two families along my row have the same name, and yet it seemed to be a stable neighbourhood, at least to my fresh eyes. Or was it that the people could always be on the move but the neighbourhood survived intact? That seems curious and yet in a sense such an experience must have been common all over Britain since the eighteenth century. At one level there was stability, at another all change. As children we must have been beguiled by permanence. If it's not interfered with unduly, childhood has something unchanging about it, and part of that must be do with our underdeveloped temporal faculty or the mismatch between our internal clock and the public face of time. When we look back we are often surprised by the extent of things changing which at the time we didn't realise. So children seem to act as unconscious shock-absorbers of social and historical change and carry part of that sensibility into adulthood.

We tended to play with children in the immediate neighbourhood; beyond the neighbourhood, such as those living on Station Road had a reputation for roughness or for just occupying an unknown and therefore potentially threatening terrain. The Ryans lived across the street, a few doors down from a laundry. David was my age, easygoing, handsome, and good company. He was more a friend than a neighbour. His other brothers and sisters had lived with their father in Canada, and something told me they would all return to Canada in due course. Two memories, both as it happens of sensory deprivation, stand out for me. One is of David recounting the story of how his father, on arriving in the dead of night from Canada, navigated all the way along Newland Road feeling his way in the unlit street from the front wall of one house to the next. The other concerns the struggles we had in communicating with David's sister who was deaf. It can't have been easy for her, a childhood reduced to lip-reading, gesticulating, and primitive forms of sign language, and I couldn't help thinking that we had to meet somewhere in the middle, that it wasn't all her responsibility to communicate. My sympathies were aroused. I was sorry to see David and his family disappear as emigrants to the new world but, in retrospect, I never once questioned my own sense of rootedness nor felt any desire to follow them. After all, I was just coming to a consciousness of my local community in New Land Road and David wasn't going to be a part of that.

I wonder what I made of that word 'Canada' when I first heard it. It was probably just a blank, an empty signifier, or out of reach and not for me. David Ryan must have talked about it but I don't recall anything he said. The fact that his father arrived in Worthing in the middle of pitch-black night and had to grope his way along Newland Road was what stands out in my memory. His father had some connection with Canada; he may have been one of the Canadian soldiers stationed in Worthing during the War and perhaps he was returning for one last time to collect his family he had left behind. I wish I could access more clearly what was going through my mind. One part of me must have been attempting to internalise an outsider's perspective of the neighbourhood. I never believed I was being invited to consider leaving the neighbourhood and emigrating. Nor did I feel David was abandoning us. It was just that his family was moving to another country. Some lines were visible, others less so. In the middle of the night the neighbourhood was invisible to the naked eye. Equally, people could break through the cordon around the neighbourhood and leave with their entire family to somewhere called 'Canada', never to return. What then were the ties that bound us together?

As I reflect on the neighbourhood where I grew up another issue is raised for me. I don't believe there was ever a time when I did not know about Mrs Long's son who died on the HMS Hood during the War. The War was a backdrop to our lives, yet I am not mindful of it bringing people together. In the comics we beat the Germans. Whoopee! Pow! Take that! *Achtung! Donner and blitzen!* In my stamp album, which somehow survived the years, I collected stamps carrying the image of Hitler and the Nazi swastika; other *Deutsches Reich* stamps boasted inflationary numbers such as 500 Millionen, which must have puzzled me or at any rate prompted me to have them valued at the philately shop on North Street. But in real life the War did not represent triumph but something we had to do as a country. Solidarity with my neighbours on account of the War was not something that impressed itself on me. I suppose I inherited my father's wry perspective on the War and how after the War he spent his time, when not working, at the cinema. Perhaps my family was no different from many others: we delighted in heroic exploits in pocket-sized comics but the War was just not talked about in our house. If I were to claim I belonged to a post-war generation, that would be conceding too much to the abstracting tendency of the biographer over-keen to 'place' his or her subject. And yet there is something in it, for, after all, I was conceived within a few days of my father being discharged from the Royal Marines in October 1946.

Relics from the War were scattered about the town, most notably the War memorial outside the Town Hall, which had been erected to commemorate soldiers who died in the Great War. On the road down to the beach and near the gasometer beside Worthing Hospital was a pretty row of small cottages. Every time when passing we would mention the bomb that destroyed some of them and how it was dropped by a rogue aeroplane returning to Germany after taking part in the blitz over London. The War, then, gave me a perspective of Worthing from the air, a town which prided itself on being between the sea and the Downs and therefore saved from the worst excesses of aerial bombardment. At Hill Barn, just north of Broadwater, we played among the huge, concrete blocks that had served to protect the coast from a German invasion, but they were never war games and they seemed to involve squeezing in between the blocks or clambering on top of them and ensuring when we didn't injure ourselves by falling off. However, only someone who had absorbed the trauma of war could produce, a half-century later, the startling, dark, straw-filled, potentially inflammable canvases of Anselm Kiefer, the German artist born in that desolate year of 1945.

My elder brother, who was born in 1945, remembers Homefield Park as a huge vegetable garden, a relic of the 'dig for victory' campaign, but I don't remember that, or ration cards. Food was never plentiful in our house, the larder often bare, rarely well-stocked, but we 'never went short' in a phrase frequently heard at the time. A half-pound of broken biscuits from the grocer's opposite – lucky dip time – would be just fine so long as most of them were not too stale. We never went in for cracked eggs; that was only for people

16

who were desperately poor. One family in the neighbourhood were rumoured to drink from jam-jars, but that was considered fairly 'low-rent' as Americans might say. The War bequeathed a legacy of austerity, but you had the impression that people's lives were governed by a longer history of want and necessity.

One door away from where I was born stood the Foresters' Hall, a friendly society dating from the nineteenth century. In the period before the Great War, the Foresters' Hall housed St George's Mission Hall and was designed to serve the 'small tenements' in Newland Road. Situated next door to the Hall in *Kelly's Directory of Worthing* for 1912 was St George's Coffee Rooms, run by Mrs Ellen Walton. At that time the 'Lily of West Sussex Court' of the Ancient Order of Foresters held their meetings on the last Thursday of each month in the Malster's Arms in Broadwater Street, Worthing. Coffee and beer. Research like this helps to create a richer context. Only now am I conscious that I was born a stone's throw from two of the traditional religious and secular missionaries to the working class in the nineteenth century, one ready to sign you up for the next world, the other determined to remind you about self-help in this one.

At the time I never did discover who the Foresters were, and I have never in my life met an ancient forester. In the back of my mind I must have imagined they lived in Sherwood Forest, wore Lincoln green, had names like Maid Marian or Little John, and sported pointed, felt hats with feathers in them. Some years ago in the early 1990s, I was in Milan when the Alpini descended on the city to hold their annual convention. It was around 15 March, the Ides of March, the time when swallows from Africa first arrive in northern Italy. A generation or so ago they fought for Mussolini but today the Alpini resemble friendly foresters who roam the Italian slopes of the Alps and dress in appropriately lively, bird-like uniform to defend the homeland against any attacks from whoever, whether modern marauding Visigoths from the north or would-be crafty Hannibals from a resurgent Africa. As I caught sight of all these Alpini coming towards me from every direction out of every bar and restaurant in Milan and calling loudly to each other, I was reminded of my childhood and the homely Ancient Order of English Foresters. 'Look out,' I felt like shouting. 'Here comes the Sheriff of Nottingham.' I sometimes think this is what childhood is for – to keep alive our sense of continuity or otherwise with the past and at the same time to prepare us for later encounters with the real thing. Whichever way we face, whether looking forward or back, it seems everything in the mind has a box to go in.

*79 Newland Road today, with no waiting sign outside. The low wall is still there. I was born in the upstairs room. Mrs Long lived at 81, the house on the right, the Ronsons on the left, next to the Foresters' Hall, and beyond that the Globe on the corner. We would kick a ball against the wall where the two cars are parked.*

Eddie Simpson, who was the same age as my elder brother, John, lived quietly with his mother in the caretaker's house adjacent to the Foresters' Hall. An only child, perhaps for that reason he needed little persuading to come out to play when invited. 'Kenny-can Eddie come out to play?' as my younger brother, Stephen, would inquire of Eddie's perplexed mother on her doorstep. One of our chief delights was to devise a play for performance on the stage in the Hall. We were the players, playwrights, directors, set-designers, producers, and, usually, the audience. It was a given that all the plays had to include episodes of thunder and lightning for we seemed more interested in the effects than in the playlets themselves. Nothing could beat the sheer excitement backstage of grabbing hold of an unwieldy sheet of metal with both hands and just managing, without falling over, to shake it. 'The gods are angry with you lot,' we would shout at the actors on the stage. The noise drowned out every subtlety of dialogue or action and brought Eddie's mother in her role as Warden rushing in, arms flailing, apron flapping, to demand an end to all our

18

revels. There was so much space in the Hall that we never fathomed what to do with it all, and perhaps that's why the curtained stage proved so attractive.

It was in the Foresters' Hall that the whole neighbourhood gathered for tea in honour of the newly crowned Queen Elizabeth in 1953. We were all on our best behaviour as we took tea and sandwiches seated along rows of folding tables which had been suitably bedecked with reminders of the occasion. It was one of the few instances in my childhood when I felt some vague kind of state intervention; school milk must have been another, as were occasional visits to the school by health inspectors. But here we were recipients of institutional charity, held in the Hall where we played on the stage. It was quite a strange afternoon as if we were being enlisted or signed up for something which we might or might not regret. We then filed out after the celebration, flags and pennants waving, still on our best behaviour with our specially decorated royal cups and saucers, which were then stored in glass cabinets for posterity along with other ornaments and *objets d'art* won at the funfair in Homefield Park.

*Coronation cups, next to an Irish leprechaun and other good luck knick-knacks, are still treasured by my mother in the family cabinet.*

Not surprisingly, there was no landau outside to take us home and no outriders in white buckskin breeches on dapple greys to accompany us on that short walk home. The occasion might have been royal but little of it rubbed off, and life quickly returned to normal in our two-up, two-down, tenement house, which faced south and which ran parallel to the railway line. Like most working-class families, we treated the newly-acquired crockery as a potential heirloom, to be admired and never touched, but when, fifty years later, they started appearing on Ebay, the auction site, no one I suspect made much money, for there were just too many pristine examples still in existence. I now think of this particular history as one of those inside jokes that links us all together as a class wherever we ended up in life. Carolyn Steedman suggests that the 1950s was a time when the labour movement 'failed to place socialism on the agenda of class politics'. That's probably true, but all those who were brought up in that period and who kept the Coronation cups share something of what can only be described as illusion, delusion, and collusion in our fate. That terrible, innocent trefoil is also what we have inherited and what also in a sense joins us together. You might say we were all to varying degrees slightly touched by royalty. I wish I knew, however, how many people of that generation share with me the regret that we lived through a time when no republican movement in Britain ever came close to being placed on the agenda.

The neighbourhood, then, where I grew up lives in my memory and, as my experience in Milan suggests, I carry it around with me. It's also somewhere I can return to with the trained eye of an academic. I wonder, for example, if Mrs Bignell, who occupied 79 Newland Road before the Great War, was ever invited by Mrs Walton into the Coffee Rooms. How many others living in that street wandered across its threshold to take a more down-to-earth cup of tea (for Coffee Rooms sounds too posh for that neighbourhood)? The tenement houses on the north side of Newland Road were occupied by what today we might judge a remarkably diverse range of trades people, including boot repairers, grocers, costumiers, dress makers, cycle makers, chair caners, saddlers, and a bath chair proprietor. On the south side of the street are listed Wenban Smith and Co, a timber and builders' merchants (which is still there), a boot maker, grocer, bakers, dairyman, tobacconist, butcher, sanitary laundry, and fruiterer. My childhood in the 1950s inherited a lively and active world, with people making things with their hands or selling things across a counter, and all within a hundred metres or so of each other.

By the 1950s the number of trades people had declined but the street retained its share of greengrocers, newsagents, decorators, laundries, bakers, hairdressers, and the Castle Hotel and the Norfolk Arms still mounted guard over the western approaches to Newland Road. As you would expect from a seaside resort on the South Coast, retired people were in evidence but not in the numbers you might imagine. In the 1950s, Worthing's population had around eighty thousand, and of these only some four thousand were under eighteen. However, senior citizens tended not to be the only conspicuous group on Newland Road. In my neighbourhood, people worked at home, close to home or away from home, and I can't ever recall anyone being unemployed or down-and-out. Resourcefulness was all around us. In one of the houses along the street lived our own Johnny Weissmuller, a talented body-builder who might have become famous. And if work was not available in the immediate vicinity you looked elsewhere. Until he was made redundant in 1963, my father worked as a boiler-man in Lancing Carriage Works, a large-scale railway employer, and my mother cleaned house for a number of better-off people in other parts of Worthing such as Park Crescent.

The high wall at the back of the house on Newland Road belonged to a small workshop on Station Road which periodically during the day emitted pungent, noxious smells into the neighbourhood. It smelt like a paint or glue factory, and the company must have been never short of complaints. Half way up Park Road and squeezed in between a row of terraced houses was a small garage. I've always been intrigued by the proximity of shops and workshops to housing, and it's why even today I'm not keen on the idea of dedicated housing estates. The terraced house where I live in York must have been a shop in the 1930s. When we bought the house there was a shop window at the front, but you could still make out where the two original sash windows must have been when it was built around 1840. Then one time when we were decorating we uncovered marks on the wall opposite the window where there must have been a series of wooden boxes for storage. On that same wall there would have been an entrance into the back of the house and where I assume there was either a door or a curtain for the family to come and go. Shoppers would then have entered the house through the front door, passed through the hall, and then turned into the front room where they would have bought whatever little things were for sale. Sooner or later, every house and neighbourhood has the potential to reveal its history to you. There's something appropriate in beginning a memoir with the word 'and'.

Across the road from the Foresters' Hall was 'next door', the Globe, on the corner of Newland Road and the Norse-sounding Dagmar Street. 'Just popping next door' or 'pushing the boat out' were phrases often heard in my childhood as relations and in-laws adjourned there with my father to be entertained and to discover what they were missing in the wider, spinning globe. My ever-respectable father may have been secretive in front of us, but wide-girthed draymen, complete with aprons and ropes tied round them, couldn't hide what they were up to as they offloaded barrels from their lorries down the iron runners into the depths below street level. The neighbourhood, then, was shared between children and adults, and we always knew our place even as we were noting down how the adults got their kicks. We noted, for example, that children were prevented from seeing inside the saloon bar of the Globe itself; they were restricted to the snug round the corner, which was, as its name implies, snug, a sober affair for quiet drinking, takeaways, and children sheepishly asking for their parents to return home or for change to get something from Wadeys, the newsagents and sweetshop opposite.

Homefield Park (now largely annexed by Worthing Hospital), where many hours of my childhood were spent, was not so much a second home as an outdoor laboratory. It was a different kind of space, one which needed constant watching, marking out, and negotiation, but it was largely free from adult interference. As we entered the park, we glimpsed through thick hedges and secure wire fencing fashionably dressed young men and women from outside the neighbourhood and from a different era playing tennis. Behind a shed in the park I lit up my first illicit cigarette, a small roll of tobacco sold in unusual packets of four for sixpence and called *Domino*. It tasted foul, as did *Players Weights*, which were sold in packets of five. I quickly switched to menthol cigarettes, which I could inhale without coughing up my lungs, a cigarette for putting a cool smile on your face and parading from side to side in front of friends and playmates. In a moody, seductive advert on television at the time, which showed a man lighting up under the glow of a street-lamp, we heard an authoritative voice inform us that 'You're never alone with a *Strand*,' but I could honestly reply that I was never alone with a menthol. The house was small and intense but the park had room for more furtive pursuits. Cool.

The Teville stream ran underground through the park from west to east. Because it was close to the surface, it turned a strip of grass a slightly different hue to the surrounding area. The stream, which once fed an ornamental lake in the park, was in one sense never on display but its subterranean presence could be felt. It rose in Tarring to the west of Worthing, flowed under the busy Teville Road, and emerged in Brooklands Lake in Lancing. From there it flowed into the English Channel, so it would have been a tidal inlet at one time in the past. When we entered the lower park from the entrance on Park Road, the Teville stream marked out a geometrical space for the eye to trace. In the centre of the park was a square roped off for cricket; to the north was a pavilion where players could change; to the south was another shed for people to sit and talk. In summer, when the funfairs arrived, they would set up camp over the Teville stream, but when the fair departed, the circular patches of grass, where the various rides had been, turned to hay, the same off-colour as the strip under which the stream flowed. That stream entered the well of my consciousness even if it took me years before I recognised it as a symbol of history quietly taking its course through my childhood.

Secrets abound in municipal parks. On the far side of Homefield Park there was a lovers' lane, where, under a tree-lined avenue of sorts, courting couples paraded in private or what they hoped was not too public. The bushes in the park, which never grew to any height, always looked threadbare, as if repeatedly man-handled. They were rarely of any use when it came to hide-and-seek, for you'd be spotted immediately. The park's clientele was inevitably mixed, as were the secrets. As children we would use penknives to cut little squares in the grass to hide coins or other precious objects. Then we would reseal the opening, note down the location, and hope we'd discover our treasure the following day or following week. 'Well, it's around here somewhere,' someone would remark, but occasionally we never did rediscover the location. When we got just a little older we would find ourselves bored and at our wits' end, and then do silly things like collecting grass in our tiny, grubby hands and seeing if we could chase the pre-pubescent girls and stuff the insides of their bras with our little offerings. That was another kind of secret waiting to be revealed.

Sometimes we resorted to forming gangs so as to conduct stone fights. We must have agreed not to use sharp flint stones, but apart from that there were no holds barred. One gang would occupy the high ground of the rockery near the swings while the other would be holed up in the shed near the public toilets at the north entrance to the park. The gang holding the rockery unquestionably had the upper hand. Most of the stones fortunately missed their target, but occasionally one would hit someone's head or close to someone's eye, as happened to my younger brother, Stephen, and then the fight fizzled out, but normally without recrimination or a visit to the hospital. The park-keeper would always be around somewhere, but only rarely would he catch us. He had just the one arm but that didn't slow him down, for, like Robocop, he would keep walking towards us across the park. We never caught him running and for that reason he never caught us. Every day he would be back, sitting in his office or on patrol, the sleeve of one arm tucked neatly into the jacket of his uniform. It must have been a miserable existence. He never managed to attract a nickname, for he was always simply 'parkie'.

The torchlight procession towards the end of summer was one of the highlights of the year and a reminder of the wider community. Seemingly all the ghouls in Worthing – and I didn't realise the town possessed so many – would come out on that evening in fancy dress. We would watch from the house, but would be forced to step back a foot or two when the masked Red Indians, complete with feathers and headbands and beating drums, would shake their flames at us or threaten to leave the procession and attack us there and then. Nothing frightened me on television as much as the dramatisation of James Fenimore Cooper's *The Last of the Mohicans* (1823). Outside the settlement was nothing but a forest of danger with shadowy figures intent on murderous deeds. For daytime frights, slightly back from the same vantage-point, behind the gate of our front door, we had the monthly excitement of cattle and sheep being driven in their hundreds along Newland Road on their way from the railway station to the abattoir on Brougham Road in East Worthing. The sheep, frightened out of their tiny minds, would jump over our low-walled front garden, desperate to discover a way back to their mates on the march to certain death and the butcher's knife. It should have been more romantic than it was, for in its own way it was our version of *Rawhide*, a Western series on television about cattle drovers and starring a young Clint Eastwood. But, close-up, the reality was less appealing.

The marble clock in the cupboard under the stairs, a working-class community in Worthing in the post-war period, neighbours on Newland Road, my childhood – all that is now confined to something we call the past. And yet I carry it all with me somewhere in memory and I can revive some of it via the long apprenticeship of writing. Writing in that sense is a tribute as well as a form of attention. In this book I focus on what happened to me as a child, while I was at school and university, during my career as a teacher, as I am now in middle age. I pay particular attention to my immediate contexts and surroundings, all the time conscious of a wider geography and history. Writing, then, possesses this capacity to breathe life into things past as well as into dead things, some of which we previously supposed impossible to revive. Not everything was intense for me as a child. Indeed, in my memory I find myself alighting on subterranean moments or images, which then glow with intensity all over again.

When I peruse the names on Newland Road in *Kelly's Directory of Worthing* for 1962, I reflect, 'Yes I remember that family, that person, that individual'. In the years to come, people will also take down the same Directory as I did in the Bodleian Library in Oxford in autumn 2009, and they will wonder about those names on a list. Some of those names will be family, but for many they will remain just a list for the disinterested eye. It is in the nature of things that thousands of names will always remain unattended, but what we can assert is that, if you start with the local and its intense moments and details, by a circuitous route you can end up with the universal and a fuller picture. As George Eliot also realised, the two go hand in hand, a belief in the larger picture and a concern with the smaller detail. In a writer's apprenticeship, too, nothing is ever too small or ever quite over and done with. In this regard you write for those who came before and for posterity. The underground stream that made itself noticed in Homefield Park will run for another generation of children like me to enjoy and it will also run in the minds of readers round the world because of this memoir. What was neglected or lost is rediscovered and, if it finds an audience or someone to notice it, it will enjoy a new lease of life. There's nothing magical about any of this, just in need of tending or retelling.

*Striking wedding photo of my parents, January 1941, on the steps of the Catholic Church in Worthing, Sussex. In the front row from left to right: Jim Pearce, Daisy's eldest son, Des Allen (friend of John Pearce), John Pearce, Daisy's youngest son, Julie Pierce, my father's sister, and Sidney Pierce, his brother. Middle row: Pat Kilmartin, my mother's brother, Lily (friend of my mother), Jane Pierce, Alf's sister, Daisy Pearce's father. Back row: Alf Pierce, my grandfather, my parents and Daisy Pearce, Alf's sister-in-law. It was a wartime wedding and the following day my father reported back to his unit in Portsmouth, and he didn't return home until 1944, by which time he had become a convert to Catholicism. For many wartime brides like my mother there was no honeymoon. When this photo was taken someone must have forgotten to say cheese.*

Chapter Two

# Writing Things Down

### Early memories

I suspect for most of us our earliest memories are like fragments or shafts of light catapulted out of an all-enveloping darkness. After all, what can we do without language? I recall being in a heavy-duty tank of a pram, whose colour was an old-fashioned, bottle green, and I am struggling to sit up. I have it in my mind that I was being pushed along the pavement on Newland Road near Wenban Smith. Perhaps there's a false memory at work here and I'm recalling a later incident when my brother, John, and my sister, Christine, were perched on the end of the pram with me inside. If so, with the passage of time, the two events have got confused and are now inseparable. Anyway, distinctions aside, I was fighting and pulling, my left hand trying to grab hold of the corner of the pram where the hood, stainless steel release arm, and buttoned plastic cover met. I must have had on a bonnet or hat for I felt I was suffocating. It was a struggle, and I am silently struggling, my upper body straining. All I sought was to throw off what was constraining me. I kept falling back and trying again, and again. I don't remember calling out or shouting but I was determined on a course of action. I was not stubborn but I was determined to slay the twin dragons of suffocation and claustrophobia.

As to what happened next, my memory is of no help and I have no means of accessing it or activating it. I assume my mother must have come to my aid and helped me sit up. It's the struggling I recall, struggling as it were for what was conceivably one of my first stepping-stones to consciousness. I say 'stepping-stones' but that isn't quite the right word, for that suggests a clearly-defined path, direction and outcome, when, arguably, it's only part of some connective tissue forged in memory. However, it must have been through such episodes that I eventually came to a full consciousness of myself and my separate identity as a person. Looked at from another perspective, and one that gives it added significance, perhaps what happened is part of some Oedipal event where the child seeks independence from the mother in order to achieve a closer form of bonding. Not so much a return to the womb, then, as a passage to an active relationship with my mother.

Memory, it has to be conceded, allows us only so much recognition or understanding. Expressed metaphorically or graphically, it's as if the abandoned or discarded torn parchment contains a fragment of writing, which is only just decipherable, in a language that contains no observable or known grammar. Whoever wrote it has fled back into the woods. S/he has infuriatingly left a trail and we feel compelled to follow its scent, but, every time we make the trip, the trail leads to the same impasse. Unlike in a play by Samuel Beckett, where the audience struggles to construct a context, here there is, or rather there was, a context but as yet no text. The reference to the pavement along which I was being pushed is I suspect part of my struggle to construct a context, whether at the time or now, but nothing that resembles a text comes back to me. As for the materials the pram was made of and the point where they met, I must have been discovering the material world not only orally but also tactilely. Suck it and see. Touch it and feel. Quite early on I must have grasped that getting your fingers trapped in the release arm was painful.

Years later, I was in the recovery ward at York District Hospital after having my gall bladder removed by laparoscopy. It might seem strange to report but something similar to what happened to me in the pram occurred. I was fighting for air and hitting out at the nurse who was shouting at me to lie back. That must be a common experience, but I tend to over-dramatise things and imagined the anaesthetic had taken a wrong course and turned ugly or perhaps the medical team had tried to revive me too quickly after the forty-five minute procedure. When I was back in the ward, I apologised profusely, but at the time all I felt was some urgent need to sit up and get some air. I had no words to communicate with anyone, just a desperate urge to save myself from oblivion, from being taken down to the morgue as it were.

A half century apart, it was as if I was back in my pram in the earliest memory I have retained. In the phrase that also in part overshadows this book, I was meeting myself again. Somewhere deep down, or out there, for I wish I could settle on an appropriate spatial metaphor to describe these events, I was undergoing a kind of pre-consciousness of adversity or, rather, I was being forced back to a primal stage of pre-linguistic experience which had never left me or which was waiting for me to rediscover or make common cause with. I can only surmise it must have been in adversity and desperation that our first ancestors came to consciousness of their identity as human beings.

The next event I recall is sitting with my mother on the shingle beach in front of Beach House Park in Worthing and enjoying a picnic. John and Christine, my brother and sister, must have been there but they are not part of the memory. We were probably eating sandwiches made of white sliced bread on some of which *Shipham's* fish paste had been thinly spread and on others *Robertson's* strawberry jam. It was always odd going out to have a picnic whether in Homefield Park or at Peter Pan's Playground or on the beach itself for we were within minutes of home. And yet for all that they were happy occasions as we gathered round our mother for the carefully divided handouts. This particular afternoon, the sun is shining, the pebbles on the pebbly beach are smooth and nicely coloured and attractive to hold in the palm of the hand as well as to press against the four quarters of the improvised table cloth, and there aren't too many people to crowd our enjoyment. In time, the tide, which is in, will drain away and reveal the sand, and then we will have a chance to build sandcastles with our brightly-coloured tin buckets and spades.

We are sitting some way back from the full extent of the high tide, midway between two stained groins periodically dipping and disappearing into the sea, and I look over the horizon beyond the pier toward the south-west. I am thinking 'This is the world. This is all there is. Beyond the horizon nothing exists. I am at the centre of the world and it's for me to explore whatever there is in it.' I put all this into such words, but at the time it was just a half-formulated thought which flashed through my mind. You couldn't speak of this as a middle voice, that voice in grammar between active and passive. To pose the question in terms of 'is something speaking me or am I speaking something' seems not quite right either. I've no idea how old I am, perhaps two, perhaps less. I'm still amazed not that I remember this but that the idea popped into my head. I suspect it's not uncommon for children at that age to imagine the size of the world could extend as far as the eye could see and no further. But I still ask myself if I was so protected or cosseted as a young child that I could suppose there was nothing beyond the horizon. One minute we don't exist and two years later we are thinking the most extraordinary things.

X-rays of elderly people's lungs can apparently reveal all kinds of scars or marks which don't affect their ability to breathe or lead an active life. Few of us die unmarked, but some cancers simply leave marks and die of their own accord. I wonder about the scars of memory. The episode in the pram and the one on the beach – are they anything more than scars of things that should be just left where they came from? Why subject them to a post-mortem or to the x-ray scanner we call memory? I wonder what purpose they serve. Some people, without knowing it, had TB as a child. My mother suffered double pneumonia in her early months and lived a healthy life with few chest problems. Such childhood diseases show up on a later scan, but the person survived it. Is this what some memories are like? Things we survive. Perhaps we should consider them as just marks on the soft tissue of the mind, marks that retain enough of the thing to be recognised later in life but not enough to make much sense of or do much with. And yet, in spite of voicing such scepticism, I am drawn to writing things down, as if to show faith with me the survivor, with the line of continuity, that is, that constitutes the self, the self, that is, which can entertain, or indeed allow for, such profound scepticism about its past.

The third memory that scars my early childhood is of pushing my four-wheeled teddy along an unfamiliar pavement. I am facing into the sun and travelling in a westerly direction as I imagine. There are houses or bungalows on my left which seem to be located below the height of the road. I am alone. It's not a busy road, it has an open aspect, and no roadside trees spoil or hinder the view. I don't know if I am crying or indeed if I am frightened. My father should have been looking after me at home but somehow I had walked out unchecked through the rarely locked front door, made my way along Dagmar Street, through the nearby tunnel for pedestrians and cyclists under the railway line, past the Nissen huts which were used as chicken sheds after the War, past Ivy Arch Road where the King of the Road coaches manoeuvred in and out of their garages to go to bed at night, on through the twittens or footpath which led up to Broadwater, and onto the road where my memory becomes live and sparks into action. I was lost but had no idea I was lost. At least I don't believe I had any such concern. No feeling of panic comes back to me. No passersby crossed my path or approached me. It transpires I was taken into the house of one of those kind people on that sunny road, and eventually the police arrived and I was escorted home in a police car with my aunt Mary who had been involved in the search.

Mary, my mother's sister from the west of Ireland, lived with us from 1949 until 1951, so I would have been between two and four years of age. As I write this in November 2009, I ask my mother, who is still alive in her late eighties, how old I was at the time, but her memory is now so patchy that she can't even recall the episode at all. 'You mean you went missing when you were a child and you were brought home by the police? I don't remember that.' I must have been welcomed home and smothered with tears of relief by my mother. My older brother and sister, upstairs at the window, must have responded somehow; I never asked them. Perhaps the neighbours stood around wondering at the boy who wandered off without permission and caused an incident. None of this has made its way back to me in memory. I never discovered until much later in life that the blame lay with my poor father, who had probably fallen asleep at the time and forgot to put up the gate at the front door.

With a knowing look as if we were co-conspirators in touch with larger forces at work in the universe, my mother would periodically remark to me, 'Thursday's child has far to go'. I don't believe it was because I wandered off at such an early age that she came to this conclusion, but I am attached to the warm glow and aura surrounding this memory. I felt no guilt at having done anything wrong. I had my little teddy and I was out pushing it toward heliopolis. On reflection, I wonder if this isn't an image of life itself. You're given something to cherish by your parents and you take off. Don't look back is the best advice. Hold that moment, I tell myself. Whatever you do, as Andrew Hodges, a dear friend in York puts it, try and avoid the parental 'wet overcoat' coming your way as one generation offloads its complex of tics and irritations onto the next. This one isn't an insignificant moment, for it contains the stuff of fiction or of poetry. I think of it as somewhere akin to the place before it becomes the celebrated spots of time that we read about in Wordsworth's verse. The moment is neither fully conscious nor an expression of the unconscious but seems to constitute part of the hinterland of consciousness where it resides, a spot in time but not a spot of time, a spot which has the potential – but not in fact the capacity – to keep expanding, a spot which indeed doesn't know when to stop resonating no matter how many times it is dragged out into the sunlight and subjected to scrutiny.

On another occasion my father was, again, left in charge of the household and, instead of dozing off, he took it upon himself to march me off to the barbers on Tarring Road to have my curls unceremoniously lopped off. Off, off, off. I was four by this time. My mother was, again, horrified when she returned home. For her, it must have marked the end of my babyhood; for my father, my entrance into masculinity. I felt none of this tension. I didn't really understand what all the fuss was about. However, as I listened to the story in the Old Testament about Samson losing his strength when he had his head shaved, I became confused. Why didn't all the stories in the world which looked similar have the same message, or at least point in the same direction? Surrounded by long shiny mirrors, jars of hair-oil and Brylcream, sharp razors and leather straps, the barber would ask my father after cutting his hair 'Anything else, sir?' Well, there is something, I would think to myself, as I sat in the chair next to him, not realising it was a question about condoms and French letters. How come Samson lost his strength whereas my cut curls signify entry into masculinity? I couldn't have expressed it like this, but I was on the road to joining a man's world.

Many of my early memories come with numbers attached. There were six of us in the family, my two parents, my two brothers, my sister and myself. Expressed mathematically, it was a case of two plus four, or six divided by four. I was the third child, not the missing child in the sequence 124 that appears in the opening sentence of Toni Morrison's novel, *Beloved* (1987), but the third child in a sequence marked 1945, 1946, 1947, and 1949. I was therefore one of a series and inserted into a definable post-war history. My place was secure and, although I might go walkabout in life, I would never go missing from the record books. My siblings were such a reality to me that I was always conscious of their shadow and of my serial relationship with them, facing out to the world together but also looking sideways at each other. Even our birthdays, which fell within the same period of each month – $22^{nd}$, $19^{th}$, $17^{th}$, and $19^{th}$ – testified to the same orbits around which we would circle in life. And we were thrown into existence in sequence, beginning with my elder brother in winter, my sister in spring, me in high summer, and my younger brother in autumn. I should by rights have worn a badge on my balaclava or woolly jumper 1234 with the 3 in bold, for my number was as brightly adorned as a nameplate or address. I was one in a series, at times enjoying co-operation, at other times competition, but there never would be a time when, on waking up in the morning, I would not be number 3.

The incident on the beach I kept to myself, and that is also part of the memory. The third child couldn't risk sharing such confidences for fear of ridicule by older siblings. There was too much at stake. Keep your insights to yourself that child learns early on. If I had swivelled my head round the other way to the left, I would have picked out the two tall chimneys of the power station at Shoreham Harbour and beyond that Brighton and the chalk cliffs at the Seven Sisters. Or perhaps I did so, only to discount that perspective. So what was I doing concluding I was at the centre of the world? Equally, I don't recall the moment or moments when I was disabused of this notion or indeed how long this incredibly naive idea accompanied me through childhood.

*A view of the beach looking toward the Dome Cinema. The hotel on the right is Warnes Hotel, where my great uncle George Pearce was employed for many years as a painter and decorator. The third boy from the left at the front looks as though he has just stepped barefoot on some sharp pebbles. With the tide coming in, seaweed strewn about the lower beach, one or two unoccupied deck-chairs, small fishing boats looking slightly abandoned, people wading gingerly in the water and shop awnings down though the sun doesn't appear to be out, this postcard from the early 1950s is full of the atmosphere of the period.*

Every child, occasionally in equal measure, attracts and constructs his or her own set of problems. An eldest child has a lot to live up to and can be made an example of. The youngest can be petted like a kitten. The second child is the first even number and for that reason can be a problem. An only child is unencumbered by the worries of a series. A third child is just another child, and for that reason carries the burden associated with sameness. In fact the third child is often haunted by the twin forces of sameness and difference. In fairy stories and folktales you always need three events to prove that things don't just happen by chance. In the Gospels, significance, such as St Peter's repeated denial that he knew Jesus, comes in threes. In families the effect is more psychological and impossible to shake off. The third bursts on the scene as if for the first time, and then you look around. 'Hey,' you shout, 'there's already a history in this family. I should have been born either first or elsewhere. There's too much water under the bridge for me to cope with.' It gnaws at the heart, you hear the cock crowing, and before long it's pretty obvious that you've been denied something. You're just another, which quickly slides into the gap formed by two words now separated: 'an other'.

I suspect this is not an uncommon experience for a third child. Exceptionally, some suffer a radical insecurity and are scarred for life. Others are happy they are the third child; that way they can let their older siblings share the responsibility for the family or ageing parents. As soon as I came to consciousness, my elder brother, John, my sister, Christine, and my younger brother, Stephen, were always there in my mind. I was always the 3 in the sequence 1234, but in turn I was always conscious of the series and my position in it. If I was rational and less maudlin, I would have seen that any child in a series would think as much. Thus, my sister would compile a very different account of our family background not only because she was second but also because she was a girl and it was assumed by my parents, for example, that she would leave school at fifteen. But for me the number three recurred in the culture and there must have been some reason for this, or at least this was as good a prop as any for co-opting this particular line of reasoning.

'Never get above your station' is something I learned with each passing month and each hand-me-down toy or item of clothing gratefully or otherwise received. 'Just button it. Wait your turn and cease complaining,' you're repeatedly told. I should have realised that life was but a game of pass the parcel and that one day the music would stop without me. For all eternity or at least since the beginning of time, the third person of the Trinity has had an enormous struggle getting noticed and should by rights complain to his master. Would I have similar difficulty in getting noticed? I recruited my own thoughts and harboured them, having recourse at times in my childhood to absconding late into the afternoon or evening and making myself invisible in order to become visible again and made a fuss of.

Some episodes from my early childhood, especially the three I describe here which took place outside the home, have stayed with me. Thousands of other moments and events have not. I am often surprised reading life narratives on sale in bookshops not at how confident an author can be in recalling childhood events but how they can assign so much significance to such fragments. I have similar doubts when reading early Freud on the interpretation of dreams. We carry around with us a discarded parchment which may or may not provide us with a satisfactory explanation of our identity. But if we had the full picture, the complete manuscript, would we not question what the fragment tells us? The White House stands for the President of the United States, but the flashes in our memories might light up nothing more than a fraction of the canvas, out of reach of metonymy and the realm of significance and security for which we, sometimes desperately, crave. In these, as in other matters, there's something to be said for not jumping to conclusions.

On the other hand, and it's reassuring for heretics like me that we have that phrase 'on the other hand' in the language, I enjoy these early memories. Perhaps the last thing my mind will alight on as my life flashes before me on my deathbed will be that image in memory of a small boy pushing a little teddy westward into the by now rapidly setting sun. If someone remembers to close my eyelids, I will hold that moment in time for eternity.


## Joseph Pierce (1919-2005)

I want to juxtapose a record of some of my early memories with writing down something about my father. I can do this by starting somewhere near a point of tentative closure with the eulogy I delivered at his funeral in August 2005. It's one of my many attempts at setting my house in order. I reprint it here more or less without alteration for it provides a more formal perspective on my family, told to an audience that included both outsiders as well as family and friends. It manages to capture something of the flavour of that occasion while at the same time it can serve as a slightly detached introduction to the family and my background. Every funeral address reaches for inclusivity and the banks of quiet diplomacy, but inevitably it carries its own set of allusions, some of which are understood only by family and friends. In spite of that, I have let this eulogy stand for the most part as it is. It was composed very quickly, within a day or so of his death, and I didn't have the usual time to spend on revisions.

Authors not infrequently observe that writing can overtake them as if it were issuing from somewhere they hadn't expected and just seems to run and run on its own accord. Indeed, there are times when we write fluently as if the whole world depended on it. In retrospect, I can now discern that there is something not so much forced as hammered out about this address, as if it bore the character of 'This is what I then thought and this is what I wrote'. I am reminded of 'Set down / This set down / This', the phrase one of the wise men resorts to in T.S.Eliot's poem, 'The Journey of the Magi', as he reflects in later life on the meaning of what he had witnessed that first Christmas. As the image of three trees on a low sky reminds us, Eliot's birth poem is also a death poem, for this was the person he was, someone who was fearless in facing up to the interconnectedness of life and death. In turn, his reflections took him to another concern and trope of his work, the terrain which my own book at times occupies, namely the tantalising disjunction or gap between words and meaning. With its broken up lines and use of a repeated deictic marker, 'This set down / This' is a brilliantly awkward evocation many authors feel in the face of the blank page and the tortuous process of saying what they mean, whether precisely or otherwise. We stutter. We try. We want to show but we can't quite get it out. This This.

How do any of us at such moments when grief is upon us review and summarise the life of a parent? 'Take this down,' declares the teacher in a dictation exercise in class. Here is my attempt at setting this down. It is part of the downward pressure that often accompanies the process of getting something into words, the pen pushing down on the page for example, or the fingers punching down on the keyboard, or the flight of the mind alighting on a branch of memory. In time, down into the earth, birth and death and writing are if not bedfellows then closely related.

'In the midst of life we are in death' – so the Book of Common Prayer in its no-nonsense prose informs us. But we have all been conscious that Joe has been dying for some time, so that each farewell over the past few months and, indeed, the past few years has been accompanied by the thought 'will this be the last'. For some 'In the midst of life, we are in debt', but this was never the case with Joe who always paid his way, careful as much for the future as for the present, investing wisely in the beautifully named insurance company 'Hearts of Oak'. While his body wasted underneath him, as his body prepared to do away with the distinction or tension between body and soul, he kept his mind lucid as those who saw him at the end can testify. His spirit lives on, thank God, and will do so while all those gathered here continue to survive him.

What can we say about Joe's long life by way of a summary? He served in the Royal Marines for some ten years, seeing action in Crete, in what is now Sri Lanka, and in the Indian Ocean. After the War, he spent eighteen years as a boiler-man at Lancing Carriage Works doing shift-work, followed by a short interlude collecting insurance premiums before ending his working life as a baker at Knowles the Bakers in Durrington. Such are the externals, but, as with most people, his life lay elsewhere. 'In my beginning is my end… In my end is my beginning.' Eliot's lines seem singularly appropriate with Joe in mind. He would want us to dwell on his childhood in Brighton and his Jewish upbringing with his brother Sid. As some of you may know, his grandparents and his mother are buried in the Jewish Cemetery in Brighton overlooking the Downs. They were a Jewish family about whom, as his sister Julie has discovered, little is known. The Van Prague surname evokes the beautiful Czech city in Bohemia, where a ford or *praga* across the River Vitava was constructed in antiquity and where merchants and Jews from all over Europe in the Middle Ages settled, crowding out the Old Jewish Cemetery. In fact, Joe's family probably came to Britain from the Low Countries (where it is a common surname) some time in the middle of the nineteenth century. They traded in shoes and cigars and, later, clothes. If you are romantically inclined – which Joe wasn't – you might imagine the family had been Sephardic Jews chased out of the Iberian Peninsula at the time of the Inquisition by zealous Roman Catholics. Or perhaps they were Ashkenazi Jews from Central Europe or the Russian Steppes, victims of the pogroms. What is known is that after a working life in Lambeth, Joe's grandparents did what all Londoners aspire to, and retired to the coast in Brighton.

Joe's mother, Esther Aarons, ran a clothes stall in Brighton before marrying Alfred Pierce. They had four children: Sidney, the eldest, who received his bar-mitzvah in his early teens, Joe, Raymond who died in childbirth or soon after, and Julie, who emigrated to Australia in the 1960s. Joe's mother, like Joe himself, married out of the tribe, for Alf was Church of England. Her early death, however, when Joe was nine and Julie but a few months old, ensured that Joe was brought up in the Christian church and that his Jewish days were over. But not quite. If you visit the family headstones in Brighton, it becomes apparent that the two boys were named after their Jewish forbears, as was Julie after her grandmother, Julia Aarons. And Joe continued in the tradition, for when he married Bridget Kilmartin in this church of St Mary and the Angels in 1941, he too married out of the tribe becoming a convert to Catholicism while stationed in Kalutara in Ceylon in 1944. Religion meant a lot to him, not so much denominations as religion in its primary sense, and he was particularly moved in recent years by his grandson Stephen Merriman's ordination to the Anglican priesthood. In one sense, after marrying, Joe never looked back, but, when prompted to reflect on his life, he would at some point return to the early death of his mother, as if he knew that in the midst of life he was indeed in death, only now it was a loss he felt he couldn't properly articulate or come to terms with.

Well, the past partly explains the present and why we are all here. Families are about life and death, a space for a never-ending cycle of hellos and goodbyes, for generation, fortunately, never stops. It certainly didn't in those post-War years as the troops abandoned weapons' drill for more domestic matters such as contributing to the baby boom. As for the Pierces, they were among the last fishing families in Brighton and their character and fate is more familiar to many of us here today. *The House of Music and the Cupboard under the Stairs*, the privately printed family book which Joe helped me with, traces some of that history. Joe possessed a strong sense in his own mind of extended family, so that as children we frequently heard mention of Dick, Jane, Hannah, Alice, and Irene in Lincoln. Alf's brother, George, who married Daisy Woolgar, had three children Jim, George and John, and they were always in and out of the house on Newland Road. In recent years Julie's children from Perth in Western Australia have also found a second home in Worthing. All that extended family, past, absent, and present, are here with us today as we bid a final goodbye to Joe.

Long before the obsession with careers came along, family was a yardstick to measure the world. What can we observe about the family who have succeeded Joe except to embark on some counting? Joe was lucky that he had so many people to mourn his passing. A wife, a sister, four children, seven grandchildren, three great-grandchildren, some twenty-two nephews and nieces, numerous great-nieces, nephews and cousins. He can't compete with Queen Victoria but it's quite an achievement nonetheless for someone who spent much of his life watching TV and John Wayne repeats. And I've said nothing about his Irish family or his mother-in-law who would address him in the wilds of the west of Ireland as 'Sir' as if he were a sahib or lord of the manor. The Irish family he married into was extensive and always welcoming – Kilmartins, Haughs, Spratts, Kellys. Mary Kilmartin was like a sister to him, and this is also the place to offer a special word of thanks to Mary's daughter, Margaret Davis. Since arriving in Worthing several decades ago, Margaret has shown remarkable devotion to my parents, and just a few weeks ago in happier circumstances she organised a splendid get-together for the family. When Joe didn't feel up to attending, it was clear the end was in sight. As for his lifetime companion, Bridie, she can speak for herself, but all the family past and present are here united, in the midst of life, in Joe's death.

Let me end on a lighter note. When Joe died on 4 August, the *Sun* carried the headline 'Let's put the great back into Britain'. I don't know if Joe followed the recent bombings in London, but, if he did, he responded in his inimitable way to the *Sun*'s hectoring stance by doing the decent thing and quietly taking his leave. Perversity – this is the character trait I most admired in him, and, like some of his other children, I have inherited this in abundance. He could always be counted on not to say or do what he was supposed to. He was part of humanity's awkward squad. When he wasn't getting his way or he was facing criticism from superiors, he knew perfectly how to give the right inflection to the English expression 'Suit yourself'. In the early fifties I would be engrossed by stories in comics dramatising heroic action in the War. Joe's view of the War chimed with the one on display in Joseph Heller's *Catch-22*, but, unlike the characters in that comic anti-war novel, he was terse about it all, and, if pressed, he would simply reply that we won the War because we possessed superior weapons. So much for a young boy's dreams of heroism or, indeed, the *Sun*'s version of GREAT Britain.

On arriving home from the War, all he sought was to draw a line not just on history but geography too. From now on Pompey, led by Jimmy Dickinson, was a football team to cheer on and no longer the naval port of Portsmouth to depart from. 'Abroad? Smelly place', he would reply, and yet he enjoyed his visits to France and the champagne country when given the opportunity to accompany his son, John. The descendant of fishermen would also insist on referring to mackerel as 'dirty fish'. Long before the phrase came into common use, Joe was there: 'Been there, done that!' In fact he hadn't, but it was surprising how much he knew given that he read so little. He knew all about tsunamis long before the big one struck Indonesia last December. And why wouldn't he, given his wanderings round the Indian Ocean with a regiment seemingly bent on avoiding war. When he worked at Knowles the Bakers and the time-and-motion people arrived to conduct an efficiency drive, he could be counted on to do the right thing and keep things slow or even-paced. And he was by nature slow and methodical, rarely flustered, but, unlike the Kilmartins, he was always on time and he always had an answer. When his daughter-in-law, Mary Eagleton, asked him when he retired if he felt rejected by society, he replied laconically, with a hint of triumph in his voice and as if the whole history of his class was behind him, 'No I have rejected it'.

Always drawing a line – this was Joe, the family man who never lost his sense of displacement or of home. The very last day he spent in the family home in South Farm Road there occurred not one but two farewells, both in a sense unwitnessed, for he was taken to hospital in the early hours of the morning only to be sent home only to return to hospital later the same day. Peace to his bones, or perhaps we should say, given his perversity about not being buried for fear of vandals disturbing his bones, peace to his ashes!

My father's world was largely offstage. It came as a shock when we went to visit him as children on an open day at the Carriage Works in Lancing, which was the main workshop of the Southern Region of British Railways for the repair of steam-hauled, electric and diesel-electric coaching stock, and which employed some 1,950 people. We knew he was a boiler-man but we had only a limited idea as to what that meant. I don't recall now if he was in overalls, but he was wearing a shirt open at the neck or perhaps it was a white vest or T-shirt. He was taking a break outside the hut where he stoked the boilers. Inside, the boilers were pounding away, the coal or coke on one side of the hut, the shovels resting nearby. It evidently wasn't a modern boiler house, and it seemed to me potentially quite dangerous on the edge of a large apron next to the fire station. But my father showed us the various dials and what his job entailed, and he also introduced his workmate to us – I think it was that way round, not us to his workmate. I couldn't, however, decide whether or not he was happy, though he looked energised. So, that's what he did when he was out of the house, and that's what he did for some eighteen years. Outside the house, at work, he felt less like a father and more like someone else.

At the Carriage Works he worked three different shifts for three weeks at a time. It was a deadly shift pattern, and guaranteed to ensure the labourer plodded homeward with a weary tread. Nights must have been particularly irksome, but the shift I remember as a very young child was the one when he had an early dinner at midday by himself before leaving to catch the train to work. There would have been a pattern to those days because I distinctly recall sitting in my wooden high-chair and calling out 'me 'ave some'. Even though he tended not to say much, I believe I was good company for my father. He had a hot cooked dinner, for he needed something to keep him going until getting home around 9.30. After dinner he would put on an off-white trench coat with two deep outside pockets at the front and a long belt which needed tucking inside. In one of the deep pockets he would insert the sandwiches which my mother had made for him, and if it was overcast or raining he would pick up his brown felt trilby and off he would go, ready for battle.

More than anything what my father possessed in abundance was stamina. He was never very good round the house and he taught us precious few skills. Nearly all the time he was in the house, he was sitting down, smoking an occasional pipe, reading the newspaper, listening to the radio, looking at the television when we got one, or staring into space. His cousin, Jim Pearce, who was a pilot officer in the Royal Air Force, rewired the house; John Pearce, Jim's brother, made us a cricket bat, which we cherished, while my father's brother, Sidney, erected the television aerial against the factory wall in the back yard. Once when I was in a hardware store seeking advice in connection with some task in the house where I now live, the assistant tried to reassure me by observing, 'You look as though you can wield a spanner.' He couldn't have been more wrong. None of my father's children could wield a spanner.

If a screw refused to turn going into a wall, it was hammered in. We knew how to change a plug, but that was about it. If something didn't work, whether mechanical or electrical, we were stumped. We tried kicking or thumping, though not like most people as a last resort but as a first resort, and when applied to the radio and television, that seemed to do the trick. Indeed, we were amazed that modern life could be so responsive to just a simple thing as a kick or a thump. In essence what we lacked was aptitude, and it is questionable if an apprenticeship in this case would have helped much. My brother-in-law, Stephen Merriman, takes delight in fixing things, but none of my father's children took any such delight. On every occasion when faced with a dilemma, it resulted in panic. There was no stepping back or reflecting for a moment or two. No, the black hole had to be filled, and at once. But as for character-forming stamina in the face of life and its many setbacks, we all possess that in abundance.

Stamina went with something else with my father. The shift pattern and often harsh working environment that he endured throughout his life made him more not less respectful of colleagues and workmates. Even as a charge-hand at Knowles the Bakers, from the 1960s until he retired, he would lead by quiet example. The only power he wielded was against the management. Such-and-such a machine would be proscribed if it wasn't safe to operate. 'No,' he would declare, 'that particular practice couldn't be introduced except by consent.' Everything in such environments conspired to treat the workforce as 'hands', but my father invariably had time to treat people as if they had a family and a life outside the factory. He stopped by the various machines in the bakery and talked to the bad-tempered Ruby on the winkler doughnut machine, to taciturn Freddie, who worked alone making Cornish pasties by hand in the morning and Danish pastry by hand in the afternoons, or to sociable Dave from Steyning, who was in charge of flour-making at the start of the day.

He was not really a union man and would never have attended meetings of trades councils, but he instinctively recognised what was right and what wasn't. 'Very Good' is how his character is abbreviated on his Certificate of Discharge from the Royal Marines in 1946; on the same document it also records 'Scar back of rt. Ear' as his physical identification mark. Wherever he worked, whether at the Carriage Works or at the bakery, there were individuals who couldn't cope or who had trouble holding down a job. When Margaret Thatcher came to power in 1979, he wasn't alarmed but he did ask a simple, and in some ways the most pertinent, question: 'Tories are past masters at looking after themselves, but what are you going to do with people who can't help themselves?' It took the Conservative Party a generation to hear that question and come to recognise (and then after 2010 to abandon) the truth of that implied critique of their social policy.

While he was attentive to others, my father struggled to attend to his own emotions. 'Still waters run deep' is an expression which could have applied to him, but it was at times impossible to discern what he was thinking or feeling. In later life, I would watch him for hours sitting in the armchair at home wondering what was going through his mind. But he never wandered off, so you would never catch him somewhere else. He would invariably come in on the right note, which was somewhere near the end of an argument when subtle distinctions gave way to forthright judgements and diamond absolutes. 'Speak when you're spoken to,' was one of his expressions to us as children, and perhaps he still felt it also applied to him.

He was always interested in what was in the news, how what (few) shares he owned were doing, how the local shops in the town centre were faring. In the 1950s, if we were in the house, he insisted on us listening to and then watching the *Brains Trust* on Sunday afternoon radio and television. But his character was governed by the alternating tides of engagement and

*My father on duty in khaki shorts, his shadow behind him. Egypt, 1941.*

detachment. One minute he was engaged in conversation, the next detached. One minute passive, the next animated. One minute smoking his pipe, the next in his size 11 shoes racing my nine-year-old sister half-way down Newland Road. Sometimes he was like a volcano erupting for little or no reason. The meal left for him was lukewarm; he couldn't locate the tin-opener; there was no bread in the house; the milk was off. But, in general, his life ran along an even course.

I suppose what you could say of my father is that he lacked a strong ambition, and when he came back from the War, like many of his generation, he retreated somewhat from the world and, instead, went to the cinema. In that respect he was blessed, for Worthing possessed four cinemas at that time, and two of them, the Dome and the Rivoli, would rotate their programmes twice a week. My mother indulged him, and he would justify his excessive devotion to the silver screen by saying that he found it difficult to settle after travelling the world on board ship with the Marines and that films filled his imagination (temporarily) with uninterrupted and wide open spaces. He was invalided out of the Marines in 1946, but I don't believe that was the reason he never spoke about his wartime experiences. As with the rest of his past, the War was something he was not going to dwell on. Equally, I suspect ten years in the services had put paid to any lingering idea he might have entertained about heroism or heroic action. *Bilko* was one of his favourite television programmes, and, watching him identifying with the men against the officers and top brass and laughing out loud, it was as if he too had been through similar experiences.

He was among the last of the Allied forces to be evacuated from Crete and he received a blow to the back of his head from a falling spar, for which he was 'granted' in May 1943 a 'Hurt Certificate'. So, before being transported to Egypt and then being posted to signals work in the Indian Ocean, he had seen action. On one occasion in later life he met up with his old comrades for their reunion, but then no more. If he had fought with the Desert Rats or had risen through the ranks, perhaps he would have been forthcoming. In keeping with his sense of detachment – or maybe I should say his sense of engagement – he enjoyed war films and watching the band of the Royal Marines on television. I remember my elder brother, John, ploughing through Churchill's multi-volume history of the war, but none of this seemed to provoke my father into discussion. Like the other episodes from his past, the War was a closed book. He must have had vivid moments recalling the War but I never once heard him begin a sentence with 'I had the strangest dream last night'.

I wish I had kept the couple of letters he sent me when I was away at school, for the content of those letters would have revealed another side to him. All I now recall is the slanting handwriting, full of narrow loops so that the letters 'l' or 'e' or 'f' were difficult to distinguish. His loops were like the arms of a signaller going through some circular motion, but it created difficulties for the person deciphering the message. He walked so upright, but when he took hold of the pen in his hand he must have imagined he was pushing something up a hill or dragging something behind him. I sometimes wish I could have done more for him. I see him now in retirement, sitting on the sofa across from me in York, waiting to go out for a drink. 'Are you right, then?' he remarks, ready for battle, and we rise together. He was one of those people who needed prodding or bringing in from the cold, but I was always conscious of protecting his space just as he had taken care, for the most part, over all those intervening years since my childhood, in protecting mine.

## The movement back and forth

Writing things down involves a movement back and forth. You scroll up and down the computer screen looking for infelicities. It's as if nothing can be set down without revision. Everything needs bedding down. This sentence is good but it's in the wrong position. This adjective is overused. This phrase is a bit of a cliché. Are you saying anything in this paragraph? You've got such an inflated idea of yourself if you believe you thought this. Be a little more honest and play less to the gallery. No one is interested in this episode. Say more about how you felt at that time. Get inside the moment and give it to the reader with more punch. Back and forth the writer goes, scrolling up and down on screen, perhaps never fully satisfied until a provisional point, a service station on the highway of writing, to adopt a tired metaphor, is reached. I can't do any more with this. I'll leave it for a few months and come back to it. I'm too close to the material. Perhaps then I can get it to sound right, for writing is also about sounds.

Why do you want to write things down? That's a question not easy to answer. In his well-crafted book of memoirs ingeniously entitled *Speak, Memory* (1951), Nabokov suggests he inherited a keen 'retrospective faculty'. It's a phrase that reminds me of his cognate interest in collecting butterflies and putting things under the microscope. The Russian exile enjoyed a special, privileged upbringing, and his account is not so much the memoirs of a survivor – though it is this – as a series of confident excursions into his childhood and family history. In an equally absorbing story of her family, *How Many Years* (1977), the French writer, Marguerite Yourcenar, who could count on her paternal side four great-grandparents in 1850, sixteen great-great-great-grandparents around Year II of the Revolution, and 4,096 relatives during the reign of François I, creates the impression that her family is a never-ending source of 'income drawdown' for her to transform into literature. My father's family almost certainly never went on the Grand Tour in the eighteenth century, and whatever tastes the fishermen acquired in nineteenth-century Brighton would not have merited the description 'bourgeois'. They certainly exhibited none of Nabokov's retrospective faculty, or if they did none of it survived. On my maternal side, the only store-room in the country house on my Irish grandmother's 'estate' went by the name of 'the long ago', and its objects had never been catalogued.

I go back and forth in my own mind and discover there only some kind of compulsion when I began these memoirs in October 2009. After finishing *Reading Joyce* in the autumn of 2007, I decided my days as a writer were at an end. I had just retired. I had completed ten books of criticism, and I didn't want to embark on any more books or any more projects. Let someone else take over. I still had things to express but there was a wider world out there and writing is concentrated on only a small part of it. But then two years later I came down one morning, sat at my laptop and began typing 'And would it have mattered if I had remembered who else was in that room the afternoon she first entered my life?' Everyone seemed to be compiling memoirs and, a little like chicken pox, it was catching. Four months later, by the middle of February 2010, I had finished seven chapters and getting on for seventy thousand words. By early April I had more than a hundred thousand words, and the book as a rough draft was more or less complete. If Annie Dillard, author of *The Writing Life* (1989), is right, and I don't think she is, I was one of only some twenty people in the world to write a book in a year. Clearly, something in my head had been waiting to be written down, a kind of downward pressure, or a movement toward some kind of postscript. That's the best answer I can offer to friends who look at me, perplexed, and wonder why, like my childhood friend June, I'm still reluctant to come out to play.

The spatial metaphors I'm using here – writing things down, back and forth – convey something of what's involved in writing memoirs. The Castle Museum in York has a living room done out in the style of the 1950s. It used to be known as the Coronation Room. One minute I had been wandering through the militaria section, bored by all the objects of war and the seemingly endless suits of armour and the ingenious ways to kill people. Next came a collection of various domestic cleaners from *Ewbank* to *Hoover* and, more recently, *Dyson*, and nearby there was a prominent notice on the wall 'Cleanliness Is Next To Godliness'. On turning a corner in the Museum up a flight of stairs I was suddenly confronted with a scene from the past, taunting me to verify its accuracy or teasing me to identify what was missing or what was in the wrong place. This was my past and, worse, my past was in a museum. That I found slightly shocking, for it was like a premonition, a deathly moment. In the midst of walking round what was nothing more than a museum, filled with objects from the past, I had inadvertently stumbled upon my consignment, my exit moment, which, to make matters worse, was closer in time to my point of entry in 1947. As I looked for the exit signs, here I imagined was the end of the long apprenticeship.

*The 1950s living room at the Castle Museum, York.*

In spite of the deliberately low lighting, with its colour dominated by brown and cream, the 1950s portrait was slightly overpowering. Presiding over the room, cluttered with objects, was a three-piece suite in brown imitation leather with pouffe to match. My eye took in the details. The three birds on the wall opposite the fireplace, arranged in ascending or descending order, served to mock pretension even as they were decidedly accurate and of their time. A small television was now beginning to take centre stage, for this was 1953 when ordinary people began to rent or buy televisions in Britain. The settee was set in dialogue as it were with the fireplace and surround, which in turn jutted out into the room and in front of which there was an arc-shaped rug. In keeping with the emphasis on homeliness, on the settee there was a stuffed ginger cat and beside the fire a copy of *Picture Post*.

The room was claustrophobic, with every space vying for attention. A large ornamental dog had been placed on top of the television; two candlestick holders made the mantelpiece resemble an altar in a church except that the candles were red not white; a pretentious writing bureau occupied one of the alcoves, its lid closed, and at the back of the room a small side table with cups and saucers had been laid out. In reality, such rooms were often suffocating, and when all the family was home in the evening, it would have been a struggle just moving around, especially if there were teenagers with growing legs stretched out.

I was struck by something else. There was, or rather there is, a kind of perversity about it all. The Castle Museum is intent on accuracy and the visitor who has lived through that period wants recognition or confirmation, that this is the world they lived through. When I first saw that room in the 1970s I was impressed by the accuracy of the details. But a decade or so later, when I visited the Museum again, I was that much older and history in more ways than one was catching up on me. Quite properly the Museum's focus is on what was typical in a respectable, working-class home for the period, and the visitor plays along. But because the room is in a museum, the past is open to display in a form that is to some extent intrusive, and I use the word 'intrusive' because some of those who once inhabited such rooms are still alive. Such people, and I include myself in their number, are in the process of being consigned to the past. Something rather terrible has been taking its historical course, for there had been no official farewell, simply my generation's removal from the scene.

Not everyone feels this way, and that can be both reassuring and disturbing. When I returned to the Museum in February 2010 to check on some details, I overheard an elderly woman beside me casually, and with no sign of dismay, announce to her companion, 'In fact, I've still got a lampshade like that.' Nearby there were other rooms on display: a Georgian room, a Victorian Parlour, a room in a Moorland cottage. The Coronation Room was, therefore, one of a series. For reassurance I suspect, as much as for anything else, you would sometimes hear an older teacher observing 'Look, children, that's how it was. That's how we lived when the Queen came to the throne.' It was worse when the 'we' was changed to 'they', that's how they lived.

Writing a memoir is also about setting down a moment in time and holding it for others to share. It is about details and arrangement and order. It's about the past we imagine is still worth recording, perhaps for posterity, perhaps for our children and grandchildren. It gestures toward a tradition, something that should be handed on, like traditional Irish music. At the heart of it all is death. 'Heart' is perhaps an exaggeration, but behind it all something is being shuffled off. The Coronation Room in the Castle Museum is dead, and, for all its meticulous planning, it was never designed to be lived in. You scrutinise all the objects and you come to the inescapable conclusion that they are all inert. Unlike the realistic texture of, say, Edward Hopper's iconic painting *Nighthawks* (1942) in the Art Institute of Chicago with its subtle play of forces in a late-night diner, there is no inherent tension in the Coronation Room.

If I turned my back to the Coronation Room and held up a Claude convex mirror, no matter how hard I might try, I couldn't transform the scene into an eighteenth-century, picturesque landscape. One reason for this is that, unlike, say, Tintern Abbey, there is nothing painterly about the Room. It is full of objects held in a deathly, period embrace. Such objects could be moved around on a weekly basis by the curator, but, whichever arrangement is decided upon, the Coronation Room would stay put and remain almost entirely untouched by responses taking place inside the passing visitor or viewing public. In this sense it is not a room with a view, and for the most part it is devoid of emotions.

Indeed, unlike the Hopper painting, no position or frame is assigned to the viewer. In both 'displays', the context is paramount, but in the Hopper canvas context serves the theme whereas in the Coronation Room the context is the theme. Equally, Hopper has managed to drain the scene of noise and to freeze the moment, and, moreover, he has deliberately provided no switch to set any of it in motion. In the Coronation Room, on the other hand, the clock has stopped and even if it were to start up again that would constitute an ironic comment on the rest of the room and further confirmation that nothing is alive. So for a visitor like myself who lived through the 1950s, there is delight and dread, but only because of an emotional charge which accompanies me.

The room in the Castle Museum also reminds me of a recognition scene in a Greek tragedy, except that in this case time is working in a different direction, from then as it were until now. Equally, while I might have committed no sin of hubris, I do bear the marks of time, which is not unlike a sin, for I have outlived my past. For those who write memoirs, we have constant recourse to an idea of recognition, of knowledge coming again or being recuperated. The three birds on the wall will provoke for another generation different associations. Writing a memoir involves a movement back and forth, and we might also imagine this in terms of a happy starting out leading at some stage to a postscript, a long apprenticeship that is. History and the present are in this way brought into a dynamic relationship, both delight and dread, both the narrowing and the broadening of the mind, both recognition and cognition, old knowledge reactivated and new knowledge imparted. A memoir activates the past, gives it life, wanders around among the gravestones and the burial urns, alighting on things to interest people. But it's not normally done in the spirit of 'As you are now, so once were we'.

The living room of my childhood is alive with noise and busy with people. Something was always happening. I am seated on an extending dining table with my three siblings as my mother readies each of us in turn to go out. I hear Phil Smith, an elderly Irish labourer who never married, put his head round the living room door 'just to say hello'. He's offered one of the wooden, dining chairs with a more secure back, and, his bones creaking, he sits down wearily. He gets out a *Rizla*, a roll-your-own cigarette paper, and manages to drop some of the loose tobacco onto the floor between his legs in front of him. In spite of spending his life on building sites with a shovel, he's in good form. He lights up his badly rolled cigarette and thinks of home in Ballyjamesduff in County Cavan. He knows, however, that Worthing is now his home where his niece, the delightfully irrepressible Julie Crouch, lives. The toes of his boots are white with cement dust. He drinks a cup of tea and is temporarily revived. Our living room is one of his ports of call. He works half-day on Saturday. He flicks ash onto the lino, imagining all floors come with the flagstones of home. We are now all ready to go out. As we wait on the forecourt for her to rummage for the front-door key in the bottom of her handbag, my agitated mother asks, 'Is the catch down?' The song that accompanied Phil to the grave was 'Come back Paddy Reilly to Ballyjamesduff', a song from over the sea that never stopped whispering to him when he was alive. One of the millions of exiles who never came back.

The museum seeks the typical, the memorialist, if s/he has any sense, the specific, frequently in the knowledge that the specific belongs to what is typical. But sometimes the specific is the interruption. In my childhood, a childhood without phones, people would drop in just as we were about to go out. The Coronation Room plays host to no visitors and to no interruption, so it can never be, strictly speaking, typical, for interruption is what is typical in many working-class homes. Putting that into words means a disruption to the narrative, so a memoir needs to strike a balance between the onward flow of things, the living room as it were, and the restraint that comes with things that stop up the flow or take a different course. A memoir in that regard has more flexibility. If it persuades us, it does so through its own kind of logic.

Back and forth the memorialist goes, drawing inferences, connections, extensions, conclusions, always conscious that things could be differently arranged. But some things have a natural order as with this chapter. Begin at the beginning with early memories and proceed through to the end with the death of your father. That way an order can be imposed on writing things down. And what can be more typical when it comes to writing a memoir than starting at the beginning not as St John does with language and the Word but with a child's earliest memories and ending with the death in this case of the child's father? A memoir, then, draws its power from being both a memento and a *memento mori*, both something with feelings attached and also a sign of something deathly and irrecoverable awaiting us all. This this. As a matter of course, it moves, at times imperceptibly, between the two poles of posterity and extinction. For this reason a memoir, in its own way a book of wisdom about the afterlife, is not only more complex but also more precious than anything encountered in a museum of everyday life.

*Wedding portrait of my grandparents, Esther Aarons and Alfred Pierce, June 1914, Brighton, Sussex.*

Chapter Three

# My Father's Family

## The Jewish connection

My Jewish roots are much more remote than my Irish roots. They are so remote that it's a little strange even speaking in such terms as Jewish roots. I don't ever recall as a child learning about my Jewish family, and it is only in recent years that I visited the graves of my grandmother and my great-grandparents in the Jewish Cemetery overlooking the Downs in Brighton. Esther Aarons was the maiden name of my grandmother and her mother's maiden name was Van Prague or Vanprague or Van Praag; my great-great-grandmother's maiden name was Joseph. The Van Praags, a common name in the low countries, were perhaps Sephardic Jews, possibly displaced, like the Jewish philosopher Spinoza, from the Iberian peninsula when an intolerant Catholicism gained the upper hand. They were prominent in Amsterdam in the seventeenth century and contributed as traders to that great trading city. Without any clear facts, I imagine a romantic past for them. Perhaps, they were classic wanderers who came to London in the first half of the nineteenth century (probably not before, for in 1800, it has been calculated, there were fewer than fifty thousand Jews in Britain). But I have to admit I don't know what year they or the Aarons arrived or where they alighted.

It would be mean to imagine that the Aarons charged at the Old Bailey in the eighteenth century with various offences, mostly of larceny, one of whom was transported for stealing a silk purse, were my family. Of course, if that were the case it would make my background a little more exotic, but I like to imagine the Aarons and the Van Pragues or the Josephs were more sinned against than sinning. I set them down in Lambeth Walk when William Blake lived in the vicinity in the first decades of the nineteenth century. Perhaps he observed their marks of woe on his way across Westminster Bridge to sell his prints and engravings in the area round St Paul's Cathedral. On the busy south side of the Thames small traders and tanning factories made use of the berths for import and export. They seem to have enjoyed a measure of success in life, from general dealer to cigar-dealer and boot-maker in two generations. And my great-grandparents had enough money to retire to Brighton, their last address being 12 Montpelier Road. But almost nothing of their Jewishness has survived – the only thing that links me with this generation is the diabetes I seem to have inherited from Sidney Aarons and memories my father had of his special diabetic loaves of bread.

The facts I have gleaned are basic. Sidney Aarons was born in Whitechapel, London in 1855. His father was a 'general dealer', while his mother signed the birth certificate with a cross. Her mother's maiden name was Solomons. Julia, his wife, was born the same year in Ratcliffe, Middlesex. Her father, Louis Van Praag, was a cigar dealer, while her mother's maiden name was Joseph. Sidney and Julia got married in March 1878 in the Great Synagogue in the parish of St James's, Aldgate, in the City of London. They were then living in Newcastle Street near the Aldwych. He was a boot-maker, she the daughter of a clerk. By 1881 they have two children, Joseph, aged 2, and Catherine, who is under one years old. Sidney's occupation in the 1881 Census of England and Wales confirms he was a boot-maker. Living in the same house at 122 Lambeth Walk in Lambeth was George Wooding, aged 15, Sidney's apprentice, and their servant Louisa Bush, aged 14.

In the 1891 Census, Sidney and Julia occupy 65/7 Lambeth Walk in Lambeth with their eight children. Sidney gives his occupation as 'boot-maker', but against the names of the children there are no other occupations. Joseph is the eldest at 18, and the youngest is Clara, who is eight months. Esther is 3. Also with them is Sidney's father, Joseph, aged 74, who is now a widower and blind, and a nurse whose name is Alice Mitchell, age 13. By 1901, Sidney and Julia are in their mid-forties. Their children are all living in the same house at 28 Kennington Road, Lambeth, which is a much more substantial house than the ones they occupied on Lambeth Walk nearby. Unfortunately, the house is no longer there, but next door there is a four-story row of dwellings with shops at street level including a William Hill betting shop, and this might have been what number 28 looked like in 1901. Joseph, now aged 22, is a boot-maker, Catherine is 20, John, 18, is a boot clicker, Louis, 17, is a boot salesman, Michael, 15, is also a boot clicker, Elisabeth is 12, Clara

10, and Isaac 6. A boot clicker was someone who cut the leather into the shape of a shoe before it was passed over for someone else to stitch to the sole. It was highly skilled work and carried status therefore. Sidney, a 'boot manufacturer' and employer, seems to have ensured that his sons had status and were assigned a particular role: boot-maker, boot clicker, boot salesman.

The family resembled a mini-factory or a cottage industry, with all the members contributing to its economic health and well-being. I assume they made the boots and shoes on the premises, and perhaps they had turned the ground floor front room into a shop to sell their wares. In 1901 no apprentice is listed, for he is presumably no longer necessary when the sons are now active workers. However, there are three live-in servants, Ada Barker, the cook, Kate Mason, a housemaid, and Annie Sims, a kitchen maid. It must have been quite a squeeze. Thirteen people plus Esther lived in that one house on Kennington Road, a road that was probably always a busy thoroughfare and that is now part of the London to Brighton A23 main road.

Esther's parents clearly possessed money and aspiration. There is an announcement in the *Jewish Chronicle* on 30 November 1894 of the birth of a son on 12 November at 65 and 67 Lambeth Walk to the wife of Sidney Aarons. This would be Isaac, their youngest child, who would have been seven years younger than my grandmother. The *Post Office London Directory* for 1902 shows the family also occupying 57 and 69, but in fact some time around 1901 they had moved to Kennington Road, which I assume they owned. Even so, their neighbours were not exactly wealthy: a music hall agent, a variety artiste, a hospital dispensary attendant, a dressmaker machinist, a house builder and decorator, a restaurant waiter. In one of the houses there is a boarder, who is a 'confectioner's forewoman'. Perhaps it is more accurate to state they were trades people who were upwardly mobile and who had not yet suffered the fate of their contemporaries elsewhere in Britain with the advent of powered machinery and large-scale shoe production.

The subsequent history tends to confirm that money didn't seem to follow them. In the 1911 Census we discover that Clara, aged 20, is a 'cashier confectioner' living with her married sister Catherine, who's now known as Kate Spurling. Kate, a 'shop assistant boot', has been married for nine years, but there is no mention of a husband in the Census. Living in the same house there is a boarder, Jack Morton, a 'labourer general'. Their brother Louis, now aged 27, is living at 12 Russell Grove, Lambeth. He has been married for five years to Ellen Parker, and they have a daughter Evelyn, aged 4, and a year old son, Sidney. Louis is still in the shoe trade and is now a warehouseman. Michael, aged 25, who is described, simply, as a manager, is single and living as a lodger at 49 Keetons Road, Bermondsey. The other five children, including Esther, do not feature in the 1911 Census.

The history of the family remains sketchy in the extreme, and the researcher feeds off any scraps s/he stumbles upon. Michael emigrated with his wife, Frances, and son, Sidney, then aged 4, to Australia. His name appears on a passenger list leaving London for Adelaide on 16 November 1922. He is buried in Melbourne Cemetery. I have discovered no other members of the family on such lists. Australia was a powerful attraction for another family with the name of Aarons, at the head of which was Louis Levy Aarons, who was born in London in 1862 and emigrated to Australia in about 1889. These Aarons were once called the Royal Family of Australian Communism, but this isn't my immediate family. My father once told me that Louis (or Lou as he was known) went with another brother to Australia and was never heard of again. That isn't quite true. Louis emigrated to the United States in 1935 when he was 51. My father was right to observe that several of the family emigrated to the States. Elisabeth Aarons, who had been born in 1889, married Isaac Rome and had a daughter, Anita. She died in Brooklyn in New York on 11 January 1964.

At times we might not have anything that can be called a personal memory (and therefore a memory as such) but there is something to be said for not forgetting our past or where we came from, even if that necessitates sitting in front of a computer screen and perusing impersonal lists of names, most of which lead nowhere. I have no particular interest in constructing a family tree as an intellectual exercise but I am drawn to the idea of connection and to seeing where that might take me or lead to. That I have Jewish cousins living round the world is not without interest, but I've never met them, never been involved in their lives, and wouldn't know what to say if we got together. I suppose what I'm saying is that I have a particular interest in the immediate family of my grandmother and this has propelled me to discover what I can about them. In the process of conducting my research I've encountered information relevant to my background, but only rarely has it been earth-shattering. I think, though, that it's important to know as much as possible about our genes and the world we've inherited, and sometimes in family research intellectual detachment acts as a counter to excessive emotional involvement.

It might be imagined that whenever I write 'I don't know' or 'lost to history' or 'it must have been' or 'I assume that', I am exercising my faculty to discriminate or that I am displaying my intellectual poise as an academic. But in fact it's an emotional not an intellectual response that is on display. What I feel is a sense of deprivation. I have been deprived of something that should be mine, for it is my family history. That I have to undertake research merely confirms my feeling of exclusion, for this is material that belongs by right to me. However, I cannot afford to over-dramatise, for if I was to blame anyone it would be my father in the first place, and then perhaps my mother for not doing more to keep in touch with her Jewish in-laws, and then my grandfather, and so on all the way through to the anti-semitism of western culture. If the Aarons were an orthodox Jewish family – which I don't believe they were – they would have blamed my grandmother for marrying outside the faith and for being responsible therefore for whatever consequences were to befall her offspring. But if I am one of those 'consequences', I am alive and kicking, a product two generations later with my own needs, wants and desires, and with my own ideas and values, a goy or a gentile but not to be defined as such, and quite capable of apportioning blame myself.

Deprivation has many aspects and here I am stressing my own particular perspective, but I am also conscious of a whole Jewish line that went into my creation. They too have been deprived, in their case of those who survived them. Why do we have children and 'scrimp and save' if it isn't connected with future generations? So I look back to my great-grandparents, Sidney and Julia, and to my grandmother, Esther, and reflect on how we have all been deprived of each other. With my Irish family, I consider below the loosening ties and the positive qualities that have flowed from emigration and an escape from poverty, but with my Jewish family I realise I have missed out on something and the research is therefore quite painful. The trouble with some forms of deprivation is that at times we cannot be sure of its extent or of its continuing legacy or indeed if it has a continuing legacy. In this regard deprivation needs to be distinguished from trauma. I sometimes wonder if my being called 'David' was an unconscious gesture on my father's part towards his Jewishness. Whatever the case, my second name, 'Patrick', belongs to my Irish side.

Missing from the family list in the 1901 Census is Esther herself. I reasoned at first that this might have been a simple omission by the returning officer, but after some more research I discovered she was elsewhere – a patient in Great Portland Street National Orthopaedic Hospital in Marylebone in London. She was 13. She had been born at 65 Lambeth Walk on 14 July 1887, but, after being dropped as a baby by her nurse (was that Alice Mitchell?), she suffered permanent damage to her spine and thereafter walked with a stoop. That was not an auspicious start, and, for Esther, the twentieth century and her teenage years began in a spinal unit. I have not been able to ascertain what the damage was or whether any treatment was successful or who paid for her. Her mother, who died in October 1926, apparently spent her last years in a wheelchair. Again, I don't know what her condition was, but I'm intrigued by all this.

In his last years my father developed problems with curvature of the spine but they were not severe enough to incapacitate him, and many people suffer a similar fate. In my mid-fifties I had a tumour removed from inside the cervical part of my spine. If it had not been removed, within a few short years I would have been confined to a wheelchair. As it happened, the eight-hour operation was extremely dangerous, and I dedicate *Light, Freedom and Song* to my surgeon by way of recognition that I can now walk, still have the use of a voice box, and can breathe unaided. I like to imagine all these events within the family are coincidental and not genetic. In 1901, treatment for spinal injuries was in its infancy, so I wonder how much joy Esther had on leaving the hospital on Great Portland Street and whether or not she had to return regularly for treatment. Looking at the details on the 1901 Census, I assume her parents possessed enough money to pay the hospital fees.

In due course, Esther must have accompanied her parents to Brighton. What she did prior to that is not all that clear. There was a story in the family that she went to the States in search of treatment for her spinal injury and that she sailed on the sister ship to the *Titanic*. My cousin Kathryn Warren in Australia, who has been researching the family history for many years, suggested our grandmother is listed as a passenger on board the *Empress of Britain* travelling from Liverpool to Quebec on 20 May 1910. I believe the ship she sailed on was the *Victorian*. That's a small correction and the sort of refinement that happens with research into family history, but it set me thinking about how our grandmother subsequently spent her time in Canada.

If I'm right, she appears in the 1911 Census for Canada as Phylis Aarons in domestic service in Calgary in Alberta. Daisy Pearce always referred to her as Phylis. Her age is 23, date of birth is July 1887, birthplace: England, immigration year: 1910. She is in service to Fred M. Trerice, aged 27, who has a wife and three young children. Place of habitation: 219 11th St Avenue. There are two other men in the house, both of whom are married and both of whom had been born in New Brunswick: Phate Hort, aged 30, and Amos Franks, 35. The census was taken in June 1911, so Esther had been in Canada for a year, had changed her name to Phylis, and possibly she intended settling there. Under the box marked 'Religion' and against her name is what looks like 'synagogue' or someone's attempt at spelling the place of worship. The religion of the Trerice family is abbreviated to 'Meth', that is Methodist. Under 'Tribal' we read that Phylis is English, but under Nationality she is recorded as 'Can' or Canadian. I should add, looking at a coloured postcard of 8$^{th}$ Avenue from 1911 which is in my collection, that, with its trams and motor cars, shops and well-dressed people, Calgary was not as backward as a Londoner might have expected or assumed.

After her Canadian excursion, Esther returned to England on 3 December 1911. The lists record a Miss E. Aarons, a domestic, travelling third class on board the *Virginian* leaving Montreal via Quebec for Liverpool. The *Virginian* was a sister ship to the *Victorian* and owned by the Allan line. When the *Titanic* sank in April 1912, it was the *Virginian*'s captain, Mr Gambell, who sent out a wireless message indicating the White Star liner had struck an iceberg off the Newfoundland coast. I assume that is how things got confused in the family. Esther didn't sail on the sister ship to the *Titanic*, but the ship she sailed on was involved in the story of that tragedy.

I am more intrigued by something else. What was in her thoughts on her return to the port of Liverpool some eighteen months after departing for a new life in Canada, especially if she had agreed to describe herself as Canadian in the Census? If she had been in domestic service for most of that time, it suggests she didn't go abroad to seek medical attention. At the same time, dealing with young children in the Trerice household in Calgary must have given her confidence to consider having a family herself. But why she travelled to Calgary and to Canada in the first place remains a mystery. Unless she had planned to meet someone there, it wasn't an obvious choice. Perhaps her return is a later chapter in the same story of a romance that turned sour. The story of the *Titanic* was then a useful ruse to stop family members from inquiring too closely as to her motivation or feelings at the time.

Esther, then, is missing from the 1911 Census for England and Wales. Her parents are shown as living at 12 Montpelier Road, Brighton, which is an elegant period house, a short stroll from the sea front, and now a guest house. In *Kelly's Sussex Directory* for 1909, Sidney is listed as occupying this address, so some time between 1902 and 1909 they had retired to the coast. This suggests they had acquired a significant amount of capital for there is no evidence they continued in trade. Hyam Isaacs is living at 12A but I don't know if this was sublet by Sidney or indeed if Sidney rented from Hyam. Needless to say, it was true then as it is today that early retirement is a rich man's game.

At some point after December 1911, Esther made her way to Brighton and presumably joined her parents. She then proceeded to open a stall on Church Street selling second-hand clothes. From this point on, the story becomes a little sharper. She met a crowd that included Daisy Woolgar (later to marry George Pearce) and her future husband, Alfred Pierce, whom she married on 11 June 1914. In May 1915 her son, Sidney, is born, followed in July 1919 by my father, Joseph. There is then a gap of six years before she gives birth to Raymond in 1925, but he was either still-born or died soon after, possibly as a result of cot-death. There is a record of a death certificate in Brighton for Raymond J Pierce for January–March 1926. We don't know where he is buried, presumably in Brighton. Her daughter, Julie, is born on 17 August 1927, and within three months she herself is dead on 13 November 1927. Julie's birth certificate bears the name of Esther's mother, Julia. So all three surviving children were named after her Jewish family: Sidney after her father, Joseph after her eldest brother, and Julia after her mother. Alf, her husband, was presumably happy to acquiesce in the names of his children. His first born was named Sidney Alfred, while in his own family an older brother was also called Joseph. And the children were brought up in the Jewish faith. Sidney had his bar mitzvah, and my father would have followed suit were it not for her death. My father once told Kathryn Warren, Julie's daughter, 'When mother died I had to go to the Synagogue and say prayers with Sid every day before school for nine months, the same amount of time a baby is in the womb.'

My father, who never spoke about Raymond, rarely talked about his mother. It was as if the trauma of loss was too poignant to find an entry-point into speech. I use the word 'trauma' here and not deprivation, for it was more than a question of being deprived of a mother at an early age. After his death I would ask my mother if he ever talked to her about Esther, but always the reply was the same. 'No, he never talked about her.' I like to think of that as the speech of silence. My father was eight when she died. Now, it is too late to put any more questions. I would like to know, for example, how she spoke, with a south London accent presumably, or if any of the family spoke Yiddish or used Yiddish words or phrases. What was it like growing up in a predominantly Jewish family? Did she read to him at night and recite for him the stories from the Bible? Were there any stories in the family that became like myths? Stories of exile or assimilation? Did she ever talk of their future or how to get on in life? Did Alf have to carry her upstairs because of her disability? I wonder if she was affectionate to her sons and how she related to Alf. Irene Hill, Esther's niece, recalls that she was a very warm person and had a sense of humour. I'm sure that's right. Was it a quiet household? I couldn't imagine it was noisy. My grandfather delighted in chasing us round the living-room table on his visits to Newland Road, but in general he was a quiet man.

My father spoke of regularly visiting his grandparents on Montpelier Road, but these seemed to be on his own or with his brother. Did they visit her brothers and sisters in London? Esther wasn't ostracised by her family for marrying outside the tribe, but there must have been some cooling with her parents. On the other hand, it was she of all the nine children who followed her parents to the south coast, and it was presumably their money which set her up in business until the children came along after 1915. I assume she and Alf got married at the registry office in Brighton and not at the beautifully ornate Middle Street Historic Synagogue. She deserved a bedecken and a chuppah, but she may enjoyed neither.

What happened to all this Jewishness? When Esther, who had married outside her faith, died, my father, who was a boy of nine at the time and being prepared for his bar mitzvah, was raised as a Christian and later converted to Catholicism when he met my mother. In my family book, which I had privately printed in 2000, I suggested that the two brothers, my uncle Sidney and my father Joseph, were named after their nineteenth-century Jewish relatives and after Old Testament figures therefore, but I suspect no one in the family realised that. And I speculated about Julie being named after Julia, her grandmother. Now I know that Julie was actually named Julia. My uncle Sidney, who was four years older than my father, was brought up to attend synagogue. I don't know when he lost his faith, but whenever he did it was irreversible. He enjoyed the comforts of no other religion and no heirs. When he learnt that I was writing books he wanted to know if I had Barbara Cartland in mind.

Apart from my father, Sidney, my father's brother, was the only Jewish relative I knew. He was born in 1915 and died in 1995. When he was fifteen or sixteen, he left home and went to work in a grocery stores in Kingston-on-Thames, and after being taken on at Smiths Instruments he made his home in west London. Towards the end of his life, when Frances, his Catholic-born Welsh wife, died, he returned to Sussex to end his days. But Sid was not the person to act as a bridge or gateway to the past. For a start, he lacked warmth and the generous instinct. He seemed to get on well with his father, but I don't recollect him ever talking about his mother or his Jewish upbringing.

Sid was the first in the family in the 1950s to own a car, a three-wheeler with plastic flaps for windows. What a day that was in my childhood when we got to be taken out for a spin! The four of us children piled into the back seat expecting a big tour, only to discover the tour consisted of a hundred metres rackety trip down Newland Road and along Chesswood Road, followed by a quick turn in the road and more of the same back to where we started out. Within ten minutes it was all over. I don't know if we managed to get out of second gear. Even as children we had no doubt this was a serious breach of something. When they ventured forth out of London for their annual holiday, Sid and Frances would send us postcards from Swanage or Weston-Super-Mare or perhaps Sidmouth or wherever, but they all seemed to contain the same message: look how far we've travelled to enjoy ourselves while you're stuck at home in what's the name of that place oh yes Worthing.

Once I accompanied my father to visit him in his flat in west London. I must have just started at university. Sid spent the time over lunch berating students in general and complaining about his taxes subsidising people who abused the welfare system. I should have tackled him, but refrained. Later, rather cruelly, my brothers and I spoke of 'sidification', that process, akin to reification, whereby the sheer joy and what life had to offer was squeezed out of you. When my father and mother went to visit him in Lincolnshire in later life, where he had gone to be near his favourite cousin, Hannah's daughter Irene Hill, they found him re-using teabags to save money. There was a streak of meanness and introversion in the Pierce family, but I hope it had nothing to do with our Jewish roots. That's why I wanted to ascertain whether or not Esther was affectionate with her sons, whether or not she hugged them and picked them up, or, more importantly, whether or not she taught her oldest child to laugh, for he just seemed devoid of humour. My father was lucky because he married into an Irish family, and most of the time he could see the funny side of things.

The lack of information about my father's Jewish family has been a problem, but in recent years, partly with Julie and her family returning from Australia to England on visits and partly from trawling through Sidney's effects after his death, a stronger picture has emerged. However, I don't have the direct contact with my Jewish family to be able to say I understand what a Jewish family is like. On the gravestone of Sidney Aarons, it reads 'ever mourned by his children and grandchildren'. Which children I wonder were responsible in 1938, the year of Kristallnacht in Germany, for that inscription? I come upon all these people on the printed page and occasionally encounter their handwriting. I acquaint myself with the various historical records, but I miss the thing called home. 'Speak about things you know' is good advice. I know my Irish family from the inside, and I wish I could say the same about my Jewish family. I own nothing of that past. Perhaps I have to be content with following a path parallel to what happened to Jewish families throughout Europe in the twentieth century, only in my case I feel something akin to deprivation but not to trauma.

Once, when living at Newland Road, we had a visit from two of Esther's sisters. Clara was the name of one, but the name of the other sister remained a mystery until, via Ancestry.com, we made contact with Howard Golden, the great-grandson of Elisabeth, who lives in Florida. I think Clara, who married Sidney Savoy in 1912, had emigrated to the States and possibly was visiting relatives with her sister, Elisabeth. The photo shows my father, smartly dressed, with his arms round the two sisters, as if to affirm 'These are my mother's sisters and I'm delighted to see them. My mother would have been proud of this moment.' Both sisters are wearing similar coats and carrying handbags. Both have glasses, one with thick lenses. They look interested in us and Clara is grasping my brother Stephen in front of her. She would have been about seventy and came bringing clothes for the children of her nephew. That was kind of her, a gesture of contact across the years and across the ocean. Unfortunately, we didn't reciprocate and thus lost contact. What I would give for an opportunity of spending just one afternoon with the sisters or with my Jewish grandmother and her parents, Julia and Sidney Aarons, who are all now buried in the Jewish Cemetery overlooking Kipling's 'whale-backed' Downs. I am sure we would have plenty to talk about. To adopt the title of a poem by Yeats, it would be a case of speech after long silence, and in its own way it too would be a love poem.

As a footnote, on only one occasion have I experienced anti-semitism as if it were directed at me personally. That was at the 1996 Frankfurt Book Fair where the German translation of *James Joyce's Ireland* was launched under the title *James Joyces Irland*. The book was much appreciated by the publishers (a joint venture between two cities, Berne and Cologne) but someone in the stand raised a question mark over a section on 'Joyce and the Jews'. This was completely unexpected and it wrong-footed me. I felt the dart going in with some personal venom, especially as the book in both editions carries a dedication to my Jewish grandmother. Joyce of course was associated at various times in his life with being a Jewish writer, and it was once assumed that he was at first refused permission in 1940 to enter Switzerland because he might be a Jew. Any introduction to Joyce I volunteered would need to include some discussion of 'Joyce and the Jews'. The matter rested there but I could see it didn't satisfy my interrogator. I came away from that giant hall, the bottles of empty Vodka strewn around the back of the Russian stalls, like a little boy fearing not so much the past as the future.

A friend I used to teach with, the critic Harry Marten, has composed a moving account of his Jewish upbringing in the Bronx in New York in a book entitled *But That Didn't Happen To You* (2006). As soon as the family arrived from Russia they had to decide on a name. Well, they had so many names in the family such as Finkelstein and Stein, but, when they arrived, the immigration officer translated Dachtiar as Doctor. When his father was about to embark on a Ph.D. program in French at Columbia University, the family gathered for a name change. Otherwise, Harry's father would have become Doctor Doctor, which was decidedly odd for a family seeking normality. That was when they decided on abandoning Doctor in favour of Marten. Martin was too English for them, but, in the insular surroundings of the Bronx and New York City, they didn't realise Martin with an 'e' sounded Danish or like a furry animal. As for a return to one of their Jewish names, that doesn't seem to have been considered by the family. The feeling I suppose was that such names would hold them back, and what they sought was to lose themselves in the melting-pot of their new country. One of his uncles changed his first name from Samuel to Carl. He was hoping to get a job as an engineer with ATT, the phone company. He wanted a name that wouldn't identify him as a Jew, and, as Harry told me, 'Carl Marten did the trick'.

Harry Marten's story is in part about assimilation, but it also illustrates the rich heritage that those Jews from central and eastern Europe brought with them to America. It's a complicated story, for on the one hand the immigrant seeks to put some distance between the present and the past. Harry, for example, was never that keen on teaching Holocaust literature or even discussing it. On the other hand, the story he tells in his memoir is riveting and has loss written over nearly every page. The sets of contrast intrigue me. The Marten family might have abandoned much of their religion but they did stay together and climb the American social ladder (one of his uncles Abe Rosenthal was a Pulitzer Prize winning international correspondent and later became the Executor Editor of the *New York Times*), whereas, in spite of all I have discovered here, my Jewish family just vanished into thin air. I wish I knew if they enjoyed life or suffered other reversals of fortune or if they were a humourless crew or careless of each other. Perhaps on the path through life, they could have taught me a trick or two.


## The Pierces

Nearly all the various marriage and birth certificates of the Pierces in the nineteenth century that I've come upon carry a cross for signature. This is one reason for the casual misspelling of our surname. If Pierce is the default position, then we started well when in 1847 my great-grandfather was named John Pierce by the Registrar of Brighthelmston (today's Brighton). His father was also called John Pierce and spelt as such; his mother was Elizabeth Pierce, and they lived at 16 Artillery Street. But then came what I can only describe as deviation. When my great-grandfather got married in 1870 at the old parish church of St Nicholas in Brighton, a church dedicated to the patron saint of fishermen, he signed his name with a cross, as did his wife, Jane Humphries. He was aged 23, she 20. The Pierce name is spelt by all the Pierces on the marriage certificate 'Peirce'. John Peirce is the father, Mary Peirce (presumably the mother) is the witness. The occupation of John, his father John, and the bride's father, Henry Humphries, is given as 'fisherman'. Their address is 12 Gerrards Court, King Street, Brighton.

In the 1881 Census, things revert to Pierce. John Pierce, living at the same address, has four sons and two daughters, all of them Pierce. John is still a fisherman, his wife Jane a 'washer'. Two lodgers are in the same house, and they share the same name Mary Bray, one of whom is 21, an 'ironer', and the other aged 14. Two years later, the birth certificate for John's son, Alfred, born 11 May 1883, my grandfather, carries a different spelling, now Pearce. Jane Pearce, formerly 'Humphrey', signs her name with a cross. The deviation, then, tends to occur with birth and marriage certificates. There would be no confusion if we relied on census details, though such an assumption is perhaps unwarranted. It could be that the family wanted to be called Pearce but officialdom in the shape of the ten-year Census didn't accede to their wishes. When my grandfather's youngest brother, George, got married to Daisy Woolgar in 1923, the name on the marriage certificate reads Pearce, and thereafter all his three sons were called Pearce and all their children are Pearce and all their children are Pearce. It happens in families. My grandfather is a Pierce but his brother is a Pearce.

Should such things worry us? After all, if we go back far enough in time we're all related. And the British royal family seem to be able to acquire new

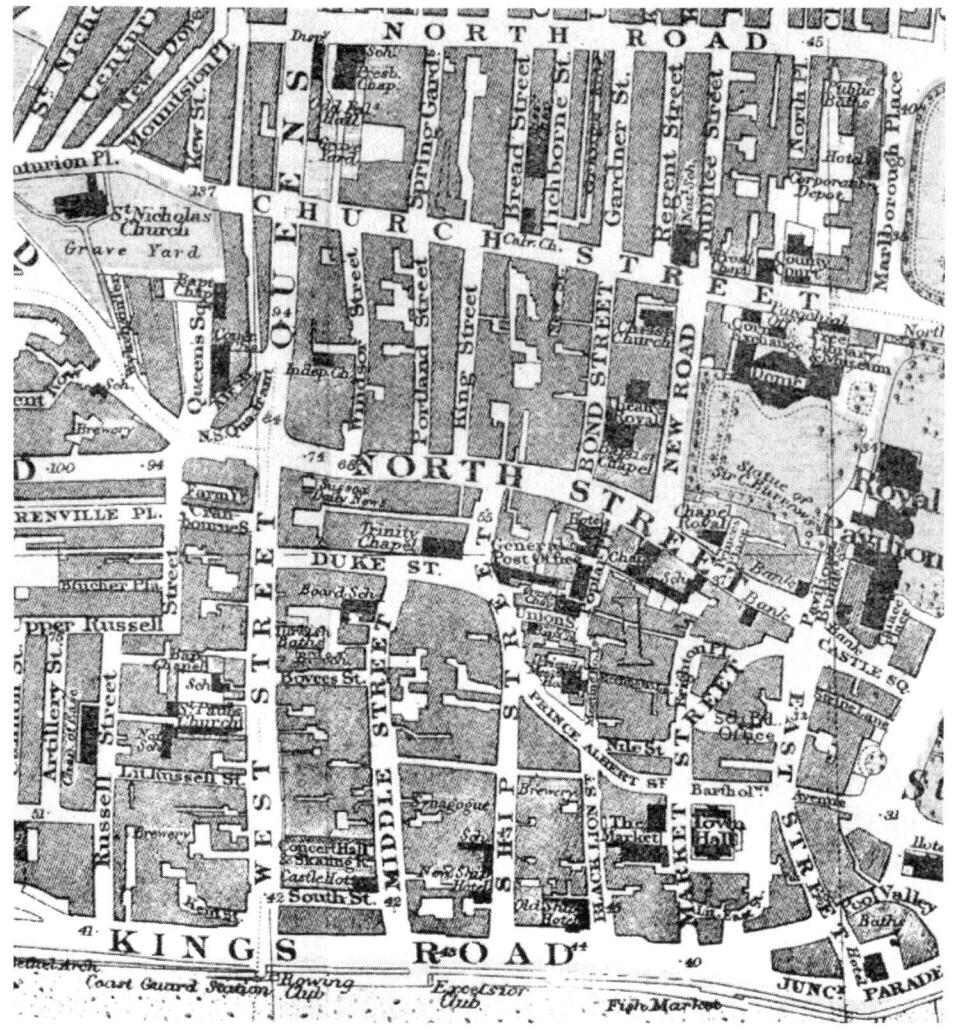

*Section of Brighton from Bacon's beautiful 1881 map. As a boy my father worshipped at the synagogue and went to the local board school on Middle Street. The Pierces lived on Bread Street, between Church Street and North Road. The Church of St Nicholas is on the left, the Royal Pavilion on the right.*

names whenever it suits them, and to do so without losing status. Battenburg to Mountbatten was a shrewd move when the country was at war with Germany. What's wrong with some members of the family being called Pierce and others Pearce? We're probably all offspring of our French father, Pierre, who came over with the Normans, which if true makes us all members of St Peter's cisalpine flock. Pierce, Pearce (three times more common than Pierce), Peirce (as in the American founder of semiotics), Pierse, Pearse (as in the Irish leader of the Easter Rising), Peirse, and on to Piercy, Pearcy, Pearson (another fertile branch of the Pierce tribe), and all the others who want to belong to us. In this regard, thinking of 'and all', it wouldn't be right not to mention here Tom Pearse's old mare from Devon on his way to Widecombe Fair in the company of uncle Tom Cobley and all (a song which I loved singing about in primary school as if it was about some distant relative down the country), or William Langland's allegory *Piers Plowman* (ca 1360-87), which constitutes a powerful plea on behalf of both righteous living and the common humanity underlying our social differences, or Thomas Nashe's witty rant of a pamphlet *Pierce Penniless* (1592), penniless being the fate of most of the Pierces I had the good fortune of knowing. And, further afield, in Ireland, Pierce is a not uncommon first name, as in the seventeenth-century, courtly poet Pierce Ferriter or the Irish-born James Bond, Pierce Brosnan. But the name change registers something for me which I find troubling. It seems to be a sign of our underdevelopment, that once we signed documents with a cross because we were illiterate or because we were too drunk to bother to get things right. So one part of me retorts 'what the hell', and another part of me, the fastidious and faithful devotee of the printed page, my rabbinical side that is, feels indignation.

Of that generation George and Daisy Pearce were our closest relatives and were always in and out of the house, but I would have felt they were closer still if they shared the same spelling. On the other hand, it's easier to spell Pearce than Pierce, or at least that's what I've found when asked. Years ago, when prompted 'How do you spell your name?' I could reply 'Pierce with a pin'. That was when the lids of jam and marmalade jars carried that instruction to release the vacuum of air. Today, people look perplexed when I reply in that fashion. 'You what?' I attempt some explanation from a chapter in the history of jam-jars and consumer culture. 'Oh' comes the response from the other person and said with a downward inflection, which is designed as a conversation stopper. The look, or the silence if on the phone, conveys it all: 'Keep that to yourself. I should, coco,' as my grandfather might say.

The 1891 Census shows the family, now living at 7 Bread Street, Brighton, using the name Pierce. John's eldest son, now 20, has followed his father into fishing, Mary, 18, is an ironer, Henry, 16, is an ironmonger's apprentice, and other children, including my grandfather, Alfred, Jane and Alice, are 'scholars'. Also in the house there is a boarder, James Pollard, 26, a bricklayer's labourer. The 1901 Census proudly confirms that the name Pierce is the proper, flagship spelling. The family has now moved from 7 to 11 Bread Street, then one of the least expensive streets in Brighton and now a cul-de-sac redeveloped as flats. Alfred is in employment as a 'wash laundry man'. John, the eldest son, is now married and living at 70 Egremont Street, Brighton, but he is still, like his father, a fisherman. Joseph (Joe), too, 24, is a fisherman, as is William (Bill). Jane, 16, is, like her younger sister Alice, 13, a laundress, while Richard (Dick), 10, and George, 6, are still at school. Mary Pierce, who was known as Polly, went to live in Bristol. I don't know the identity of the two children indicated on the 1911 Census who died. Possibly one was Henry or Harry as he was called, who died of tuberculosis when young. He had once been a champion Sussex fist fighter.

The 1911 Census affords us a further insight into the family, who are still living at 11 Bread Street. John, now aged 63, and his son Joseph, 34, are now 'smack owners'. A smack was a large fishing vessel for bringing fish to market. A small number remained in use until the Second World War. Some had a topsail on a mizzen mast and the sails were usually ochre in colour. That sounds quite romantic, but I'm sure their work was anything but. Jane Pierce, 60, had a reputation in the family for being the equal of the men and for banging heads. Jane Pierce of Bread Street was not a person to tangle with. William, 32, is a 'licensed waterman' and 'boat owner'. Alf, 27, who signs the form for the family, is a 'gas stove tester' at the Gas Company in Brighton. Jane, 26, is a laundry maid, Richard, 19, works in a mineral water bottle factory, while George, 16, cleans bottles in a brewery. The six children are still single and living at home, testimony to something, though I'm not sure to what exactly, for they were all crowded into five rooms (excluding scullery and bathroom). Alice, now aged 23, has flown the nest.

I grew up in Worthing but Brighton occupies another centre of gravity for us Pierces. It's as if there is in the genes some emotional attachment which never left us as we travelled the ten miles by rail along the coast to relocate in Worthing. As children we loved rides on the Volks narrow gauge electric train, which ran along the sea front in Brighton between the Aquarium and Black Rock, or sliding down the helter-skelter precariously perched over the sea on the Palace Pier. When it was first built in the 1890s, the Volks electric train ran through the waves like a daddy longlegs. The town was like a giant playground or amusement park. We always had to stop along the front when passing a whelks stall for my father to taste the local catch. He was then in his element. We discussed the respective merits of the two piers and listened to the raucous shrieks issuing from the seagulls and day-trippers on the beach. Daisy Pearce believed that the Pierces were descended from the wrong side of the blanket when the Prince Regent slipped out of the Pavilion through a secret door in the bedroom. I'm not sure if being so well-connected has helped much, and I suspect half of Sussex entertains such far-fetched and fanciful notions. As can be observed from the records already outlined, in the nineteenth century the Pierces were fishermen, and not just fishermen but the last of the old-style fisherfolk in Brighton. Which sounds equally romantic and certainly more legitimate.

To repeat, the modern story of our family begins in 1870 with the marriage of John Pierce to Jane Humphries, who went on to produce eleven children: John the fisherman, Mary, Henry, Bill and Joe, who also followed the family tradition into fishing, Alfred my grandfather, Dick, Jane, Hannah, Alice, and George, the youngest, who later married Daisy. They lived in one of the little houses on Bread Street, which was home to fishermen with big families. The one event to stand out above all others in the life of John Pierce, the paterfamilias, was an injury at sea, as a result of which he had a steel plate inserted into his head by a Chinese doctor. Towards the end of his life as a fisherman – or perhaps it was in the middle, or perhaps at the beginning of his life – John would come home, put the money on the table, and proceed to drink all the trophies he had collected from the sea. More tragedy followed in the 1920s when his eldest son, John, drowned at sea while fishing. In the photograph I have of him, he is dressed the part with seaman's cap and jacket, and, underneath, a waistcoat buttoned up over a scarf at the neck. I wonder what he made of Brighton and fishing for a living. Except for his sad eyes, the photo gives nothing away, and there is no hint of a smile.

Alfred was born in May 1883, and, apart from a period in the army during the Great War, he spent his working life in the gasworks in Brighton. When he enlisted with the Royal Garrison Artillery as a reservist in May 1917 at the age of 33, he stated his trade was 'stove testing (gas)' and that his address was Crown Gardens. That was to be his address for most of his life. Gentleman Alf was bred in Bread Street and later crowned, but he never tasted luxury. Toward the end, after a short spell in a first-floor flat in Chesham Road, Kemp Town, where he grew to be a shadow of himself, he came to live with us in Broadwater. He liked nothing better than watching the afternoon races on TV and reaching down for his conical bag of *Wilkinson's* snuff. It was the responsibility of myself or my younger brother, Stephen, to replenish his stocks of snuff. One morning in December 1964 when we went into his room we found he had passed away – he must have died in the night. My mother held a mirror up to his mouth to catch his breath and my father, after collapsing at the end of the bed in homage to his dead father, closed the curtains at the front of the house. He was eighty one.

'Lord love-a-duck' was one of Alf's sayings as he chased us round the table as children. We had no idea what it meant and never bothered to ask. As it happens, it's a phrase that also graces Joyce's 'Edwardian' novel, *Ulysses*. A dapper man with a white silk scarf, shining grey hair, and polished black shoes, he loved coming over on the bus along the seafront to see us, and he was always a favourite with us. In one of his photos, taken in middle age, he is sporting a bowler hat and is smiling. It's a natural pose as if he has just won a bet on the horses. With age he developed a kind of husky voice, but he always gave the impression of being independent and self-contained. Even after the National Health Service was established in 1948, he made it a point of never going to see a doctor, for he always associated medics with fees and butchers.

I take down again his wedding portrait photo on the eve of the Great War. He is standing behind Esther, who is sitting on a chair beside a table with flowers on it. She rests her right arm on the chair's upholstered support. The forefinger of her right hand is touching her face toward her ear. She is wearing gloves. Her left hand is folded on her lap, but no fingers or wedding ring are showing. She is wearing a slightly heavy, plain jacket which is buttoned over. The jacket has a striking flower trim at the collar and hem, which matches her flowery blouse. There are flowers everywhere. On her head is an extraordinary plume-shaped, feather hat, which reaches up to Alf's left shoulder and which fills out like something out of the circus or music hall. She has prominent features, a square jaw, full broad mouth and lips, and inquiring eyes. The expression she has on her face is as if to affirm 'This is my special day and here is my quiet, animated, pose to the world. Whatever the future brings I have someone to care for me. The man behind me will do as he's told.'

Alf is wearing a three-piece suit with stiff, detachable collar and tie tucked in. His hair is brushed down straight to his right and he is looking with bright, penetrating, dark eyes just to the side of the camera. He has a look on his face as if to say 'This is my best pose, not a hair out of place. I've got my hands in the pockets because I was asked to. We're a handsome couple and I can't believe my luck. Lord, love-a-duck. She could have got a better catch if her back hadn't affected her. But here I am, a gas stove tester, ready to face her people and to attend to her every need.'

This of course is my interpretation, but the issue of class difference is I suspect close to the mark. There was another, barely articulated, view or prejudice in the family and it was Daisy Pearce's. She held many decidedly strange views but none stranger than her belief that Esther wouldn't have been able to solicit a marriage partner among her own because of her deformity since 'you see it was against Jewish law or custom'. I'm sure this was an unconscious form of displacement away from the more obvious class position. We were wrong to tease 'Charleston' Daisy in later life, but we did so on almost every Sunday when she came to the house. She was someone who believed it absolutely wrong to consider the possibility of a Britain without the monarchy. Sipping her tea from a saucer, she would caution us, 'You shouldn't think such thoughts. It's not right.' She was happiest when reading Bri's tealeaves (Bri was how she addressed Bridie, my mother), but, equally, she was of a generation which believed that, whatever their purpose was, the purpose of ideas and thinking was not to threaten the State.

George Pearce, her husband, who worked for most of his life as a painter and decorator at Warnes Hotel on the seafront in Worthing, was at times 'half crazy', as the song has it, over his Daisy, but he found refuge in football and gardening. I, too, was fond of her and looked forward to her Sunday visits in the years before she died. She was the family's most eccentric character, and she doted on my mother, but became very protective of her husband in his final illness when she imagined my mother might be attempting to steal him from her. In 1963, she lost two sons in the same year in separate accidents, Jim, her eldest, while flying for the RAF during the Malaya emergency, and John, her youngest, while driving for a haulage company, Hall and Co. She and George were never the same after that tragic year. She always gave my brother, John, the best Christmas present, a matching pair of socks, for example, and ten shillings in money, whereas for the rest of us it was odd socks and five shillings if we were lucky. Of course John should have the best. He was the eldest boy and his name was John.

The marriage between Alf and Esther lasted thirteen years and produced four children. They lived at Crown Gardens, near the junction of Church Street and Upper North Road, near to where Esther had sold clothes when she had come to Brighton. This was where my father grew up, and his early years must have been stable and happy. There is a photo of him with long hair, slightly dishevelled, brushed to one side, his head up, smiling as if there were no tomorrow. His loose-fitting jacket suggests it is one of his mother's, who might have been the person taking the photo. All I know about his schooling is that, after attending Middle Street School, he then transferred to Pelham Street Secondary School for boys. He had a natural intelligence and, later, would enjoy conversation about all manner of things with his three sons who went on to university, but we had precious few books around the house as children and he was rarely seen with a book in his hands. I wonder what sort of house Esther kept. She was apparently a good cook and an accomplished seamstress, someone who made shirts for Alf and clothes for the children. Whatever the case, their family life together was short-lived.

Esther died one year after her mother and eleven years before her father. Alf survived her by thirty seven years. As with nearly every such photo, their wedding studio photo gives no indication of what was to come. She had something about her. That's the impression she conveys, someone who understood style, clothes and the theatre of life. Did she deliberately wear a plume of a hat for her wedding photo instead of a more traditional Jewish veil? Alf recognised what best meant, but that was it. He was someone who assumed that an image for a man was set in stone, but Esther I am sure, with her adventurous spirit of living abroad for eighteen months and changing her name, was into fashion and changes wrought on the individual by a change of appearance and just walking out down through the Lanes or wherever. She was in that sense a modern woman driven on by her interest in exchange. I've got this, what you got? What's more, she must have loved children and the future if she felt compelled to have a fourth one in spite of being told by her doctors not to risk another pregnancy.

When she died Alf decided that his new-born daughter, Julia, would be raised by his sister, Jane Shoosmith, with the stipulation that he would take no further part in her upbringing. This was an extraordinary decision even if he meant the best by it for the child. What motivated him was the belief that Julia would have her own family from the start and would enjoy home comforts with a woman's touch. He couldn't cope on his own with a baby; the two boys were old enough to help themselves, but the prospect of a new-born child must have spooked him. So Julia moved to her aunt's basement flat on Rugby Place in Brighton and, before she was three months old, she lost both a mother and a father. Now, out of the reach of her Jewish mother, Julia became Julie and was raised as a Methodist. Only after the War, when she applied for a passport to visit Switzerland, did she learn her real name. As a footnote, Julie's daughter, Kathryn, came to our grandfather's defence in an email she sent me from Australia in January 2010: 'Give Alf his due, he was supposed to have "kept" his dad, John Pierce, in the mental hospital (I think it was Haywards Heath). I was told no one else in the family contributed to his upkeep (your dad told me that).' For whatever reason, my father never spoke about this to us, his children, but the reference to Haywards Heath sounds right, for that was the location of the Brighton County Borough Asylum.

We often went to see Jane in her sunny basement flat before Julie married Jim Terry and moved out to Woodingdean on the outskirts of Brighton. Jane, who I believe was childless and then a widow, was a very kind mother to Julie, who in turn always spoke warmly of her. On his deathbed in August 1935, Jane's husband, Harry, insisted that Julie be bought a dolls pram for her eighth birthday. Harry was always 'uncle' to Julie, never 'dad'. But then the distancing began. Jane grew apart from Alf and refused to attend his funeral in 1964; she also didn't allow Julie to attend.

I suppose you have to concede that years ago these things happened. In Ireland at roughly the same period, as we will see in the next chapter, John Burke was being brought up by his aunt, my grandmother. Put yourself in Alf's place. Your wife has just died, you have a new-born baby, your mother is dead, your mother-in-law is dead, your wife's siblings live in London. There is no social security system and no one to advise you. So you turn to your own brothers and sisters, and one of them agrees to bring up your child. The only thing that's wrong is the stipulation not to see her (or, I assume, make over an allowance), but that was Alf's peculiar understanding of human psychology.

Alf suffered terribly, like my father, from the death of Esther. Home comforts were now at an end. I don't know why Sid left home when he was not long into his teens but I suspect it was to do with the change in family circumstances. Sid wasn't going to delay. Some time in that period after her death, Alf made perhaps the worst mistake of his life, and initiated a trauma which had long-term consequences for the family. He met up with a woman working behind a bar, and, for whatever reason, he took pity on her, perhaps because of her drinking habits. He must have calculated he could cure her. I believe I'm right in saying that within a short space they got married. My father never mentioned her name but, from the little piece of research I've conducted, I suspect it was Beatrice and that she married Alf in 1931 and died, aged 50, in 1937.

She made life miserable for Alf and my father. All the furniture was sold off to feed her alcoholism. My father, then in his early teens, tried to reason with her but without success. 'There's no point,' insisted the fatalistic Alf. 'Just let her drink herself to death. That's all you can do.' And she did apparently drink herself into an early grave. But not before my father had lied about his age and joined the Royal Marines when he was just seventeen. 'Why did I join up?' he would repeat when asked. 'To get away from home and to get myself a pair of boots.' In that sense, perhaps not unlike many before him and since, the future marine jumped ship to sail the seas. On his enlistment at Southampton on 5 August 1936, the boy who was brought up to be a shop assistant was 5 feet 8½ inches, his complexion 'dark'. On his discharge ten years later in October 1946, he was 5 feet 11 inches, my own height, and his complexion has now turned 'fresh'. The facts speak for themselves: when he enlisted, he was still a boy and almost certainly under-nourished. Indeed, he was so young that 337 days were not counted toward his service pension because he was officially 'under age'.

The time with his real mother was heaven, but with his step-mother it was hell on earth. Of neither mother, however, could our father bring himself to talk to us as children, for they were both consigned to those inconsolable regions where language offers no help. No talking cure could be invoked, no known medicine or therapy of any efficacy. Alf, meanwhile, gave away his daughter and lost two other women, one he adored, and one he initially pitied but then abandoned to her fate. The irony was he always insisted in a pub on the bar staff filling his glass to the brim. Now he had more than his fill.

I return again to my father and to the portrait he transmitted to us of his family background. As children, when we were bored, we fiddled with the ivory tusks in two ornamental black elephants that sat motionless on either side of the mantelpiece, a memento of his War years in the Indian Ocean. Every time I put an age on him when he was injured on Crete, it surprises me, for he was no more than I was when I left university. Twenty-three. His first child was born a few years later. I see him again in khaki shorts on some tropical island and picture to myself what he was thinking. After the War came the years of shift work, then retirement, then the stroke, followed by care homes and death. But what intrigues me is this: until the end there beat the heart of a little boy who dearly missed his mother and who would have gone to the ends of the world to call her back. If he had compiled his own memoir I wonder if he would have portrayed it like this with the fulcrum of his life set so early.

There are few people today who don't enjoy such mixed backgrounds as mine. Odd, not odd, abnormal, normal – these words shade into each other when it comes to describing families. Indeed, if we're honest, how do any of us know what is a normal family? As Harry Marten puts it in the title to his family book 'But That Didn't Happen To You'. Yes it did, replies every historian brought up in such families. Yes, that did happen in my family, if not to me then to one of my relatives. Obscurity intensifies such feelings. Precisely because it is an untold story you want to shout it from the rooftop. 'Listen, everyone, listen you chattering classes, stop what you're doing. This is my story. Forget the headlines. Here amid such neglected spots and sequestered vales lies the real inside story of what took place in these islands (and elsewhere) as the modern world came to pass.' To my mind, wherever it ends, for millions like me, this is the source of the radical impulse and revolutionary thinking.

Now as I look back, I do so with equanimity and without anger or indeed sentimentality. If my name was Beatrice Webb, the pioneering English socialist, and I wanted to insist on tracking a clearly defined if positivist path from my family to society, I might have been tempted to call this memoir 'My Apprenticeship', and then proceeded to insert sections with titles such as 'My family typical of the Industrial Revolution'. But, unlike Webb, mine was not a class to give orders or indeed to order the world. The English side of my family was indeed a product of the industrial revolution, but I lacked the confidence or the conviction of someone emerging from the Victorian dark to do more with such a clinical observation. I try and understand the past, but there is something resistant about it all.

'Yes I see where you're coming from,' people often say to me. Perhaps they know more than I do. When I lose my temper I blame my irascible Irish nature, but then I realise my father had a fierce temper. I am the child of two or three or maybe four ethnicities, religions, and cultures – Irish, Catholic, English, Jewish, Church of England. One of my father's aunts became a Christadelphian. Among my relations in Ireland I count small farmers, agricultural labourers, drovers, nurses and teachers, and in England cigar-dealers, boot-makers, boot clickers, shopkeepers, fishermen, smack owners, gas-workers, shop-workers, painters and decorators, a pilot in the Royal Air Force whose name is listed in the National Memorial Arboretum, a physiotherapist, a popular member of the crew on *EastEnders*, a lorry driver, taxi-drivers, a bus driver, an airport security officer, bakery workers, secretaries, a prison officer, school teachers, a sheet-metal worker, a scaffolder. Whatever the future brings, this much I own.

*The village of Caherbarna in County Clare, Ireland. Looking west towards the Cliffs of Moher. Pat Dunleavy's thatched house is in the foreground and beyond that to the left is the Kilmartin house. The white gable immediately to the right of the Kilmartin house is the remains of the old house where I took my first steps in 1948, now open to the sky. I took this photo around 1985. The cows would have belonged to John Kilmartin, being driven from the 'mountain' for milking in the cabin adjacent to the house.*

Chapter Four

# The House of Music

## Caherbarna

For whatever reason, many of the episodes in my life I forgot to remember. I had no internal camera as it were to record things. Of course, there are just too many events to keep in memory or, indeed, to want to preserve. I took my first steps at eleven months in the kitchen of my grandmother's house in the townland of *Cathair Bhearna* or Caherbarna, in the parish of Liscannor, in the barony of Corcomroe, in County Clare, in Ireland, a couple of miles from the famous Cliffs of Moher. June 1948. That was a memory I couldn't possibly have, so I am obliged to rely on the witness of my mother and other family relatives. Yet, it means a lot to me that my fate as an academic has been tied so firmly to my mother's people. In this book I focus for the most part on my English roots but I have never been able to forget my Irish family or set them on one side, and I keep returning to them as if to a language once familiar but no longer spoken, drawn on by something profoundly elegiac. At the same time I ask myself what is memory when so much of it depends on things we read about or things we are told.

'Cherish what you have' was a motto often heard in the family, and I do so again as I look back to that time before time began when I was fated to wander into a County Clare house of music. I write about that attachment in the introduction to *Irish Writing in the Twentieth Century: A Reader* and in various places in *Reading Joyce*. Most of my books testify to this particular filial obsession. Recently, with this book of memoirs in mind, I have undertaken some more research into my Irish family to reflect again on that heritage of continuity and discontinuity, of roots and uprootedness, of loss and struggle.

In the 1911 Census for Ireland, which is now online, I notice that the entry for my Irish grandparents indicates that they spoke Irish in the house where I took my first steps. They could also read and write. For the purposes of the Census, their address is given as 13 Caherbarnagh, Ballysteen, County Clare. House numbers are clearly a bureaucratic if necessary imposition, for they were never used in that part of the world, and the district was spelt by our family without the –gh, simply Caherbarna, the townland of the gap. To distinguish my side of the Kilmartin family from the other one nearer St Bridget's Well, we sometimes used Caherbarna East. In the 1920s there were eleven houses in Caherbarna East and nine in Caherbarna West. More importantly, my grandmother's age is given as 35, when in 1911 she would have been 29 (she was born in 1881). That must be a simple error on the part of the returning officer, Constable John Sheehan. There was nothing to be gained in exaggerating your age, unless you were close to pension age. It seems unlikely that she wanted the age gap with her new husband to sound less dramatic. It's quite possible, on the other hand, that she didn't know her own age or miscalculated when asked by someone in authority.

Two other people occupied that house on the night of Sunday 2 April 1911: Thomas Kilmartin, who was a year old, my grandmother's first born, and who died in infancy, and Robert Greene, aged 72, who was my grandfather's father-in-law. My grandfather had married one of Robert's daughters and moved into the house at Caherbarna, and effectively the house switched ownership from the Greenes to the Kilmartins. When she died, the house was occupied I believe for around two years by just Robert and Patrick, and then my grandfather married again. The house itself had been there for some time because in *Griffith's Valuation* of 1855 there is a house in Caherbarna registered to Robert's father, Michael Greene, who paid rent, as did most of his neighbours in the village, to Captain Francis MacNamara.

In 1911 Patrick Kilmartin, aged 55, a farmer, is recorded as Head of Family, and we learn that Robert Greene couldn't read or write but could speak two languages. In the 1901 Clare Census, Robert's age is recorded as 55 and at that time he could read and write. Make of that what you will. Robert's wife, Margaret, was 46 and they have four children, two boys, Patrick and John, and two girls, Katie or Kate, aged 17, and Lizzie, aged 7. Patrick died the following year in 1902 aged twenty one, the same year as Robert's wife, Margaret. John emigrated to the States and in 1913 married Mary Flannigan in Somerville, Massachusetts. Kate was also supposed to emigrate to the States, but she was too frail to go, so her sister Margaret went instead.

Some time after 1902, Kate Greene married my grandfather. The marriage was short-lived and she died on 28 December 1907 at the age of twenty four. There is a story in the family that she may have died giving birth, but she might have just been always frail and in poor health. She is buried near the entrance to Kilmacreehy Cemetery, where many members of the Greene family are interred. In April 1908, when she was fifteen, and four months after the death of her sister, Lizzie Greene emigrated to the States, being vouched for by another sister, Margaret. That would have meant Robert was then living in the house alone with my grandfather. Margaret's grand-daughter, Nancy, recalls her grandmother telling her what is part of a classic emigration story, how Robert Greene sat down on the side of the road and began crying. 'Some people passing by offered him help, but he told them he was all right, just sad that he had just sent the last of his children off to America, and would never see any of them again.' In 1913 Lizzie herself got married and lived all her life in Massachusetts. Some time between April and June 1915, Robert died at Caherbarna, surrounded by none of his own family, who were all either dead or in America.

So in 1911, three years before my English grandparents got married in Brighton, my grandmother (Minnie as she was known to neighbours) is living at Caherbarna and has a young son by a man who was, according to the 1911 Census, nearly twice her age (he was born in either 1859 or 1867). Until the 1901 Census went online the family thought my grandfather originated from somewhere near Doolin. The Census confirms this, for in 1901 he is living with three other siblings in his parents' house in Cronogort West, which is near Doolin. Regarding his age, this is given as 34, which would suggest he was born in 1867. But that doesn't explain how he put on twenty one years between 1901 and 1911! I think the view that was handed down in the family was that he was much older than my grandmother and that when he died he was in his seventies, not his early sixties.

As for his marriage to my grandmother in February 1910, that was like many at the time, namely an arranged one. I wish it was more romantic. The spa town of Lisdoonvarna was famous for its matchmakers, who plied their trade at the end of the harvest in the month of September, but the practice would have been widespread in Ireland. One woman in the village, who later married one of my uncles, was rowed ashore from the Aran Islands in the hope of marrying a rich farmer, only to discover the rich farmer was none other than the boatman himself, who earned his living as a 'blocker', that is the intermediary between farmers selling cattle. This is an extreme case by any standards, but the number of arranged marriages suggests that love wasn't uppermost in many people's eyes when it came to a partner for life, and it was for life because divorce was unheard of in rural Catholic Ireland. An arranged marriage I should add was not a forced marriage. My grandmother had the right to say no.

As for the house itself, this was a typical one for that part of County Clare, with thatched roof, thick lime-washed walls, flagstones for a floor, three rooms, and cow cabin attached. There was no running water and no electricity. Creature comforts were few. The bedrooms tended to be damp and the thatch periodically leaked. Oil lamps and candles nightly transformed the interior of the house into a stage for ghosts and shadows where it proved at times difficult to discern who you were talking to across the room. 'Is that you, Maggie? I didn't see you come in.' Outside, there would have been a stack of turf for the fire, and a pile of dung mixed with straw from the cow cabin. Drinking water was fetched in a white enamel bucket from a trickling spring a little distance away, and water for washing from the *log*, as it was called, an Irish word meaning well. The house faced south with stunning picture postcard views down to the Atlantic Ocean and Liscannor Bay and then across to Mount Callan where before the coming of Christianity in the fifth century fires would be lit to the ancient god Lugh. I suspect the room my grandmother slept in when she arrived was nearest to the setting sun, the best room in the house. The kitchen was large enough to be a living room, somewhere to cook, wash, entertain, and dance the night away. I cannot imagine what went through her mind the first time she crossed the threshold and took the holy water from the font near the door. What I can report is that almost immediately she became pregnant, her oldest son being born in December 1910.

Her father, my great-grandfather, was John Kelly, who migrated to Liscannor from the area of Gregan's Castle near Ballyvaughan in north Clare, settling in Ardnahea in a little cabin upon marrying Mary Cross from Ennistymon. The cabin is still there, but it would be more accurate to describe it as a hut. In the 1911 Census he is recorded as speaking Irish and English but he wasn't able to read or write and signed the form with a cross. Under his occupation the record states he was a shepherd, but, according to my cousin Margaret Davis, who has taken over as the family's historian from her mother, he was known as a 'drover' in that he drove, herded and lived with his flock. In the 1901 Census he is simply a 'caretaker'. Whatever the case, the shepherd, drover or caretaker had ten children, six of whom survived. His daughter,

Margaret, emigrated to the States and married John Shannon. Years later, in a letter written in 1960 from Tewkesbury, Massachusetts, Margaret's husband asks my mother what it's like living in England. Such comments are like ripples in time, there to be noticed as part of a longer passage of history.

In *Wild Life in a Southern County* (1879), Richard Jefferies suggests that shepherds know their fields like a book, studying and lingering over every letter. By degrees 'a habit of observation grows upon him'. The only real shepherd I have ever encountered was in Avila in Spain in February 1971. He had wandered down from the mountains to the raised slopes overlooking the beautiful, mystical city of St John of the Cross and St Teresa, a city which at that time in 1971 was nearly completely surrounded by medieval walls. I was with my student, Fernando Bauluz, on a weekend away from the polluted city of Madrid. Fernando approached the shepherd, who was wearing loose-fitting garb and home-made sandals not unlike huaraches worn by Mexican peasants. It was apparent that the shepherd lived away from human society for he struggled to talk about anything except the weather, but he spoke like a visionary, someone in touch with the movement of the stars. Fernando told me afterwards that these shepherds lived for six months of the year in complete solitude with their animals, on account of which they were recruited by Australian sheep farmers in the outback. I wonder how I would have engaged in conversation my great-grandfather. Four generations apart, would we have anything in common or would the water under the bridge have drowned all meaningful contact? In 1971 Fernando constantly spoke of taking to the mountains like Che Guevara and leading the revolution against Franco and western capitalism. But John Kelly I suspect was no Ned Kelly.

John Kelly, my great-grandfather, is like a figure out of ancient myth rather than history. He wanders down into the Liscannor area and spends his life wandering with his sheep and livestock. At the same time he begins to put down roots and has a large family with Mary Cross, a woman from Ennistymon. From that union comes my grandmother, then my mother, then me, and then my son. But we know precious little about the paterfamilias or indeed his wife, though my mother remembers her in her last years being looked after at Caherbarna. Recorded time took a long time to catch up with my family or hunt us down. John Kelly's family went unrecorded in history; there is no mention of the Kilmartin family until the 1901 Census. Indeed, in *Griffith's Valuation* of 1855 there are only some twenty two references to Kilmartin as a name in the whole of County Clare.

It always amuses me to see T-shirts or postcards emblazoned with something like 'I have Irish roots'; for many of us, I suspect our roots in Ireland are indefinable or take quite a research effort to define. John Kelly drifted into Liscannor and set up home in a hut in Ardnahea. My grandfather, Patrick Kilmartin, had the good fortune to take over a house in Caherbarnagh that belonged to the well-established Greene family. Hardy's Tess could trace her history back to more blessed times. Beyond a certain moment, my roots are unknown and the only thing I'm now sure about is that we came out of the Irish dark. I delight in that. We were the real thing, close to the bogs of Ireland, unmixed with anything that was above our station and, moreover, untraceable. As I write this memoir, in an act of revenge against the forces of history, I take delight in setting straight whatever record we possess – or don't possess.

When I first examined the 1901 Clare Census, I couldn't locate my grandmother's name Mary Kelly, and for the best part of a year I assumed she was lost to history. She would have been eighteen at the time, and I searched the whole of County Clare for her name, initially without success. The assumption I made was that she was in domestic service and hence away from home at the time of the Census. If that was the case she would have been registered as a domestic servant. There is a Mary Kelly in the Carmody family of shopkeepers in Ennis, but I didn't believe this was my grandmother. She did work for a time in Ennistymon Hospital, but about any other work she may have undertaken before her marriage that was unknown. As far as I know she only travelled once to the county town of Ennis, twenty miles away, to visit a chiropodist. She frequently visited the spa town of Lisdoonvarna, which is about ten miles distance. She would walk there and back from Caherbarna to see her sister-in-law, Susan Madigan, who had married into the hotel trade. She didn't get to peer over the Cliffs of Moher until we took her there by car in the 1960s.

Six months later, in the summer of 2010, I returned to the 1901 Census when it went live in Ireland as a whole, and after further perusing the records I came across a person who had been transcribed by someone in the National Archives as 'Mine Kelly'. I was pretty sure that first name was a mistake, so I got up the original return. The handwriting is not terribly distinct but to my eyes it looks as though the name should be 'Minnie'. Her age is given as 20, she is a domestic servant. She can read and write and speaks Irish and English. The house where she resides belongs to Bridget Thynne, aged 39, a shopkeeper in Liscannor, who is a widow with one son, Peter, 14, and a mother, Maura Liddy, 75. Pat Maguire, 24, an agricultural labourer, who is described as a 'servant', is also living in the house. I would be surprised if 'Minnie' wasn't my grandmother, and if I'm right it would be the first time she is mentioned in the history books and archives of Ireland. Little by little the past returns to us. Appropriately, it was a struggle for me to identify her. In the family, we all knew she was called 'Minnie' and we all knew her real name was 'Mary'. What we didn't know was that from her earliest years she was called 'Minnie', and what we never imagined doing was looking up 'Minnie Kelly' in the various Census records.

Minnie's brother, Michael, or Mikie as he was known to us, was a frequent visitor to the house in Caherbarna trudging up the long, sodden field in front of the house like a survivor from a different age to see the sister he had grown up with in the last two decades of the nineteenth century. In 1911 he is registered as an agricultural labourer. In the 1950s, he was never at home when we would be entertained by his smartly-dressed wife, Nora, in what became a ritualistic feast. 'Now eat ye all up,' she would insist hovering over us before returning to the kitchen for another dish to serve up. At Caherbarna there was only a crackly radio but Nora possessed a gramophone and a collection of old 78 LPs of traditional ceili music, and it must have been in the front room of that cottage that we first heard 'Miss McCleod's Reel' and other favourites from the pre-war period.

In his engaging play about memory, *Dancing at Lugnasa* (1990), Brian Friel focuses on something blind and desperate about music and that generation in the 1930s in rural Ireland, but this was never my experience in the 1950s and 1960s. Perhaps we were slow learners in my family and couldn't see the break-up that was coming. The children and grandchildren of Mikie and Nora had music running in their veins, and it still had some way to run. Their son, Tommy Kelly, was a prize-winning dancer. Mikie's daughter, Mary, who was married to Paddy Haugh, always threw house dances for us when we were home on holidays in their tiny cottage on the hill at Ballyhean. Theirs was a hospitality that let you into its heart, and it was invariably associated with music and with songs.

In that tiny, rented, low-ceilinged cottage on the hill, there would be a pause in the dancing, and from out of nowhere the songs would start up with no introduction, and everyone would hush. 'Where the River Shannon Flows', sung as always with perfect pitch by Mary herself, was one I remember:

There's a pretty spot in Ireland
I always claim for my land
Where the fairies and the blarney
Will never, never die.
It's the land of the shilelah.
My heart goes back there daily
To the girl I left behind me
When we kissed and said goodbye.

This would be followed by her daughters, Nora Donoghue and Maura Ball, launching into 'The Cliffs of Doneen' and the topography of the west:

Take a view o'er the mountains, fine sights you'll see there.
You'll see the high rocky mountains to the west coast of Clare,
Where the town of Kilkee and Kilrush can be seen
From the high rocky slopes round the cliffs of Doneen.

There was something unashamedly direct about the words of the songs and it was matched by the seemingly impersonal style of singing. That combination of unaccompanied singing, utter stillness and bleeding hearts was captivating, constituting a form of ownership over their culture as well as over their locality and way of life. Old style, or *sean-nos* in Irish, is how it's often described. Where the tradition came from I don't believe anyone knows, but it was everywhere in evidence. Nothing is ever rushed and everything is somehow suppressed and at the same time expressed. No matter how tragic the song, the singer never broke down.

Micho Russell, who can be heard on several cds, played the tin-whistle and flute in similar fashion. Give each note its due and end on a long note. Before becoming famous, he played at our house dances in Caherbarna and Loughloon. I remember taking him to see Patrick Kelly in Cree, south of Miltown Malbay, in County Clare. I'd picked him up from outside his house on the exposed coast road high above Doolin. His mother, who was a concertina-player herself, was never keen on him spending any time away from his jobs around the farm, and she would have 'roared' at him, as they say in those parts, if she'd seen her sixty-year-old, grey-haired son tiptoeing out for the day across the field in front of the house. The fiddle-player, Patrick Kelly, who was no relation, was one of the custodians of the tradition and consulted by leading musicians; it was Patrick who passed on one of the missing parts of 'The Foxhunter's Reel'. We found ourselves in his kitchen one afternoon toward the end of the 1960s. On account of his ill-health Patrick spent much of his time in bed but came down to greet us. He had been born in 1903 and had learnt his music from George Whelan, a blind fiddler who came to Clare from County Kerry some time in the nineteenth century,

He had heard of Micho, who was then finding an audience beyond his immediate neighbourhood in north Clare. Patrick needed no priming but began by reminiscing about teachers of traditional dancing and how he could discern who had taught a person to dance just by watching their movements. In that part of Clare, around Quilty, they produced not only tons of kelp, from which they extracted iodine, but also an amazing crop of lively and distinctive dancers, who would delight in bold, swirling movements, picking up their feet, and clicking their heels. Micho beamed and I listened. At Caherbarna in the 1920s, my mother recalls a travelling dance tutor called Hennessy staying at the house while he was giving a course at Ballycotton School. Patrick's kitchen filled with afternoon sunlight from the south ruffling the still air.

Patrick asked Micho to play a few tunes. 'John of the Fog' or *'Seán sa Cheo'* was one of his favourites at that time. Patrick then took down a tin-whistle from the dresser, rested his elbows on his knees, and cleared his throat. 'That tune you've just played. What name have you on it?' He waited for Micho's reply, and then said, 'This is how I would play that.' We were in the presence of a master. His playing was forceful and designed to allow you, the student, to discern how the tune was structured. Where Micho would coax the notes to perform for him, Patrick attended to the phrasing, deliberately forcing the air out of that humble, little instrument of the poor. Micho couldn't read music but he was absorbing all he was being told. Nothing, however, altered his style. In that regard, he never married but always had a twinkle in his eye and lived in hope that he would one day reel in a pretty colleen. I always found it interesting to watch the encounter between traditional musicians, and my only regret was that no one encouraged me to take up an instrument as a child.

In 1911, John Kelly's youngest daughter, Bridget, was 18, and she would have been conceived when my great-grandfather was about 60. After the Great Famine in the 1840s such late marriages became common, which meant that there was a significant age gap between fathers and children. Again, there is a discrepancy in the 1901 and 1911 Census about the age of my great-grandmother, Mary Kelly. In 1901 she is 50, in 1911 68. If we accept that latter figure and the age of her youngest daughter as 18, then she would have given birth at 50, which is unlikely. If we accept the 1901 figures, she would have given birth to her youngest surviving child at 43. My grandmother's last child, Susan, was born when she was in her mid-forties. Late pregnancies and males who married late increased pressure for families, but there were some advantages. For a man to start a family in his fifties meant care by his partner in old age, time to enjoy his young children, and handing on the tradition. My mother remembers being coached by her father in the art of step-dancing and the Clare half-set. In his later years my grandfather suffered from rheumatism and the farm was neglected, but I never heard any member of the family say anything other than positive things about him. After all, it was he who bequeathed to us a house of music.

Children, rather than love, were at the heart of such marriages. By way of contrast, but not unrelated, at the heart of the parish was the celibate priest. In the 1911 Census, our relations, the Kilmartins in Caherbarna West, had seven children under 13 and their parents were just 43 and 38. Most of the children in that family never married, but the ones I met as adults were all delightful. Lizzie and Katherine retired to Ireland after being in service to a shoe manufacturer in Boston, Massachusetts; in the 1950s, when home on holiday, they would come to our house dances wearing galoshes to protect their shoes from the treacherous roads. Their brothers, baby-faced John and Jim, were inseparable when I would join them on market days in Katherine Kinnane's pub in Ennistymon. Whenever we stopped by to visit them at their farmstead on the way up to Donegore and the Cliffs, the slightly innocent Mary Ann would greet each of us twice, once at the gate and then again inside the house:

'You're heartily welcome. Come in.'
'Come in. You're heartily welcome.'

Tyrannical fathers, on the other hand, were all around us, some as neighbours, some within the perimeters of our own family, and one father abandoned his family for a campaign of drink and years of homelessness in London. As children we would compare notes on the lie of the land in our respective families. One group of cousins lived in constant fear of their lives because their father got the youngest child to spy on the others. Occasionally, when they had done something that might be misconstrued by their father as misbehaviour, such as inadvertently dropping a large stone on someone's foot or dirtying a pair of shorts, they would plead with us not to say they were responsible. But, on the whole, the families I knew well and the Kilmartins in particular tended to be very affectionate with their children. My uncle Pat Kilmartin, for example, was an exemplary father, ever attentive to his children's needs.

How much love developed between my grandparents after they married, I couldn't say. I hope they enjoyed years of tenderness in between the time of sorrow and death of five of their children. My cousin Padraig, John Kilmartin's son, has recently erected a tombstone at St Bridget's Well to the five who died. Thomas, the eldest, fell into a bowl of boiling water which had been left on the kitchen floor. He was three years old. Two other children died within a week in April 1918, perhaps from measles. We believe a daughter Mary, born on St Patrick's Day 1914, who had been farmed out to a family in Lisdoonvarna, died of a broken heart, of 'pining' as it was called, when she was eight. Some of these children, such as Mary and Bridget, have the same names as those who survived, so their uniqueness has been partly obscured. The Susan born in 1926 replaced the Susan who died in 1916, but she too died in infancy. It's as if my grandparents wanted to replace sorrow with joy by a simple process of renaming. In the first year of her life, my mother, the second Bridget, survived double pneumonia, that is pneumonia affecting both lungs. So some of the children were lucky to survive childhood. The story duplicates what happened to Robert Greene's family who lived in the house in the previous generation. Robert had ten children but four of them died in infancy. In that house you had a more or less even chance of not surviving childhood. And it didn't stop there. Two of Robert's children in their twenties, John and Kate, died in that house. I describe number 13 Caherbarnagh as a house of music but in many respects it's more accurate to call it a house of death.

We don't possess a photo of my grandparents together, and indeed I don't know what Patrick looked like. I've always assumed his eldest surviving son closely resembled him. All the time I knew her, my grandmother wore reams of ankle-length, cotton, black clothing, tied up her long black hair into a bob at the back, and couldn't hide the fact that, as with all her children, she had none of her own teeth. Every summer when we returned, her voice became huskier and the arch of her spine curved ever closer to the ground. In her middle years, she never flinched from lifting heavy sacks of flour and animal feed, and that was the result, a bent back in old age. When I read about Mother Ireland and ancient Irish mythology or the revolutionary appeal of Cathleen ni Houlihan, I recall my grandmother with a goose-wing feather reaching down to sweep the dust off the Moher flagstones into the grate or shouting at her son, John, in the settle bed in the early morning to get up for fear he would be late for the creamery.

For her party piece she would sing 'The Trees They Do Grow High', a ballad about a bonny boy who's young but he's growing. Was that a lost love of her youth, or why would she spend time with a boy who married at the age of fourteen and was a father the following year? One verse is about an arranged marriage, and I wonder if subconsciously she was trying to reveal something about her own fate when young:

> Father, dear father,
> You've done me great wrong.
> You married me to a boy who is too young.
> I'm twice twelve and he is but fourteen.
> He's young,
> But he's daily growing.

I never saw my grandmother dance, but every summer when we were there at Caherbarna, she would ensure we enjoyed at least one house dance. Friends and family and neighbours from around the parish would be invited, some by special invitation, while others would get to hear of it and just turn up. Singers, dancers, and musicians from the various neighbourhoods of Liscannor including St Bridget's Well, Loughloon, Ballycotton, Ballyhean, Ballyvorda, and Luogh would all descend on the house. Preparations for the evening were carried out as if it was a familiar routine. Bottles of Guinness and porter would be carried over from St Bridget's Well, sandwiches made. The kitchen would be enlarged by repositioning the table near the door. The wooden chairs would then be placed on the kitchen table for the musicians, and the remaining *súgán* chairs would be pushed back against the wall or used for those taking tea inside one of the bedrooms. Extra oil-lamps would be hung from the rafters, the floor swept, the settle bed folded up to become a bench, and we would then await the visitors after dark. In *The Scenery and Antiquities of Ireland* (1844), N.P. Willis and J.S. Coyne observed that 'The love of dancing appears to be inherent among the Irish, and constitutes a striking feature in the national character'. A century later, in the early 1950s, I was an inside witness to that scene from antiquity and, if asked, could confirm that observation from my own experience.

Some years ago I got my Aunt Mary to commit to paper some of her memories about the house of music, and this is what she wrote:

As far back as I remember the old house was popular for dances, music, card playing and story telling. Dad was good to tell stories and was often invited to neighbouring houses to entertain them with his stories. Mummer dances, collection dances and gambles were held there. Dancing continued until the early hours of the morning. Tea and cake were provided and at mummer dances they had a couple of casks of Guinness. At other dances only the musicians got drink. Auty Linane was the usual musician; he played on a concertina or tin whistle. Later, Paddy and John Kilhourie and the Russells provided the music for the big dances and the house was packed with people. Much later, John Kilmartin, John Guerin, John Burke, accompanied by the Kilhouries and Russells, entertained us, and they were a joy to dance to their music and listen to. There was also step dancing while the musicians had a break and songs were sung. My earliest memories of the songs which were sung were Jacky Russell singing 'The Shawl of Galway Grey' and Martin Flanagan singing 'Eileen McMahon' and 'The Boys from the County Mayo'.

By the 1950s mummer dances, where people danced to the sound of an instrument imitated by the human voice, were a thing of the past. There were always musicians at the house dances I recall, and they were always revered, as they were for Mary when she was growing up. Among the neighbours Danny and Norrie Malone with their son, Michael, would be among the first to arrive. Dan Considine, with his darting, deep-set eyes, accompanied by his wife, would follow. Then the Guerins and the nearest neighbours, along with the many branches of the Haugh family from every direction. Michael Gorman, one of the richest farmers around and a great help to the family when it came to harvesting and bringing home turf from the bog, would also show up. The music would start and four sets of couples would take it in turn to dance the Clare half-set, a series of dances including reels, jigs, and a hornpipe which lasted for about twenty minutes or so. I didn't realise at the time that I was witnessing the end of the era of house dances in Ireland.

Nearly everyone could dance, but from my vantage-point, seated on the wooden, folded-up settle bed, it was plain who had music flowing through their veins. Great dancers like Michael Malone were the complete thing: extraordinary nimbleness on their feet, from the waist down all movement, from the waist up as solid as a well-made, dry-stone wall, perfect timing and anticipation, and always utterly in control as they avoided the dresser and the edges of uneven flagstones, and negotiated with their partner round the enclosed space that during the day was a multi-purpose kitchen and living room. Such dancers were a delight to behold, and you could tell by their expressions how much joy their bodies gave them. In those intimate surroundings, they were never showy but they recognised they were special, and they would in turn lift the music.

The adjectives frequently employed in my family to describe great music were 'fierce' and 'brutal', words which I always considered rather odd and not that easy to define. Fierce and brutal had nothing to do with wild or savage. The Aran islanders who turned up at St Bridget's Well for Garland Sunday at the end of July and who wore ropes for belts looked fierce. Fierce music was music that would wear you out, that showed no mercy that is. It was as if the dancers were in a competition or determined to do justice to what they heard, and it seemed to involve taking things to the limit, how only in that way could the full joy be experienced or extracted. You couldn't sit it out if you heard good music starting up. 'Leppin' like a hare' or 'handling the fut' is how Percy French puts it in his gently humorous take on the Irish poor and their love of dancing in 'Phil the Fluter's Ball'.

In between the sets there would be unaccompanied singing, or people would be invited into the room inside to take some food or drink, or they would make for the door, desperate for the air outside. Among others, I recall Dan Considine singing moodily about 'The Waves of the Silvery Tide', and Michael Malone the beautiful Fenian song, 'Down Erin's Lovely Lea'. Throughout the night, to keep the dust from rising, the Moher flagstones would be sprinkled with water, and the turf-fire would be allowed to die down. Just before dawn, people went home to milk the cows and go to the creamery or adjourn to bed. I rarely got to that point, for some time in the night I would be carried like a sack of potatoes over the shoulders of one of my aunts into bed. Maudie Kinnane, who never married and lived on her own, would have the last word: 'The poor crathur's tired and past his bedtime.'

Some time in the 1930s the local priest invited himself to one of our house dances. There had been a clash of timetables and no one had deigned to attend the dance he had scheduled in Liscannor. Discovering his parishioners were all at Caherbarna, he decided to come up to the house and harangue them all for their non-attendance. This was the decade when the Church was attempting to influence the morals of the people by taking control of dance halls and to raise revenue in the process. The priest in this case, whose irritation must have increased with every pothole in the road he failed to negotiate, got more than he bargained for, because my grandmother was a determined woman who was a match for the red-faced priest. That confrontation must have been some sight, worthy of a scene out of a novel by Emile Zola.

Perhaps she recalled the incident ten years before, during the War of Independence, when the Black and Tans, in pursuit of Michael Collins, searched the house for weapons. This time, with a sickly, young son, John, in bed, her response was immediate, and she hunted them, but their irritation was such that, before departing, they cut her hair in revenge. That, too, would have been a triumph of sorts for my grandmother against the male aggressor from over the sea. The English soldiers had not got what they were seeking and she had stood firm against them. I remember as a child watching her in the evening unfasten her black hair to comb it and being struck by its length for it reached down to the small of her back.

In the case of the priest, I assume my grandmother was initially confused by the entry of the uninvited guest, but then her hackles must have risen as soon as she realised what was happening. Part of her anger must have been fuelled by the annual humiliation of having her name read out in the local church and her meagre contribution to the clergy of the parish broadcast. It seems she went for him, and, in the scuffle which ensued, she grabbed his collar and hunted him out of the house. I can hear her shouting and see her arms flailing, 'Out, Father. Take yourself off. You're not welcome in this house. Who do you think you are coming in like that?' I don't know if the crowd then cheered or if they continued with the dance. I suspect there would have been an embarrassed silence. After all, their instinct was to welcome visitors, and what they all understood was something that Hely Dutton had observed in 1808 about County Clare: 'In no part of Ireland is hospitality more practised than in this county.' Anyway, the following day my grandmother walked down to Liscannor to return the collar to the priest, and in the process she presumably apologised. I don't think that particular priest interfered again with the house dances of his parishioners, for he must have realised he had overstepped the mark.

When her husband died in 1931, my grandmother was on her own, approaching fifty, with responsibility for her mother, Mary Kelly (who died in

1935), and for five surviving children, Patrick, born in 1912, Margaret, born in 1917, John, born in 1919, my mother, Bridget, born in 1921, and Mary, born in 1924. One morning, then, in March 1931, aged perhaps seventy two, my grandfather, who was one of nine children who survived and the eldest son of John Kilmartin (b 1831) and Susan Scales (b 1838), collapsed with a thud on the flagstones of the kitchen floor. The first thing my grandmother did, after ascertaining her husband was dead, was to put on her coat, embark on the hour-long walk down to Liscannor, and collect his pension. If that is considered unnatural or the act of a devious and scheming individual, then it is also the recourse of someone who is emotionally tough and determined to survive. In her final years she clubbed to death a fox which had broken into the hen house. Her father, born about 1833, had survived the Famine, as had her mother, born about ten years later. And she was married to someone whose parents had survived the Famine, but on neither side of the family had their economic fortunes shown much sign of improvement in the century between the 1830s and the 1930s. My grandmother and her dependants were still one week away from hunger. The only thing they did have was the rarely used key to their own door. A clear-eyed cynic might with justice conclude they were no longer tenants but were now owners of their own poverty.

From the outset, my grandmother, a drover's daughter, must have recognised that the world owed her something and nothing, a little something, that is, but largely nothing. She was in turn driven by the need for shelter, and for shelter in all its forms. Constantly hemmed in, she didn't have the luxury to experiment or to step back and discover her true self, and, as with most of her generation, she was not one to practise indulgence. I think of her as someone whose childhood and youth was spent in aligning character and personality for the long road ahead. When she moved into Caherbarna she gained security and a roof over her head, but she had an old man to look after as well as a husband nearly twice her age. The pattern of care followed by more care continued. The creamery was a cooperative venture in rural Ireland, and there was a tradition of people helping each other with harvesting and various forms of exchange and barter (*meitheal* is the related Irish word used for a gathering of people for work), but all this can serve to mask social differences and distinctions. The poor frequently faced utter isolation in a cruel world. 'Save yourself' was a phrase I never heard in the family, but in effect this is what 'community' sometimes amounted to.

Laying out the bodies of those who had died provided my grandmother with some income. She also received some money from the Flanagans for doing their laundry. This necessitated a journey through rain-soaked, treacherous fields to Luogh, which was some miles away. Then there was income from the milk which they took to the creamery, but, again, this too was fairly meagre since they only had a few cows and the land where the cows grazed was known to us as 'the mountain'. They were at the bottom of the pile known to historians as the rural poor. Only agricultural labourers, who tended to have no land or very little land such as my uncle Jack and my aunt Mary, faced a more precarious existence. The oil lamp near the fireplace was lit only when there was no more light in the sky.

On that walk to collect her husband's pension in the spring of 1931, a knitted, black shawl round her, the years must have spread out before her and behind her. A quarter of a century divided her from her husband in terms of age, but she lived for another forty years. The following ten would be crucial in terms of giving her children the best start in life, but by 1940 three of the five would have left home, never to return except on vacation. I wonder if she passed any prying neighbours as she hurried on down to the pension office and whether there was any panic in her voice when she stepped inside the office and confronted the official: 'I've come to collect my husband's pension. Patrick Kilmartin. Caherbarna.' Perhaps the rural poor, and their offspring, always have something to hide.

No account of Caherbarna would be complete without mention of John Burke. He was one of Bridget Kelly's children who was brought up by her sister, my grandmother. To distinguish him from the other John at Caherbarna he was always known by the name John Burke, never simply John, a sign perhaps of his ambivalent status. With tremendous persistence he taught himself how to play the violin and to accompany John Kilmartin on the flute, and the two could sometimes be heard at Considine's pub at St Bridget's Well. He had an innocent, fresh, ruddy face and combed-back hair. One of the few early photos we have of him was taken in the summer of 1948 in a meadow during haymaking. It shows him looking directly at the camera with an infectious smile on his face for he was always cheerful. He has an arm around my mother. My aunt Margaret, who suffered from multiple sclerosis in later life, is also there in the photo with her first-born, Christina. My grandmother is sitting upright in the middle with my sister looking up at her, while my curly-haired brother John is, characteristically, looking away at something that has caught his eye in the distance. I have another photo, an internal one in my mind, and it is of John Burke on the cabin roof whitewashing the gable end of the house as we arrived one summer from England for holidays, for they were always late in Caherbarna and had been caught out. 'You'll be late for your own funeral' was one of many catch-phrases I grew up with. Like his cousins in that household, John Burke spent most of his life as an emigrant in England, in his case playing Irish music in pubs 'off the Harrow Road' as he used to say.

He was a sweet musician like his namesake, the famous Kevin Burke, and would play at our house dances alongside Denis Guerin perched on a kitchen table inside the door in the corner near the holy water font. Years later, with my aunt Mary I visited him in a dark, ground-floor, council flat in north London, but emigration and years of poverty had taken its toll. The family had given him everything except the means to adapt. I can still hear him now singing to his own accompaniment 'Fare-thee-well Lovely Mary', a beautifully tender emigration song which seemed to suit his temperament and to give him comfort away from home, which in his mind he had never left:

Fare-thee-well lovely Mary, for it's now I must leave you,
To the distant West Indies, my long course to steer,
I know very well, love, long absence will grieve you,
I'll be with you, lovely Mary, in the spring of the year.

So don't let my long absence bring any trouble to you, love,
Nor any foolish notions run into your mind,

For although we are parted, we'll be true and loyal hearted,
And whene'er I return, love, 'twill be just like old times.

The big ship is sailing, lovely Mary is wailing,
Her red rosy cheeks now as pale as the snow,
Her gay golden locks she's continually tearing,
Saying, 'I sigh, love, I'll die, love, should I ne'er see you more.'

As for neighbours, the Guerins lived next door. Denis, their youngest, was a lively dancer and sensitive fiddle player. He would enter the house unannounced, bless himself with the holy water and stand by the door. 'God bless all here,' he would declare like a priest from the altar, and stay standing with hands in pockets, grinning. Later, he emigrated to New York to become a liftman in a block of apartments. His impossible father shouted at me as a child when I brought in from the field a frog that had one leg missing to show him nature's capacity to adapt when scythed down. 'Take that thing out of the house, and leave it where you found it.' The elderly Nora McDonagh, another neighbour in the village, would sit by the hob of an evening and smoke her pipe and take not the slightest notice of children pointing at her beard or refusing to kiss her.

Tom Wren, who was the wildest man in the parish, one day rode up to the house on a huge red stallion that he had difficulty controlling. Once I spent a day helping him with the harvesting near the Cliffs of Moher. When I arrived at his cottage, he went to collect something in the room off the kitchen, but had to force the door. So much straw tumbled out that I wondered where the pig was. For lunch, we shared warm tea in a lemonade bottle and thick, white bread sawn off by Tom's blunt knife. Overhead, we were distracted by the call of a pair of curlews flying high on their way south. I never knew anyone in those parts whose face didn't light up when the name of Tom Wren was mentioned.

Our immediate neighbour, Pat Dunleavy, was the exact opposite. He possessed one of those classic faces of the west, full of the passage of time where the lines registered both the harshness in the environment but also a softening. I can still hear him asking after my family in England 'How are all over?' even though, as far as I could tell, he had never set foot outside of his native county. Blessed with an abundance of native charm and lively conversation, Pat would lend me his bicycle when I was around on holiday. He and Maggie never had any children and I wonder on reflection if I brought out the father in him. In the long ago there is no recourse to evidence or corroboration and the world just slips away from us. My mother recalls Pat's father, Tom Dunleavy, conversing in Irish with my great-grandmother at the house in Caherbarna. Then there was Paddy Carroll, the intellectual in the village, who used to spend his days playing chess with me or John Kilmartin or with anyone around, until one day he decided to emigrate to Canada. His tiny house by a bridge over a stream has been a ruin for the best part of half a century.

## The loosening ties

The world of my Irish childhood is one that links me almost directly with the childhood of Thomas Hardy in Dorset in the 1840s and 1850s. Hardy was born at Upper Bockhampton, near Dorchester, in a house built by his great-grandfather and where he lived until he was 34. When growing up, the novelist would accompany his father to local house dances and play the violin. Perhaps it is for this reason that few modern writers have understood better than Hardy the powerful attraction of both ties and loosening ties. Like Hardy, I have been in touch not only with a traditional way of life that once was common in these islands for generations but also with the break-up of such a way life.

Some things in Ireland such as agricultural machinery lived on long after they had been abandoned in England. In *A Song for Every Season* (1971), Bob Copper's father, who was born in 1882, recalls gathering hay into rows with a machine they described as a 'tumble-down-dick'. That would have been in fields near Brighton at the end of the nineteenth century. In the 1950s I recall working such a machine at Caherbarna. I can't remember what we called it, perhaps just a hay rake. You sat on a cushion on a metal seat and, reaching forward, with the reins in your left hand, you steered the horse in a neat circle, anti-clockwise, round the uneven meadow, while with your right hand you periodically lifted the 'comb' as it gathered the spread-out, cut hay. I managed just the one circle before being ridiculed by my elder brother and conceding defeat to what I concluded was nothing more than an instrument of torture.

The wooden, flat cart my uncle John owned was also from a much earlier period. According to the historical geographer and social historian Estyn Evans in his classic survey *Irish Folk Ways* (1957), they were in use in Scotland in the late eighteenth century, but to the small farmer in the west of Ireland until a generation ago they were invaluable for all kinds of farm work. Thus, every morning, after being harnessed to our incredibly stubborn black pony, the Scottish cart carried the two or three large, heavy cans of milk down to the creamery in Liscannor along lanes which struggled to do justice to that term. As we waited in the queue for the cans to be offloaded at the creamery, I would look enviously at carts which had rubber tyres.

Always you felt the world lagging or dragging behind, but the time difference for me makes itself felt in another way, for I am conscious that all the people mentioned here would be surprised, perhaps horrified, if suddenly they rose from the dead and saw their names in print and translated into a narrative such as this one. 'They were happy days' is the phrase Mary uses in recalling those times, and I have no reason to disbelieve her or to dismiss her comment as simply nostalgia. In evoking the past, that generation believed there was once a glow or aura surrounding them, which contrasted with the more prosaic or less happy present. *'In illo tempore'*, at that time, the priest would say at Mass introducing a reading from the Gospels, a marker to separate off a blessed time when Jesus walked the earth. Nostalgia, too, shares something of the sacred about it. In the long ago, the cycle of the seasons, the pattern of daily life, must have given meaning and comfort to their lives. In the morning you milked the cows and went to the creamery. On Sundays you put on your best clothes, polished your shoes, and walked to Mass, shoulders back, head high, after which, if you were a man you adjourned to the pub nearby, and if you were a woman you hurried home to prepare dinner.

It was, however, a happiness based on circumstance and 'making do'. It wasn't a lifestyle of choice but of necessity, and, with the advent of modernity and the demand, especially by women, for self-fulfilment whether in terms of relationships or careers, it has passed away. Those of us who have inherited that lost world are never free from a certain hesitancy as we reflect on the past, a certain tension, that is, between the head and the heart. With my neighbourhood in Worthing it was possible for me to ask about the ties that held us together; with the neighbourhood surrounding my Irish family there was never any doubt about the ties (nor about the claustrophobia). At the same time, to the patient observer and social historian, the injustice of it all as a way of life can be overwhelming, and not just on account of the poverty. Young labourers were driven from home for stealing paltry sums from the farmer for whom they worked; young women were forced to give up an illegitimate baby or to undergo an abortion in England for fear of the shame it might bring on their family. Not everyone left Ireland in search of work or because of the colonial encounter.

Some sharp, and at times painful, things, then, have to be said by the next generation, judgment exercised, and lines drawn. Take away the music and the all-night house dances, and what was it but 'the sigh of the weary', a lifetime of duty and drudgery but precious few rewards. For those who face it day in day out, there's little to be said for poverty. My mother was the exception, but it would sometimes surprise me the bitterness I heard among members of my family against those who were better off. They would slip into that mood almost without prompting. I say mood rather than attitude, for it was not a noble rage but more like some irritant they wore next to their skin. In Lancashire and the industrial north, you'd hear a comment such as 'It's well for some', but among my family in a face-to-face community the inequality was more pointed: 'They're the people with the money, the big Moher farmers, and we have nothing. 'Tis all right for them.' For whatever reason, perhaps because she had emigrated at an early age, my mother shielded us from such sentiments. 'Never let the sun go down on your anger' was one of her favourite expressions.

It's not surprising I spend so much time in *Light, Freedom and Song*, my cultural history of modern Ireland, on loss and struggle. I stress both loss and struggle, because it wasn't simply loss. Loss dwells on sentiment and gives too much to the forces of inevitability. Struggle allows room for human response and for solidarity. It also calls attention to the idea of witness, both at the time and on behalf of the future. Not everything comes under the heading 'loss', and one of those things is 'struggle'. My grandmother's struggle through life has value for me and for my family. The poverty she endured was as close as it gets to the edge of human existence without falling into the abyss. She belonged to a generation whose parents had survived the Famine in the 1840s when over a million of her fellow citizens either perished or emigrated. Like many grandmothers, she was an example to us all of how not to succumb even as adversity strikes.

As I lay out the bodies of that generation in this memoir, I see her again trying to stretch her back. Resting on the table in the kitchen, she pulls herself up to full height and, with the corner of her black apron, she wipes the rheum from her eyes. Unseen, her grey-black hair tied in a bob and brushed back from a pallid, care-worn forehead, she pauses for a moment, peers out of the low window across the uninterrupted, sodden fields strewn with clumps of reeds to the south, and, with a sharp intake of breath, mutters a comment to herself about the weather. 'Never give in. Never give up.' That's the lesson she taught us, the determination to keep alive the generous instinct and not to let go of our sense of belonging.

The ties of family, then, loosened over time. Pat, my grandmother's eldest surviving son and an early pathfinder in the family, who would cycle forty miles down to Limerick to a dance, left 'Paddy's green shamrock shore' in his twenties, never to return. But in this case, unlike Robert Greene's children who emigrated to the 'green fields of Amerikay', the destination of choice in the 1930s was England. With his friend, Joe Culligan (who later emigrated to California), he worked his passage across the Irish Sea to Liverpool, then, after working his way as a farmhand through North Wales and the English Midlands, he arrived in the London area, eventually settling in Burghfield Common, near Reading, and close to the Atomic Weapons Establishment at Aldermaston. As soon as he approached manhood, Pat, who was never that keen on farming or killing animals, must have realised that Caherbarna was quite simply the 'back of beyond', as we used to say, and no place for someone who wanted to get on in life or make a go of things. The eldest son normally inherited the farm, but Pat had other ideas. Not that he betrayed any signs of triumph over his origins or indeed any resentment against the new Irish Free State that couldn't provide for its own. Even though it was forced on him, his adopted country provided him with a new life, and he ensured a certain continuity with his past. He married late for example, had a large family, and never lost his smoking habit or his rich, throaty voice and distinctive accent.

For most of his working life, Pat was a labourer with Laings the builders, who provided him with a very small pension but were generous in looking after him when he retired, fitting out a new kitchen, laying new carpets and so on. He never complained. Like his father, and indeed like my mother, Pat was a great dancer. Indeed, according to Packie Russell, the great concertina player from Doolin, he was among the finest dancers he had ever played for, which was a real compliment coming from the frequently irritable brother of the angelic Micho. Without music we would have been lost as a family, for it was like a religion, something which Maxim Gorky once observed about the Russian peasantry in the nineteenth century.

The new field of Migration Studies must be full of such accounts as I am here recounting. Within a few years of arriving in England, Pat found openings for two of his sisters. In October 1937 my mother left Ireland when she was just fifteen and the following year went to Worthing to work in Pearce's Dining Rooms, a bed-and-breakfast near the town's railway station and run by George and Daisy Pearce. '70 Vic' as she used to say, that is 70 Victoria Road. This was where Pat had lodged when working locally as a labourer on the roads. Here she met my father, who was George's nephew, and they got married on 11 January 1941 when she had just turned nineteen and he was twenty one. The following day my father returned to his unit in Portsmouth and in the following weeks my mother, a wartime bride, could be heard by the Pearce boys crying herself to sleep. Margaret, the saint in the family, was delayed. Otherwise, she would have ended up in Worthing. But Margaret fell hopelessly in love with Patrick Spratt from Limerick, and eventually settled near Heathrow in Feltham, Middlesex, where she raised a large family at the end of one of the busiest runways in the world.

John Kilmartin stayed home and never married until late in life. He was the one member of that generation in the family who would have benefitted from a university education, for he was always reading late into the night and always displayed an interest in history and ideas. Mary, the custodian of the family's history and indeed of the history of the parish since she acted as clerical officer for Kilmacreehy Cemetery, spent two years in Worthing, as I mentioned in a previous chapter. On returning to Ireland, she married Jack Haugh and raised a family of four in an agricultural labourer's cottage overlooking the same graveyard where she is now buried with Jack and where her own mother was interred in 1973. They chose well, for they all lie beside the restless Atlantic Ocean and near the ruins of a church dedicated to a saint who flourished in the sixth century. There are portraits of Mary in my other books, for she was my favourite aunt and taught me more than I know about the sympathetic imagination. It was in keeping that the three songs she should recall as part of her earliest memories were emigration songs, the view of Ireland that is from exile.

My mother survived them all, but she didn't survive to tell the tale for her memory is now very patchy. I have many cousins from that side of the family but it's only on formal occasions such as funerals and weddings that I get to see them. Families now are more like dispersal points without the spark which once lit up the world. I don't mourn the passing. We live a long way from each other, I no longer call myself a Catholic, and my academic career has taken me further from home than perhaps I would have liked. Along with the Church, distance enabled me to get on in life, but, wherever I go, I am accompanied by a sense of absence and echoes of displacement. These feelings of emptiness come at me all the time and trigger something that I can only describe as perfectly understandable but strictly irrational. I resist brassy talk of 'community' or, for all the intensity of my own working-class family background, strong expressions of community, preferring instead something less visible and more ruminative. I like to imagine, however, that not forgetting, while not the same as always remembering, is a tribute to something that still defines me. When I attended the funeral of Margaret Spratt's eldest son,

Patrick, in August 2011, it shocked me to see the large turnout, especially among his colleagues from the crew and cast of *EastEnders*. Patrick left school at 15, but, wherever he went, he was surrounded by a heightened sense of community, something I rarely encountered in my working life as a teacher.

I haven't been inside the family home at Caherbarna for some forty years now. In the early 1960s, around the time we moved in Worthing from the intense, working-class community of Newland Road across the railway tracks to the quieter area of Broadwater, my uncle John Kilmartin received a government grant and built a new house alongside the house of music. I can still see the excitement on his face as he spread the architectural plans on the table and discussed the layout of the rooms. It was to have a slate roof with wooden floors, electricity and a porch. Gone were the whitewashed walls, the thatched roof, the open hearth and the flagstone floor. With the new house came something else: there would be no more house dances in Caherbarna. The end of tradition was to be the price of modernity. In turn, within a few years, a new uncle, now in his forties, emerged in our absence, someone who was to cut his links with the rest of the family for years to come.

In 1967, aged 48, John got married to a neighbour in the village, and he did so at seven o'clock in the morning. It was the first sign of a determined recluse in the making. Thereafter, his three sisters and their children were not welcome at Caherbarna. It was his wife's second marriage and she was determined to have John for herself. Every Sunday from then on, the two of them attended Mass not in the local church of Liscannor but in the seaside resort of Lahinch. We considered her behaviour quite bizarre and couldn't really understand why John, who was so close to us, let it happen. It reminded me of a plot in a nineteenth-century novel. Perhaps she wanted to create something akin to a 'perfect misanthrope's heaven' in the words of Mr Lockwood at the beginning of Emily Bronte's *Wuthering Heights* (1847). I don't believe John was ever late again for the creamery.

When he was dying of cancer in the county hospital in Ennis in 1996, John told his wife to end the feud, and she did so. I met her once thereafter when she was introduced by my aunt Mary at a funeral in the parish church in Liscannor, but I didn't recognise her at first and found myself fumbling for words. The children by her first marriage were reluctant to involve themselves in the feud, and we have retained friendships we enjoyed as children. The two sons she had with John I don't really know, even though they are my first cousins and now live in the house next to the abandoned cabin where I took my first steps. John himself is buried in a large corner plot under an ostentatious headstone in the cemetery at St Bridget's Well. I wish life had turned out differently.

As I write this, he comes back to me reaching for his tin whistle from the shelf beside the radio in the old house and readying himself to play some of his favourite tunes such as 'The Sligo Maid' and 'The Longford Collector'. Music in his heart and music to the ears. At the time we were both in our different ways 'looking away', to quote that moving phrase from Hardy's poem 'The Self-Unseeing', but I like to think that nothing can violate the aura of that stored memory when the past knew absolutely nothing of the future. Perhaps, in my own way, I share his independent spirit as well as his single-mindedness.

I pick up again the letter he composed in his mid-thirties to my mother at Christmas 1955, which is at once full of brotherly love and a reflection of his generous self. The new curate in Liscannor, Fr Kelly, had set up a new *ceili* band, and John writes: 'He is a lovely young priest God bless him you could say anything to him.' The times were blessed when you could write like that about the clergy. John expresses so much anticipation in the letter about the church and the new school in Liscannor. It was to be called 'St Brigid's Ceilidhe Band' after St Brigid's School and St Brigid's Well, the local shrine once visited by Lady Gregory in research for her book *Visions and Beliefs in the West of Ireland* (1920). Members of the band included John himself and Micho Russell (flutes), John O'Loughlin (Patrick), Denis Guerin and T.J. O'Driscoll (fiddles), Mikie Flanagan from Luogh (Pátie), Joe Leyden from Doolin (accordions), Paddy McCormack (drummer). The Kilhourie brothers would join them later after their period of mourning with the death of an uncle. 'If you were over at school Sunday night you'd have no *shoe* coming back if you heard that music. The priest and people said it was *terrific*. OH BOY.'

Some things were meant not to last, and perhaps the world I associate with my childhood and adolescence is one of them. Why shouldn't the ties of family and neighbourhood loosen? After all, I took my first steps in a place that knew all about gaps: Caherbarna in Irish means something like the townland of the gap, the gap between the stones or cliffs. Toward the end of her life, my aunt Mary, the inhaler beside her, would wonder aloud to me, 'How did we end up like this?' It was a remark that seemed to sum up a whole generation overtaken not so much by a lifetime of smoking as by the forces of history itself. If my name was Thomas Hardy or Frank McCourt, I could write some of these stories as examples of tragedy. But that too would be misplaced or part of an exaggerated response. How could anyone in their right mind want a return to the hard times and restricted lifestyle of my grandmother's generation? How could her children be blamed for alighting for the new territory, wherever that might be and however it turned out? Today's younger generation have their own sets of problems and it could be they won't be comforted by traditional supports of old such as music and religion. But this doesn't mean they won't discover other support networks.

You can observe a small reminder of difference in first names for their children. Within a generation or so there won't be a need to include brackets after a person's name or place-names such as Doolin and Luogh as John does in his letter, for the labels individuals wear round their neck, a sign of an altered, less tribal view of the universe, will be much more distinctive and perhaps sufficient, at least for the present. One of my cousins, for example, who now lives in Limerick, has just named her daughter Ava Grace, a name which can only with difficulty or clerical perversity be traced back to the 'Hail Mary' in Latin (*Ave Maria, gratia plena*, Hail Mary, full of grace). In the 1970s, an Art teacher I knew in Ennis bravely named his children after left-wing leaders such as Salvador Allende and Rosa Luxemburg, but that was in some ways a more political decade.

Good things, then, can come from loosening ties, and it's on that note I want to end this chapter on the house of music. My thoughts go back to the early 1980s when I visited the ghost town of Bodie in California, which in the second half of the nineteenth century was a bustling mining town where prospectors came from all over the world, including Ireland, in search of gold. In 1879 its population rose to ten thousand. Now it is among the best preserved ghost towns in North America, complete with saloons, classrooms and cemetery. I was there with my California friend, the novelist Kirby Wilkins, and we began to talk about all the people who had pitched up there. I was impressed by the poignancy of the scene and the evaporation of dreams in the harsh landscape on the edge of the desert. 'Not at all,' was Kirby's response. 'These were people who abandoned Europe for the prospect of a new world, and what drove them must have been stronger than what they found.' I hadn't been expecting that response from Kirby, for his natural cast of mind was for *lacrimae rerum*, for the tears of things. But I must confess the point of view has stayed with me, not as a comfort but as a corrective to any maudlin sentiment to which I am occasionally prone. As Joe Culligan discovered, one winter spent in shorts on the warm California coast is enough to convince most emigrants from the west of Ireland to abandon any plans of ever returning home.

*1950s postcard view of Sussex radiating out from Brighton. Nearly all of the county's treasures are away from the coast. On the South Downs above Worthing are the ancient forts of Chanctonbury Ring and Cissbury Ring, and nearby is a Saxon church at Sompting. Anyone brought up on the coast is constantly invited to explore what the county has to offer, especially the chalky remains of its woodland history in its villages and place-names. The softness in the landscape and in the sea air is sometimes mistaken for a softness in the character of its people. There is nothing effete about Sussex.*

Chapter Five

## Sussex by the Sea

Good old Sussex by the sea.
Good old Sussex by the sea.
You can tell by the smell
That it stinks like hell.
Sussex by the sea.

It is as well from the outset to get an upside-down view of my early schooldays. Only much later, in the afterlife as it were, did I appreciate just how beautiful the countryside of Sussex could be. The coastal strip, which is for the most part now fairly undistinguished, is another matter, and you need to get north of the Downs to see what the county has to offer. As children growing up in Worthing, where only rarely was the beach free of the smell of seaweed, nothing would have persuaded us that we were living in a 'fashionable watering place' as Thomas Allen describes the resort in his *History of the Counties of Surrey and Sussex* (1829). We gave no thought to the fact that it was Princess Amelia and the 'illustrious house of Brunswick' who put Worthing on the map in the early decades of the nineteenth century. To us it was simply 'Wervin', a town whose Latin motto, *ex terra copiam e mari salute*, meaning 'from the land plenty and from the sea health', was clearly excessive in its claims, at least in regard to the word 'plenty'.

On the other hand, being brought up in Worthing did give us a perspective on the world, but nothing could shake our belief that the town was a 'once-fashionable watering place'. 'The tide's in, so the ball will swing now' is a comment frequently heard on the radio when Sussex are playing county cricket at Hove, but for us, whether the tide was in or out, the obnoxious smell would always swing about inside our nostrils when approaching the seafront.

Inveterate scoffers that we were, we enjoyed mocking the pretensions of our native county and town borough.

All around us in the air we breathed there was a downward pressure. According to the *Blue Guide England* (1989), Worthing is 'a resort with a mild climate, a shingly beach and an atmosphere made sedate by the large number of retired people'. And if that were not enough for downward pressure, from his Olympian heights the editor cruelly adds, 'It has little of interest apart from the Museum in Chapel Road.' At Saturday morning pictures at the Plaza cinema, we never sat directly below the front edge of the upper stalls or anywhere within firing range of what could be dropped down from the kindly souls above. Popular songs didn't escape the downward movement either, as with one which was in the charts at that time:

> Lady of Spain I adore you.
> Right from the night I first saw you
> My heart has been yearning for you.
> What else could any heart do?

That song of noble yearning and male desire, sung with gusto on *Sunday Night at the London Palladium*, got waylaid almost as soon as we heard its inflated humbug:

> Lady of Spain I adore you.
> Lift up your skirt, I'll explore you.

I'm not sure how the rest of it went. Maybe there were only two lines, but those two lines convey an impression that as children we enjoyed our own republic free of adults, and, on our way home from cubs, chips in hand, we belted out such numbers down the streets of our respectable town twixt the sea and the Downs.

By rights, we should have been reported for disturbing the peace. All these years later I catch myself, coming downstairs in the morning, singing lines such as:

> O, she wears red feathers and a hooly hooly skirt.
> She lives off just cocoanuts and fish from the sea.
> A rose in her hair, a gleam in her eyes,
> And love in her heart for me.

That was part of my early sex education – women wearing red feathers and hooly hooly skirts. I would have been five when Guy Mitchell released that song on an unsuspecting world in the spring of 1953. The lyrics must have been designed to evoke the islands in the South Seas, but I gave no thought to what such women looked like or what red feathers signified or indeed if I would ever encounter someone with love in her heart for me. Somehow I knew I was listening in to an adult world. For anyone still in the infants it was a time for words rather than dreams to work their magic. After all, the closest word to 'hooly' in my vocabulary was not 'hula' but 'hooligan', a term of disparagement repeatedly heard at school on the lips of masters when a fellow-pupil was misbehaving. Girls wore hooly skirts but boys were hooligans. Whichever way, it was a man's world, or so I must have thought.

In the context of 'Lady of Spain', I dread to contemplate what might have been lying dormant in my mind on my first visit to Spain as an eighteen-year-old seminarian or later in my fifties walking down the Ramblas in Barcelona and being accosted by an attractive, female pickpocket who wouldn't take no for an answer. The provincials we were, we moved from 'adore' to 'explore' in just one line. Would that it was ever that simple, but in those innocent pre-teen days before the real action began we just sang along with our own lines to accompany tunes we heard on the airwaves.

*Humorous postcard, dated July 1925, poking fun at Worthing. The person writes to her daughter Aggie, 'Altho you can see by this card that I am so happy, can't you see the homesick look on my face. Love, Mum.'*

If the weather and drawing water from the well governed our lives in Caherbarna, in sunny Worthing our lives were overlooked by park-keepers, policemen on bicycles, and a general notice-board called municipal. The word 'municipal' was everywhere, insisting on ownership and exclusion in the name of community: the municipal gardens, the municipal dance hall, the municipal pier, the municipal library. Worthing's appeal was strictly limited, unemotional, low-key and nothing if not full of repetition. Coaches, lining up along the front near West Buildings of a summer evening, advertised 'mystery' tours into the Sussex countryside. Old people, many of whom wore dark glasses all the year round, retired to Worthing to escape adventure, the exotic, the unknown. What could be more bracing to blow away the cobwebs of the mind than a walk along the pier and hearing the municipal band strike up *Good Old Sussex By the Sea*!

## St Mary's

I spent the first seven years of my schooling in Sussex by the sea. The fourteen-year-old Veronica Holloway, who was in her last year at the school and lived nearby in Stanley Road, took me by the hand and in turn handed me over to Miss Nevin and Mrs Dear, the teachers of the infants. I was four, what today would be called a rising five. The first year at St Mary's was conducted in a shed next to the Church of St Mary and All the Angels on Richmond Road. We played out in a tiny, cramped playground round a tree with exposed roots, and, after lunch, rested our heads on our hands on the desk in front of us and listened to the traffic outside. 'Put your head down. I can see you,' shouted Mrs Dear. 'And shut your eyes.' But, unless it was me, I couldn't determine who was misbehaving. Miss Nevin and Mrs Dear were a well-established, double act, on stage, and we were in the audience. A lit stage and a dark auditorium where the audience were sometimes forbidden to look up. The elderly Miss Nevin was a dear and the younger Mrs Dear was married to a policeman. Nevin and Dear, Devon and Ear.

They seemed to delight in collecting silly remarks made by the angels in their care. The school magazine for Christmas 1958 includes their report, complete with knowing exclamation marks and capitals. Sidney Roberts now says that because he does not go home any longer to dinner, that his mother 'has put him out to school dinners'. 'Mrs Dear apparently cannot go to Anne Griffin's house until they get some biscuits in. The very little infants were heard to be asking mummy for pennies for the ORGANS instead of Orphans!! Stephen Sands and Christine Leggett are sure they'll be able to go to the Big School at Goring when they are 100!' I could never imagine them referring to their pupils as 'two sheets to the wind' or 'nothing between the ears' or some other term of contempt, phrases I often heard in staffrooms when I became a teacher myself.

I don't remember the content of those early lessons, but within a year or so I was asked on Monday mornings to take the dinner register and the attendance register across the busy Richmond Road, past Park Crescent, and along the cul-de-sac of Amelia Road to the tiny office of the headmaster, Mr Joy, at the main school. He would run his finger down the dinner register, adding and carrying from one column to the next, and so arrive at the total income for that week's dinner money. Twelve pennies make a shilling, twenty shillings make a pound, I would hear myself reciting in my head, but what is one and nine and one and nine? That would fox me. The attendance register was neatly filled in, full of noughts and crosses. His anxious-looking secretary, who gave the impression of living on her nerves, would stand hovering about the room by a one-bar electric fire. Then the accomplished mathematician would pick up his mug of tea and return to whatever he was doing on his cluttered desk, and I would hurry back to the shed with the wooden floorboards which bounced. When I got to the juniors, I would go home for dinner.

A memoir now gives me an opportunity to rearrange the tables and to put my teachers together for a classroom portrait. The kindly Mr Joy, who was a big, unseen influence on my education, lived in Park Crescent, the most prestigious row of Regency houses in Worthing. He took assemblies in the hall and signed the end-of-year reports with his full name 'Albert E.Joy B.A.'. If you were chewing gum or smiling when you shouldn't have been, Mr Joy would raise his voice. He gave the impression of knowing things about you that you weren't aware of, as if your future was in his hands. My mother cleaned house for him, so the family were well-known to him. One evening as children when he was recovering in Worthing Hospital after an operation, we went to visit him in an open ward. He was sitting up to welcome us round his bed and showed us the ear-piece he had for listening to the radio. He never stood on ceremony and could, even when not at his best, step out of his public role with no loss of dignity. We were to him 'a happy hardworking jolly set of youngsters', the words he used to sign off his Headmaster's Notes in the Christmas 1958 issue of the school magazine.

The house where Mr Joy lived belonged to the Church and attached to it was Canon's Patch, an acre of grass surrounded by a high wall, which the unworldly Canon Westlake made over to the school. Some of my jolliest moments were spent in that sunny retreat surrounded by Sussex cobble flint-stone set in mortar. Inside Canon's Patch was like being outside of time. It's where many of the school photos were taken and where we played all kinds of sport in summer. As you crossed into Canon's Patch from the school, you moved magically from in time to out of time. With tall trees from a shady Park Crescent peering on the other side over the plot, it was like a Walter Crane watercolour alive with the spirits, fauns, and little people of the earth. Later, Mr Joy allowed the basement of his house to be used as a Catholic youth club, and it was there, on the eve of the 1960s, that we learnt to jive and smooch and twist under the watchful eyes of the clergy.

Mr Stiffneck, his deputy, who took the examination class, was known as 'Gandy' on account of the way he kept stretching his neck inside his tight collar like a gander. I suspect he had some Irish background but this was never visible, for no one got anywhere close to him, and he never dropped his guard even when he was about his personal business. From somewhere near the Headmaster's Office, he would pick up the large key to the outside toilet located in the playground reserved for the teachers and adjacent to the boys' toilet, and return it when he had performed his duties. I don't ever recall him taking over the role of headmaster. He lived quietly and at the end of the afternoon made his way out of the school gates quietly. Cracking a joke or becoming flustered was not part of his bag of tricks. That would have been too much effort I suspect.

Mrs Dragon, by contrast, loved the crackle of her own voice. When the school was split in two and a new senior school created at Goring-by-Sea under the name of the Elizabethan English martyr, Robert Southwell, (now Chatsmore), she took up a senior appointment. I spent a week there on finishing St Mary's before Monsignor Porsche, the parish priest, decided to send me away to boarding school, but not before I was bawled out after lunch by her. I had been enjoying myself playing football on the field and had come in sweating. My face reddens easily and this was held against me and made worse by the embarrassment she had caused. 'Pierce, come out here. Go immediately to the washrooms and get yourself cleaned up. Never come into school like that again. And wipe that smile off your face.'

Mr Dishevelled was the music teacher, who also played the organ at the

Church. With his projecting nose, 'Beaky' was a very sad case and it was cruel to see him the object of so much abuse on account of his looks and classroom indiscipline. The very worst time for 'Beaky', which, fortunately, he may have known nothing about, was when we would pass a chained parrot perched in a garden outside someone's house on the street opposite Victoria Park. 'Pretty Polly. Do re mi,' went the parrot. This was innocent enough, but in time the parrot, who was a model pupil, became familiar with all the questions and all the answers and performed them accordingly and without pausing for breath: 'What's your name? My name's Beaky.' This was followed by a string of swear words and other responses which suggested a perfect ear. It was as if the whole school over time had made its way past the house with the parrot in the garden and discharged its collective bile and resentment against the school as represented in the figure of poor 'Beaky' and his articulate spokesperson. Mr Dishevelled was a talented musician but St Mary's wasn't the best place for him.

Mr Distracted was a softy and could have suffered a similar fate to 'Beaky'. He had been in a Japanese prison-of-war camp during the War, and would no doubt have kept this to himself except that half of the middle finger on his right hand down to the knuckle had been removed by his guards. We must have been quite cruel and unsympathetic as children for when he struck you on the back of the legs for, say, idling with the classroom pencil-sharpener, you would concentrate on the moment when his hand made contact to determine if you could feel the oblong bit of the finger that was missing. He had dark, brown, liquid eyes which couldn't hide a distracted soul inside, but it was quite a shock in later years to find him conversing with you with genuine interest and to learn that he wrote poetry.

Miss WW was a study in the relationship between character and personality. Her character was ever-present in the way she conducted herself, but there was something resistant about her personality. Everything she did suggested a prim and proper attitude to life, but it would have been nice to have seen her in some other colour than blue, for blue seemed not to express but to hide her personality. When she died she was buried in the same row at Offington Cemetery as my father and grandfather and Canon Westlake.

The tall upright figure of Mr Sideburn was sports master, and, while most teachers never moved school, you could tell he was on an upward career path. A disciplinarian, he would use the slipper to gain attention, or, with his right hand, he would lift you off the ground by the sideburn. He had a soft spot for the girls, and my sister, who represented the school at running, would babysit for him when he had small children. Mr Sideburn's signature is on various certificates I won at school, including the one for the high jump which became a school record in 1957, beating the previous best which dated back to 1954. I believe my record stood for a number of years, and for all I know it may still be a record. Three feet eleven inches (or 1.143 metres in new money), and at the time I could have been only about four feet six inches in height. Of all my achievements at St Mary's, this is the one that gives me most pleasure. The girls in their navy-blue knickers did the scissors, but I preferred the western roll. There seemed to be something about the sideways movement over the bar. The scissors, which involved just the legs and the crotch, didn't allow for flight, just keeping the back awkwardly upright. Give me the more composed, sexy, western roll anytime, I deliberated. The Fosbury flop, which turns the body into a projectile, hadn't yet been invented. Not the embarrassing scissors, nor an absurd flop, but a delightful roll onto a well-placed and convenient mattress to break the fall.

My favourite teacher was Miss Sweetheart. I would have moved heaven and earth to please her, deliberately graze my knee, anything, to get her to show pity or any sort of emotion toward me. In my school report for July 1955, she observed: 'David is well up to standard and works with enthusiasm.' Not surprisingly, I was 'a happy and helpful member of the class'. Miss Sweetheart lived somewhere near us on the other side of the railway line, and one day on the way home I attempted to keep up with her, me running on the uneven, red brick pavement and she so sedate on her bicycle with a wicker basket and glancing occasionally over at me. She had the smoothest knees I had ever taken the trouble to notice, and when I stood next to her at her desk, while she was marking my exercise book or fielding some cooked-up, private question, I felt something stirring. I was seven, another prime number to go with my beloved three. I think my attraction to her was reciprocated, but I must have instinctively known she couldn't disclose that to me. I never did discover her first name.

When she married a Dutchman and left to teach in the British Embassy School in the Netherlands, I felt a sense of betrayal. Today, I punch her name into Google expectantly but nothing comes up. Perhaps she changed her name again or perhaps I've got wrong the Dutch name and spelling. I wonder if I ever came into her thoughts again. The smoothness of her sweet knees I realise now must have been because she had stout legs, but who cares when she's the occasion for your first sexual experience? In the school photo for that year when she was our form teacher, she is wearing a three-quarter length skirt, a zipped-up cardigan, and a bangle round her neck. She has strong features, wavy hair, and a subtle or knowing smile. I can see why I took to her.


## My contemporaries

What about my contemporaries? At the end of his life in his last book of poems, *Endpoint* (2009), the genial American novelist, John Updike, reflects on how his classmates at school in small-town Shillington in Pennsylvania provided him with a

> sufficiency of human types: beauty,
> bully, hanger-on, natural,
> twin, and fatso.

That was true for me as well, though at the time I couldn't have known it. In primary school you are in the default position called looking forward, and you spend little time reflecting on who will accompany you into later life. Apart from six months repeating 'A' Levels, I never lived in Worthing after the summer of 1958, so I rarely met up with my old classmates. I always resist joining sites on the net such as Friendsunited in case I might have to confront changes to my rear-view mirror, for I enjoy the control that memory brings to my past and almost certainly I would have to adjust my impressions to a different or more nuanced order of reality. These classmates circle around in the various, distant spools of my mind with not one blemish or ageing mark to show for their troubles. There's a lot to be said for losing touch.

It was generally acknowledged that Audrey Gilbert was the brightest star in class. Every day she commuted on the bus down from Dial Post in the middle of Sussex. She was a giggler, but she gave the impression that she understood from the start she was going somewhere. I think she was one of the very few to get to university. There was a period when she found herself being harassed on the way to catch her bus by one of the toughies in the class. She spoke to me about it, and I volunteered to accompany her along Richmond Road to her bus stop near the Post Office on Chapel Road. I did that for about a week and that seemed to do the trick, for the toughie didn't bother Audrey again. Instead, he would chase me through the school in a rage. I don't know what it was about, and I didn't know at the time. There seemed to be some fierce resentment which only a fist fight could settle.

Margaret Sullivan, who came from a big Irish family, lived in a poorer neighbourhood near the school. We enjoyed each other's company, me in my grey short trousers and grey pullover and she in her yellow, summery, cotton uniform. We would go head-to-head in the competition of being awarded stars for our tables, but there was never any nastiness between us. After secondary school at the Sion Convent, she continued on to teacher training college. You could imagine her staying the course and teaching, for, from an early age, she showed courage and tenacity and, more importantly, a sense of humour and a lightness of touch. Her brother John went into shipping and worked for Lloyds in the City.

Some people were naturally talented, and others had to work at things. I had difficulty deciding which category I fitted into. I'm surprised when people tell me I'm very bright. All I know is that I'm not bright enough. Perhaps that's to do with being number 3 in the family. Did Jesus, who was number 2, know he was the Son of God is one of those questions which continues to intrigue me. When he was dying on the cross and resorted to crying out 'Why hast Thou forsaken me?' we should perhaps take him at his word. That he had been abandoned by his father. When one morning my mother came upstairs to the bedroom to inform me I hadn't passed the interview to get into the local grammar school, I felt strangely abandoned. I was always top of the class or near the top at St Mary's and should by rights have followed my elder brother to Worthing High School, but it didn't happen.

Virtually none of the boys in my class went on to grammar school. I never discovered if there was a prejudice against Catholics among the masters in their tweed jackets at the grammar school, but I suspected as much. Girls in my class went on to the Convent, which was to all intents and purposes a grammar school, but the boys lost out. Tony Harrison, the Leeds poet, cultivated a long-burning resentment against his grammar-school masters, and he deploys it to good effect in his 1978 sequence 'The School of Eloquence'. But Harrison was fortunate, for the West Riding scheme enabled a small number of bright boys to enjoy a grammar-school education. Because I didn't get to have an opportunity of being taught in a grammar school, I was never able to train a bitter or sceptical eye on the disdainful smiles of such masters. I fell through whatever nets were not there. But I never blamed St Mary's. There was never a day when I didn't want to go to that jolly school at the end of a cul-de-sac by Victoria Park, whose entrance on a road named after the nineteenth-century reformer, Richard Cobden, looks more like a back than a front entrance.

If someone by way of reproach were to argue 'You should have stayed where you were among your class. All your education is but proof not that you've betrayed your class but that you never had it in the first place' I suppose I might half-agree. Is intelligence a measurable commodity? Or is it something that you acquire on the journey through life? As can be seen scattered throughout this book and indeed my other books, I have a fondness for qualifiers such as 'perhaps' or 'seems' or 'could' or 'might' and other examples of stylistic hesitation. One of my philosophy tutors at university would cross out 'seems' and write in the margin 'Things are or they are not'. I've never sufficiently found an answer to that question as to whether such qualifiers suggest a discriminating intellect or a lack of confidence. Confidence, after all, is a class marker, as is resentment.

If Monsignor Porsche hadn't taken it upon himself to send me to boarding school, thinking I might have a vocation to the priesthood, I would have left school at fifteen and entered the labour market as unskilled working class. You, dear reader, wouldn't now be reading what I am now this minute in December 2009 writing. The educational system, which is another way of saying the class system, was intent on crushing me, but it didn't manage to, and I have lived to tell my story. So this memoir is in part a narrative of survival and coming through. But, unlike Harrison, I carry few resentments around with me. I have lived on the outside of things. My accent, for example, moves between Received Pronunciation (or the Queen's English) and Southern English, and, whenever I want to emphasise my class background or to vary the impression people have of me, I slip into using glottal stops. So I occasionally say 'me[ʔ]al' instead of 'metal'. Unlike politicians from the middle class who alight on such an accent for political effect, I enjoy the complicity my working-class accent brings. I refuse to systematise my speech, therefore, preferring to link my fate with all those others who carry a number of selves inside them, the one that was assigned to them, the one they adopted, the one they aspired to, the one they refused, or the one they spent a lifetime unsuccessfully veering away from. 'My mother bathed me as a child in a me[ʔ]al tub.' You can sometimes tell that a person doesn't come from Brighton when they pronounce the 't' in the middle of that place-name.

*St Mary's Primary School, Worthing, Sussex. Class photo, taken in the 1950s. We must have been told to say cheese. It was unnecessary in my case, for I was always animated in the presence of my favourite teacher.*

I look again at the black-and-white photo of those who shared that year with me and Miss Sweetheart. I am sitting in front, the nearest boy to her. There are some forty one in the class, formed into three rows across the school playground. The class was evenly divided between twenty one girls and twenty boys. We had no teaching assistants in those days, but the faces tell a story not of impoverishment and neglect but of hope. Not one child looks overweight. There were no fatsos or Billy Bunters in my class, and only one child is wearing glasses (though that could be for other reasons). Behind us are the backs of houses on Cobden Street with their stack pipes and chimneys. Also behind us is a solitary netball post, waiting for playtime. In front of us there is the cover of a large drain, which would have been at the junction connecting to the outside toilets just out of shot of the camera. If I wasn't in possession of what is an inside story, I might wrongly assume the photo resembled a period Northern scene by Bill Brandt or, if I gave it a slight twist, an image by the contemporary satirical photographer, Martin Parr.

That photo was taken in the mid-1950s. I am about half-way through my years as a junior. This is the world coming to pass. Expectant, cheerful, without colour. In search of colour, some of the older teenage pupils at St Mary's skipped school in September 1956 to witness the arrival of Liberace in Southampton on his first trip to Britain. In the photo there are some who are giggling, and a gangly boy is looking to his left, distracted by something. But everyone else is looking forward. I am sitting in the front row and close to my beloved teacher, who is standing. Next to me is the quiet Philip Hamlet, a little mouse who came from the nearby, sleepy village of Sompting. I am wearing a jacket which is buttoned, loose-fitting long socks which come up to my knees, a school tie and jumper, and sandals. It must have been a dull day in summer. Like the photo of my father as a boy, I am smiling for all eternity.

I must have persuaded many of my classmates to sign their names on the back of my photo, some a little uncertainly, some with capitals, some slanting downward across the page, some sprawling indiscriminately, and some I suspect someone else, perhaps Miss Sweetheart, has transcribed for them. Each letter is distinct and separate and I can read them all. As if they were determined never to be just one in a series, their names are as distinct as their image in the photograph. Some, such as Audrey Gilbert, just signed with their first names as if that was enough for posterity. Mary McVeigh, Janet Pipkin, David Davidson, Mary Hill, Hilary Chipchase, Eileen Fitzgerald, Margaret Ahern, Paul Forbes, Stephen Mander, Christine Byrne, Denise Burke, Frances Gillespie, Frances Clark, Danny Keegan, Philip Keane, Malcolm Shaw, Philip Davey, Patrick Laycock, Philip Hancock, Ian Wood, Philip McLaughlin, Ursula Martin, Carole Oakley, John Baker, Yvonne Seacombe, Frederick Girdlestone.

Most of my classmates I don't recollect terribly clearly, but the photo has helped me bring some of them back to life for the first time in over half a century. Malcolm Cool lived in a dark house facing Victoria Park. His mother was cub mistress for a time. His slightly severe father was old style, and he reminded me of someone who had been in the military. Some years later on New Year's Eve I must have been in the house and he led our formal, prayer-like, celebrations ushering in the new year. We stood up round the table in the dark living room next to the kitchen and wished each other well for the coming year. Malcolm was the opposite, easy-going, full of banter and riding out storms, for he never pushed himself academically and therefore found himself periodically having to apologise for his shortcomings. He would never have done anything formally and was the first in our group as teenagers to wear outlandishly modish shoes.

I don't know why I remember that particular New Year's Eve when I spent so much time with Malcolm and should by rights have recalled other happier times. Perhaps in the hinterland of consciousness we remember things that strike us as odd or in need of incorporation into full consciousness. Later in life when I got to know the English critic and Keats scholar, John Barnard, I was somehow reminded of Malcolm's father. Perhaps at school we learn all the various types of people we will encounter later in life. Perhaps the astrologists are right about the limited number of star signs (and therefore personalities) available to us. What did the absence of Malcolm's mother signify? I wonder if my mind was sensing the signs of a marriage in dissolution. Or was it that Malcolm's father died soon after and that the new year did not turn out well for that family? So, looking back, I am recalling something that contained as it were a later moment in time. Perhaps I was also half-recalling something about my cub mistress and how she took me home one evening after I had nearly drowned at the swimming baths, buying me a bag of chips on the way to assuage her guilt.

Once, when I was trying for one of my cub badges, I rang my cub mistress from the public phone box outside the Foresters' Hall on Newland Road. In those days there was an elaborate system of lifting the phone, inserting four pennies into the slot, waiting for an answer, and then pressing the button marked A. This would then ensure a proper connection. When Arkala picked up the phone at the other end, I became confused and forgot to push the button marked A. A few minutes into the conversation, she shouted something down the phone line about speaking up because she couldn't hear me very well. When I returned home and began recounting what had happened, my brother John jumped up, rushed out, and returned a few minutes later with the four pennies. 'They're mine,' he shouted in triumph. 'You idiot, not only did you forget to press button A, but you also forgot to get your money back by pressing button B.' I was more than usually crestfallen especially as I was convinced I had flunked it and wouldn't get to add to my collection of badges. As it happened, my cub mistress relented and awarded me the badge, commenting that it must have been down to the poor line.

As her name suggests, Christine O'Brien came from an Irish family. Mary O'Brien, her elder sister, went on to marry one of the Phelan brothers from County Cavan. She smiled with her eyes and was always welcoming, as indeed were all the O'Brien sisters. Once I stayed with the Phelan family in County Cavan. They lived on a farm in that hill country near the border with the

North. This was before the Troubles began in 1968. They would regale me with stories about the illegal cock fights that took place in the locality between farmers from the South and the North. Such fights, so close to the border, must have carried political or sectarian overtones, but here was an Ireland close to the people and one that had a certain ancient devilry and freedom from constraint that I responded to.

The Phelan family was touched with tragedy. One of the brothers, who was a singer of traditional songs and great company, died underneath the tractor he was driving. That toppling over was one of the first deaths to register with me when growing up. Another brother, Ben, the one who had married Mary and moved to London, died from cancer some years later. Before he returned to Cavan, Frank Phelan got me a job on the buildings one summer vacation and, in between offloading breeze blocks and filling in trenches, taught me how to drive a dumper. My very first driving lesson, however, I managed to demolish a wall when reversing. The dumper escaped unscathed, and Frank kindly rebuilt the wall. I passed my test the second time round.

If I had stayed in Worthing, the passage from school to adult life would have taken on a seamless character, but as it is I have to work with my memory to remember it all and put it back together. I should remember more things about Christine O'Brien than I do, and if I were to meet her now she would remind me of the times we shared, how she wore her hair in a neat beehive like Dusty Springfield and danced in the basement in Park Crescent at the Catholic social club with not a single hair out of place. Bridget Gant has kept in touch with my mother and whenever we meet up she always reminds me of something I'd forgotten about St Mary's, how so-and-so is now in a wheelchair or someone else died of an overdose. 'You remember so-and-so,' she begins, and I haven't the heart to reply 'No'. But then Bridget never strayed far from her neighbourhood.

Nowhere among these class photos can I discover the girl who was extra special to me. Perhaps Pat T——— joined the school in the upper juniors. You could guess she was trouble from the way she shook her pony tail from side to side and from the way she teased you and then scampered off. But there was something about PT that made me want to follow. She was lively, intelligent, and athletic. Perhaps she wasn't the black sheep in her family but that's the impression she conveyed. She had the demeanour and confidence of a wayward child in a fairy tale, and I loved her every movement. I see her now turning her darting tease of a glance toward me and then away from me and I want to run after her and touch her. In my final year at St Mary's I tried to summon up courage to ask her out. I considered an excursion to the Downs would mark the beginnings of our betrothal. But it never happened. Perhaps I feared a refusal would signify the end of my quest and the irretrievable breakdown in our relationship. I'm sure PT had hundreds of admirers but, as with Miss Sweetheart a few years earlier, I entertained the foolish notion that I was special. When I left St Mary's, I left behind unfinished business, and it came as a shock to learn, five years later, that she had married and had a child.

What I'd give to start it all again. The afternoon sun high in the sky shining into the warm classroom, the catkins we grew in bottles on the red-tiled window ledges, the yellow cotton summer uniforms of the girls, the rude jests and passing comments in the playground, Chinese burns, piggyback fights, sports day in Victoria Park, throwing bean bags at each other in the school hall without a care in the world, observing the individual peculiarities of our form teachers, playing up when students from the local teaching training college at Bognor took class, singing the words of the chorus with a guitar-playing young female trainee teacher about coming from Alabama with a banjo on my knee, experiencing the danger and exhilaration of climbing onto the flat roof to retrieve tennis balls and peering down magisterially at the school in the playground below, basking in the praise of a favourite teacher, feeling the heat on your face when being bawled out or, better still, when someone else was being bawled out and made to stand in the corner, appreciating the solidarity with classmates when collectively punished, collecting empty jam-jars for the missions and wondering how much money that would translate into, noticing the van pull up in late morning with the hot dinners, dawdling along Cambridge Road on the way home and sucking the sweet honey from pink fuchsias dangling over someone's garden wall – what I'd give to relive it all again. As Wordsworth also realised, there's nothing quite like the prelude to something.

By rights, a sizeable chunk of this chapter should be devoted to the day of my First Holy Communion at the age of seven, the highlight for some of a Catholic childhood, but the special day seemed too much of an adult invention to suppose or feel it was in any way natural. I didn't take to the mantle of innocence draped over everything, and felt awkward being surrounded by so much good behaviour and being dressed up like a mannequin with hands joined and photographed. Holiness was fine, but how could I converse with my classmates or kick a ball around or chew bubble gum when I had just received Holy Communion? With its downward pressure, First Confession, which we went to the week before, was more natural even if I couldn't decide on what sins to confess. I had reached the age of reason, so an important milestone had been crossed. The trouble was I didn't feel different, only that I had been told I was different.

It's clear to me now that while at primary school I was in my most 'iterative' phase, that is my least self-conscious, individuating phase, the self-unseeing. Custom, routine, repetition encouraged me to fit in and not to stand out, and it is this side of me I remember. There were few actual moments that I recall sharply. It was as if I was beguiled by customary experience and on my way to being enlisted into the lower ranks of Britain's labour market. What I used to do, rather than what I did – this is what has stayed with me. I was running but gave little thought to my shadow self keeping up with me. I hit the triangle in music lessons, raised my hand when the class was asked a question, and stood up smart when the headmaster or a visitor came into the room. 'Miss, Miss. Sir, Sir. Me Miss. Me Sir.'

I was internalising things all the time, not so much about books as about the world and how it operates. What I recall about my teachers is not what they taught me but what their behaviour told me about their character. I was in the audience, happy and helpful, and they were lit up on stage. Child-centred learning was unheard of. Instead, every week we were reminded that empty vessels make most noise. As an educational experience it was patently deficient. There was no science taught, no drama lessons, no exposure to foreign languages. I particularly enjoyed perusing maps of the different countries of the world and not just those marked in the red of Empire, but that should have given way to something more challenging. Long before I heard about plate tectonics and continents shifting, something had come away in my mind, for I would trace the shoreline of Brazil protruding into the Atlantic Ocean and reflect on how it fitted into the map of West Africa. On my way home from school I stopped off at the municipal public library to pick up story books such as Jim Corbett's *The Man-Eaters of Kumaon* (1944) and to watch the librarian jealously stamp them. Except for an oblique view on things, I owned nothing. And it was not a school to acquire contacts for use later in life, but I suppose what it gave me was a developing idea of myself in relation to others – and not too many tears.

I delighted in sport and sporting achievements. Dennis Toner recovered from polio as a child to become a talented footballer and cricketer. We were joined in juniors by a boy from the West Indies, who surpassed us all at sport. His name now escapes me, but we had never encountered anyone who could bowl a cricket ball so fast and so accurately, and he was equally good when it came to the bat. Outside of school, six years or so ahead of us, there were the Bonetti boys, whose family ran an ice-cream parlour store near the Dome cinema on the sea-front. Peter, who later kept goal for Chelsea and England, became a name to conjure with. With his agility and economy of movement, there was never a time when the quiet and modest Peter didn't show promise as 'the cat' he became. We caught up with him when we trained for a short while with Worthing Catholics FC under the management of the pipe-smoking Larry Stoppard, who lived near us on Park Road and who was I believe a commercial traveller with piles from the way he was given, while discussing tactics, to scratching himself.

I remember walking self-consciously into school after the Munich air disaster on 6 February 1958, which involved the deaths of my childhood hero, Duncan Edwards, and some of the team I had watched playing at Fratton Park against Portsmouth. It felt strange to be touched by so public an event and to know that my classmates felt something similar. Passing the stacked crates of milk bottles near the entrance, I wondered about the way impressions could suddenly become rank-ordered, how some impressions were more important and some less important than others. It temporarily slowed me down, being the first such moment when I felt time freeze and at the same time expand. The next public event to affect me in that way was the assassination of John F. Kennedy five years later, but by then I was at boarding school and my consciousness had altered significantly.

Once while sitting on a bench seat in class, facing in toward my mousy sparring partner, Philip Hamlet, I fell back and hit my head on the radiator, which necessitated a visit to the hospital and a stitch. I broke no arms or legs playing football. There are school photos of me where my right eye is closed due to some undiagnosed ailment, perhaps conjunctivitis, but I didn't miss school if I could and never played truant. When the weather turned cold I would wear a balaclava knitted by my mother, and when I moved from infants to juniors I swapped mittens threaded through the sleeves for gloves threaded through the sleeves. One day my elder brother, John, fell over in the playground and knocked his head on a raised drain. He suffered concussion, was put to bed, and the doctor sent for. Were it not for Dr Rosenberg, who immediately rang the hospital, he would have suffered more serious consequences. John was always getting into trouble and needed quite a lot of contact with the sheer resistance of things to come to his senses.

## Keeping faith

It was a Catholic school with a Catholic ethos. In the period after my First Communion I must have been turning over in my mind the issue of faith, and in my final year I told Fr Corcoran of my wish to become a priest. While serving Mass and Benediction, I was coming into close contact with role models among the local clergy. What attracted me to such a lifestyle I couldn't say. My sister believes the idea was planted in me by my mother, but I don't recall any such moment or conversation or indeed feeling such pressure. Moreover, although I was closer to her than to my father, I don't believe I was a mummy's boy. Needless to say, there wouldn't have been any pressure from my father, who was never very approachable when it came to discussing personal matters. Perhaps it was no more than being a good Catholic boy from a good Catholic family. My elder brother showed no such inclination, and I wish I had followed him, but, a third child, I was always more reserved and of a reflective turn of mind.

Once when we arrived in Lahinch for our summer holidays after a twenty-four-hour trek from Worthing, we came upon Fr Corcoran with his mother, who was looking for a retirement home somewhere in the west of Ireland. It was the only time I ever saw Fr Corcoran slightly careworn. Working abroad in England must have given him a certain zest, but there must have been a darker side to his character. One of his contemporaries who was ordained with him was recruited by a diocese in the United States, but, before he arrived in New York to take up his appointment, he had met an attractive young woman on board the Atlantic liner, and that marked an unbelievably dramatic end to his career in the Church. As a boy, I didn't encounter enough of such human stories or 'falls from grace' as the Church insists on calling them.

Perhaps the path I was to adhere to for some eight years had its roots in my sense of Irishness. The local priests, most of whom were Irish, and some of them trained like Fr Corcoran at All Hallows in Dublin, carried 'home' in their voices. Fr Coleman Quinn, who came from County Clare, was determined to put down roots, as, unflustered, he established a new parish in East Worthing, offshoot from the main parish. The quiet-spoken Jesuit, F.X.O'Sullivan, came over for his summers from James Joyce's old school, Belvedere College, Dublin, and galloped through Mass so that he could have his daily swim at the beach, intent, like a good Jesuit, on enjoying parish life without a parish. School, too, gathered all the Irish names together, not only the surnames but also the first names, particularly of the girls – Bernadette, Theresa, Patricia, Mary, Deirdre, Eileen.

Irishness in Worthing found its focus in the church and school of St Mary's and in the Sion Convent, an order dedicated to the conversion of the Jews, which was ironic given all I write about in a previous chapter about my Jewish family. However, Irishness was a pale shadow of its former self. It was more a badge than an umbrella, and it couldn't hide from its estranged quality. We were a clan without a clan, a community inside a community. The world was essentially indifferent to our plight – whatever that plight was exactly. Adapt, it kept saying. You might sing in your hymn books about the faith of your fathers, but England was never going to return to the old faith. Learn the value of being separate, of not sharing your cherished beliefs and culture with others. So there was always the certainty and, at the same time, the attraction of estrangement if I continued with my idea of a vocation. As a footnote, it was in keeping that, when passing St Andrew's (High) Anglican church on Clifton Road on our way to Mass, we would be cautioned by our mother to avert our eyes.

In all kinds of ways, the summer of 1958 marks a profound break in my development as a person, and before I could absorb what was happening the ground under my feet had shifted. Perhaps that's as it should be. In later years, I managed to negotiate serious wrenches by means of a retreat into reading or through the intellect. But at eleven I had no such resources. I woke up one morning to discover that the intensity of home life together with that jolly school had disappeared for ever. What I gained, however, was something unexpected, but this took time to be revealed and it revolved around not so much religion as my native county. I didn't appreciate it at the time but what I was learning was a different kind of faith, one that took me back to my roots twixt the sea and the Downs.

Largely through education and the passage of time I have discovered an affection for what Richard Jefferies and Edward Thomas call 'the south country'. Jefferies himself, who was a notable defender of the southern landscape against London prettification of village life (what he termed 'primrosing'), spent the last year of his life at Goring-by-Sea and is buried across the road from my parents' house in Broadwater. In a plot nearby is also buried the prolific naturalist, W.H.Hudson, author of a fine appreciation of the Sussex countryside, *Nature in Downland* (1900). For a time Hudson lived in Park Road on a site that in my childhood was occupied by Hall and Co, a builders' merchants who employed John Pearce, a much-loved cousin, who was tragically killed in an accident at Horley in Surrey driving one of their trucks. W.E.Henley, who was also a model for Long John Silver on account of his amputated leg and forceful temperament, moved to Worthing in 1898 and spent the last years of his life at St George's Lodge, Chesswood Road, which is a continuation of Newland Road. A leading figure in literary circles in Edinburgh and London in the 1890s, he was a strong influence on Yeats as a young man.

*'I wonder to myself how they can all get on without me – how they manage, bird and flower, without me to keep the calendar for them. For I noted it so carefully and lovingly, day by day.' Memorial to Richard Jefferies, at the entrance to the church cemetery in Broadwater, Worthing.*

As the run of his name suggests, Oscar Fingal O'Flahertie Wills Wilde, son of a woman who wrote inspired Irish nationalist verse under the pseudonym 'Speranza' for Thomas Davis's newspaper *The Nation* in the 1840s, came out fighting, and went on to compose part of *The Importance of Being Earnest* (1895) in Worthing, as references to Jack Worthing, a handbag and a third class railway ticket serve to remind us. Shelley's *The Necessity of Atheism* (1811), for which he was rusticated from Oxford, was printed in Worthing, a reminder of a radical tradition which, two hundred years ago, embraced Tom Paine in Lewes, William Blake in Felpham, and Shelley in Goring Castle (where, nearby, we picked jar-loads of bluebells as children). Here was a cultural legacy to crow about and one that helped me discover a sense of place reconstructed through reading about the past.

Sussex by the sea, the ancient Kingdom of the South Saxons, has been for me, therefore, a mixed estate, at once a birthright and also an acquired taste, somewhere to escape from and to return to. I would never have become a writer or academic, however, if I had stayed there for, like many people, I needed not immediacy and involvement but distance and perspective to learn how to think for myself. Let me jump forward to December 1962 when we moved to South Farm Road, Broadwater. The actual distance was only about a mile from Newland Road but the social and emotional distance was much greater. The first time we went upstairs and looked out of the front bedroom window, we were greeted by our new neighbours opposite resting under their headstones in the cemetery behind a flint-stone wall. There was something else. We were now living on a busy, fairly brutal, main road, and this also militated against communication with our living neighbours, so at a stroke the intensity of our former neighbourhood vanished into thin air. In relocating, we had gained extra living space but at a cost. I suspect we believed that as a family we could make a home anywhere and that loosening ties would not unduly affect us. At fifteen years of age, it was apparent that my sense of place was set to be filtered through the past and recollected through the tranquillity that comes to many of us only with the passage of time.

If I had been familiar with the work of Jefferies at the time I could have made more use of him not only in extending my local sympathies but also in keeping faith with where I had grown up. I only had to raise my head after turning into Clifton Road on the way home from junior school to be greeted by the 'fungus-like roundness and smoothness' of the Sussex Downs, as the keen-eyed Hudson describes them, and the character of that greeting was always personal, a gentle beckoning to those who are native to the area. In *A Song for Every Season* (1971), a classic account of a family of sheep-farmers from Rottingdean near Brighton, a family who did indeed have a song for every season, Bob Copper suggests the Downs are a 'great moral educator' and notices how a shepherd's work 'breeds patience in a man'. That, too, is right. The great sheep farms have long since disappeared, but, even though they are largely empty, the Downs continue to exert some ancient pull, a legacy perhaps of their former inhabitants patiently looking for company.

In her old age, whenever we took Daisy Pearce for a spin in the car and passed Chanctonbury Ring on the road between Storrington and Steyning, she would sit up and wave. 'Hi Chank,' her thin voice would sing out. Then she would sit back, adjust the pins holding her hat in place, and carry on the conversation where she had left off. It was only a brief interruption but she spoke familiarly, as if she was visiting an old friend from her youth. Needless to say, Chank, or Chenkbury as he is known in Roger Gough's 1789 translation of William Camden's *Britannia* (1586), was unmoved and, indeed, disinclined to show any response. Chenk, Chank. However, what I needed was someone to turn the visual accompaniment to my life into music. In his evocative journal of the soul, *The Story of My Heart* (1883), Jefferies, musing on top of the Downs, suggests the clock 'may make time for itself; there is none for me':

Now is eternity; now is the immortal life. Here this moment, by this tumulus, on earth, now; I exist in it. The years, the centuries, the cycles are absolutely nothing; it is only a moment since this tumulus was raised; in a thousand years it will still be only a moment. To the soul there is no past and no future; all is and will be ever, in now.

Before I embark on the religious journey that would take me away from Worthing, it is right to pause and hold onto this moment in time. I am back where I belong and where I began with the cupboard under the stairs, the Teville stream, and with the phrase 'in and out of time' under which my book in part shelters.

*John Fisher School, Purley, Surrey. This photo was taken in 1958-9
in front of Woodcote when I would have been eleven. I am twisting something in my
hands.*

Chapter Six

# Boarding School

## Away

Away is such a powerful concept and at its most powerful in childhood. In Irish folktales a child, especially a boy, could be taken away from his family by the fairies and never returned. That is why you see photographs, as late as the 1920s, of boys in rural Ireland dressed as girls. Jane Urquhart called her Canadian-Irish novel on emigration simply by the one word *Away* (1993). In English novels from Charles Dickens to Angela Carter, away is not only a continuing theme but also one of the great conveyor-belts for characters to learn about themselves and appreciate the nature of difference and the limits of change. In an engaging opening to 'The Bloody Chamber', Carter's modern rewriting of Perrault's children's story, the protagonist is carried by the train through the night 'away from Paris, away from girlhood, away from the white, enclosed quietude of my mother's apartment, into the unguessable country of marriage'. I love those prepositions, three 'aways' followed by 'into', and then the adjective that lifts the opening away from Perault and children's stories toward an altogether different kind of writing and psychological inquiry: 'unguessable'.

*David Copperfield* (1850) is no less an exploration of psychology but this time it is a boy's story, filtered through the eyes of a boy who tells us what he knows but more than he imagines. Here he informs us about going away to London for the first time:

We had started from Yarmouth at three o'clock in the afternoon, and we were due in London about eight next morning. It was midsummer weather, and the evening was very pleasant. When we passed through a village, I pictured to myself what the insides of the houses were like, and what the inhabitants were about; and when boys came running after us, and got up behind and swung there for a little way, I wondered whether their fathers were alive, and whether they were happy at home.

David is under the illusion that he is doing the picturing, but it is we who are doing that. We are picturing David on his journey from Yarmouth to London. Equally, when David mentions 'insides' we can't help the association with food and with what is happening inside David's stomach and inside David the person. That phrase about the insides of houses also reminds us of how a boy might express this. A more articulate or educated person might be expected to say 'I wondered what their houses were like on the inside'. Or 'I wondered what the interiors of those houses were like'. It's a risk, but Dickens creates his own readers or rather he relies on them, certain in the knowledge that they, too, are responsive to how language works and to what are in effect a composer's arrangements.

Through his choice of words, all these associations come to us and with them David's take on things. In that regard we are not just picturing David but accompanying him. Again, the use of 'inhabitants' in this passage is unexpected. The word is slightly awkward, as if David is trying to generalise, as if he were a traveller or a foreign observer. The word thus keeps the description descriptive, but there is then another switch as the boys clamber aboard the coach and 'swung' there for a while, at which point David immediately begins wondering about their families and what they were about. In four sentences we move from starting out from Yarmouth to home again.

David is searching for the right kind of register and he doesn't quite settle on it. As we look back, do any of us know for sure what words we deployed in certain situations at the time when young? Isn't it the case that what intervenes is nothing less than the history of our competence in language? *David Copperfield* is the work of the imagination in full flight, and part of that concerns getting things not wrong but in this passage not quite right (and therefore precisely right). It is also a novel which draws on Dickens's own life story, so it has an added personal dimension and accompanying tension for the author. The sentence structure, the grammar, conveys a boy's perspective; the vocabulary betrays words which are in struggle with memory and correct usage. Some things convey our world and some things betray that world. What did the boys do after clambering behind? They 'swung there for a little way'. Is that their legs or their bodies swinging? They didn't just hang on but swung there, as if the coach was designed to be used like something you might come upon in a playground. I wonder if it's a word that belongs to the adult author rather than to the fictional character telling the story about his childhood past, for it seems to move between the two poles. Even though it's an illegitimate question, I find these boys so intriguing that I can't help wondering what happened to them in life and how their own destiny obscure played out.

Unless your name is Simone de Beauvoir or Marguerite Yourcenar, memoirs are never quite so layered or integrated as a fictional narrative, and for the most part we wouldn't want them to be. These are my memoirs, not Dickens's, but, leaving on one side the even more complex question of the novelist's trespassing on such forms of narration, you can discern how complex is the art of writing memoirs, or indeed how much threatens to get out of hand or to slip a gear when you embark on the task of writing about the past. Should I deploy only a vocabulary that was available to me at the time or should I seek to impose on that early experience the sentence structure and vocabulary of an adult? A mixture of styles will be the response of most people I suspect who at some point will have recourse to that phrase 'as if'. Seek to convey something of those early years as Dickens does, but avoid the dramatic plunge into the first-hand as announced by Joyce in the opening sentence of *A Portrait of the Artist as a Young Man* (1916).

In 1958 I went away to school, courtesy of Monsignor Porsche, the local parish priest, who as his name implies drove fast cars, said Mass at a side altar in under twenty minutes, and who was in every sense of the term a secular priest. Before returning to school I would stop by at the presbytery to pay him a courtesy call. My benefactor, who paid my school fees and my boarding fees, would generously put his hand into the deep pockets of his purple-edged cassock and pull out a fistful of notes from the parish collections. Unlike his predecessor, the ascetic Canon Westlake, Dennis Porsche understood the value of money and how you made more by sprinkling it around. 'Here, take this. You'll need some of your own pocket money.'

Since 1958, I have returned home only for the most part as a guest or former resident. The first day of my holidays I would be immediately asked by my sister when I was going back. At school I would cross off the days and weeks until the end of term. All the time I was learning the difference between here and there, how, as the train pulled out of Worthing Central station on the way back to school, life continued without me. It took me a long time, until the first half-term, to register the meaning of away.

That first September when I went away to school, I was accompanied by my mother. Like Copperfield, my journey was from the provinces and the coast to 'near London'. We caught the fast train from Worthing to East Croydon and changed there for the three stops back, past Purley Oaks, to Purley itself. Alighting from the station, we walked the mile or so up Foxley Lane to Peaks Hill Rise, where we turned right onto Peaks Hill itself and the John Fisher School, a school which was about a hundred metres above sea-level. I don't recall what we talked about on that journey. I remember as the train pulled out of the station at Worthing noticing out of the window the back of our house on one side and the twittens and Nissen huts on the other. Part of me lingered in the past with the cerements of my childhood, with thin curtains and red skies at night, while another part of me was being carried forward inexorably to a new life.

It didn't occur to me on that first journey but it did on every subsequent return to school: how come Worthing would continue without me? Wasn't I then necessary to its life? With each subsequent journey back to school that passing thought accompanied me, and it retained the same character of withering intensity. I wasn't at the centre of the world as I had imagined on the pebbly beach or, worse, I wasn't at the centre of any world. Some thoughts, especially existential ones about not-being, are best dealt with when you are older. It is the mismatch between age and consciousness that is destabilising. Today, I wake up to the noise of traffic passing outside and give thanks that the world is continuing without me. But at eleven years of age, 'away' had the stench of extinction about it.

In the chamber-like entrance-hall to the school we were welcomed by the school secretary and one of the priests, and almost at once I was saying goodbye to my distraught mother, who was clinging onto me with open arms. She just wouldn't let go and pressed me to her. 'He's mine. He's mine, and I can't let him go.' The school secretary then took it upon himself to hold back my poor mother while I was shepherded by the priest through another door into the refectory. That must have been an awful moment for my mother, and I've often reflected on it since. As I discovered on bidding goodbye to my own son when he went away to university in London, the wrench was worse for her than for me. At eleven I didn't appreciate the difference between home and away. My mind was probably a blank as regards what to expect from boarding school. Children's books spoke of pillow fights, midnight feasts, and apple turnover beds. Full of merry japes that is. I don't think I was convinced by any of that. If I had any idea that such a word existed in the language, it would have been Carter's 'unguessable'.

When the door to the refectory from the entrance hall swung open, the world changed for me. I had left behind the intensity of that living room in Newland Road, and, when next I returned home, the house would have shrunk in size, the stairs grown steeper and their tread even narrower. I had embarked on a course of defamiliarisation, where what was once familiar and unconscious would be returned to me as once-familiar and sharply conscious. I immediately put to one side what had just happened with my mother and slotted that painfully exposed farewell into a space marked 'Frozen. Leave well alone'. A different kind of spotlight was now trained on me, but as I stepped out onto that new stage I was not quite sure of the part I was to play. However, the phrase I would never have used was one that comes to David Copperfield on his way to London about 'trying situations' facing his heroes such as Roderick Random or 'that Captain in the Royal British Navy'. I had no such heroes or indeed such equivocation in my character or make-up. As I made my way in life, my family would never be an embarrassment to me. That much I did know about the next scene in my self-dramatisation.

It must have been afternoon teatime when I arrived. Term had already started and I had to slip into whatever routine had already been established for the new boys. The boarders were all taking tea, crowding round an urn at the end of the room. The talking momentarily stopped when I walked in. Then came the rush of silence as I made my way down past the long tables pushed up against one side of the room, acutely self-conscious, glancing at the boys ahead, desperately trying to take it all in. I was introduced as a new boy and handed what looked like an oil-stained plastic plate and a chipped mug. Fortunately, the noise picked up, and I stood around waiting my turn for some tea. Someone must have told me what to do but it wouldn't take me long to get into the routine.

I cannot record here that I felt special, and the entrance test confirmed as much. I was placed in the bottom stream. I remained there until the following year when something happened, a more determined person began to emerge, and I ended in the top stream. Boarders, however, were special because we were only some thirty in number, out of a school population of around three-four hundred. There was something also special about the school itself. John

Fisher was a Catholic school, run not by a religious order but by the secular clergy. It seems extraordinary now, but of the thirty or so teachers on the staff, sixteen were secular priests, who were at that time considered surplus to parish requirements and eight of whom had degrees from Oxford or Cambridge. The ethos was Catholic and English, not Catholic and Irish, and much was made of academic and sporting achievement. It regularly got pupils into Oxbridge and each year it would take part in the English Schools sporting events. At the school entrance on the right was the newly built chapel and on the left the school playing field, which was just big enough for a football pitch in winter and a cricket pitch in summer.

It was a compact school set among the trees – oak trees, maple trees, pine trees, silver birch trees, poplar trees. It was also in a residential area above the valley bottom where ran the A23 trunk road and the main railway line from London to Brighton. Only now looking at Google Maps do I realise how small it was, squeezed as it is into an oblong space between Peaks Hill on the south side, Great Woodcote Park to the north, and then Woodcote Drive to the west and Church Road to the east. Two hundred metres south to north and about three hundred metres west to east. No wonder I considered it compact. The main building, which housed most of the classrooms, overlooked the playing field, and behind that building were three temporary classrooms, each with their own coke-fired stoves, where the whole of the second year was taught. Inside the main building, exposed to the elements, there was a small, open-air, swimming pool, which was a cool blue when first filled but thereafter an unappetising, warmish green.

On each of the three floors of the main building, corridors carried the whole life of the school. On the ground floor were the toilets, where you never knew as you entered the cubicles what would be scrawled on the walls, for this was a boys' school I kept reminding myself. That's what boys do. Shock you. On another floor was a room where there were four baths for the boarders, which we would fill to the top and jump in, turning a room with four baths into a noisy splash room. Across the corridor was Mr Flogger's small office under the stairs where 'Flaming' Flogger would administer the strap, after which boarders who were soft like me would have recourse to a fast-running cold tap in the room opposite to absorb the sting. Down another corridor on the third floor was the science laboratory where one lunchtime an enterprising fifth-former, unsupervised, made an explosive device and ended up in hospital.

There were quieter quarters I should add, for it wasn't really like Dotheboys Hall as described by Dickens in *Nicholas Nickleby* (1839). Fr Compson was a music buff and, to improve the sound quality of the acoustics, he had covered the walls of his room with egg cartons. He was only too pleased to share his passion with pupils. In the classroom he was at the centre of chaos, but in the intimacy of his own surroundings there was no one kinder. In that sense 'Compo' (as we called him) reminded me of Mr Dishevelled, one of those teachers who deserved better. His account of a pilgrimage to Palestine in the school magazine is a model of its kind. He was a teacher with insight, vision, and humanity, but none of that was visible at the time, for he always looked harassed and unable to let us into the ground zero of his mind. His account ends on a reflective note:

> And what of the political situation? The city wall that separates the two peoples is fulfilling its ancient function, and there is an atmosphere of menace in its shadow. One listens with a sympathetic neutrality to the propaganda that is offered on both sides. We saw the hovels of the tens of thousands of Arab refugees and we remember that the Jews themselves were refugees from persecution in many a land. The situation is a terrible threat to world peace and yet humanly speaking insoluble. There are, however, the monks at Latroun praying day and night.

All that is nicely put. 'One listens with a sympathetic neutrality to the propaganda that is offered on both sides.' The use of the indefinite article before 'sympathetic neutrality' draws my attention. That captures something of the deliberateness of 'Compo' in both his speech and his gait, for he carried himself slowly like a bald-headed, medieval monk and wore his cassock for months on end until the food stains became too much for the eye and someone whispered something in his ear. As for 'propaganda' being 'offered', that again conveys something of his patience in dealing with the world. You can hear him listening to the complaints of both sides but then deciding that the complaints were essentially propaganda. However, he doesn't let the matter rest there. Yes, it's propaganda but it's being offered and therefore not to be condemned out of hand. This is the gentle 'Compo' I remember.

As it does today, the Palestinian issue did look insoluble in 1958, but I am struck by his use of 'humanly speaking'. The Trappist monks are praying. On the other hand, more than others, religious people can contemplate extremes, in part because the world doesn't belong to them. Whatever the case, 'Compo' was right about the threat to world peace. To mark some anniversary or perhaps he was our form teacher, my class clubbed together at the end of the year and bought him for a present a felt-tipped pen, which were just coming onto the market. It cost us 21 shillings (in today's money, probably about £25 or more). Poor 'Compo' was clearly touched.

The bell for afternoon lessons would sound and we would emerge from our sojourn with 'Compo' into the noisy corridor outside. 'Keep to the left and straighten your tie.' I began my career in the corner of a dark, internal classroom on the first floor, which was just reward for being in the bottom stream, and how could I complain when my fees were being paid by my kind benefactor? I remember plucking up courage and asking my French teacher when we would be able to speak French. 'When you get to the fifth form and Monsieur Mogford's class' came the reply. So that was it, just hang around and wait until you got to hear Monsieur Mogford's French accent mauling the English language: 'Wight, lady, come out ear and get sex of the beast.' My companion on the back row was a boy called Duckling, whose first name has been blotted out by the second. Duckling. I think he and his brother had appeared in a television food advert. Somehow we were all boxed in or waiting to be roasted.

Mr Bumptious taught me English that first year. He would set for homework creative writing exercises and we would write at length about an autumn day for example. He responded favourably when we consciously went over the top and invented words and phrases that flowed with the sounds of the natural world, as when the rain ran in rapid rills down the mud-filled streets, or when the sun's shiny beams spilled through the amber-coloured skies. To set the scene at the beginning of one essay, I wrote, 'It was a cold, frosty, bitter Saturday morning in the late autumn,' and then, as if to add to its invented quality and please teacher, inserted 'murky' between 'cold' and 'frosty'. The young teacher, down from Cambridge where he read English, was trying desperately to awaken something in the bottom class. Perhaps not surprisingly, he would get angry very easily. 'Come out here, you b-b-b-b-b-bumptious b-b-boy,' he would stammer, his face reddening with rage at the boy and at his own inability to get out the words. In retrospect, I think it would have been less demeaning if he had banned all initial plosives from his idiolect. He would have commanded as much attention if he had called out, 'Come out here, you irritating, young man.' For greater effect, he could then have jumped up and down or stamped his feet. He didn't need all that stammering embarrassment, but none of us had the courage to take him on one side and tell him.

He moved me from the back row and positioned me near the front just below his dais so that he could keep an eye on me. But he must have observed there was something really sluggish or dormant in me, for one day, without warning, he called me out. 'I'm not happy with your attitude, Pierce. You don't seem to be trying your b-b-best. Here take this chit down to Mr Flogger. And let me see some imp-p-provement in your work.' I was confused. I didn't consider I had done anything wrong or was underperforming, and yet how could my teacher be wrong in his assessment of me? I saw him write 4 in blue ink on a scrappy bit of paper. That meant two strokes on either hand. 2 would have been enough, but 4 on his part was just vicious, and for me potentially painful. He must have known I sniggered at his stammer outside class.

I would definitely be heading to the bathroom opposite for the cold tap on my red hands, and I would make sure I had plenty of time afterwards to come to terms with my punishment and to hold back any tears. I don't recall if the punishment did the trick. All I know is that the impetuous Mr Bumptious was fairly unp-p-predictable, and that within a short space I had made significant advances in my academic studies. In my school report at the end of that first year, he observed in passing: 'An excellent worker. He has plenty to say and continued effort should bring fluency of style.'

The boys, as much as the masters, ensured the school exhibited little charm, but I liked the fact that it was not a pretentious school. There was no long drive, no white knobs on gateposts, and the elderly headmaster, Canon Byrne, who never raised his voice, lived quietly in his rooms with a beautiful red setter at his feet. When he appeared at an event, the reports in the school magazine speak of him 'gracing' the event. There aren't enough headmasters or those in authority who conceive their role as an absent centre. Unpretentious. 'No high horses here' would be a good school motto and there would be no need to translate it into Latin either.

When the English Martyr, John Fisher, was canonised in 1935, the school retained the name it started out with six years before in 1929, simply the John Fisher School. The school badge, which carried a fish against a blue background, was a deliberate pun on the name of the sixteenth-century cardinal who refused to accept Henry VIII as head of the Church and who paid for his defiance with his life. If I was to become a priest I, too, would become, like the apostles, a fisher of men. The world was rebounding on me again. I went to a school which took pride in the definite article and never bothered with a saint's title. I didn't keep the faith, however, and, the only time as a boy the great-grandson of one of the last smack-owners in Brighton went fishing, the tackle, which cost me a week's pocket money, got caught under Worthing Pier. It's probably still there.

## This sporting life (cont)

What was it like going away to school for the first time? When I'm feeling upbeat, I can supply an immediate answer: more opportunity for sporting activity and organised games. On the very first occasion I walked into the first class in PE (physical exercise), held in the school hall for there was no proper gym, Mr Danahar the master was already there walking on his hands across the parquet floor. The thought momentarily occurred to me that I had mistakenly enrolled on an apprenticeship with Billy Smart's Circus, and I wondered if I would soon be in training for floor exercises or perhaps the high wire. Eventually Mr Danahar, dressed all in white, righted himself, dusted himself down, and, in spite of being no taller than any of us in the class, addressed us as if he had completed his formal education and was an accredited teacher. But I could discern this was serious. This was more than determining who could run the fastest to the four sides of the gym in a game of port and starboard or sitting cross-legged and seeing if you could touch the ground with your forehead or had the agility to put your big toe in your mouth and suck it. The masters at this school were lucky, for as it happened some of my classmates had been born acrobats and flew through the air as if they were in their element.

I kept a copy of the school magazine for 1959 and see the name of a certain 'D.Pierce' keeps recurring. For academic subjects I was put in the bottom stream but my real ability lay elsewhere. I was in the right school. In 1958 the rugby pitch had just been laid out in an area adjacent to Woodcote, the house where the junior boarders slept. The pitch at that time had no proper drainage and consisted of a muddy slope with lengths of wood, roughly hewn from pine trees in the grounds, acting as goalposts. Rugby wasn't my sport, charging up or down a slope in the mud. It was difficult enough with conditions under foot just standing and watching a game. Besides, the pitch was only large enough for seven-a-side rugby. However, I feel a sense of pride that fifty years later my old school produced Paul Sackey and George Skivington, two members of the recent England rugby team.

That first term, or perhaps I should correct myself for it was as if I was attending a sports academy, that first season I played for the Under Twelves at football. According to Mr Doyle in the school magazine, 'D.Pierce, the vice-captain, made a very good right-half with a powerful shot which sometimes surprised opposing goal keepers.' I like that sentence. It doesn't read quite right, but that's what I possessed: surprise. Leave out 'powerful' and it reads fine; otherwise, if you keep it in, put a comma after 'shot', for it's a non-restrictive relative clause giving additional information. I thank Mr Doyle, however. I had forgotten I was vice-captain, so all my kicking a ball around Homefield Park in Worthing had paid off. In the photo reproduced in the magazine I am sitting cross-legged with folded arms next to the captain, Kevin Duffy, whose family enjoyed daytrips to Brighton at the weekend and whose older brother was to die tragically in a motorcycle accident on Purley Way. Jeff Norton is on my right and behind me is my pal Geoff Older, his head to one side following his straight hair, which would never stay in place when brushed back. Of the twelve games we played, we won seven, drew three, and lost three. We drew against Westminster Choir School and St Joseph's Beulah Hill, but we beat St Thomas's Sevenoaks 13-0. Caterham Prep School we blew away, but we lost twice at home and away to St Mary's Croydon.

I particularly enjoyed playing at home on the right side of that compact pitch bounded on one side by a row of tall poplar trees and adjacent to the school chapel where I served Mass in the morning. Part of its attraction was that in spite of being on the top of a hill there was no horizon, so everything conspired to create a feeling of woodland intimacy. I took corners and floated the ball into the goal mouth area and watched as my team-mates belted it hopefully into the back of the net. I took command coming forward and saw the game opening up. In defence I learned the art of sliding tackles and when to go forward and when to stay back. Overall tactics was something I left to others. I just loved the feeling of solidarity and being part of something.

The following year we were beaten 13-0 by a team we were convinced were over the age limit, but that didn't seem to unnerve us. We took defeat in our stride. We were good but not that good. 'Your turn to bag one, Dezzi. No, you go, Vinnie.' Well, if you win 13-0 you should share things out. It was just the cocky way they went about it as soon as they entered our half. We, too, had our special victories, but nothing can ever be counted on when it comes to sport, and recurring problems with knee cartilage suggested Walter Winterbottom, the England team coach, wouldn't be sending for me anytime soon.

After Easter came the season of cricket. I knew I possessed talent with football but cricket is different and requires more than natural ability or aptitude. There was so much pressure on you even before you started. You claim you're a batsman but no one would know if you were any good until you ran up a score. For whatever reason, at the start of that first cricket season, I was selected to play in the Under Twelves against Balcombe Place. I went in at number 6 and scored 20 runs out of a total of 66. We then bowled out our opponents for 30. From then on I was promoted up the batting order. In the school magazine written by my fan, Mr Doyle, there is this comment: 'The batting was dominated by D.Pierce and G.Older, both of whom made over two hundred runs in the season for an average of around twenty.' And if that wasn't flattery enough it turns out I was also a good fielder: 'The fielding was always keen and aggressive, especially by Pierce at silly mid-off.' Silly mid-off is just in front of the batsman and you have to be a little silly to field so close to the bat. Of the thirteen games played, we won eight, lost two and drew the others. Balcombe Place is now a retirement home, but we saw off more prestigious schools such as St Benedict's Ealing, Worth Priory, St Peter's Guildford and St Thomas's Sevenoaks.

*I have kept one my school cricket bats. Made by John Wisden of Penshurst, Kent.*

Cricket, then, was a special kind of team game. 'That's not cricket' is a phrase with its own meaning, and in one respect the comment has nothing to do with cricket. 'That's not football' has never entered the language, except when it applies to football. Cricket in this sense is about character and the formation of character. In his celebrated novel, *Netherland* (2008), Joseph O'Neill uses the game to provide a critique of American culture post 9/11, showing how cricket abroad serves as a home for exiles, a place of longing, and even 'an environment of justice'. Mistakes in football can often be rectified. If you lose the ball you can run back and perhaps retrieve it. If you miss a scoring opportunity, another one will come along. Of course, mistakes by goalkeepers are different, for these can result in a goal to the opposing side and undermine morale. But with each ball bowled in cricket, the life of the batsman is under threat. As you go into bat you have the whole team on your shoulders as it were, and, for those charged moments you are in, it is you versus the whole of the other team. You can score a four and be cheered, but, equally, you can be out first ball and forced to face the long walk back to the pavilion with only a bit of useless wood for company. Shot selection is also an art. Do I defend this ball coming at me? Do I square cut it or drive it into the covers? Each ball demands the utmost concentration, therefore.

In life as in cricket you should play with a straight bat, or carry your bat though all kinds of adversity, and, at the end of it all, people might well recall fondly how while you may not have made a century you had a good innings. At the crease, there's nothing quite like playing the late cut, which is like a bang on the head of the ball as it passes you by. Such a stroke is a form of contempt, not unlike a cheeky glance down the leg-side to help the ball along, hopefully to the boundary. A six over the head of the bowler is a way of indicating to the bowler, 'Take that, and if you try it again you'll get more of the same. Smack.' Batting, then, is a form of speech, a form of aggression by another name. No wonder ex-colonials and semi-colonials have a thing about winning at Lords, the home of English cricket.

During the winter of my second year at John Fisher, with my pal Geoff, I received a series of coaching sessions with the Surrey and England cricketers, Tony Lock and John Edrich, paid for by the school. In the late afternoon, we travelled into Croydon by bus, and at the back of a department store, whose name I've now forgotten, we found the indoor nets. John Edrich I seem to recall had broken his finger that summer and so wasn't always available but Tony Lock was. Geoff had great fun with him cracking adult jokes but I tended to be quieter and more respectful. I just wanted to learn a few things, not to mix it. Given that he was really only a bowler, Lock, who with Jim Laker was among the handful of great spin bowlers in the post-war era, was a surprisingly good coach at batting. The much younger Edrich, who went on to open the innings with distinction for his country from 1963 to 1976, tended to be more dour and fairly remote as a person. As I travelled back and forth to those sessions with my cricket bat, guard and whites, I wondered, out of season, if I was indeed special or where this sporting life might lead.

Around the age of twelve I was at my best as a sportsman. So much promise and quite a lot of achievement. I won a cricket bat from the school and a cricket ball from the London evening newspaper *The Star*. In the school magazine I read I was good at other sports. 'Pierce surprised everyone by winning the under 12 high jump.' That is such a backhanded compliment by the head of boarders, who obviously didn't know anything about the reputation I brought with me from St Mary's, my primary school! I also won the under 12 long jump in the annual sports day that year, and from the Fisher House notes it transpires that I established a new school record. As for boxing, 'among the novices one noted immediately the two brothers Catley, as well as Burr, Older and Pierce'. I won all my bouts, beating among others a boy who within a short time became South London champion. As if that wasn't enough of me, my name is also mentioned in the section on Chess as a promising newcomer.

There was, then, no end of encouragement for me at John Fisher. I ran for the school at Motspur Park in sprints and relays. I took up hurdling round a makeshift course in the garden of Dunningley, the house in the school grounds where senior boarders were accommodated. In myself I was never so confident, and it is only returning in my mind to that period and reading the school magazine that I feel any sense of confidence in myself. At one athletics meeting – it might have been at the Royal Military Academy at Sandhurst – I came up against an Army side, and realised immediately the limits of my career at long jumping. The boys in the Army school were six inches taller than me, jumped like seasoned champions, and gave the distinct impression that sport was a version of weapons training. Boxing I knew I wouldn't pursue beyond those early years, for all of us valued our looks too highly to allow them to be permanently damaged in a ring. Football, as I've already indicated, also had a limited shelf life due to cartilage trouble. I suppose cricket I could have pursued into adulthood and made something of.

But none of this happened. One afternoon in the summer term there came from the playing fields the loudest scream I had ever heard. In pulling a javelin out of the ground, a boy had somehow managed to put his eye out and blinded himself. My group were on the cinder track with our elderly hurdling coach, and when we eventually arrived on the playing fields an ambulance was already taking the poor boy to hospital. Perhaps episodes like that was one of the reasons which led me to reflect on the downside to this sporting life. Hammer-throwing and pole-vaulting were, with javelin-throwing, things to avoid, and I never did pursue them, but the sports I was involved in began to lose their shine, in part because of the amount of time they took out of the week. Mr Ferguson, the master who had played for QPR or some other professional football team and who was responsible for arranging inter-school sports matches, was none too pleased when I gently remonstrated with him about playing in another tournament. Even now I can see the disappointment on his face as we stood at the edge of the playing fields in a kind of negotiation. He failed to understand how anyone could turn down an opportunity of representing the school. 'It could count against you in the future. Just give it some thought.' That kind of threat wasn't terribly persuasive, and I dismissed it as just a form of crude thinking. Indeed, no one ever got anywhere close to me coming from that angle. I was then in my second year and turning my attention to academic subjects and to spending more time with my books and working my way up to the top class.

## Boarders

At boarding school nearly every hour was accounted for. The day began at 7 o'clock with the grizzly rattling the door handle to our room to wake us. Mr Grizzle was a maths teacher, who had a room upstairs. We weren't allowed any talking or food anywhere in Woodcote and if we broke the rule we were slippered by the grizzly, who entertained no excuses as he stole into the room. This was particularly painful if we were wearing pyjamas, and more so if our name was De Galliard and we came from France and wore thin, silk pyjamas. De Galliard was regularly beaten and it was apparent to us all, De Galliard included, that he was a bit of a wimp as he danced round the room trying frantically to get the sting out of his backside only to end his display by sobbing into his pillow. About five of us shared that dormitory, my pal Geoff, a boy named LeFebvre, whose family must have come over with the Normans for he was true-grit English, and two other boys whose names I've forgotten. Woodcote was a place of imposed rather than natural silence. We moved in silence from the bedroom to the wash room and toilets. Only when we were on the cinder pathway outside the house could life assume a more natural shape.

I kept a black-and-white photo from that period (see p.128). I am standing in front of Woodcote, my focus trained on something in my hands. It's a sunny day, the back of the house is bathed in light, and the windows of the washroom and of the masters' rooms upstairs are drawing in fresh air. I am in shade, my eyes fixed on whatever it is I am holding. I am wearing the blue jacket of the school uniform with a badge of something in my lapel. Perhaps that was the Fisher House badge. My hair is parted low down on the left. I don't know what I am thinking or who took the photo or why. That boy, who resisted for as long as he could before he started wearing long trousers, went away from me, and just vanished into thin air. He is now beyond recall. I have no idea where he went or why he disappeared, and I miss him more than I can tell you. When I followed my teddy out of the house on Newland Road, I was lost only temporarily, for the police came and brought me home. But the boy in the shade just left home and never returned. There was no official farewell, no search party was dispatched to retrieve him, and no moment in time when I could say 'This was the month or year that he went away and never came back.' Of all my photos this is the one I cherish the most.

The year I spent in Woodcote clearly strove to impress itself on my consciousness. Perhaps that's what I was thinking: a memento of a year out of my life and a prelude to something. The house offered no retreat from school life, and it was out of bounds during the day. Indeed, there was little that resembled home in that first year at boarding school. The only kind thing that happened to me in that house was the attention of one of the domestics, who would always have something to say to me as if I was one of her children. But of course that was out of earshot of the grizzly. Perhaps I shouldn't be too harsh on my housemaster for once I caught him propped up against the bark of a tree in a large park somewhere near the disused Croydon aerodrome. With his peak cap on, old Charon was off-duty, by himself, watching a game of cricket. He didn't see me or my companion, Rudy, but I was struck by his lonely appearance, a Yorkshire lad who grew up to lead a lonely life without a home or family and who is now remembered for his lack of humour and the way he rattled doors.

My bed in Woodcote was against the wall on the opposite side to the latticed bay windows. When I woke in the middle of the night I would turn toward the windows and the quiet of the street outside. Then I would be drawn back inside. The wooden parquet floor ensured noise travelled through the whole mock-tudor house. As its name might suggest, Woodcote was a place for forbidden secrets and it was there I learned the facts of life, or rather I learned where babies made their entry into the world. That was one conversation the grizzly didn't manage to interrupt. So women had a cleavage down below the waist and another entry-point into the body. That first lesson in female anatomy still didn't clarify everything for me and it omitted any reference to the pleasure principle, so any understanding I might have developed concerning real contact between the sexes remained in the dark, as did the embarrassment over my ignorance. A good Catholic boy, I must have been a slow learner, for no other questions came to me at that stage.

One day, waiting in the corridor for Fr Killjoy, the priest in charge of boarders, my companion in the queue, who normally devoted all his time to talking about cars and Wolseleys, pressed his thumb flat against his index finger and showed me the back of his hand. 'What's that?' he wanted to know from me. 'Your thumb pressed against your finger.' 'No. Look again. That's what a girl's got. See.' I was learning all the time from my contemporaries. That boy wasn't the best tutor to have, for he was himself subject to passionate outbursts, as when waiting for Fr Killjoy he, suddenly, for no apparent reason, turned on the priest and kicked him in the shins. Wow, that was something, and by rights it should have merited the stocks or sackcloth and ashes for the rest of term when he should have been formally excommunicated by the Church and then permanently excluded from the school. Nothing like that happened. He was told to see Fr Killjoy after supper. There was clearly form between them. Perhaps he was overcome with boredom waiting in the corridor or angry with Fr Killjoy for being regularly singled out. Latticed windows and versatile vaginas, sedate-looking Wolseleys and abrupt kicks in the shins – at eleven years of age I never knew what was coming next. But what I did know was that that boy without a name had more than one interest. Perhaps in time I would follow him down that dark corridor and discover passion and sexuality for myself or whatever it was he imagined I or the opposite sex was missing.

In the second year I moved across to Dunningley, a large detached house where most of the boarders were accommodated. I shared a room on the first floor with around seven others. It was a cold room and when the nights were at their longest we would have a little competition to see how many serge blankets we could have on our bed and still be cold. That was like sleeping with a heavyweight boxer or wrestler on you and the springs tended to give way under you so that just a tiny head in a hammock-like structure could be made out. It gave a new twist to the merry japes idea of boarding schools. Heating by paraffin stoves was always potentially risky, more so when a pillow fight broke out and one of us accidentally kicked one over and flames started leaping round the room. Once, after lights out, we decided to climb out of the window with the help of sheets tied together. That was more like boarding school. At midnight we were strolling round the grounds by the light of a full moon with no one to stop us or check our courtly progress as we made our way past the row of tall poplar trees swaying in the wind by the playing fields. It would have been even better with a bag of chips in hand.

The long nights had benefits. Fr Killjoy allowed us an hour of television in his room if we could squeeze in. That was where Quatermass entered our consciousness and banged on the quaking frame of our little lives. A fifth-former, whose surname was Barnes, allowed us to listen to records on his *Dansette* player, and it was there that I had my first opportunity of handling records by Cliff Richard and the Shadows, Buddy Holly and the Crickets, and Bill Haley and the Comets. That seemed so grown-up, waiting for the next record to drop down, always making sure the player was only moved or transported when the stylus arm was clipped down. I felt vaguely that in the act of consumption I was contributing to a ritual shared by all my generation, for this was youth culture in the making, and something was stirring. In retrospect, shadows, crickets, and comets were simply the first acts in an extraordinary procession that should have played a more formative part in my adolescence.

As for ginger Barnes in a line-up of boarders, he was the last person you would associate with rebellious youth. He spoke gently and expressed an interest in you. He had an impressive collection of records and let you sift through them, but none of the fashion the new stars were wearing rubbed off on him. And neither did their gestures of defiance as captured on EP covers. He was as plain as the room he occupied, but when he jumped into the swimming pool, his legs tucked up underneath him, he was an expert bomber, and he threw a cricket ball further than anyone in that school. He would have been three or four years ahead of me but he possessed absolutely no authority.

There was no veil to pierce, no aura which held me. That was what living with a small group of boarders was like. You mixed across the age range and occasionally you encountered a wall which collapsed in front of you. I think it must have been his gentleness which was out of place, and this was interpreted by some as a sign of weakness. Away from home, I'm not sure what I thought.

In another room A.P.Jensen, one of two brothers, standing on his bed, would show us how to insert two fingers into a light socket and jump when the switch was turned on. 'Look, no damage,' A.P. beamed, holding up his paw. Cheeking older boys was also part of the fun because everyone knew that authority existed to be mocked, and yet it couldn't be done with impunity for there was no such thing as off-duty at boarding school. I remember being chased through the house by a heavyweight of a guy named Van Ryssen, who appears in the school magazine as a hammer-thrower of note. I got as far as the boot room before my fingers were trapped in the door leading outside. He relented at that point and deemed my punishment was enough. 'That'll teach you, you little runt,' he shouted as he disappeared back into the house.

Every evening after supper we played games downstairs for an hour, and in the weeks leading up to Christmas we had competitions among ourselves. The snooker tables were always waiting for us, the green baize a blaze of light in an otherwise dark and musty room. Cues would be rolled on the table before the start of a game to select one which was straight and true, and away we'd go potting everything in sight. Table-tennis in another room was always popular. Around bonfire night on 5 November, I had my back to an open window scoring freely against my opponent when a local teddy boy threw in a lighted banger and stood grinning as it exploded. Fr Killjoy rushed down from upstairs but was told by some of the fifth-form boys to relax; they would attend to matters, and they did. There was no fight; they went out into the night sky and simply told the Mohicans that the reservation was their territory. At least that's what they reported back, and the south London 'teds' never bothered us again. That was the way to do business. French teddy boys, who carried razors and who were reported to be heading our way across the Channel, were more terrifying than their English counterparts, or so we believed. The world was pressing in. If Quatermass didn't get you upstairs, the 'teds' would downstairs.

I had little affection for Fr Killjoy and he had none for me. He had his favourites and my pal, Geoff, was one. Indeed, when Geoff was seventeen Fr Killjoy lent him his Austin 7 when he was home on leave from the Junior

Leaders Royal Army Corps. Fr Killjoy I'm afraid was someone I took an instant dislike to, initially because I couldn't see what there was to like. He wasn't effeminate but, like the unpolished Demosthenes, he spoke as if he had a pebble in his mouth, and what made it worse was his limp handshake. As for the boarders, I particularly admired an older boy named Soyka, whose first name was Paul, but we always called him Soyka. He had perfected a beautifully precise bowling action, like a windmill silhouetted against the sky, and he took a fair share of wickets when playing for the school Colts. Magee, a rugby player and a hammer-thrower, was another older boy I took to. When in charge of homework sessions in the evening he would help me with my English composition. 'Couldn't you start this in a little sharper fashion? Put this sentence first, and then proceed.'

As for the oldest boys, they have shaded into the other boys in the school. I use the term 'boys' but, looking at the photos in the school magazine for that year, it is evident they were anything but boys. They scored centuries in cricket, as did Rupert Lister, one of the giants at the school when I was there. So it must have been the fifth-formers who were the seniors I was most in contact with. The most senior boys appeared too old to be posing in school photos playing for the school, but they, too, if they were boarders would have been subject to the same regime as me. Not that they were models of behaviour. There were always stories that went round about what they got up to, such as lying down in the road with legs in a V shape and holding up the traffic. Inside the school they exercised restraint, but outside the school they were at times seemingly out of control.

A comment in the Boarders' Diary in the school magazine appears to have escaped the editor's censorship. It reads: 'I would first like to thank our previous matron Miss I——- for all that she did in our interest.' 'All that she did in our interest' sounds slightly odd, as if she did more for the boarders than was expected. I recall two matrons in my time, one was middle-aged and fierce and the other was young and fetching. It was this last one who always had a queue at her door in the evening as boarders stocked up on toiletries like shampoo and yet more bars of *Imperial Leather* soap. I can't remember what phrases we used about putative relations between this flirt of a matron and the older boys but they wouldn't have been very pleasant, and I suspect completely without substance.

I wonder what happened to all those boarders. Roderick More O'Ferrall, or 'Mof' for short, was a year ahead of me and our paths were to cross again in later years. His passion for cricket was quite something. Rudy Markham, whose family I seem to remember were woollen manufacturers in Yorkshire, was one of my pals and we perhaps should have stayed in touch. Miss WW at my primary school was a study in the relationship between character and personality; Rudy was a study in the relationship between character and intellect. I admired the way he held back from full-blooded engagement in things, as if he realised school was simply part of a long-term process. He had a slightly old-fashioned face which lit up when something interested him, but almost as suddenly it would revert to its default stillness. You could detect he was watching the world even as it sought his active participation. But there would be no leap of faith; he would always insist on certitude before making a move. I never had a row with Rudy. A year ahead of me, he commanded respect and, besides, he would never do anything to upset me. Some boys convey the impression that they are already young men even though they are still boys. It isn't that they are in advance of their age but somehow looks and age aren't quite in sync. I liked that about Rudy, more so in retrospect.

As for my pal, Geoff, well we just seemed to go our different ways. I tried to stay in touch after school, and I met up with him some years later. He invited me up to Purley, where he was staying with Fr Killjoy, and we went down to a new entertainment complex on the Brighton Road in Purley. It had a revolving lager bar, where you sat on a stool next to the bar and the whole thing slowly revolved like a merry-go-round. The dance floor sparkled with brilliant spotlights and I, a gauche seventeen-year-old seminarian, sat drinking with another girl Geoff had invited along with the girl he was seeing. I felt awkward, completely out of things, tongue-tied, unwilling to make a first move. I kept putting myself in her shoes, someone who had dressed up to be noticed, not a hair out of place, and me too embarrassed to compliment her. After all, Jesu was the joy of man's desiring; women I had been informed were a source of temptation. Besides, I had absolutely no chat-up lines on which to draw. It was the last evening I was to spend in the company of my pal, Geoff. We had two good years together between 1958 and 1960, but we probably reached the end of our friendship in that time. Perhaps he knew that celibacy wasn't for me and that he was nudging me in a different direction.

So came to an end the diversions of Purley and my two-year sojourn on an escarpment among the Surrey trees. When I descended from that peak of sporting promise, what had I learned about the world of learning? An exposure to foreign languages is what has stayed with me. French, Latin, Greek,

Spanish, all these languages were taught me during those two years. The Latin master was Fr McLean, who was utterly fierce and uncompromising. *Ut* plus the subjunctive was one lesson he insisted on as if your continued existence on this planet depended upon it, but I still struggle when asked to translate a sentence such as 'He returned home to discover a change of circumstances'. Did Labienus return home in order to discover a change of circumstances, or is it as a consequence of returning home that he discovered changed circumstances? In one there is a purpose, in the other a result. Should *ut* plus the subjunctive be used or *et* followed by the indicative form of the verb? *Ut* would signify purpose in this case, followed by a subjunctive verb; *et* plus the past tense of the verb would signal that he returned home and discovered changed circumstances. I don't think I've got that right. Perhaps I'm still utterly confused and still can't distinguish purpose and result from the intimidating classroom atmosphere in which the distinction was first introduced and my equanimity threatened.

In the tussle between English and Latin, you had to admire the logic of the classical language, but you felt it lost something of the subtlety and ambiguity of the new language. My classics teacher would have a view on this, but this was not up for discussion. No one came out of his class unscathed. With his jet-black hair and a face which suggested that he shaved not just once but two or three times a day, the warrior possessed so many weapons in his armoury, but one look was normally enough to do the trick. As Director of Studies, he was clearly a forward-thinker for while I was there, in those years of the Sputnik, he introduced Russian, which looked as if it was the coming language.

I received only a smattering of ancient Greek and Spanish. The content of other subjects has largely escaped me now. I remember seeing a frog pinned down, its poor heart still beating, and some lesson being drawn. I learned about Bunsen burners in the lab and calculated where the flame was at its hottest. In Geography lessons we learned that rivers have three courses. 'The upper course,' I wrote in my exercise book, 'is like a child, panicky. The middle course is like a youth, steady. The lower course is like a pensioner (flow if you must).' We would wait for Mr Flogger's catchphrase to emerge. We had no idea if 'by and large' suggested a mind at its most profound or one that was locked in like ours. I don't recall doing any music or drama. There was, however, a drama festival in my first year where I saw fourth-year pupils stage *Twelfth Night* and Shaw's *Pygmalion*. That has stayed with me, watching a boy in buckskin boots swagger across the stage as Sir Toby Belch. Stepping into or out of roles appealed to me then as it does today. I suppose it was a case of anything to escape the rule-book which governed school life. For if my teachers were severe, my fellow pupils were never short of tricks.

In the summer of 1960 I returned home to Worthing and discovered that there would be no going back to the John Fisher School. Monsignor Porsche, who did everything quickly, was economising and that was that. If I imagined I was in for a five-set match over five years at John Fisher, I was mistaken. I just made it through two sets and then rain stopped play. I didn't even have time to bid farewell to my friends and teachers. When my kind benefactor discovered my continuing interest in becoming a priest, he took it upon himself to contact St Joseph's College, Mark Cross, near Crowborough in Sussex, and so one afternoon we drove over quickly in his nifty, low-slung Porsche, touching speeds of 80 miles an hour, the *Esso* signs of my childhood flashing by, and met the Rector, Monsignor Westlife, who was supervising joinery work on the school stage.

I sat no exams, a perfunctory, limp shake of the hands was enough, and in the middle of September I found myself in a junior seminary on the edge of Ashdown Forest, on course for the Catholic priesthood. It was that quick. The boy with the glottal stop, who grew up in a tenement house parallel to a railway track, was now someone else's burden. There was no time to adjust or draw breath. One minute I was wearing a blue cotton jacket with cap to match, the next a black woollen jacket with cap to match. One minute I was swinging idly among the Surrey trees, the next I was signed up for crocodile walks, three abreast, in a column, making determined sorties into the canopied lanes and ancient forests of the Sussex Weald. It was another wrench to add to all the others that made up my short life of wrenches since leaving home in 1958. I was away again, but now I was going back in time to the Middle Ages and to the age of religion.

The Convent Mark Cross, Rotherfield

*The College began life as an orphanage for girls run by nuns. Here in this Edwardian postcard the symmetry of Pugin's Victorian building stands out together with its austerity. After five years here I, too, felt like an orphan.*

Chapter 7

# A Retreat in Time

## The path not taken

For most people as they look back on their lives they must be struck by the thought that things could have turned out differently if an alternative path had been pursued. For some there will be the realisation that particular mistakes had long-term consequences. Rectifying such mistakes can present its own challenge; equally, how to write about such mistakes constitutes another kind of challenge. All the way through my teenage years I imagined I had a vocation to the Catholic priesthood and I took the necessary steps to pursue my chosen career. But it wasn't to be, so now I look back not in triumph but to some extent in failure mixed in with a certain puzzlement as to why it took me so long to discover the Church was not for me.

I could abide by convention and structure this chapter as the triumph over illusion, as a narrative of liberation, where I escaped from the nets which threatened my ability to swim freely in the world. With Simone de Beauvoir in mind, I could have entitled it something like 'memoirs at their most intense of a dutiful son'. If I was in my early twenties I am sure I would have been tempted to follow Joyce's line in *A Portrait of the Artist as a Young Man*. But now, at the end of my academic career and in my sixties, I am keen to rethink that period of my life in terms other than one leading at the end to 'Welcome, O life!'. Certainly, I wish I had adopted a different path, but such a wish is almost immediately accompanied by something else. If I had opted for another course, I would have attended the local Catholic secondary modern school, left at fifteen, and, whatever else might have occurred, it would not have involved university and writing books. Memoirs would have been, simply, a thing of the past for others to pursue. Perhaps I would have remained a good

Catholic, joined the Knights of Saint Columba, and taken the collection at Mass. I might have become a taxi-driver like three of my Pearce cousins, taken an office job, joined the Marines like my father. I would never have had an opportunity of meeting up with my lifelong partner for we would have mixed in different social circles at opposite ends of the country. I would, however, almost certainly have developed diabetes in my early fifties and suffered all the other health problems, for in that sense biology is destiny.

When I look back – and I do so all the time – I am never free from the realisation that things might have been different. In joining the seminary, I had embarked on a prelude to some other kind of narrative. Equally, I am aware that the stepping-stones that make up my life could not have been predicted, and that they can only be set down, if at all, in retrospect. In this chapter I seek out lines of continuity particularly in regard to the self underlying all that I experienced in my teenage years, but I'm not sure if I can bring it together. In some respects it would have been easier dealing with physical acts of aggression or abuse from those in authority, for there's nothing more taxing than extricating the self from the soul or the mind after it has been messed with by others.

In everyone's life there must come a time if you embark on a memoir when analysis takes over the account. In the previous chapters up to this point I have allowed the narrative of my life to unfold without too much interference, organising the material under certain sections or headings and allowing it scope to breathe. But as I approach my five years in the junior seminary and the one year or so spent in the senior seminary at Wonersh, the narrative stalls and I find myself wondering if I can go on writing as I did in the last two chapters. Was it all a lie? Did I live those years with a self or the dream of a self that was not me but something that threatened to become me? Was I a conformist, identifying with my masters and the Church, and is that my true self? Did I lose myself or find myself somewhere along a trail which eventually I didn't take? Or did I lose a shadow self and find my true self somewhere down a path which eventually I did take? Is anything to be redeemed now from all those years when I lived an illusion? Can I double back on myself and discover something that has the distinctive marks of my own character and personality through all this period when I was training for something I no longer believe in?

In the small hours I am haunted by such questions, which now look impossible to resolve. 'Move on,' some people might at this point interject.

'The relationship turned sour. Waste no more of your time and energy on trying to get it back or do it justice. Walk away. Like your grandmother you grabbed hold of the priest's collar and sent that boy packing. It's gone, David. You gave it your best shot. You're better off as a person, living a more normal life. You took the wrong path but now it is the path not taken. Enjoy what you have left. Forget the idea of "prelude" and write "postscript".'

What intrigues me is that the path not taken is also the path I took for a while. Perhaps that's the best way I can write about those years, full of contradiction where the cogs don't quite mesh together. In *Apologia Pro Vita Sua* (1864), a frequently tetchy defence of his life, John Henry Newman refers at one point to 'the true key to my whole life'. For him the intellectual move from Anglican clergyman to Roman Catholic priest was in one sense part of a single, seamless journey. My journey was away from Rome to somewhere outside the Church, but I never felt anything of the confidence of Newman in defending my position or claiming it was anything but a struggle to find myself. Moreover, unlike Newman, I had no companions, no friend such as Newman had in Ambrose St John, to support me. In retrospect, what I don't want to do is give an inch to the religious ideology which held me, and I have always believed or felt that to some extent rebellion or resentment, whether passive, tame or vicious, are markers that betray a continuing involvement. I want to be free, wholly free, even of those attitudes which smoulder or linger around the field of battle long after it is over. In common with that merry band of ex-Catholics, what I have sought is never to be identified by the prefix ex-. Equally, I am keen not to be too harsh on my contemporaries and on those who sought to enhance me as a person. Without the Church I wouldn't now be writing this, so there is a continuing debt which I acknowledge. But as it turned out I have effectively destroyed all contact not with that period of my past but with my contemporaries and with my teachers, and that I now also acknowledge is a failing on my part.

Every year friends in Leeds and York, some of whom are into their seventies, meet up with their contemporaries at school or university, but I don't have that comfort. When I abandoned my religion I seemed to abandon not only my youth but also the companions of my youth. That seems sad, especially as many of them, I suspect, also abandoned their religion, so we would have much in common. It's too late now to renew friendships. Of course, I could arrange to meet up again and compare notes or see how far so-and-so got in life, who died young or in middle age. But that would be like a revenant disturbing former friends after long absence and we'd all be playing roles in the graveyard of our past in that respect. I try googling but then realise most people never feature on Google. I now accept the line is broken, and realise or recognise another truth. For I have to concede this one victory to the Church, who persuaded me to think that independence meant burning all the bridges behind me.

My old college, which was built to a design by Edward Welby Pugin in 1865-9 to house an orphanage for a hundred and twenty girls and which became a junior seminary in 1924, no longer exists. It ceased operations in 1970 and was succeeded first by a ballet school and then by a Jameah Islamiyah school, an extremist school which was closed down by the authorities in 2007. For sixty years or so it was an orphanage for girls and then for sixty five years or so a seminary for boys. In time, no doubt the building will be a ruin and its fifty-four acres, six miles south of Tunbridge Wells, put to some other use. Perhaps it will return to the farmland from whence it came, the cricket pitch, lovingly tendered when I was there, torn up, the pond allowed to become once again a gathering place for nature's excess, the work of my Classics teacher, Fr Maurice Finnan, and his cohort of weekly waders and dredgers come to nothing. So much useful labour to become so much useless toil.

There was very little by way of folklore surrounding the previous occupants of the building. One fragment I recall concerned the holiness of the first Rector, Fr Corbishley, who was spoken of in hushed tones and who I believe had a withered arm, and the other concerned the death of one of the orphans who fell over the banister from the top floor, which necessitated erecting a security guard made of brass to prevent anyone from toppling over or sliding down. For a spiritual community it might seem surprising when I report that few of us believed in ghosts, or perhaps there was the willingness to believe but there were no sightings recorded in my time. It was a case of 'I believe. Help my unbelief'.

We were looked after by nuns, who with a small band of women, some with learning disabilities, in their care would do the cooking, cleaning, and washing. With heads bowed, they would scurry along the corridors if they passed us. Throughout my time at College, there was then this parallel, ghostly community of sisters and maids, shadowing our paths, doing all the menial jobs, who would be glimpsed through food hatches or through windows into rooms where they did the ironing. In a little garden known as Carmel at the side of the College and largely hidden from view, the nuns filed slowly up and down along narrow gravel paths, reading from their breviaries. But I don't think I got to know the names of any of them or indeed to engage any of them in conversation. One boy was expelled when he was caught with one of the younger maids in a disused room above the print workshop. I can only guess what Margaret Atwood would have made of it all.

In this chapter I return to something which has waited dormant inside me for nearly half a century to be dealt with. My intention is to offer a glimpse of a community many of whose participants, especially among the teaching staff, are now dead. It is in truth only a glimpse, being nothing more than a personal memory by an orphan who fell by the wayside, but for all that there is merit in playing a descant on something that is now for me part of my long apprenticeship, a prelude to something that never happened.

## Obedience

By rights, I should commence my account of these years with the classroom education I received, but everything to do with a junior seminary revolved round the moral issue of obedience, or what cynics might call submission. The rule of St Benedict, channelled through the seminary of St Sulpice in Paris, governed our lives. There were rules for everything, as if there had never been any pruning but only accumulation and desuetude. These rules must have been at one stage to do with the Latin word *regula*, which is more like regulations than rules, regular rather than rule-bound. A regulated life sounds more in keeping with an aspiring Church starting up than with a series of abstract rules which have become divorced from something that lives and breathes. For in time rules became a thing in themselves, or reified to use a vocabulary deriving from Hegel and Marx. I must have sensed as much at the time for in the margins of my copy of Thomas Dubay's *The Seminary Rule* (1953) I took constant issue with what I was reading. Thus, against the sentence 'Every time the bell rings in the seminary it offers the seminarian an opportunity to conform his will with God's' I facetiously wrote, complete with a colon and exclamation-mark, 'Bell-ringer: God!'

The rules we followed needed to be explained by the Rector, Monsignor Westlife, in his little homilies in the Oratory, but, at times, they were brandished by the teachers like weapons to get us to submit to them and to their control therefore. 'My dear students,' he would begin in his heavily nasal fashion after lumbering down to the front of the Oratory in his squeaky, buckled shoes, 'there is a rule about special friendships and that is why when older boys sign up for walks in the afternoon they do so in threes and not in pairs.' We never did have that rule properly explained to us.

He was given to blundering and at times didn't realise what he was saying. 'Check to see there is no fluff under your bed,' was another remark he came out with, but this was received with an impossible-to-smother guffaw from the seminarians in his audience, who had been transformed at that moment into adolescent, male, gawking onlookers. That occasion must have been to do with the rule governing personal hygiene or cleanliness. Inside a junior seminary, soft power was best but, if not, there was the stick administered by the priest in charge of discipline, Fr Butcher. I never heard any of my contemporaries speak fondly of the rules and how they might have been designed for our benefit, for they were always considered an imposition. It's difficult to believe Jesus came all this way down to earth to bring us the rule book and to tell us to check under our beds in the morning for any odd bits of fluff that might be gathering there unnoticed.

The *magnum silentium* or great silence is the big rule governing religious institutions. From the end of evening prayers – or Compline if you were in a convent or monastery – until breakfast the following morning, silence was to be observed. With the strains of *Salve Regina*, the motet to the Virgin Mary, sung every night in chapel ringing in your ears, you climbed in silence, one at a time, the four flights of stone steps up to the top of the building on the third floor. There you collected your towel from your room, again in silence. You brushed your teeth in silence in a washroom shared by around fifty boys. If you accidentally bumped into someone in the washroom getting your wash-kit out of the shared locker facing you, you apologised by way of a gesture, but no words passed your lips. In the individual wooden cubicle in the great dormitory where you slept you arranged your clothes on the chair beside your bed always doing your utmost to let nothing by way of words or casual expletives pass your lips, for this was the period of the great silence when the focus of your mind together with your emotions was to be trained on thinking exclusively about religious matters and particularly on preparing yourself for Mass the following morning.

If, with your pyjamas on, you took a minute or two to peer south out of the high window at the grounds of the College, the tall conifers surrounding the swimming pool, toward what used to be known as Orphanage Wood, and beyond that the encircling gloom of the Sussex Weald, it was only to reflect on God's goodness, for everything – blood-red sunsets, screeching starlings in the eves now settled, owls silently swooping, hawks roosting, the night-time chatter of nature – belonged to Him. In time, in reading more widely in English literature, you would discover confirmation of a connected world even in the hyphens of the Jesuit poet Gerard Manley Hopkins, 'womb-of-all, home-of-all, hearse-of-all night'. On reflection, it would have been more comforting if Hopkins had written 'hearth-of-all', but not everything hunkered down for the night.

More down-to-earth and less open to divine intervention, it was apparent when there was a full moon outside because there would be an increase in dream talk among your fellow seminarians, which was another kind of impulsive chatter, outside the realm of guilt or innocence. At Dunningley, when I was at John Fisher, I remember participating in such talk by putting questions to the dreamer in the bed next to me and trying to discover an entry into the dream sequence, but at the junior seminary the rules and the cubicles prevented that. I was learning the habit of silence and interiority. I was on my own in the great silence of things.

Silence and therefore repression governed our lives. Some misdemeanours such as talking in the dormitories were considered so serious that it was as if they were almost on the same level of moral turpitude as to merit the description 'mortal sin'. Other examples of breaking the rule were assigned to a lesser, more venial bracket. Walking down corridors, always on the left-hand side, never running, was undertaken in silence, as was waiting to see one of the 'profs' (teachers) in their rooms in the evening. The ritual of distributing letters in the playground before lessons began was conducted in silence, but that was only to allow Fr Butcher to be heard above the buzz and excitement of news from home. Silence was the norm for most of the time lunch was served in the refectory when there would be a reading from the Bible followed by a (censored) passage from a frequently tedious novel or travel book or biography. *Prester John* by John Buchan was one such book I remember or, as one of my contemporaries let slip to a delighted audience in the refectory at the start of the reading, '*John Buchan* by Prester John'. To break up the silence we pounced on anything untoward.

Bells would be rung to usher in a period of talk or to signal a period of silence. After supper there was a half-hour slot for 'recreation', which consisted in high-energy talk and anxious glances at the watch. When the bell sounded, the default position resumed. The face dropped like Bell's palsy, for you couldn't smile when you were in a period of silence. In time it was apparent that joy was being squeezed out of you, as if in a parallel way the reification of rules was finding an ally in Max Weber's routinisation of everyday life. If the rules didn't get you, routine would. Indeed, what the routine of our lives amounted to was a series of brief interludes of animated talk against a background of grinding silence.

The annual three-day retreat in the days around Halloween was conducted entirely in silence. That was a real test for anyone embarking on a career in the Church. Of course I admit it was nothing by comparison with the forty-day ordeal endured by the Jesuit novitiates I once met at Heythrop College, their former magnificent pile in the Oxfordshire countryside, but it was still something for me at thirteen. No talking for three whole days and nights and each day filled with meditation, prayers, rosary, litanies, services, and sermons sometimes given by Jesuits brought in for the occasion because of their ability to strike fear into a captive audience. Seated in front of the altar next to a table and a lighted candle, the retreat priest, wearing a black cassock and white surplice or stole, would take delight in announcing, 'The four last things'. Then he would exhale a deep, heavy sigh, look up into the dark, roof space of Goldie and Child's Gothic-inspired chapel, and continue, 'I want to begin with the four last things'.

And that was just the beginning, a beginning near the end, a retreat in time back, as I imagined it with all the deliberate pauses, to the Middle Ages. Death, judgement, heaven or hell. If he were teaching a creative writing class, our retreat priest would have delighted in quoting Annie Dillard's remark in *The Writing Life* (1989), 'Write as if you were dying'. But he stuck to his more austere task. 'Life is a preparation for death'. This would be spoken as it the sentence read 'Life is but a preparation for death' and had been lifted out of a late Medieval devotional manual such as Thomas à Kempis's *The Imitation of Christ* (ca1418). We were back to a period when people didn't just fear God but *dreden* Him as Wyclif's Bible in 1395 has it. In a chapel with underground heating still waiting for half-term before it was switched on, the priest was warming to his topic. The rest of us were shivering as we waited for the fires of hell and other delights to slide into view. 'For all eternity…. Remember, God is not mocked.'

What does so much silence do to you? If he were still alive, the Trappist monk, Thomas Merton, would come into his own at this point, for he belonged to a contemplative order of monks where speech was called on only when necessary. From my limited exposure to silence I would suggest its positive quality was to allow you to spend more time listening to the sounds of the natural world, developing the habit of observation, and reflecting on language and experience. In periods of silence words and phrases have time to rebound and to be absorbed by the mind. Let me give an example. The title to the *Salve Regina* (Hail Queen) motet contains the English word 'salve', a balm or medical ointment. As I climbed the flights of stairs to bed I found myself wondering about the connection between the Latin word for Hail and the English word for balm. Mary as the balm for sinners like myself, an ointment for the wounds I have inflicted on the body of my Saviour through sin. Or I could find myself thinking about the translation for another phrase in that motet: *Mater misericordiae*. Mother of mercy. The word *misericordiae* is the one that intrigues me and I had time in a period of silence to allow my mind to go over and to settle on its associations and meanings. Heart of mercy. *Cordiae*, the genitive of *cordia*, heart. Cordial, our Latinate English word, is linked to it. A cordial reception, nothing too expansive, since its meaning has changed over time. *Miserere*, to have mercy. *Miserere mei*, the penitent prays. Lamb of God have mercy on me, for I am a sinner. And you can't help hearing the English word 'miserable'. Mercy, sin, miserable, but Mary is the heart of mercy and therefore can dispense mercy and lift our hearts out of miserableness.

Silence, then, allows the subject or sinner time for such thoughts – or associations, for that's what they are – to emerge into consciousness. Back and forth and then a turn, sometimes decisive, whereby it all begins to make sense (or otherwise) for the person silently meditating on words and phrases encountered during the day. This was but a short distance from meditation as such, where a scene such as the *Stabat Mater*, where Mary stands at the foot of the Cross, is called up and worked on by the religious mind. In turn, meditation, which I once heard compared by Langton Fox to a bone given to a dog, was supposed to lead naturally, after much chewing, to the higher state of mental prayer.

This is the best kind of gloss I can put on silence. By way of contrast, whenever we were afforded the least opportunity, we would indulge in noise just to show we were still around and that, in spite of all the training in restraint that came with being in the choir, there was nothing wrong with our vocal chords. After Mass on the last morning of term we would belt out the *Magnificat* as if that motet to the Virgin Mary was our *nil carborundum* ('don't let the bastards grind you down'), a comforting catchphrase of solidarity frequently heard in the seminary as it was among service personnel in the Second World War. We had survived another term, through noise our souls had been magnified, and we hadn't let the bastards grind us down. The steam train at Rotherfield Station in the valley below was beckoning to transport us away, back to civilisation, away from the rule book, away from timetables, cruel routine and the great silence. The Rector, who was an Arsenal supporter, imagined College was home and in that way justified keeping us over Christmas, but we all knew that was something which commanded little assent. On Boxing Day the College choir sang carols for wayward teenage girls in the care of nuns at a convent in the nearby village of Frant, but nothing was sweeter than hearing the *Magnificat* pressed into service on the following day. We may have missed Christmas but we were intent on making up for it somehow, and wherever that was it would be away.

'Away' never lasted long enough, but in time something worse started to happen to me. I began to lose sense of what was return and what was away. Was it home where I returned to or was it the College I returned to? Where was away? Was that home? Was I away from home when at College or was I away from College when I was at home? Something was going wrong; fortunately, it cut both ways. As the years progressed, during term we had increasing recourse to the momentary lift that accompanied noise and letting rip. Yes, I was away; however, I could also feel something of being away from the institution. It was always refreshing to hear the call of the moorhen and to realise it was indifferent to my plight.

In the recreation room used by Poets, across from the Rector's office and next door to Fr Davy, the quiet-spoken prof who took us for history and games, the record player would be turned up to full volume so that nothing could be heard except the lyrics in tune with the insistent melody about trying to see it my way. Whether or not we could work it out was a question that was usually answered in mid-flow by the dramatic entry of one of the profs, who would swoop down to switch off the devil's music and proceed to read the riot act. The warning usually worked for a week or so, and our nerves would be soothed thereafter by the low notes of gentleman Jim Reeves, at six in the charts, singing about someone who had to go, but then the noise returned in earnest to the impossible-to-silence sound of my generation.

Noise was threatening and promiscuous, silence was repressive and ordered. Noise never bothered me but silence did. In the refectory we sat at the same place for every meal, six on one side of a table and six opposite. Each week we moved up the table in pairs, eventually arriving at the place next to the prefect for breakfast and supper or to the priest for lunch. It was the responsibility of the pair adjacent to the priest to make conversation for the limited period at lunch when dessert (and cheese and biscuits for the priests) arrived. Some priests had lots of small talk but some such as the disciplinarian, Fr Butcher, had none. So for that week when my turn arrived to make conversation it became an ordeal. I would sit anxiously during the preceding period of silence trying to think of something to say, some (preferably non-religious) topic that might interest the disciplinarian such as the decline of the wheatear or the activity of moles at this time of year or the singular pleasures of grass-cutting by moonlight. Rather than waiting for the bell to suddenly announce the arrival of chat, I would have been better off spending the whole meal draped in silence or composing a silent ode to boredom. Chat, what chat? This was punishment, forced chat, and I had become a slave to chat, chattel. O boredom! Get me out of here.

I recall one particular lunch, sitting at the table next to the window overlooking the gravelly front drive. Fr Butcher started on about the idea of the remnant and how Jesus would have been quite happy with just a few committed followers. Putting down his cheese knife and turning to me with his world-weary, pained look, he inquired, 'Wouldn't you agree that was a persuasive idea?' I knew what the crop-headed cleric was getting at and where he was coming from. Looking at his cheese knife and the broken remains of his cream cracker, I wanted to say something about extremism, but I realised that would just give him further ammunition to detonate somewhere in the empty space above my head. Ardent people, especially those tinged with fanaticism, are never easy to tackle for they tend to have no respect for the disinterested intellect. How I despised those occasions. The butcher was a cleaver, and he treated conversation as an opportunity to display how he would go about dividing the sheep from the goats.

It became clear that Fr Butcher was a big fan of the Trappists on Caldey Island and also of St John Vianney, the Curé d'Ars, the French priest who refused to absolve people in the Confessional unless they agreed to relinquish the sinful pleasure of dancing. Indeed, Fr Butcher, who made a point of wearing his own tapered, French vestments, taught us French as if we would be some day making a pilgrimage to Ars. You can always tell people by the company they keep, in this case the spiritual company, and I had no intention of following him down that dangerous path, which entailed a further retreat from a world already uncomfortably close to the edge. On the other hand, he was conceited enough to think of himself as a model, so I felt in my mind he had to be in some way countered. I disliked him as a person and as a priest, but I never felt able to tackle him. He would take one look at my bookbinding efforts and cast them on one side. 'No, we can't use these for the College library I'm afraid. Next.' There was a problem with the sewing or the glue or the gold leaf lettering on the spine. 'Many are called but few are chosen.' I kept hearing that phrase when I was queuing for his approval, and in the end he was right for I was not in fact chosen and, as I explained in a previous chapter, I never could wield a spanner.

The contemplative order was always a possibility or a possible temptation for someone training to be a secular priest. Fr Killjoy at John Fisher went on to join the order of Carmelites, another retreat from the world. There may have been others among my contemporaries at Mark Cross who ended up in monasteries or friaries but I remember only one. He was several years ahead of me. His first name escapes me – it might have been Bill – but his second name was Hodges. When he joined the Cistercian monastery of Mount St Bernard in Leicestershire, a Trappist monastery, he changed his name and became Brother something, so in one respect it was appropriate that I forgot his real name. Periodically, when the electricity substation in the village suffered a power outage, we would be left in the dark, and on one evening I was in an outside classroom with Bill and a group of boys. It was an occasion for the future monk to exercise his considerable gifts as a storyteller. It was a ghost tale he told to a rapt audience which ended on a high note, with all of us screaming inconsolably when he came to the final scene and the entry of the ghost. If it hadn't been pitch-black outside we would all have rushed out of College, past the fields of startled sheep, down the steep hill toward the Saxon settlement of Rotherfield, and we would never have stopped running until we managed to shake the story out of our woolly heads.

On another occasion I was with him again, this time also in an outside classroom but now it was daylight and things had calmed down. We must have got onto the topic of our futures, and I believe at that stage we knew about his future intentions and that he was soon to leave College. The future monk had money in his family and, with deliberation, he pulled back his sleeve, displaying in the process a thick, hairy arm. Then he removed his expensive, gold watch, placed it on the desk between us, and, with the heel of his heavy shoe in his right hand and as if his whole life depended on it, he smashed it to smithereens. So powerful was the blow that not a single shard of glass escaped from underneath. 'That's what I think of the future,' he calmly informed us. That eloquent shattering put us all in our place. Here was someone who needed to spend the rest of his life in silence, away from the world, in obedience to the higher goal that was driving him, perhaps seeking, in the words of Christian at the beginning of John Bunyan's *Pilgrim's Progress* (1678), 'an inheritance incorruptible, undefiled, and that fadeth not away'. He seemed to be in touch with something which was deeper or more charged than the numinous or Rudolf Otto's idea of the holy, and I was certain it was something I would never be able to experience in a month of Sundays. If that's a monastic calling I reflected afterward as I was dropping off to sleep fingering my cut glass rosary beads, give me the secular world any day. Desert religions have a lot to answer for.

Devotion to an ideal, then, meant submission and lowering the head. Silence could be terrifying. You spent your time meeting the self, sometimes locked inside the cupboard of your mind, a mind that you soon discovered was by turns uninspired, cheap, inane, trivial, repetitive, remorseful, conceited, and also in need of others. Looking round at the other silent objects in the cupboard, all I could feel was estrangement. The mind gave the impression of not belonging to anything or anybody but at the same time of being only too ready to jump to conclusions. Every day we spent seven minutes in the Oratory before lunch on something called Particular Examen, which was the equivalent of looking at your body in the mirror in the morning if you were so inclined and finding fault with particular areas. This was a very picky time when we would inspect our consciences and resolve to do better. Whatever St Ignatius of Loyola in the sixteenth century intended by the practice, seven minutes a day on finding fault ensured that most people fell prey to scruples, the scourge of the religious life. Did I make a good confession? Did I tell the priest about that particular impure thought that made a brief passage through the corridors of my mind and that lingered there for more time than was proper? Did my teeth touch the Host? Did I mean to hurt someone by such a passing remark or did I hurt him by mistake and how much responsibility should I take for his hurt? Did I really envy my classmate for that A mark he received and was it the cause for my wishing to achieve higher marks? Was I aiming higher because I was competitive and wanted to come out on top or simply because I wanted to do my best? O God, come to my aid. I can't cope with all this agitation and the scruples infecting my mind.

I wish it was true that *amor vincit omnia*, that love conquers all, and for that reason, according to Virgil, that we should yield to *amori*. In my experience in a small college of some hundred and fifty souls, even though it was sinful, you could really hate people. Hatred was something, unlike the mind, which you could own. I did not sympathise with her but I quite understood why Chaucer's Prioress wore that motto about love conquering all on her wrist, for she liked sending out mixed signals, and perhaps she knew how spiritual weapons played a part in the conquest of material things including the heart. After all, she was a woman who wanted all. The spiritual Prioress, the beautifully named Madame Eglantine, probably had few scruples, but I had many and I never did learn the art of warding them off. They would come and go of their own accord, like the spots on my face. Try not to nick them when shaving is good advice. Hatred of others was easier to deal with. I just kept at bay those I disliked and never stopped admitting in the Confessional to sins against charity.

My best year, when I felt on top of things, was coming up to 'O' Levels, what used to be called the fifth year at secondary school. At Mark Cross, that particular year was known as Syntax. I began life in College in the class of Upper Rudiments, then came Grammar, and after Syntax we found ourselves rather grandly among the Poets, followed by Rhetoric, the apex of an education among the figures of speech. After Christmas in Grammar, before I reached Syntax, I experienced a period of depression which lasted for three months. It should have coincided with the following year when we were snowed in for three months, for that would have shown me what the signs outside were telling me, a confirmation of sorts from the gods. I wanted to leave College and return home. I gave no thought to the future, simply to cutting and running. In Syntax the following year for English 'O' Level we read Robert Browning's poem 'A Grammarian's Funeral', but that seemed like an intellectual exercise on Browning's part. He was right about his subject being 'nameless', but the year I spent in Grammar threatened to destroy for ever my appreciation of English grammar and the way language is structured.

I felt a burden to myself, but I ascribed this not to being a sinner as John Bunyan does in *Grace Abounding to the Chief of Sinners* (1666), but to something that felt like depression. It was psychological rather than pardonable or unpardonable. Day and night, night and day, night and day, day and night. It made no difference which order you put them in, for sequence was not the issue. Night brought with it no blessings and no gathering round the hearth. Every day seemed like a week and every week like a month. Three months took on the character of three years. I never experienced one moment when I was free of the insistent monotone in my head. As Hopkins puts it in one of his dark sonnets, 'I wake and feel the fell of dark, not day'. 'Fell' is the word that best describes it, something fallen or cut down like a tree in the road, a word between a verb and a noun, knocked off course, its Anglo-Saxon etymology (where it meant skin or hide) now obscured. Wake feel fell dark pause not day. Soulless. This was the story of my heart at that period of my life. This that.

I told my classmates to count me out of the end-of-term play. *The Best Days of Your Life* or something out of that stable didn't seem right in the circumstances. How I despised plays about school which ended with a play on the title of the play and a *tableau vivant* by the cast. I must confess I found the gap on the stage where the closed curtains failed to meet more beguiling and in tune with my mood. Dejection, Coleridge and the Romantics called it. That was to dignify it, for it was more like abjection, when I encountered an unwillingness to connect my life with anything around me. John Stuart Mill 'found' himself through such a crisis in his mental life. It was my nineteenth-century moment, but I can't claim I came through it in triumph. Time became duration, empty, inane, and nothing could shake me out of this black mood or 'Giant Despair' as Bunyan calls it in *Pilgrim's Progress*.

Most evenings I would take my concerns to my austere confessor, Fr Coldheart, with his rimless glasses and Roman tonsure, and each time his response was the same, 'Give it time'. What was time I reflected when it could slow down so fast and for such a long time? That wasn't playing the game. I had obeyed the rules but look where it had got me. However, and for this I have to thank my confessor, supposing I had left College during that bleak spring term of 1962 and returned home? What then of my great expectations? That was another path not taken.


## Omnium gatherum

One afternoon in my rudimentary first year at Mark Cross we formed into two groups for a cross-country run. One group went with the Head Boy, someone called Brian O'Dell, the other with another prefect Martin

Straightlace, who would have been in Poets, that is one year behind O'Dell. Those two were like archangels who sought to exercise influence in the College. Straightlace was intense and religious, O'Dell, with his double-breasted jacket and leather holdall, articulate, together as a person, and at the same time remote and impossible to read. I can't remember why but they seemed to attract support and opposition in equal measure. Well, this particular afternoon, the two packs set off in opposite directions. I was with Archangel O'Dell and we headed off down a stream directly opposite the back entrance to the College. The stream at that time of year was fast flowing, in spate, and in parts the icy water came up to our waists. So this was to be no ordinary run. The Archangel knew where he was going and we followed, pushing back the briars and brambles on the banks that were in our path. Eventually we came to a clearing among the trees and waited for something to happen. I glanced down at my thighs oozing little spectacles of blood from scratches, but I took no notice.

Word spread that the other group would be making a rendezvous at this same spot, and when they did so we would come out from behind the nearby trees and assault them. This was more like a boys' school I reflected, an adventure like the boys imagined they were going to have on the island in William Golding's *Lord of the Flies* (1954). There was a clash, first of all some words between the two rival Archangels and then sticks around the heads and legs of our opponents. 'I'm sick and tired on your prim attitude,' so spoke our leader to the young pretender. 'You're a confounded nuisance. Keep your nose out of things that don't concern you.' Martin Straightlace probably couldn't believe what was happening for he was a simpleminded disciplinarian, and he did have an unfortunate predilection for poking his crooked nose into everyone's business. I, too, had difficulty believing my rudimentary ears, for this wasn't supposed to happen in a junior seminary. The puritanical Archangel had been ambushed by the worldly-wise Archangel, and, lost for words, he had been put on the back foot. The packs locked horns, the yelling started, but it was over in a matter of minutes. I don't know who claimed victory. It was one of those events outside the school bounds which didn't seem to have any consequences, whether short-term or long-term, and no one was called to account when we returned to base after our excursion into the more savage parts of the High Weald. The following year the Archangel with the celebrated nose became Head Boy.

The episode impressed me not so much as a clearly understood allegory but as an example of currents in the life of the College which had nothing to do with religion and everything to do with beings boys and doing what boys do best. I was back in Homefield Park with rival gang warfare and stone throwing. You didn't need religion to enjoy that. At the end of that year we learnt that O'Dell didn't continue on to the senior seminary even though as Head Boy he was expected to, for after all he was supposed to be a model pupil. I liked that about him, what I imagined was a thoroughgoing secular attitude to life hidden inside someone going through the motions like a character out of a John Banville novel. He fooled us all, and afterward we wondered what was in his holdall, which he protected with a lock and key, and whether it was full, as some suspected, of top-shelf, imported magazines.

Sincerity was what we all aspired to, but O'Dell suggested another way of being or another way of coping, for the two were closely allied in the seminary. Only very rarely did we encounter the institution making light of religious beliefs. One was at the end of September in the first year when there was a big fanfare and a procession on the feast of St Michael the Archangel. The procession formed in the corridor outside the Chapel, with Fr Coldheart dressed in a cope and humeral veil and clutching in front of him the wing of the saint as if he were holding a monstrance with the Host. From there, accompanied by chants and hymns, acolytes and swinging incense, the procession filed along the dark, polished corridors of the ground floor, past the nuns' quarters and the refectory, up the stone steps to the first floor, past the Oratory, through the long study where we did our homework and into the recreation room reserved for older pupils. It was all an elaborate hoax performed for the benefit of new boys to the College. I never saw Fr Coldheart, who was Director of Studies and normally fairly pompous about things, look so amused as he did when, at the end of the service, he passed round the filthy-looking, mottled goose wing and told the assembled gathering always to remember there was a lot of mumbo jumbo about religion and that the Catholic Church was a grown-up religion and took care to keep relics and miracles in their place.

Sincerity is necessarily blinkered. It needs eyes in the back of the head, but if you possessed such eyes that might mean the end of sincerity. One of the texts we did for 'A' Level English was Oscar Wilde's *The Importance of Being Earnest*, but most of us didn't find it particularly easy to write about and we were given few clues or insights by the cold heart who taught us. The play just seemed a bit of a game, like a board-game where the pieces moved round the board bumping into each other or advancing if they landed on the right square or were discovered in the right handbag. We assumed that somewhere buried beneath the light-hearted humour there was a serious play, but, no matter how hard we tried, its essential meaning, if it had one, eluded us. Bunburying intrigued us but simply as an invented word. The gay theme was never detected or mentioned and nothing was made of the critique of sincerity that the play embodies or hints at.

Unlike Browning's poems, which could be a struggle to make full sense of because of the tone or external references, Wilde's play was my first encounter with a text which resisted interpretation as such. At the time this didn't unnerve me. Mysteries in the Church were in one sense or to some extent understandable or at least explicable. They could be explained by the Church Fathers or someone more intelligent than me or they could be just explained away. How come 25 March is celebrated as the feast of the Annunciation, strictly nine months before the Nativity, when within a few short weeks, if Easter was late, Jesus would die on the cross? Does it matter that the Church's calendar sometimes obeys different rules and cuts across two liturgical years? It was rare to engage in discussions about the historical Jesus and I never heard anyone indulge in speculation as to whether or not the 'Son of Man' had a human father, but as someone brought up within the Catholic fold that is a heresy I now find quite intriguing.

I should have been pursuing similar questions or doubts about the English set text, but the whole environment tended to close off such moves, so they never got going. What do you do with someone like Wilde who refuses to obey conventional rules of interpretation or who indeed stands there in the roadway or out in the desert daring you to interpret him? But that never arose. Our provisional solution, as we entered the exam room that June, was probably sufficient for the day. Avoid answering on Wilde or, if we had to, deploy him in the comparative essay and, if we could not show insight, then show knowledge.

For anyone studying literature or searching for the habit of perfection, how far would sincerity get you is a pertinent question. How is this relevant to my life? Is there a line of continuity between this and that? Can this be paraphrased in terms that makes sense, whether for me or for the average reader or sinner? But there is a difficulty. Sincerity seeks to abolish or narrow the gap between being and meaning. Things should mean, not just be. Modern literature from Flaubert to Wilde, from the Imagists to the postmodernists, has steered its own challenging course, but in all my years at the junior seminary I assumed religion and literature could be studied as distinct spheres of influence without discerning any clash on the horizon or indeed making much of any overlap or any unifying categories such as myth and symbol. If there was a conflict or if irony threatened to get out of hand, I would have retreated behind the unfurled banner of religion, which occupied territory more ancient than Homer and the classics. And at that time I would have justified my retreat with a retort or a conceit such as this: literature was simply struggling to express something that religion already knew.

In the nave of the former Anglican church of St Mary's in York, next to the Jorvik Viking Centre, there is a grave belonging to someone named Elizabeth Blanchard, who died in 1789. On it we read how Elizabeth was 'a sincere Christian' and 'an exemplary mother'. The adjective 'sincere' intrigues me. It couldn't read 'a sincere mother', but why would anyone feel the need to emphasise that she was a 'sincere Christian'? In the seminary I would not have taken much notice of the adjective, believing that sincerity was what we all aspired to as Christians. Now, fifty years later and more appreciative of the variety of religious (and non-religious) experience, I find myself reflecting on the contexts surrounding the cult of sincerity and linking it in this case with the emergence of Methodism in the late eighteenth century and the importance attached to interiority and enthusiasm. York was a particular prize for the outdoor preachers, and, in 1759, thirty years before Elizabeth died, John Wesley opened a Wesleyan Methodist Chapel on Aldwark in the city. Elizabeth, I assume, was exposed to this new influence, so she didn't just go through the motions of being a Christian or mechanically following its observances, but was a person whose religion was driven by the need to connect Sundays with the other days of week, and therefore it meant something to her.

In my seminary career, connectedness also dominated my way of thinking, but I spent those years never once discussing Wesley or indeed the contexts surrounding the cult of sincerity and how that cult might have fed into or informed English Catholicism in the modern period. As a result, any critique of sincerity developed of necessity either from personal observation or from within, and it took years for a more rational and historically grounded appreciation to take over. I shouldn't be too harsh, for in my subsequent career as an academic and writer, without a strong exposure in adolescence to sincerity the forcefulness of my critique of the world would have been significantly attenuated.

I pick up again the photograph of my twenty classmates in the summer of 1963, taken outside the main entrance to the College. This was the class of Syntax, the fifth year at secondary school. As the person with top marks in the class, I am seated next to our form teacher, a smiling priest whose name I have forgotten. He taught us science in the new laboratory next to the gym, but obviously he didn't make that much of an impression. On his left is seated Dermot MacDermot, who was one day older than me and who was also as it happens wiser than me. By wiser I mean more cynical. You can tell by his looks in this and every other College photograph when he's with me that he knew more than he's letting on. It was Dermot who suggested I read Joyce's *A Portrait of the Artist as a Young Man*. He had a feeling I might get something out of it, like J.D.Salinger's *Catcher in the Rye* (1951). For my part, when he sat in front of me in the Chapel or Oratory I would study the unbelievably flat shape of the back of his head and wonder about his eleven other siblings.

*St Joseph's College, Mark Cross, Crowborough, Sussex. Class photo, summer 1963. I am sitting on the right of the priest. It was the last time we were together as a group, for many of my contemporaries never returned to the sixth form.*

Dermot, the College's supreme ironist, enjoyed ribbing me and testing me but there was no malice in him, simply impishness. He wore his tie tightly pulled as if it were a piece of string, a signal to all and sundry that his compliance was under strain. At some point in a conversation, if given the chance, he would have tackled me over my deployment throughout this book of a mixture of real names and pseudonyms. The question would have been essentially about the ethics of concealment but it would have been couched in terms of a matter of interest. 'As a matter of interest, did you have anything in mind by mixing real names with pseudonyms?' And my reply would be the one the distinguished critic, Christopher Ricks, reputedly gave when, after a public lecture, he fielded a hostile question as to whether or not he had actually read Spinoza with 'Yes, next question'.

As I inspect my other classmates from the perspective of a new millennium, I am struck by their hair styles and the grooming that must have gone into the appearance of those who were supposedly on a path toward life-long celibacy. I think we all carried combs somewhere about our person and would periodically during the day find time to do some grooming and at the same time take care to brush off the dandruff from the shoulders of our jackets or cassocks. If you possessed straight hair like Martin Shaw you would comb it back and keep it off the face. Charlie Reid, who was a control freak on the football pitch but who was otherwise cheerful company, had a crew-cut on top and brushed back at the sides. His throat cleared, he loved crooning about scarlet ribbons for a little girl's hair. Nick Simon, who took up a position at the back of the group for the photo, has a Machiavellian half-smile on his face, his straight, ginger hair also contributing to the effect. One boy stands there in the photo next to Nick, his shoulders slightly turned as if he were part of some mean pop group and this was the publicity shoot for the album cover. With his exaggerated quiff, he must have been imagining he was Billy Fury, the next Elvis or, better still – for we all suffered terribly from such delusions – God's gift to women.

In an act of premeditated defiance, another boy, even more disaffected than the boy with the exaggerated quiff, is deliberately refusing to look at the camera. Smudger, a dear friend of us all at the time, is squatting at the front, again in conscious pose, his left arm on his knee, his thick, black hair parted on the left, but all of us recognised the pose was nothing but a pose and that, as soon as he stood up or opened his mouth, the pose would collapse into its constituent, frenetic parts. The camera had a stilling effect on him. Also squatting at the front is the blonde-haired Stephen Dean, who always looked younger than he was and whose musical ability set him apart from the rest of us. It wasn't surprising that twenty years later Stephen went on to compile popular collections of hymns sung by the faithful in churches all over the country.

Nobody is sporting a short hair style, but, as I say, several are going as far they could under the rules with the new fashion. Indeed, if the camera allowed you to see the backs of their heads you would be able to discern some with DAs or some with hair that could be quickly shaped into a duck's ass as soon as the vacation arrived and you were back in civvy street. Several sported a Boston, which was a square-cut back, a style that was always considered more acceptable than a DA. Summer 1963. Beatlemania was taking off in the States, Bob Dylan's 'Blowin in the Wind' was blowing indiscriminately everywhere in the prevailing wind, Cliff Richard and the Shadows were about to go on a summer holiday, and the Rolling Stones released their first single, a cover of Chuck Berry's 'Come On'. At Westminster, the Secretary of State for War in Harold Macmillan's Cabinet, John Profumo, finally confessed to an affair with a call girl who was also seeing a naval attaché to the Soviet Embassy in London. Meanwhile, I was busy in retreat from the world on the edge of Ashdown Forest with the companions of my adolescence, many of whom were busy grooming their appearances and shaping their hair, ready to take their place in the world or, if not, on the look-out for any bit of fluff that might be collecting unnoticed under their beds, for this was the last time we would all be together as a group.

I don't know whether any of us in that photograph made it through to the priesthood. I believe the same is true of the photograph taken the following year showing the ten cassock-wearing prefects with Monsignor Westlife and Fr Butcher. I'm going to assume I'm probably wrong and that at least one person is now saying Mass every morning perhaps at a side altar in a quiet country church for those who kept the faith of their fathers. It would indeed be extraordinary that none of those being trained for something completed the course, for it doesn't seem possible that an organisation like the Catholic Church, which has been in existence for two thousand years, could not renew itself in the modern period with specially chosen, fresh recruits. *Spes messis in semine* was our Latin motto, the hope of the harvest is in the seed. We were the hope but in our case there was to be no harvest, only a storehouse of potential seed destined for stony ground. It now seems extraordinary but inside the seminary we would joke about Solomon with his seven hundred wives never losing any of his seed. Some of my classmates I know went into banking, retail management, their family's business, medicine, the Metropolitan Police, education. I assume others went into the caring professions such as social work, for so much grooming and idealism among that group must have eventually found its proper outlet. However, someone must have lost a pile of money if they imagined we would now be the mainstay of parish life in London and the southern counties of England.

I return to the question that might be put to me: how many of your year, not the College as a whole but your year, made it through to the senior seminary and then through the six years to the priesthood? And the answer is: at the most, one or two. A generation earlier it was not uncommon to encounter after a priest's name his brief biographical details such as: After studying at St Joseph's College, Mark Cross, Fr so-and-so went on to St John's Seminary, Wonersh, and it was there that he was ordained in 19—. They were indisputably a different generation to my generation, the baby boomers, born around 1947, who dipped their toes in the waters of religious experience and who decided for the most part they would prefer to try something else.

When I transferred to St John's Seminary, Wonersh, in the summer of 1965, the year Rotherfield Station and with it the branch line down to Polegate was kindly axed by Dr Beeching, I did so with few regrets. The College was now more cut-off than ever. It had never managed to generate any real affection inside me, and I have never been able to call it my alma mater, my nourishing mother, my soul. Perhaps not surprisingly, I never made a return visit, and, coincidentally, it was closed five years after I left. My younger brother, Stephen, followed in my footsteps but I think he had even less affection for the place than I did, and we never speak about our time there. Throughout my College career I was looked up to for my sporting achievements, but I deliberately don't emphasise those here, for I am more intrigued by something else. In retrospect, though this was not apparent to me at the time, it was at College where the tussle between self and soul took hold and intensified. As I say, I felt an orphan, or at least my days at Mark Cross had made me feel like an orphan. My real home I could always return to in Worthing even if the separation over seven years of being away had altered me and put iron into my soul.

In one of his last essays, 'The Hours of Spring', which he wrote in 1885 when living at 'The Downs' in Crowborough, Richard Jefferies complained about the wind as 'sharp as a scythe'. If he was younger and in good health and had been in my shoes, he might have discovered some spot in the nearby vicinity of Mark Cross and Rotherfield to return to, and he would have relished writing about it in terms such as: This was the prelude to my adult life. This is where I found myself, where I developed a twin affection for Gregorian chant and the natural world, where I delighted in some babbling brook or fast-running stream, beside which I wandered in spring and meditated on life's course. This is where, in following an abandoned path through a forgotten field in search of the eye-catching yellow hammer, I disturbed a skylark nesting on the ground, and made my way back to the secluded pond behind the cricket pavilion, where a heron, fearing danger, its spindly legs dangling helplessly under its body, struggled to take off. This is where on blustery afternoons in winter, protected by a woollen vest hidden beneath a cotton shirt, I charged up and down the brow of a hill playing a noisy game of football and periodically glanced across the valley to notice the smoke from the chimneys of cottages among the trees. Eventually, this is where I discovered, as if it were there all along, a cross with a mark on it, a bitter-sweet moment, as sharp as a scythe, held in time and held in time for as long as I survive to recall it.

Every spring while I was at College, in a well-established tree overhanging the back lane to the tradesman's entrance, a wren made its nest. High above the ground, a tiny, well-camouflaged, tawny-coloured bird, which you could miss as it flitted from branch to branch, built a dome-shaped nest, which was impossible to miss and which looked about five times the size it needed to lay its eggs. At the end of my five years in College, what had I built around the walls of the self to withstand the ravages that might be coming? One of the mild-mannered profs frequently called me 'facetious', without realising this was a form of self-protection given the environment. There is no more comforting structure in Latin grammar than the cognate accusative where the verb's object is etymologically related to the verb. Transposed to English, I was still dreaming the dream, thinking I might have the key to my life. Equally, my race had some way to run and I didn't have the luxury of building by habit or instinct and neither did I possess the comfort of knowing my future destination only the hope I would succeed in my chosen path.

Like my Irish family in history, I was a slow learner, always conceding more to the opposition than it deserved and at the same time leaving myself open to attack. I never bothered preparing answers to potential questions that might be put to me, trusting to a wrong kind of instinct. If I was confident about anything, it was that I would never have to endure another night on the top floor of Pugin's Gothic-inspired building that was formerly a Victorian orphanage. But as I reflect on this period of my life, a period devoted to self-reflection and soul-searching, I have to admit I had no idea what lay on the horizon or how much further I would have to travel to discover my true vocation.

*1920s postcard of the monastic-looking refectory at St John's Seminary, Wonersh,*
*Guildford, Surrey, with the light flooding in. The fifteen months I was here in 1965-6*
*I don't ever remember hearing anyone complain about the food.*

Chapter Eight

# The Ferment of Ideas

## Wonersh

Toward the end of the Second Vatican Council, which was called by Pope John XXXIII to open a window onto the Church, I abandoned the Victorian Gothic orphanage in the Sussex Weald for the late-nineteenth-century, Dutch Jacobean building of St John's Seminary, Wonersh, Nr Guildford, Surrey. Sussex to Surrey again. September 1965. In *The Prelude* (1805), Wordsworth writes about how in the early days of the revolution in France he felt 'bliss was it in that dawn to be alive'. 1965 wasn't one of those heightened revolutionary moments, but things were stirring, and I was in one of those centres where it was happening. I had just turned eighteen. Change, and possibly tumultuous change, was in the air. In his letter to the Corinthians, St Paul had affirmed, 'The letter killeth, but the spirit giveth life', and that spirit we felt was alive and kicking again. You could feel it everywhere, in the wide ambulacrum that greeted you on arrival in the entrance hall, in walks in the grounds, in the refectory across the table for lunch or supper, in weekly trips into Guildford, wherever two or three were gathered together.

There was also evidence that battle lines were being drawn when I arrived. Among those in authority you could sense a generalised fear, which was as good an indicator as any of something untoward blowing. Rumours circulated that uppermost in the minds of English Bishops, returning from Vatican II, were the seminaries, for a fuse had been lit in Rome by the Pope whose image we had captured on his coronation seven years before in the cold, tenement house on Newland Road, and there was no knowing what ravages might follow if the fires caught hold among the young and the impressionable. When the post of Rector became vacant, it was filled for a brief period by Langton

Fox, who had written pamphlets for the Catholic Truth Society on the infallibility of the Pope, the Immaculate Conception, and the Shroud of Turin. He held himself erect, as if in lofty prayer, and sang the praises of the burgeoning evangelical movement, which was just then emerging as a force among English Catholics. You could discern at the time that this was one of the means the authorities had of limiting the spread of new ideas, namely the recourse to traditional belief and to the cult of interiority rooted in personal experience. Before the end of my first term, Fox, a safe pair of hands, had become Bishop of Menevia. He was followed by another safe pair of hands, whose name I have now forgotten but he had a special devotion to the Virgin Mary. 'Catholic Truth' was a collocation that always made me uneasy.

Institutions have a life of their own but, unlike Mark Cross, Wonersh possessed a lifeline to the outside world. The architect, F.A.Walters, had ensured there were no dark corridors and our lives were filled with the light of hope. Fr Eamon Casey, later the famous disgraced Bishop of Galway, moved us all with a talk on his work with the homeless charity *Shelter*, which he helped to found with Des Wilson. In the recreation room, first thing in the morning after breakfast, daily newspapers were devoured, together with the first three cigarettes of the day. It was in that room where we conducted weekly debates in the evening as if we were at the forefront of a new ideological movement where classical authors such as Socrates and Cicero would be quoted alongside the new theologians such as Karl Rahner, Hans Küng, and Charles Davis. As to where it was all heading we were all pretty clueless, but that gave our debates more urgency, not less. In one sense we were not unlike junkies waiting for the next fix, but in another sense I found myself for the first time on a high simply from the exchange of ideas.

As is evident from the notes I took at the time, I read voraciously in philosophy and the history of ideas. Frederick Coplestone's remarkable multi-volume *History of Philosophy* (1946-1975) was a like a *vade mecum*, but in my case it assumed the character of a sceptic's companion. For I was particularly impressed by what I saw as the Achilles heel view of how philosophy evolved, how one philosopher latched on to the weakness of his predecessor and proceeded to take the subject in new directions. Alongside Coplestone, I read Thomas Aquinas's *De Veritate*, Jacques Maritain's *Degrees of Knowledge* (1937), and Richard Aaron's *Theory of Universals* (1952). I was also reading more widely outside religious and philosophical frameworks, and I made notes on J.K.Galbraith's *The Affluent Society* (1958), Paul Hazard's *The European Mind*

*1680-1715* (1964), and Emile Burns's *A Handbook of Marxism* (1935). All the time thoughts were percolating somewhere inside me and often without conscious direction from me. I was involved in a kind of passive reading where I was casting about and seeing not only what I hooked but also what hooked me.

If I run together pell-mell some of the sentences I transcribed in a notebook at the time, it becomes apparent how varied were the ideas then laying claim to my soul: 'God is that than which no greater can be thought' (Anselm). 'Does every truth come from a first truth?' (Aquinas). 'The real essence of a thing is unknown' (Locke). 'One cannot demonstrate that one knows, for the ultimate basis of our knowing is not necessity but contingent fact, and the fact is established, not prior to our engagement in knowing, but simultaneously with it' (Lonergan). 'Marx's materialist conception of history revolves around the fact that social existence determines consciousness' (Burns). And in notes on a series of lectures on Psychology I wrote that 'the human soul is naturally immortal and *de facto* will live for ever'. Not absolutely immortal, for only God is this, but naturally immortal, so the sentence has to be completed by *de facto*, for God could annihilate the human soul. My teachers assumed they had answers to everything, but, even as I faithfully took down what they were saying, my maturing mind was beginning to gaze elsewhere.

In memoirs of the time he spent in the seminary at St Sulpice in Paris in the 1840s, Ernest Renan speaks of a similar moment in his intellectual development: '*Penser me paraissait l'objet unique de ma vie*' (it seemed to me that the unique object of my life was to think). This passive stage couldn't last, and for both of us the next stage involved a series of questions. Was it possible that the intellect could determine the course of your life? Could the intellect transform your whole life? Could that one stem, here identified by the French word '*penser*', come to provide the means by which you would change as a person, to exit the seminary as happened to Renan? Nothing held me back, not even the cautionary note the Church struck when it called the bringer of light 'Lucifer'. I was in that regard pensive, waiting. I was launched on a headlong course which in time would also lead to the door marked 'exit'. Because it hovers between the physical and the metaphorical, 'headlong' is a word in English that invariably draws attention to itself. Only time would tell whether the course I had embarked on was foolhardy or courageous.

The subjects we took that first year included Logic, Epistemology,

Cosmology, Metaphysics, and Church History. In those days the first two years at a senior seminary were devoted to philosophy, the second four to theology. Philosophy was conceived as the handmaiden to theology and was used to provide a grounding in natural theology, that is in securing an approach to God through natural means as opposed to the theology revealed through Scripture and the Church. What could be apprehended about the Divine independent of belief? That was the kind of question we kept returning to. In Cosmology we studied the pre-Socratics, those philosophers before Socrates, who were among the first in western culture to formulate ideas about the nature of the universe. All the time the implication was that such thinking needed the supplement that came with Christianity, so there was a pincer movement at work, one that was strictly philosophical, and one that was historical in cast. In turn, the image kept coming to me, especially when I encountered the Latin word *sicut* followed by some prophecy in the Old Testament and meaning 'see it all fits together and makes sense', that Christianity was more like a bolt-on than a natural completion to philosophy and history. At the same time I never quite freed myself from the thought (later to become a doubt) that perhaps this was a form of rationalisation on the part of the Church after the event, or as the Latin adage has it *post hoc ergo propter hoc* (after this, therefore because of this).

Fr Jim McConnon was a thoroughgoing neo-Thomist, someone that is who followed the teaching of St Thomas Aquinas, the medieval theologian who had interpreted for the Church the teachings of (the newly discovered) Aristotle. In his classes on Cosmology and Metaphysics he regularly posted a warning-sign above modern science, and we took note accordingly. It was an education in the traditional fashion, with caveats and cautionary signs and markers, where debates took place only on terms already demarcated as outcome-already-known. I remember composing an essay in Latin on the distinction between potency and act in the philosophy of Aquinas (which I've kept), but I never once imagined my ideas would potentially carry me away from the being I once was. Even as he sought to distinguish them, no one understood better than Aquinas how close potency was to act.

Knowledge was an edifice and, with the help of scholastic philosophy, we were invited to reconstruct the building from the foundations up. The ambition was laudable, but I would switch on the light in my study-bedroom of an evening and wonder, 'I know nothing about electricity or how it is generated. With an 'O' Level in Physics-with-Chemistry, what gives me the confidence to pronounce on how science is conducted or to question what might be some of its foundations?' System-building, whether pure or applied, I would leave to others more capable than me. Outside of class, I dipped into Bernard Lonergan's *Insight: A Study of Human Understanding* (1958), which provides a modern defence of Aquinas against the Kantian and Heideggerian traditions in philosophy, only to plead ignorance. I would never be able to come to grips with a philosophy with so many propositions set out in terms of a hierarchy of building blocks. I responded positively to the idea of insights, openings, *aperçus*, that beautiful, whispery, French word, but not to insights when they were systematised. I am drawn to the consciousness of things which are just out of focus, as with the hinterland of consciousness. While they attracted me as subjects, it began to dawn on me at this time that I did not have the intellectual capacity or the disposition to become either a theologian or a philosopher.

Some instinct or pressure, which I now discern was a movement away from universals and towards words and things, was preventing me from throwing myself wholeheartedly into the building of foundations. Let the ruins of the Forum in Rome remain as ruins. That thought, once I heard it clanging, seduced me. The classical world had its own pressures and concerns. I wanted to engage with the modern world but my teachers at Wonersh were insistent in their warnings about the modern. Such suspicion of modernity ran deep in the Church, yet to me there was nothing which stipulated that the expression of religion had to be clothed only in the past. Equally, why assume the modern was in itself more fallen, more sinful, less sound intellectually than a previous period? That was similar to an old debate which engrossed thinking minds in the early seventeenth century and which Jonathan Swift participated in during the early decades of the eighteenth century, but then in its later stages it took the form of 'classic versus modern' and it concerned culture rather than religion.

'Modernism' as a term first raised its head in the work of the Jesuit priest, George Tyrrell, and others in the late Victorian and Edwardian period. They were attempting to turn the Church toward science and the modern world. Today the term is normally used to describe a popular undergraduate module and not a religious heresy. The Church outlawed 'Modernism', for the modern world was to be confronted not accommodated. The prevailing attitude was that the modern world had taken a wrong turn. Depending on the topic of debate, that moment could have been the Reformation, the rise of modern science in the seventeenth century, the age of the Enlightenment and in particular the work of Kant, Freud and modern psychology (an exception was made of Jung), the spread of newspapers, contraception and the pill in the 1960s.

Modern was invariably modish or, if it was judged a gloss or a bit of humour was needed, enclosed in inverted commas. A modern setting could be assigned to something as long as the essential qualities were retained. The new fashion for the priest to face the people when saying Mass was just coming in, but an altar would need to be erected in front of the High Altar. That was considered adjusting to 'modern' needs and a recognition of the rise in importance of the laity and a visible and metaphorical nod in their direction. Centuries after its erection, the Medieval rood screen, which was designed to keep the sanctuary largely invisible to the people in the nave, was being dismantled. But there were limits as to how much clerical power could be relinquished. The current valuing of the word 'modernity' in the humanities would have met with silence, indifference, or antagonism in the Wonersh of my time. Not so much among my fellow students, but among those charged with upholding and transmitting the doctrines of the Church.

I recall purchasing several books by Karl Rahner, and it must have been because I perceived in him a theologian trying to make sense of modernity and not just rejecting it out of hand in the name of some older set of principles. My confessor, the theologian Fr Peter Harris, was also someone I respected for his insights into the modern predicament and for his attempt to align the Church's dogma with the modern world. The subtlety of these thinkers particularly appealed to me. For the mind was not just a receptacle for received knowledge; it was also involved in altering the world especially through speculation. The Trinity, after all, which Harris has spent a lifetime reflecting on at a Canadian university after he was laicised, is either a fantastic belief or a fantastic human invention. Whichever way, it remains fantastic, and worth a minute or two of anyone's time.

Renan's *'penser'* carried him through to the other side. The intellect enabled me to stand on my own two feet, and it was at Wonersh that I began to put it to real use. In Logic I was taught by Fr Tony Lovegrove, who had been a pupil at my old school, John Fisher, and who had studied philosophy at Louvain, writing his thesis on Hobbes's *Leviathan* (1651). He instilled into me the principle of contradiction or non-contradiction. It was something I had absorbed in passing already but now I had a term for it, that things could not be true and not true at the same time. At Wonersh it was an important lesson for me to grasp that there was a principle which was not governed by religion, a principle which at a stroke could lay waste whole armies of prejudice. If x, then y, we learnt in symbolic logic. An excluded middle would lead to a false conclusion. A grounding in syllogistic argument was useful, but it was the principle of non-contradiction which excited me. The proposition A is B cannot be true if A is not B. Those two propositions are mutually exclusive, and in all worlds. Thank God, I heard myself murmuring, not for God but for Aristotle and those ancient Greek thinkers.

My understanding of modernity suggested complexity at work everywhere, that things could have many meanings or exhibit polysemic discourse, to adopt a current critical term. But that was in the future. For the time being, something that was true for all worlds was a step on my road elsewhere. My education was paying off, for I was at last being given the tools to critique my own religious background and general ideological disposition. Concerning my experiences at Mark Cross I wrote in the last chapter, how 'the mind gave the impression of not belonging to anything or anybody but at the same time of being only too ready to jump to conclusions'. To have inside you a principle that was not you, or at least which gave the impression of not belonging to you, was something that I now value, perhaps above all others. For the mind has the ability to awaken the soul to its task and to redirect a person to their true vocation. Precisely because of its detachment and at the same time its attachment to principles such as that of contradiction and non-contradiction, the mind can give the necessary push to round on the self, change beliefs, and alter behaviour.

What else happened to me at Wonersh? Or, rather, what do I now recall from that year or so I spent there? It mostly concerns the students who joined me at the senior seminary, some of whom are now priests or are now deceased. Late vocations at Wonersh were quite common. Fr Peter de Ath, who died in 1997, was in my year and we struck up a friendship which should have lasted beyond my time there. Peter rarely became exercised by intellectual ideas and didn't seem to be plagued by intellectual doubts. Equally, I never saw him reduced to anger. I could have learnt more from him than I did, for I never encountered anyone so intent on seeking out the common ground between people, something I was never that good at, being more concerned to give voice to my own opinions. He had what the best Catholic priests possess, an unassuming commitment to service in some neglected spot, and he bore in himself witness to the view that the world could be other than what it is. You could rail at Peter but he would come back the following day with something like 'Yes, David, I can see what you're getting at. I wonder how we might use that idea in our future work in the parish.' That first year, he had purchased a new kind of typewriter with cursive script, and he was so proud of it, for it seemed to embody an aspect of his personality. I like to remember him as someone who was always given to seeking connections and who always felt the need to keep up-to-date.

There is often something remarkably constant about the pattern of human behaviour through time. What has impressed me googling my contemporaries is discovering obituaries which I could have composed forty years and more ago. It was in keeping that Pat Olivier, who died on a walking pilgrimage in 2007, should be remembered as a priest who welcomed the poor into his presbytery in Guildford to serve them tea and sandwiches. It was also in keeping that, when he was laicised after getting married in his fifties, he would take an active role in a group dedicated to helping the clergy who left the ministry to marry. His singing voice was full of character and integrity, and everything he did when I knew him suggested a gentle commitment to an ideal, even when that ideal changed direction. Unlike me, he would never have just walked away from a previous incarnation but he would have brought his whole life with him in an attempt to make sense of changes as if they were all part of the one journey.

There is a photograph of Fr Christopher Pritchley on his parish website in Surrey. I recognise the same 'Pritch' I knew when at Mark Cross and Wonersh. His face, which recalls Griff Rhys Jones, the Welsh comedian, is still slightly craggy, and you can tell there is the same readiness to engage with the world but not to judge. In the seminary he was a couple of years ahead of me and opened the bowling when we played cricket. On his parish website there is mention of the First Communion programme, which is only proper, followed by a notice about his parishioners getting involved in cricket if they so wish. As for 'Pritch' himself, we learn that 'His interests are rugby, cricket (Kent), following the fortunes of Arsenal and photography'. I could almost have penned that forty odd years ago, for that was the person I knew in my seminary days, someone for whom the sacred and the secular were intertwined. His looks have changed with the ruins of time, but the character and personality have remained as fresh as the first occasion he bowled me out with a ball that cut back inside.

Although it was a word we avoided, Wonersh was full of interesting 'types', and I could fill a chapter with them, but as I seek to understand that period in my life something else is required than a series of pen portraits. Architecturally, the building contained so much light that it's difficult to believe how much it concealed. But that was in the nature of the training where the emphasis was on spiritual development in a community where so much was shared. It was an odd kind of existence with your head bowed pacing up and down polished corridors or meditating in chapel facing in to the pews opposite, all the time aware that you were being watched. The contemplative monks in the Carthusian monastery at Cowfold in West Sussex would have their meals in their cells served though a hatch and they would dig their own individual graves. St John's was different. Your spiritual life was tested in and through contact with others.

How much you revealed or let slip was not always easy to determine, but there were always two sides in play. Ideally, the social or public self was supposed to mirror the private self, but in reality what occasionally happened was that the private self became buried or concealed or just lay dormant. The people I admired sought integrity even though it was a constant struggle to achieve or maintain. For others, the public image seemed to occlude any sense of interiority, as if they couldn't distinguish a true from a false note. These were the kind of individuals who, before they had received their tonsure at the end of their second year, would begin wearing the clerical collar outside the seminary. Integrity, on the other hand, meant you lived your life forgetful of the mirror of vanity and ensured as far as possible the public self was anchored in the private self.

We seemed to be so preoccupied with integrity that we missed what else was in the frame, particularly in regard to sexual identity. As we stood in front of the mirror putting on cassocks and adjusting sashes, we gave little or no thought to what we shared in our attire with women. I recall Fr Lovegrove mentioning how cassock-wearing clerics in Louvain were shouted at in the street, '*Les jupes!*' (the skirts). I just dismissed this as an example of Continental anti-clericalism and something we wouldn't have to face on the parish in Britain. But the image of skirts returns to me with some force, for throughout my childhood and adolescence I was surrounded by men dressed in clothes resembling what women wore.

Black was fairly neutral but those higher up the Church ladder wore purple, red and scarlet, and, when dressed in clerical garb for the street, would show sensual flashes of colour. As if he were on the way to becoming a female man, a bishop in addition enjoys an elaborate set of clothes including stockings, rings, gloves, pectoral crosses, mitres, a mantelletta for covering his rochet or symbol of Episcopal authority when outside his diocese, and a mozetta or short cape which can be fastened across his breast. I suppressed all such gendered thinking at the time, made nothing of the extraordinary layers of meaning behind the word 'defrock', and yet it's so obvious to me now. It's as if when I was in the seminary I fleetingly registered things but put them completely out of my mind. The only issue I had with a biretta was putting it on the right way round.

How I didn't notice all the mixed signals being given off remains a mystery unless it's akin to class consciousness being tied to class horizons. I understood the power of clerical clothing but gave little thought to the issue of gender, simply that it was different and belonged to the period when Jesus walked the earth. Metaphorically, there was so much light in the building at St John's that I couldn't discern the many layers of concealment, some of which were linked, ironically, to the issue of display. Sexual orientation, for example, can be disguised or concealed (or find its true expression in crossing gender barriers). In the seminary before 1969 and the Stonewall riots we were taught that our sexuality could not be expressed, that celibacy signified no sex and no contact, and it was always assumed that sexual contact referred to women. In June 1966, relations of a friend who attended his ordination ceremony for the diaconate asked him quite innocently if he'd 'had it done'. He wasn't quite sure if they meant a vasectomy or castration, but he was in no doubt it was one or the other. For anyone exposed to the heady mixture of celibacy and display, gender identity should have received full and open discussion, especially since it was close to the question of integrity, but it remained one of those things we observed in passing and then put out of our minds. We spent time dressing up and disrobing, and we dressed in what Belgians saw as 'skirts', but sex was for others, not for us.

Many people reading this memoir will be thinking 'What about all the abusers you must have come across while you were in those two seminaries? For the sake of honesty and a more complete picture, why not tell your reader about these people?' I must confess the number of abuse cases that have come to light in recent years has made me wonder the same thing, especially as I was mixing among so many with Irish names. All I can report is that I must have been fairly sheltered or didn't have the gumption to notice things. At Mark

Cross one of the prefects, who had an obsession with the pop singer Lulu, would tuck in the bed-clothes of one of the first-year boys in the dormitory, but I judged that was just a passing phase and gave it no further thought. I'm sure it was fairly innocent and nothing more than a sign of affection in an emotionally frozen outpost that once housed an orphanage.

No one ever touched me or made sexual advances and I don't recall any behaviour that could be described as grooming. One late vocation at Wonersh, who was coming up to the subdiaconate, would invite groups of us to Harveys department store in Guildford for afternoon tea. His Irish family had money and he was keen to play mein host. That we all felt was fun and a mark of generosity. I don't believe he made it through to the priesthood, and perhaps there was a question-mark about his character. Such a doubt would invariably arise when someone was 'blocked' for promotion whether for minor orders or for major orders such as subdeacon, deacon, or the priesthood itself. I think he might have applied to another bishop to ordain him. But he was the nearest of anyone I encountered who suggested there might be something slightly suspicious about his character. There used to be a joke in the seminary that if you had been blocked and agreed to undertake a (despised) course in Canon Law in Rome, you might get to proceed.

While engaged on this memoir I quite naturally began researching the names of my contemporaries, and what surprised me were the clergy who did not appear on diocesan and parish lists. I began to wonder if most of my contemporaries at Wonersh never made it through or if their names had been deleted from the select list of those who had been chosen, perhaps because they had abandoned the ministry to get married. I left Wonersh in 1966, so that's forty-four years ago as I write this. It was during this research that I came upon a list of abusers among the clergy and discovered there the name of one of my contemporaries. That was quite a shock, for nothing had prepared me to encounter at first hand so much innocence and idealism trampled on and betrayed.

In November 2007, at Lewes Crown Court, Fr Dermot Keaveney was found guilty when he was seventy two of sexually abusing two teenage brothers in a series of attacks conducted between 1975 and 1982. He would have been in his forties when he committed those offences, and that must have constituted part of his defence, that they were a long time ago. It was obviously a very serious case, with his victims suffering long-term damage. Found guilty, he received a prison sentence of sixteen years. The BBC News report carries a photo of Keaveney with the caption 'The judge said Keaveney gave no thought to the damage he caused'. I look again at the photo of the fairly brutal face of an old man with a cast in his left eye. He might have given no thought to the damage he had caused to those two boys but you could see in his face, the window onto his soul, something terribly unresponsive. In the police mug-shot, it is as if his past actions, and indeed his character, had caught up with him.

This was the same person I sat next to in the light-filled refectory at Wonersh nearly a half century ago when he was a deacon and coming up to ordination to the priesthood. I remember he was difficult to engage in conversation, and I must confess there was something about him I didn't take to. I couldn't quite determine if he was pious or just withdrawn, but, with his head bowed, he gave the impression he would never put a foot wrong. I remember receiving his blessing on the day he was ordained, together with his ordination card. 2 June 1966. 'Hoping that you will pray for me at times, David,' he wrote. His hands had been freshly anointed with oil and he was now a priest for ever after the order of Melchizedech. I wished him well. Nine years later he is sexually assaulting two young brothers in a parish in Brighton and Hove.

When I look back, I wonder was he already a potential abuser and just biding his time? Or did the abuse commence when he was in a parish and had the young in his care? Was he attracted to a celibate life because then at least part of his life was under control? Or did his celibacy act as a foil to deceive his victims and put them off their guard, and did he think this or half-think this somewhere in his mind while he was preparing for the ministry? However you attempt to understand the motivation, it's ugly. Do I have any sympathy for his current fate, spending possibly the rest of his natural life in prison? Probably not. My sympathy is drawn toward the lives of his victims, now in their forties, the age Keaveney was when he was abusing them. But would I have had more sympathy if he had been someone I took to? That I don't know. Some things seem unforgiveable.

My second year at Wonersh came to a fairly abrupt end in early October 1966 when I mentioned to my confessor that I would like to take time out at the end of my second year to pursue a degree, possibly in philosophy or English. 'If you feel that way, perhaps you should seek a second opinion from Canon Arbuthnot, the spiritual adviser to the seminary.' I booked an appointment for a day when the external adviser was next visiting and we met in the Rector's office for no more than two minutes. When his South London presbytery received a direct hit during the Blitz, Arbuthnot had been miraculously dragged out alive, and thereafter he had an aura of holiness about him as if, like one of Calvin's elect, he had been specially chosen. 'If that's the way you feel, you can't have a vocation,' the holy man coldly informed me. That was pretty final or about as final as it gets. I had only just sat down when I was departing the way I had come in. It was obvious that there was no room for discussion in that room. God had spoken and I had no intention of outstaying my welcome. Within a matter of days, I was gone from the seminary.

My mind had been made up for me, and, until I began writing these memoirs, I never gave that quittance notice more than a few minutes of my time. I did hear myself saying by way of reproach, 'This is where intellectual ferment gets you, David,' and yet an accompanying thought sustained me. I didn't need all that institutional baggage to weigh me down. '*Ite, missa est*,' as the priest says at the end of Mass. Go, the Mass is ended. Now I could go. I had received my mission. I would cast aside the key, but, unlike Newman, I would discover my true vocation elsewhere and it would be a pilgrim's progress on my own, perhaps of necessity away from God and not towards Him. After all, it was said at the time in the 1960s that some of the best Christians might be among those who believed in the death of God. I was a marked man, an outsider, no longer chosen or indeed called.

I searched inside for a settled or mature response above the fray, but discovered only a person who was by turns impassive, light-headed, and angry. I found myself facetiously thinking of parts of speech again and of the position I occupied in a dead language. From a cognate accusative, dreaming the dream as I suggest at the end of the last chapter, I had become an ablative absolute, that Latin construction perilously detached from the main clause. All things considered, what kind of institution was it that could abandon me because I had expressed an interest in going to university? That was so absurd that I was lost for words. And why on earth did the authorities assume God supported them in decisions which were profoundly anti-intellectual? Did they imagine God was simply holy and had no intellect? It was just the push I needed to clear my head of all the nonsense I had tried patiently to make sense of over the years.

Renan exited the seminary with continuing issues about inconsistencies in the story of the historical Jesus. Some of the Church's teachings he couldn't accept, but he insisted he was still a Christian. Indeed, in his struggle against theology, he found support in the character and personality of Jesus, and it was this view that underpins his *Vie de Jésus* (1863), his life of Jesus. However, Renan was particularly exercised by the question of how far it was possible to reject one aspect of those teachings without rejecting them all. In the weeks following my departure from Wonersh, I didn't need all this. I just needed space to allow what had happened to settle. I was on my own, in between worlds, dangling. I had been rejected by Mother Church and cast out, but it would be a few years yet before I rejected that august institution and before I no longer regarded myself as a reject.

I returned home to Worthing, embarked on a course of 'A' Levels at the local further education college, and applied in November to read English and Philosophy at university. In the spring I had interviews at York, Keele, and Sussex, but was unsuccessful. At Sussex the philosophy tutor took a sideswipe at my interest in continental philosophy: 'Do you not realise that Heidegger supported the Nazis?' At York I waited in a corridor where F.R.Leavis had an office, and at a short interview was asked to explain: 'Do you mean to say you have destroyed the English essays you did at 'A' Level?' As was the case in my junior seminary, there existed no room for facetiousness in the groves of academe. Apart from an offer from Liverpool to read Philosophy, a letter which I never had the courtesy to reply to, the rejection slips confirmed my feeling of abandonment, and it was left to the people administering Clearing in August to offer me a place at Lancaster University, which was, like York and Sussex, a new university. It might be considered facetious but I had to look on a map of Britain to ascertain whether Lancaster was north or south of Preston. As I discovered, it was a long way from a fashionable watering place on the south coast. Watford Gap by comparison was only up the road from London.

## University

Autumn 1967, my teenage years over, I arrived at the shining city on the hill, otherwise known as the University of Lancaster. That summer the first cohort of students had graduated. Newness was in the air. It was so new that there were still no halls of residence, and most students lived in bed-and-breakfast accommodation in Morecambe and commuted into Bailrigg by special double-decker buses. We were welcomed by Tom Lawrenson, a professor of

French, at St Leonards Gate in the city of Lancaster, which was the first home of the university. After furnishing us with a potted history of universities in Europe, starting with Bologna, he ended: 'Spend your three years with us wisely and please remember there are some of us who will be here long after you've gone, so give some attention to the community that will survive you.' That seemed to be a jibe about the new generation of students who might take it upon themselves to wreck the place. As I came away from that opening session I wasn't sure if I had received a welcome or a warning-shot. I do recall that it was a common belief at the time that the new universities were deliberately sited a couple of miles outside of town in case there was trouble.

We were required to take three subjects in the first year. I was signed up to read English and Philosophy, so I had a choice as to my third subject. The first person I noticed on entering the room where the subject specialists were advertising their courses was Adrian Cunningham. We had met the previous year in London at a Catholic-Marxist conference under the auspices of *Slant*, and he had been recruited in the meantime by Ninian Smart to teach in the newly-founded Religious Studies department, the first such department in Britain. I had initially no intention of returning to the sources of friction of me, but, somehow, that chance meeting reminded me I still had unfinished business, and I signed up. I was slightly apprehensive about that decision, but was almost at once reassured when I embarked on a course entitled 'Nineteenth-century Religious and Atheistic Thought'. This was the most invigorating course I took at Lancaster, largely because of the stimulus provided by Cunningham, who as it happened was closer at that time to being an anarchist than a Marxist.

I needed time to reflect on my religious upbringing and education, and what could be better than by focussing on the group of thinkers who emerged in the 1840s to take apart the monolithic system Hegel had erected. That was quite invigorating to spend time turning things upside down, to watch as one century unwound into another, and it fitted in with my mood. Week by week in fairly rapid succession, we analysed the idea of projection in Feuerbach, that our idea of God was simply a projection of our needs, wants, or desires, Marx's view that religion was the opium of the people, and the concept of authenticity and the leap of faith in Kierkegaard. Everything excited me again, not least the intriguing (short) title to a book by the Danish philosopher called *Concluding Unscientific Postscript* (1846). I needed that postscript to what I had been through. I also needed to conclude something, and almost certainly it would be unscientific. So Kierkegaard, the forerunner of twentieth-century existentialism, was a rich source of comfort, as he has been to many over the years who for whatever reason have felt abandoned.

In seminars, Ninian Smart would reach for a tall copy of Aristotle's *De Anima* from the bookshelf behind him to explain something, or he would notice me reading Lucien Goldmann's *The Hidden God* (1964), which had been recently translated into English, and ask me after class what I made of it. 'Well, "hidden" sets up a different set of associations and therefore a different kind of discourse to "invisible".' At lunch in the bar of Lonsdale College, the distinguished professor would stand me a drink, and converse with me, an unsophisticated freshman, as to an equal. I could see why Cunningham, a student of Raymond Williams at Cambridge, would want to work with him, for all of a sudden the field of the humanities broadened out yet again and in new directions. It was quite extraordinary in the middle of a damp winter's afternoon to encounter on the wind-swept campus Buddhist monks in saffron robes, who had come across from Sri Lanka to study their scriptures under the Anglican professor. If Williams had emphasised a common culture within Britain, Smart was a reminder of the common ground, regardless of culture, that all religions occupied.

The New Testament scholar, Robert Morgan, struck a more traditional religious note but, again, even when tackling issues over, say, the meaning of the phrase 'Son of Man' we were taught to see where biblical scholarship and textual criticism might lead us. Only years later on a visit to the Chester Beatty Library in Dublin did it strike me with some force, firstly, that interpretation is close to the heart of Christianity and, secondly, that there is something inherent in the tension between history and belief. Peering over a dimly lit display cabinet at a fragment of St Mark's Gospel dating from around 200 AD, several thoughts came to me all at once: the precariousness of the transmission process, the surprising lack of a single source for the story of Jesus, and, perhaps above all, how there is something attractive about a religion that begins not with the unsullied, monolithic truth but with different and occasionally competing versions of its origins. The resulting 'scandal' is either all too human or all too divine, but to my mind it undermines any idea of conspiracy on God's part or any idea that Christianity at its outset had a single story to tell. By rights, we should pay more attention to the phrase 'according to' when the Gospel is read out in church services.

At Lancaster, until the arrival of a Northern Irish Protestant tutor, who would cavalierly refer to 'kraut' philosophy and 'kraut' theology, the emphasis throughout the department was on openness and critical inquiry. For the first time I could write about religion without putting in the margin at the top of the page 'A.M.D.G', *ad majorem dei gloriam*, for the greater glory of God. I recall writing an essay on Paul Tillich and on whether it was possible to study theology without believing in God. I can't remember what conclusion I came to, but I am sure no one wrote 'rubbish' in the margin. It was a small department that first year, but it was a real powerhouse in the generation of ideas, and none of the original three tutors were proselytisers.

Philosophy was less inspiring. We covered a lot of ground in that first year, sampling the various areas covered by the subject including moral and political philosophy, the philosophy of religion, the theory of knowledge, and a short introduction to the philosophy of mind. Almost no continental philosophy was covered, but we received a grounding in English empiricism from Locke to Berkeley and Hume, in nineteenth-century ideas about moral discourse from Bentham and Mill onwards, and in forms of linguistic or ordinary language philosophy. Ideas about the nature of individuals were also touched on in the work of P.F.Strawson and others. In the philosophy of religion we concentrated on arguments for or against the existence of God. I recall a public debate between Smart and Colin Lyas, who had been a student of Anthony Flew at Keele, on the existence of God. Staring up into the two corners of the room facing him, Lyas would taunt Smart about his childish beliefs. Smart adopted the unflustered stance of someone completely at home with his subject. 'Philosophy could only take us so far in certain debates, and religion was one of those debates.' But such skirmishes were few and far between, and departments tended to keep to their side of the fence.

After Aquinas and metaphysics, or indeed German Idealism and existentialism, ordinary language philosophy lacked something. In the wake of my experience in the seminary a more sceptical reading of the world should have appealed to me, and yet it didn't. It was as if the pendulum had swung too far. When invited to interview at Sussex I was asked to write an essay on the sentence 'The sky blues'. I suspected that was a trick question and I couldn't bring myself to do the necessary preparation. I suspect now it was a similar kind of sentence to Strawson's 'The King of France is bald'. Are such sentences true or false or are they neither? Throughout my teenage years, I had been struggling with the mystery of Creation or with St Anselm's ontological argument for the existence of a being greater than which cannot be thought, and now I was being asked about adjectives functioning as verbs or contexts which made something true or otherwise. That seemed such a let-down. Perhaps under the right kind of tutelage I might have continued with Philosophy but at the age of twenty there seemed to be better things I could do with my time. I am sure Sartre and de Beauvoir, on the barricades or sipping coffee outside a café on Montparnasse in May 1968, would have agreed with me.

English as a subject at Lancaster combined the study of both language and literature. Contemporary linguistics was particularly strong and I was privileged to be taught by, among others, Geoffrey Leech, Anne Cluysenaar, Christopher Candlin and Norman Fairclough. All these tutors made a significant contribution to my understanding of language and linguistics. Leech's book on stylistics had just appeared and he was grappling with the issue of semantics and its centrality or otherwise to the study of language. His book on the language of advertising I found less impressive. Coming in the wake of Vance Packard's populist *The Hidden Persuaders* (1957), its ideological neutrality seemed gutless and out of keeping with the times. Fairclough's formulation of critical discourse analysis and his work on language and power was still some way off, but we felt that something was taking its course, and he was very patient as we struggled to comprehend the more rarefied aspects of transformational grammar as propounded by Noam Chomsky.

After I graduated, Linguistics eventually established its own department, and I notice from the University's website that it now has over thirty members of staff. English, meanwhile, took creative writing under its umbrella. So that particular moment when language and literature and the integrated approach to English studies were studied in the single department is now past. I lament nothing. Both sets of tutors developed my appreciation and insight into words on the page. Linguistics was a more lively subject at Lancaster, partly because it was new, partly because of the personnel, and partly because it saw itself more as a science with discovery methods than as an arts-based subject. This meant it was responding to developments in the subject in a more immediate way, especially through journals. It takes a long time reading literature before you have the confidence to say anything new.

The professor in the department, W.A. Murray, who was intent on keeping things together, would speak airily about Lancaster becoming a world centre for English studies, where equal attention would be devoted to both language and literature. Once, when I had been invited on my own to his large, detached house near the University, he took care to show me all the ornamental objects and wall-hangings he had collected from his travels round the world, particularly from Africa. The ambition he had for the department was probably inflated from the start, for the two branches in his empire were pulling in different directions, and the course on Linguistic Stylistics, the 'bridge' course, was just not going to be strong enough to hold things together. Put simply, the linguists believed in description, the critics in the Department in evaluation or, if you were a Marxist critic like David Craig, in explanation. Cluysenaar, who was herself a poet, fought a valiant battle to show us how you could move from description to evaluation, but she was a lone voice, and when she published her book on the topic it carried the word 'literary' in the title, *Introduction to Literary Stylistics* (1976).

The critic was interested in whether or not this was a good poem, the linguist in what contributed to the effects in our reading a poem. For a linguist with a communication model of language in mind, where the metre in a poem changed course or where the rhyme scheme deviated from an established pattern, there you would encounter a higher incidence of communication or meaning. But the linguist, who could make some valuable observation about the tension between poetic metre and prose rhythm, would hold back from declaring if the following lines from Yeats's poem, 'The Man and the Echo', were good or bad or weak or powerful:

Did that play of mine send out
Certain men the English shot?

Larger questions, such as if the lines or the half-rhyme drew the reader into the poet's predicament and the history of modern Ireland, would also remain untouched, but these are precisely ones the critic, whether cultural or literary, would want to discuss.

The linguist, then, was as happy dealing with an article in the newspaper or an advertising jingle or an entry in a telephone directory as with a Shakespeare sonnet. It was simply language in use. The critic on the other hand was looking to discern shifts in the culture or how values, whether cultural, social, or individual, manifested themselves in language use. In tutorials, with four or five us round a table in his room, Craig, who was himself a student of Leavis at Cambridge, would get us to date small extracts lifted from different periods of English Literature. That could be quite enlightening and at the same time quite embarrassing when you discovered you were a century out, and instead of Mrs Gaskell in the 1840s you had foolishly opted for Samuel Richardson in the 1740s. The interpretation of a passage would hinge on a particular word which carried a shift in sensibility or in its structure of feeling or in its scientific outlook or its historical reference.

I enjoyed being in the dark at the beginning of these exercises in dating, and was never especially upset by the charge from colleagues in Linguistics about reading out of context. After all, it was only a teaching tool, and, besides, reading literature is a constant challenge not least when confronted with an unknown context. As you listen to the opening lines of Robert Burns's 'Song: Composed in August' ('Westlin Winds') you need to be alert to the tone from the outset:

> Now westlin winds and slaught'ring guns
> Bring Autumn's pleasant weather.

The use of 'slaught'ring' puts us on our guard. Indeed, the reader suspects there is an irony in the collocation, pairing, and rhythm in the first line and waits for the poem to shed light on the implied, broader relationship between the human and the natural worlds, and we are not disappointed for, as Dick Gaughan's rendering reminds us, this is among the youthful Burns's most moving songs on the unity of life. Literary texts, whether they are songs or plays or lyric verse, often involve performance, and part of that performance or event begins with a challenge not only in how to establish the right tone but also in how to supply a context.

Later in the poem when you hear the line 'Some social join, and leagues combine', you find yourself, if you are conversant with the making of the working class in Britain, jumping forward from the year when the poem was written in 1775 to the Combination Acts of 1799 and 1800 and the legislation at Westminster which was designed to prevent 'unlawful combinations of workmen'. Whether we read it looking back or looking forward, Burns's love song to Peggy Thomson resonates against its historical context and 'Tyrannic man's dominion' over nature. Any linguistic description would need to address at some point the values that inhere in the poem and its vision of 'man's' place in the world, but that was a move tutors in Linguistics tended to steer away from as lying outside their domain.

From the beginning, I must have always felt closer to Literature than

Linguistics. Unlike studying Linguistics, 'Doing English' is something most of us are familiar with from early years at secondary school, and most of us have some facility or ability in commenting on texts. Perhaps that's one of the reasons the crisis in English studies when it arrived in the 1980s proved so profound. That crisis was just beginning to emerge when I was an undergraduate at Lancaster, and it manifested itself around the issue of interpretation. Repeatedly, linguistics drew attention to the limits of what it was legitimate to say about a text. The limits of interpretation coincided with the limits of description. At the same time, Ferdinand de Saussure, the founder of modern linguistics, had drawn a line between history and function, so it was now possible to study a language without referring to its history for example. No recourse to history and no recourse to evaluation – this seemed like some kind of clarion call as the attack on criticism began to gather force. From another direction at Lancaster, there came the attack on the liberal-humanist critic from more theoretically advanced positions, especially in the work of a Marxist critic like Craig. But you didn't need to have a Marxist around to detect the under-theorised nature of criticism at that time. Whenever they encountered the word 'problem' or felt they were on the back foot, tutors in English should have substituted 'opportunity' and stepped forward. In that way the topic could have been approached less fatalistically and more imaginatively.

I wish I had taken a more lively interest in the battle within the Department at Lancaster between the two sides, for in many ways it anticipated what happened later on in English studies. But at the time I felt I was being invited or coerced to choose between the two approaches, and I was reluctant to commit myself. The linguist is quite naturally interested in systems and structures, the critic in the particular, the concrete, perhaps by extension in the typical or the universal. As the American pragmatist, Richard Rorty, might have noticed, they are embarked on doing different things. Of course, some critics imagined they existed on a higher, more sensitive, plane, but that, too, was absurd. Tolerance, for example, is not a virtue with which literary critics are particularly blessed. Equally, in linguistics at that time there was the implied belief that literary language could be explained or reduced to its constituent parts. Again, this was an act of hubris or simple vanity, for no one from linguistics taking a powerful poem to pieces can say that they've explained its power.

In retrospect, the areas of English Literature I enjoyed the most centered more on sampling than on surveying. Even though it looked as though it was a survey course, the history of the American novel since 1850 was really a sampling course. Each week, we studied a 'big' novel and the module acquired momentum accordingly. The American novel, for example, was a collection of redskins or pale faces, with writers like Mark Twain looking west toward the frontier of language, or writers like Henry James turning their gaze inward toward consciousness and in James's case to the heritage of Europe. Novels such as Upton Sinclair's *The Jungle* (1906) or Theodore Dreiser's *Sister Carrie* (1900) could be discussed in their own terms or as examples of new literary movements such as naturalism or inheritors of older literary movements such as realism. Symbols in such a module were everywhere, so that kind of approach also came into its own. What did the scarlet letter symbolise in Hawthorne's novel of that name? We could all discover something to say about that. And the same was true of Herman Melville's *Moby Dick* (1851). Truman Capote's documentary novel, *In Cold Blood* (1966), completed this module on a slightly unnerving but upbeat note.

Another module more obviously to do with sampling was an introduction to forms of criticism and different kinds of critics. The list of names and topics included Viktor Shklovsky and Russian Formalism, I.A.Richards and the concept of practical criticism, Cleanth Brooks and New Criticism, W.K.Wimsatt and his attack in *The Verbal Icon* (1954) on the intentional and affective fallacies, Sartre's *What Is Literature?* (1947), Georg Lukács and his Marxist contribution to literary studies, the work of F.R.Leavis, and a strange, little book at the time which didn't seem to fit in with the course, Roland Barthes's *Writing Degree Zero* (1967). I wasn't quite sure I understood this last book, so I went away and read *Mythologies* (1957). What an extraordinary mind I thought. The essays were so striking that it was at first difficult to discern not only the direction but also the origin and intellectual foundations of such a mind. Today, we are more knowing and could write our own essays on signs and signifiers in the culture along the lines of the French master, but in the late 1960s it came as quite something the comparison between wrestling and boxing or a disquisition on the shape of Marlon Brando's head. This was new subject matter and it wasn't certain under which academic discipline we were supposed to assign such a form of criticism. It was in keeping that one of the exam questions asked us to discuss Barthes's (quite impossible) claim that 'Modernism begins with the search for a literature which is no longer possible'.

Like most students at that time I was unsure as to the rationale or logic that lay behind my subject as a whole, and only later did I even consider such a question. But on reflection there was something else blocking my view, and that arose from the issue of choice. As a student it felt as though I had been invited into a room full of goodies on a table and asked to pick and choose whatever took my fancy. I enjoyed that aspect, but now as I look back I wonder if that wasn't part of the dilemma and part of what I can only describe as a wider deception. And yet how could it be otherwise? We are all in that regard consumers as students, and if we are involved in production it is because we are initially consumers. At Lancaster the emphasis seemed to be on student choice at the expense of some overall insight into the subject. I assume my tutors would claim that if I didn't enjoy my studies or found them wanting that was because I had made the wrong choice(s). You had opted for the Romantics instead of the Renaissance, for the Victorians instead of the Eighteenth Century. Tough. In the seminary I had no choice as to what I studied or consumed, but as soon as I arrived at university I was confronted with one choice after another. It's not for nothing that when asked about the principles then governing English Literature at Lancaster, I hesitate before responding.

Coverage is a related matter, and most tutors in English over the last thirty years have been less than comfortable with the general acceptance of the model of the smorgasborg, of pick and mix. But as an undergraduate the tempering of my enthusiasm for English stemmed I believe from something closer to home. I had devoted much of my time at Wonersh to stepping back and trying to obtain a perspective on the world. I had been given a training in what now I would describe as a form not, as might be supposed, of Christian idealism but of radical scepticism, focussing in particular on questioning what constituted knowledge and how it is constituted. Upon entering university I threw myself into all things modern, assuming a new university was at the centre of all things modern, but I soon discovered the lack of perspective, particularly in Literature, an obstacle. 'Forget meaning and just accept being. A poem doesn't have to mean anything; it can just be.' That Modernist dictum or false dichotomy also seemed to be what I was being offered from some quarters. One of my English tutors wanted to know if I was in the right subject. 'Wouldn't you be better doing Sociology or History?'

I had come north imagining a key to knowledge would be unlocked and that I would be in touch with the most up-to-date ideas around, but, somehow, while I had developed considerable expertise in reading, that overall perspective had eluded me again. If the room I found myself in was claustrophobic, it was a different kind of claustrophobia to the one I had experienced at Wonersh, and its character was one I didn't sufficiently understand at the time.

Outside of class, throughout my undergraduate career, under the tutelage and encouragement of my friend and contemporary Derek Noonan, I pursued an interest in Irish writing, but it was never an overriding one. I recall being engrossed for a time in the six volumes of Sean O'Casey's *Autobiographies* (1963), and I read more widely in modern Irish verse, and, prompted in part by Cluysenaar, I even gave some consideration to pursuing research into Austin Clarke. In later life I went on to write three books on Joyce but *Ulysses* we did in one week in my third year, with none of my tutors showing any real interest or knowledge when it came to the Dublin writer. Scottish literature was more available and I enjoyed reading Lewis Grassic Gibbon's trilogy, *A Scots Quair* (1932-4). For whatever reason I managed to miss the occasion when Craig invited down the legendary Scottish poet, Hugh MacDiarmid.

Among my contemporaries, there was a strong interest in creative writing, and poetry readings were well-attended and lively. We had entered university with our heads full of Dylan Thomas's *Under Milk Wood* (1954) and Richard Burton's 'bible-black' reading ringing in our ears. Then along came other insistent voices such as the Mersey Sound, and poets such as Allen Ginsberg and the Beats and Kenneth Patchen from the American underground. Late at night, the candles flickering in empty Chianti bottles their sides covered in newly-melted wax, we would put on the record player and listen to Leonard Cohen ('Canada's export to culture') singing moodily about Suzanne taking him down to a place near the river.

Adrian Mitchell, who was in residence for part of my undergraduate career and who was then editor of the newly launched radical newspaper *Black Dwarf*, ensured that politics carried a sharp edge. The front page of the first issue in May 1968 was dominated by words in red and black and carried an unmistakeable message from the time. At the bottom of the page a caption read: 'Go on, you lads,' as a French shipyard worker told Daniel Cohn-Bendit. Workers and students united. A later issue contains a poem by Mitchell celebrating the colour red and the importance of red paint. I remember on one occasion watching Mitchell chalk in large letters in a single line across the blackboard in Bowland lecture theatre, 'Now is the time of darkness when only light should be seen'. The Blake-inspired, performance poet then returned to the centre of the podium and began 'To Whom It May Concern (Tell Me Lies About Vietnam)'. It was one of those rare moments when I felt the earth move under my feet, and, significantly, it took place outside official class time.

*The front page of the first issue of Black Dwarf, June 1968.*

'It's wasted on the young is education,' you hear people at bus-stops say, and I understand why. I should have made more of my days as an undergraduate, and I wish I had, for it might have shortened my apprenticeship. I never much liked Lancaster as a university nor indeed the seaside town of Morecambe. In winter when the snows came, the view from Bailrigg towards the Lake District was inviting, as were the broad if treacherous sands round Morecambe Bay. But in myself I wasn't at my best, still beset by awkwardness, and I was too dismissive of things around me. My clothes told their own story for I paid almost no attention to my appearance and let my hair grow without care. If she had survived into old age, my Jewish grandmother would have whispered something in my ear, and, hopefully, I would have listened.

I fell into a certain routine and couldn't afford to be extravagant. Every week I got £10 out of my account at the National Westminster Bank in Alexandra Square, a sum which I hoped would be enough to cover meals, cigarettes, beer, and the occasional book. Few of my contemporaries had cars, and I don't believe any of my circle of friends felt particularly special, or if they did they didn't show it. Many of us, after all, were accepted into university under Clearing. We did a lot of sitting around, waiting for something to happen, and I rarely studied after 6 o'clock in the evening. In the junior seminary, every night I listened into the great silence of things, but at university I did everything I could to avoid hearing that deeply disturbing, existential note. I have a 1960s postcard of the iconic Forton Service Station on the M6 near Lancaster. It's difficult to believe now but, when this service station opened, students from the university piled into cars, and raced down the motorway to spend an evening soaking up the ambience in what looked like a control tower and watching the cars zoom by below. To save money, at the beginning and end of term I would hitch-hike back and forth to university from Worthing, a distance of over three hundred miles.

It was a period in my life when I was physically in one place but my lyrical Irish heart (or whatever it was) lay bleeding elsewhere. I was good at joining things and then leaving or saying goodbye. I participated in events at the Catholic chaplaincy, but then stopped going altogether. I helped out in social work activity such as adventure playgrounds, or the claimants union, or just visiting lonely elderly people in their homes, but none of this lasted for any length of time. It hurts me to confess that, while I was at university, I smoked on average twenty *Senior Service* cigarettes a day and played absolutely no sport.

Today it looks cramped, but in the late 1960s one of the attractive features about Bailrigg as a campus was its intimacy, and it was possible therefore to get to know a fair proportion of the student body as well as a cross-section of the staff. I mixed in all kinds of circles across a range of disciplines and was rarely on my own. I developed my talents as a folk-singer and enjoyed other evenings socialising in pubs around Lancaster. Among my contemporaries were some distinguished people who went on to make a mark in their respective fields, in academia, in the unions, in adult education, in journalism, in left-wing politics. I should have spent more time with them instead of pulling back from engagement, but that must be a common regret among those who are the first generation in their family to go to university. I made no attempt to attend the degree ceremony in July of that year and had my certificate posted to Worthing.

Was it a revolutionary decade is a question that is sometimes asked, and it's often assumed that it was. Towards the end of May 1968, one of the Paris student leaders came up to Lancaster to rally support, but any enthusiasm at the public meeting I seem to recall was restrained. That was perhaps not surprising. The most political students were driven by a need to identify with the shop floor worker, and, for a handful, this led to distributing leaflets at factory gates and, later, to securing employment as car-workers or dock-workers or wherever the seeds of militancy were pushing through. But most of us, I suspect, especially those among my contemporaries who read the tabloid newspapers in the Junior Common Room, were in denial or refused to address the question of our relationship with the working class. At best, we were troubled by the huge social divisions in Britain, but we couldn't identify a path to take us forward.

Some students who identified with the working man took to wearing donkey jackets. Hunched over the shoulders, the black jacket, with an oblong piece of imitation-leather stamped across the back staring at you like an empty billboard, evoked the world of the hod-carrier on a building site, though the softness of student hands suggested a different story. Some of my colleagues spoke gruffly of lighting a spark, as Lenin had done two generations before. In the late 1960s and early 1970s, the Trotskyist tactic of entrism re-emerged with some force, but to my mind such a tactic reflected a dilemma rather than a coherent strategy. 'Workers and students' was a good slogan, but nobody knew if the class was behind us or in front of us. For myself, I had no wish to return to the shop floor or to the kind of deadening routine which had sucked the life out of my father, and I winced when middle-class students spoke glibly about vanguards, or, more generally, when they substituted analysis for experience. At the same time, coming from a once-fashionable resort which was fairly bulging with active right-wing groups such as the recently formed Anglo-Rhodesian Society, I hated the thought of things continuing as they were, and I longed to destroy the system underlying everything.

May 1968 was the month when the so-called 'Craig affair' flared up on campus after David Craig had suggested that the accommodation at one of the colleges then being built might include mixed dormitories. The minutes of this particular meeting were leaked to the national press by one of the students present, and within forty eight hours huge sums of private investment were withdrawn from the University. The siege mentality which ensued distorted politics on the campus. It was bad enough being a student without having to face the hostility of the national and local press or the contempt of Morecambe landladies and the wider public. But, in advancing your cause, as was the case when I exited from Wonersh, you cannot always pick your moment – that was the lesson I drew from all this. It would have taken quite a leap of faith to connect the May events in Paris with the dispute over mixed dorms at a provincial university in the north of England. Craig's suggestion was patently not what Trotsky called a transitional demand, for today, at universities in Britain, mixed dorms are the norm, whereas capitalism, perhaps not as strong as it was, is still limping along.

I kept a copy of the 1968 summer issue of *John O'Gauntlet*, the student newspaper, and I return to it again to capture a flavour of the period and to revive my memories. The lead article is about a strip show which was to have been staged in Lonsdale College and the repercussions which followed when it was abandoned. It is accompanied by an article about a computer dating competition on campus, which had also run into difficulties, but this time as a result of a faulty computer programme. Also on the front page is a letter signed by three hundred and eighty people at the University condemning Enoch Powell's racism and his 'appeal to ignorance and prejudice'. In an editorial the newspaper properly came to the defence of Craig and the University against the sensationalism of the national press over 'Free Love College'. Elsewhere, under the heading 'Revolution 1789 to Weekend 1968', there is a dismissive review of Jean-Luc Godard's film *Weekend* in which the reviewer crowed about the French director's 'ideological impasse'.

What also catches my eye is a short piece on *Black Dwarf*, which was just about to be launched with Adrian Mitchell and Tariq Ali on the editorial staff.

In an interview, Mitchell indicated it would be a 'non-intellectual, broad-sheet type attack'. *The New Statesman* was 'too intellectual and out of touch with socialism: what they wanted were forthright articles and not book reviews'. The correspondent, in what was a typical kind of reactionary comment at the time, couldn't resist adding that rumours of a split among the editorial board were unfounded. It wasn't a particularly sporty university, so I don't know why so much prominence was given to the York v Lancaster sports weekend, an occasion which, as the report indicates, resulted in very little damage to University property.

My contemporaries continued reading the tabloid newspapers in the Junior Common Room, recoiled from anything which might suggest solidarity with causes, whether working-class or otherwise, and went home for weekends. Perhaps I'm being a little unfair, for, as I should be the first to recognise, being a student generates its own set of problems. It's a time when people are not at their most, but in my experience often at their least, radical. There's too much at stake in your early twenties. Lecturers have the freedom to give vent to their unease with the world but students have essays to hand in, financial worries, emotional worries, worries about their identity, troubles with landlords and with friends and associates. They also have a career in front of them, and that too in the late sixties was troubling, for my generation were among the first to realise that there were more of them as future graduates than there were interesting jobs to go round. In the previous generation, that is anyone graduating before say 1960, there was probably some sort of match between interesting graduate jobs and graduates. But with my generation all that was about to change, and some of us, especially those with a working-class background, sensed this would be the case.

It would be wrong, however, not to recognise that the world at that time was undergoing profound changes, some of which could not be defined in straightforward political terms whether in the number of sit-ins or taking to the streets in protest. I was not a reliable witness to events in part because of my background and in part because I was not fully committed to anything. In the seminary I could sense what the mood was among my contemporaries, but at university I was ever alert to the prospect of betrayal and I never trusted the student union at that time to spearhead anything I would want to follow. At the same time, there was new territory being mapped out even if it was not always visible. What seemed to come through all those years was the need for a different way of doing things. It wasn't yet the age of entitlement, but in some respects that made it all the more radical, for the exercise of power was draining away from those in authority and toward those who increasingly felt the need to be empowered. Any political party which secretly or brazenly identified with the slogan 'What we have we hold' must have been sweating.

When I departed from the shining city on the hill in June 1970, I had no intention of returning. I shook off the dust from my feet, drew an imaginary line under my years as an undergraduate, and, glancing back at the newly-built Chaplaincy Centre on the edge of the campus, headed south. By rights, from all that I had been told about the value of a degree, I should have been blessed with an abundance of confidence to face the world, but I was still the same inside, not quite sure of my identity as a person and lacking, not least, direction. That summer marked the end of a long-term relationship and at the same time a search for a new focus to my destiny obscure. I was at a loose end and I returned to Worthing to reflect on my future. I had a hankering to continue with my studies and I had no intention of going into school teaching. Within a year I would be back at Lancaster.

The five years from when I began my studies at Wonersh to finishing a degree at Lancaster had altered my view of the world and changed me as a person. They were years of intellectual ferment and emotional turmoil, but they were not years of increasing self-possession. Having said that, there was a significant amount I had either consciously acquired or unconsciously absorbed, and I believed, given the right circumstances, I would discover my voice again. Feelings of guilt, however, troubled me. That must be quite common at that age, to sense that with your first surge of freedom you had not lived up to people's expectations and that you had let yourself down. In my mind I moved back and forth rarely settling on a fixed position, but this in turn allowed a temporary solution to emerge. It became apparent that I still had some way to go before I reached a plateau in my life. An omega point, such as Teilhard de Chardin might have envisaged for the individual, was out of reach, but a plateau might be possible I reckoned. The question was: could I pick myself up and start again? I may not have been as special as I imagined when called to the priesthood in my teenage years, but I did still consider there was something special about me. Perhaps the only special thing about me was that I was a slow learner.

That summer I was hired by Brian Graver to teach English as a foreign language at a language school in Brighton. He had written a standard textbook on the subject, and it was a properly accredited school. I was grateful for all my linguistics courses, which suddenly came into play, and I felt a degree of confidence explaining tenses in the English verb or the use of phrasal verbs or the distinction between restrictive and non-restrictive relative clauses. I met with some success and, moreover, the teaching took me out of myself. Among my classes were two lively and intelligent Spanish students, Almudena and Fatima, who suggested I might go to Madrid to teach for a year. At the end of so many years of compulsion this seemed like the opportunity I needed, just on the spur of the moment to do something. A change of circumstance, a change of country, and the risk of going without having secured employment in advance. If it wasn't Kierkegaard's leap of faith, it was certainly the next best thing, a leap into the unknown.

So in early October 1970, at the age of twenty three, with thirty pounds worth of pesetas in my pocket, I caught a plane from Gatwick to Madrid to begin my Spanish interlude. The interlude might not have come to pass for I was nearly sent back without setting foot in the country, not because of my politics but because at the airport in Madrid I found myself being ushered into a line which was departing for London. Through a glass dividing compartment, I glimpsed Almudena and a welcoming party which included I think her Chilean boyfriend, Hernán, waving, but none of the officials could understand the difference between 'to' and 'from'. All they heard was 'Londres' and, from the smattering of the language I had received at John Fisher over a decade before, I couldn't supply them with an appropriate preposition. I just kept seeing in the mind I was searching an upside-down, back-to-front question-mark. 'From,' I kept repeating, 'I've just arrived from London.' Eventually, my efforts succeeded and I was allowed into the country. In spite of the welcoming party, I was effectively on my own again, this time in a city, two thousand feet above sea level, where the military and ill-mannered officials reigned supreme.

MADRID. - Puerta del Sol

*Postcard of the Puerta del Sol from around 1900, the afternoon sun high overhead, casting strong shadows everywhere. Reading a foreign city was for me essentially a struggle for perspective. This is why I like this photo, which evokes the beginnings of the electric tram and an era before the explosion of advertising hoardings. No sound distracts me, nobody clutters my view; everything is still, awaiting a novelist like James Joyce or Alfred Döblin to bring the shadows to life. And then I start recalling memories of constant noise and bustle which assaulted my senses when I was the city's guest in 1970. Next door to my flat was a* pollería, *a shop selling nothing but chickens, their dead eyes staring at me from their extended necks. In an adjacent street, a man-mountain of a butcher, his apron stained with a month's supply of animal blood, would pat a huge slab of ox liver as he served me: '¿Si, señor? ¡Dígame!' In a bar across the road I would watch as refuse collectors on their morning round stopped off to down a complimentary glass of cheap brandy; then, clambering aboard their truck, the medicine taken, they would shout back to the* tio or barman *something about receiving* ganas por la vida, *literally, appetites for life. My timetable was defined by the British Council, but everything else in the culture needed to be seen or heard.*

Chapter Nine

# A Period of Adjustment

## Spanish interlude

Madrid was the first European capital I spent any time in, and to this day, although I consider it a harsh city, I still retain an affection for it. In some ways the most remarkable thing about Madrid is that its main gathering-point is named not after some military victory or naval commander or some other kind of human triumph but after the sun: *Puerta del Sol*, gate of the sun. New Year's Eve is celebrated at the port of the sun, as are less formal parties and gatherings by families and groups. It is the hub of the city and a tribute to the pagan god which Spaniards have worshipped from antiquity. Whenever I spoke about England to my students, I could see they were thinking about the sun, or rather its absence or its puny rays in those northern latitudes. They would have been decidedly unmoved by the phrase 'when soft was the sun', a phrase used by Langland in the fourteenth century to describe Piers Plowman on settling down to enjoy his vision on a May morning among the Malvern hills. Their sun was masculine and strong, adding colour to their lives. *Sol*, hear that majestic word, high in the sky, each letter given equal weight, not to be dismissed, or trivialised, or turned into 'sunny' or 'sunset boulevard'. If that wasn't enough, it is from the *Puerta del Sol* that all parts of Spain take their measurements. Santiago de Compostela or Extremadura are so many kilometres from the *Puerta del Sol*. The whole country is in one sense defined or, under its big top, guyed thus. See the sun high in the sky, see its gate, this is our capital city. He belongs to us and we belong to Him.

My hosts had kindly found a temporary pensión for me in Argüelles, an area to the west of the city, adjacent to the wide open spaces of the Casa de Campo, and popular with university students. The pensión was a large room on the third floor with some six or eight beds in it. That first morning, I woke with the sun in my eyes and immediately checked to see if my thirty pounds' worth of pesetas was still in my pocket. Then from a narrow, sun-filled balcony, I looked down on a narrow side-street. So this was abroad, I discovered myself thinking, and much as I had imagined it, the sun also rising à la Hemingway, but then something caught my eye: a band of city workers was busy hosing down the pavements and gutters. Since February that year there hadn't been any rain. Some nine months' gestation and none of the rain which is supposed to fall on the plain in Spain had fallen. I watched as the water trickled round the tyres of the parked cars, moved along the gutters, and carried on further down the street. It was in keeping that my first impressions should focus on the city's detritus and the passage of time, accompanied almost at once by another passing thought: street-cleaning was a job that would need to be done whether or not the fascists were in power. I was hungry, so I walked up to Calle Princesa at the top of the street and soon found a welcoming restaurant, which became my home for a week or so. I pointed to what I needed and within a short space could order things without too much guilt or embarrassment.

That first week was a slightly anxious period because, without any income or bank overdraft facilities, I realised that I would be returning home if I didn't secure a teaching appointment. So I began that task in earnest. My hunch was that language schools, for whatever reason, would be short of teachers at the start of a new academic year. At one language school, which had been recommended to me, I was interviewed by an accountant and offered a position, but I didn't take it. I judged that with my degree in English from a good university in the UK, where I had undertaken courses in both language and literature (I now felt something akin to pride about my studies at Lancaster), the least they could do was ask me about how I would go about teaching English to a lower intermediate class. My next interview was at the British Institute on Calle Almagro where I was offered a split appointment, half-time in the evening teaching in the British Institute School and the other half in the morning teaching adults at the Institute itself. And so, in the middle of the Iberian Peninsula, where the picaresque novel in part originated in the work of Miguel de Cervantes, my teaching career began and with it a phase in my life that came closest to a series of memorable adventures.

In 1937 at the time of the Spanish Civil War, Auden imagined Spain as:

On that arid square, that fragment nipped off from hot
Africa, soldered so crudely to inventive Europe...

For his generation Madrid was at the heart of the struggle between the forces of democracy and fascism, and it was a view that survived. Spain's former iconic status for the European Left accompanied me during my time there, but I believe I was always more respectful, or indeed more sceptical, than Auden. Spain was more than a European invention. It was certainly never a 'fragment' and, while the Pyrenees tended to cut off the country from its northern neighbours, I wasn't terribly convinced by the patronising image of soldering or of 'inventive' Europe. Like me, Auden must have spent too long as a child studying maps. The real understanding of Spain, a country of regions and contrasts, comes not from above peering down but from long association with its history and people. I seemed to be apprised of this much from the outset.

I needed little persuading when I came across Gerald Brenan's *The Spanish Labyrinth* (1942), a thoughtful inquiry into the background to the Civil War written in its aftermath and within a few years of Auden's poem. As he suggests in his Preface:

> Spain, both economically and psychologically, differs so greatly from the other countries of Western Europe that the words of which most history is made – feudalism, autocracy, liberalism, Church, Army, Parliament, trade union and so forth – have quite other meanings there to what they have in France or England. Only if this is made clear, only if each piece of the political and economic machine is separately described, only if the provincial questions are gone into and the interactions of all the local and sectional organizations on one another are brought to light will anything like a true impression be arrived at.

In that phrase 'quite other meanings' Brenan captured something which also chimed with me. My first reaction, however, that first week on moving into my interior flat on Calle Carranza was to remove all the bulls and other heavy ornaments scattered around the room. I was English; I could do without all that. Lighten up. But then I recalled Picasso and Goya and their fascination with bull-fights. The culture was not just different; it was strange. I had my work cut out to understand it.

My salary was enough to get by and to pay for my accommodation. I was about ten minutes' walk from the Institute. I could now wander the streets like a flâneur, perhaps not as Francisco de Quevedo's *Don Dinero*, Mr Moneybags, did in the Spanish Golden Age but, at least, in the best English traditions, for I had the wherewithal to pay my way. In time I might be able to toast my Madrilenian hosts and wish them well. 'Down the hatch', or, more properly, *Salud y pesetas y tiempo para gastarlas* (health and pesetas and the time to spend them), or more simply, given that Spain once enjoyed a peasant culture, *pan y agua* (bread and water). As for sharper comparisons closer to home, my salary was as nothing compared with the riches expended on the long-haired Director of the British Institute, whose flat alone on the fashionable Paseo de Rosales was rumoured to cost the British Council in rent about twice what the highest paid teacher at the Institute earned. So much for Spanish inequalities I reflected, for Drake's children were more than able to match them.

I was expected to play the role of the Englishman abroad, telling my charges all about how the language works, along with information on the British way of life, its history and civilisation. 'You mean to say you've never seen the Cambridge colleges,' a group of my students wanted to know. 'No, I've never had the pleasure.' 'And Edinburgh? Surely you have been there? Not seen its magnificent Castle or the Royal Mile?' It was evident that this was not a well-travelled tutor standing in front of them. I was there to learn, and, as is often the case with ex-pats, I was learning as much about my native country as the one I was in. I knew, however, my place, and that was reserved for someone who had no doubts about his outsider status both in Madrid and in his own country. I was 'away' again but now I had no one to share my plight, no comrades in arms, and the only solidarity I encountered was with those students who responded to my detachment.

Increasingly, I was forced into the role of a passive and single-minded observer. In my dark flat I woke in the mornings to the sounds of pulleys and women conversing as they hung out their washing to dry in the interior shaft of the building which was open to the sky, and for some five months I entertained in my mind what they were saying about their husbands, me, and other neighbours. In my silent world I was the guest listening in to the rhythms of the host language but as yet no drops of meaning fell from the sky.

The year I spent in Spain after graduating developed my skills as an observer, and, although I didn't ever get inside the culture, I did learn to appreciate the many meanings of cultural difference. When listening to Paco Ibañez singing *'Andaluces de Jaén'*, a poem by the Thirties poet from Andalusia,

Miguel Hernández, I thought I could hear the cry of a people that in its directness was quite unlike anything I had encountered in English or in Irish writing in English:

*Andaluces de Jaén,*
*aceituneros altivos,*
*decidme en el alma: ¿quién,*
*quién levantó los olivos?*

Andalusians of Jaén,
proud harvesters of olives,
tell me from your soul, then,
who made the olive groves? (trans A.S. Kline)

While Auden imagined an 'arid square', the question posed by Hernández, who was brought up as a goatherd and farmhand, concerns ownership of the land. Indeed, the simplicity of these opening lines belies their revolutionary appeal. What do olive-pickers do but pick olives? Yes, but *'en el alma'*, in the soul, there is something else at work, and it is prefaced by *'decidme'*, tell me not what's in your mind but what's in your soul. The repetition of *'quién'*, *'quién'*, who, who, is not so much a query as a form of insistence, that it is not the owners of the *latifundia*, but you, the olive-pickers, the landless peasants who raise the crops, who are the rightful owners. 'Decide me', a phrase that moves between Spanish and English, is one we might legitimately hear hovering around these lines, for it is a poem about commitment and consciousness-raising.

Hernández, the poet from the South, is a reminder of cultural difference within Spain, but to the stranger Spain itself is a potent example of cultural difference. I enjoyed these many layers of difference. As I wandered about Madrid in those first days I was captivated by all the sweet-smelling aromas. You'd imagine with its dry, hot climate that the smells would be odours but this wasn't the case. Among my female colleagues, Spanish plumbing was a constant topic, how you couldn't know what might appear under your feet in the shower, but that I dismissed as just so much prejudice by ex-pats, who wanted the experience of an exotic country but not contact. My facetious side hoped it was indeed something real and pleasant and not a ploy by the military to pollute the air with something akin to Huxley's 'soma' in *Brave New World*

(1932). It seemed to be a mixture of flowers, scent, sugar, saffron, and sweet-smelling tobacco. I don't know where it came from. Everywhere I sauntered, there were tempting cake shops and bakers making bread on their premises and flower-sellers in brightly coloured, long skirts and older women out shopping in their slippers.

Pollution, then, wasn't the first thing to strike me about Madrid, but it soon made its presence felt. Shortly after eight o'clock in the morning, I would descend the dark, narrow stairwell of my apartment block into the fast-paced and noisy street, turn east along Calle Carranza, negotiate my way across the busy Glorieta de Bilbao, stop at a pavement café for a light breakfast, and then glance back at the way I had come. The Sirens had disappeared. Within about forty minutes the pollution from the build-up of traffic had become so visible that it covered my tracks. I was still breathing normally, or so I imagined. After all, I couldn't really complain. I took to smoking *Ducados*, a strong cigarette with black tobacco, which cost me around twelve pesetas for a packet of twenty. Only once did I suffer a coughing fit and that was returning to Madrid on a Sunday evening after a weekend in the pure air of Avila.

Unlike the unbelievably cheap *Celtas*, which came away in your hands, *Ducados*, or ducats, had, as the name suggests, a certain currency, and nothing could make me believe otherwise. Smokers after all were in the majority in those days and were well-provided for. In the hall outside the classroom students and their teachers exchanged cigarettes without a care in the world though they would inhale as if their life depended on it. You would sometimes hear people claim that brown tobacco, *tabaco rubio*, might give you cancer but black tobacco, *tabaco negro*, was fine. My throat thought otherwise and I was rarely free from the rawness that accompanies smoking cheap cigarettes. '*Córtelo*', I would hear my students shout at me when I developed laryngitis or pharyngitis. Cut it. I imagined it was a knife they were referring to, or perhaps cut it out, meaning smoking as a habit. But it was true, you have to catch throat infections early or they will give you trouble.

In English we catch things, in Spanish they cut them. There was rarely a moment when I wasn't learning about cultural difference. *Negro* and *rubio*, black and white, English and Spanish, that dramatic series of oppositions impressed me about Spain, and you could tell by hand and arm gestures in the streets that points were being made forcibly. Leave subtlety to perfidious Albion and the undemonstrative English. Students would invite me back to their family homes and show me their collection of Marx and Engels or the burn marks on their arms where they had been tortured in the prison at Carabanchel. The law students I knew, who sought a career in the diplomatic service, were more conscious of treading a fine line, and they would become irritated when the riot police entered the university campus and chased them into the bars and restaurants of Argüelles. Other students were bolder and would tell me of their *manifestación* at the weekend where they would suddenly appear outside a popular metro station such as Goya to distribute leaflets calling for the overthrow of the system and then as suddenly disappear into the metro. It was one of these courageous students, Javier, who showed me round an abandoned prison somewhere in the city. In one room we stumbled across card index files of former prisoners dating back to the 1930s and 1940s. That was quite a shock, picking up cards with a name and the offence and the prison tariff. One prisoner I remember received forty years for *rebelión militar* while a woman was given a similar tariff for having an abortion. The authorities had grown careless in the years in between, leaving evidence of their brutality.

One evening I was invited to a showing of Eisenstein's *Battleship Potemkin* at the university. The large hall was crowded with an audience expecting trouble. There were no seats, so we were all standing, with one eye on the doors for the *guardia civil* or the university police to burst in and flail us about the head with their truncheons. With every scene, the audience became more tense until the Odessa Steps sequence locked us into the revolutionary moment the film was commemorating. That was an unforgettable occasion and a reminder that solidarity creates its own audience, who in turn come to embrace works originating in wholly different historical and political contexts. In the 1930s, Louis MacNeice judged that Spain was 'ripe as an egg for revolt and ruin'. Leave aside the idea of ruin (for there was to be no repeat of the bombing of Guernica in 1937) and that is the Spain I remember in 1970-1: 'ripe as an egg for revolt'. You would have to be blind not to notice something was hatching.

I got to know Manolo better than many of my other students. The son of one of Franco's generals, his main focus in life was caring for his false finger-nails and playing the Spanish guitar. He was always in good form when we met up and voiced no convictions except to be free of convictions. In every cupboard in every room in the family apartment there were racks of quality wine. It was as if the good things of life needed to be accumulated against a possible time of scarcity and drought. One of his sisters, Belén (Spanish for Bethlehem), had been educated either in Paris or in the French school in

Madrid. His siblings were all in their early twenties and betrayed no sign of doing anything with themselves apart from living off their father's pension and drinking his wine. They were so at ease with the world, Belén in particular, with her fluent English and sophisticated manners. She made me feel very gauche whenever I met her. '*Oye*, David. Do you know Georges Moustaki?' Silence. 'In that case, let's listen to him singing "Le Temps de Vivre".' For the children of one of Franco's generals, it was indeed the time of their lives, acquiring languages, learning musical instruments, catching the night-train to Paris, and playing out in the lengthening shadow of the Generalísimo. So much sophistication based on so much brutality, the gauche boy reflected. I've often wondered what happened when Franco died, for I always associated Manolo's family not with the march of history but with the counter-movement we know as tragedy.

The closest friendship I established was with Fernando Bauluz, whom I mentioned in Chapter 4 and whom I write about in passing in *Reading Joyce*. At weekends we spent quite a lot of time exploring the cities of Castile, and then for *La Semana Santa* or Holy Week, we visited Córdoba and Seville. All those trips were memorable, not least because I was seeing Spain through the eyes of a future film director. Fernando was someone genuinely interested in people and he was keen to share his enthusiasm with his English teacher without being overbearing. But I should preface all this with some remarks about the context, for this will help when I say that my trips with Fernando allowed me some rare insights into the Spanish labyrinth.

The year I was in Madrid a famous trial of ETA members took place in Burgos. There was an embargo on news, so the court proceedings were effectively *in camera*. It was a powerful lesson I learnt, that the only way really to get to know Spain was to keep travelling, for not only were the regions decidedly different but at that time you couldn't trust the state-controlled media. If a demonstration or mass strikes were planned, the television stations would show re-runs of popular films or famous soccer victories to keep the people in their home or at work. The streets of Madrid were full of the military in uniform as they made their way to their offices or parade grounds. On-duty or off-duty, their presence was a constant reminder they existed not to protect Spain from enemies without but to suppress any opposition from within. The secret police were also probably everywhere, and I was advised not to speak too freely especially in taxis. In addition, Madrid was the administrative capital of the country, so it was top-heavy with civil servants. All this apparatus of the State contributed to the feeling voiced by some of my more politically conscious students that Madrid was not so much a special as a despised place, a centre of power which would be used against the people of the city and against the other regions of the country in particular the Basque country and Cataluña.

My first excursion into the Spanish labyrinth outside Madrid occurred one Friday afternoon in January 1971 when I caught a bus with Fernando to Cuenca. It was a month into a cold winter, and when we arrived on the outskirts of the city the first thing to greet us were what I imagined picturesque fires outside caves on the side of a mountain. These turned out to be gypsy encampments, and they formed a kind of ironic comment on the *casas colgadas* or overhanging houses, built to withstand the Moorish advance from the south, for which Cuenca is celebrated and which we had come to see. In polite society, gypsy music, the music of the *gitanos*, had a continuing attraction. Manolo, the general's son, delighted in playing such passionate music on his guitar, and one of my colleagues at the Institute, who was from what is now Zimbabwe, had come to Spain to become a flamenco dancer. The reality of course was something other, with Romany people here in Cuenca living in caves on the side of a mountain with a fire at the entrance for warmth and to ward off wolves and other predatory animals. Through the touristy eyes of a foreigner, what, I judged, could be more scandalous for a modern European country than its people living in caves. It was a shocking indictment and a throwback to a world when the first settlers arrived in Spain, and Fernando agreed, adding it was probably more shocking that people were attracted to their music while giving no thought to the social conditions which produced it.

Thankfully, there was more to Cuenca than caves, just as there was more to Madrid than blind people selling lottery tickets at street corners or others without limbs begging on the steps into the metro. It was all part of a labyrinth, designed to get your moral nerves jangling but inviting you to explore further if you could get past your initial prejudices. Fernando had the right temperament, and in the spring we were in front of a class of *gitanos* on the northern outskirts of Madrid, teaching English to a group of teenagers. It was a dangerous venture and we both knew it. We caught the metro to the terminal station and then a taxi as far as the cab-driver would dare go. Then we had a walk of a mile or so through an unclaimed landscape to the gypsy encampment where there was a garishly lit classroom with a blackboard. It was dark when we arrived but that didn't stop us. The children enjoyed our sessions and we would have continued but, as we half-expected, one of the older boys pulled a knife on Fernando and that marked the abrupt end of term. Neither of us I should add regretted our attempt to make contact with Spain's outsiders, some of whom we had observed living in caves in Cuenca.

It was a country of contrasts. In Avila of the saints, cake-shops advertised 'las yemas de Santa Teresa', the egg yolks of Saint Teresa, which, with my religious or was it my incorrigibly facetious mind, I imagined had something to do with the mystic's menstrual cycle. One afternoon when we were there, we observed a ritual which the saints must also have witnessed. On one side of the main plaza, young girls in their teens paraded up and down while on the other side paraded Avila's young men. Up and down the opposite sexes went, their darting eyes working overtime with secret glances, their fingers jabbing as they pointed across real and imaginary lines. It seemed to be the closest the sexes came to each other in that pure air, and I couldn't help being reminded not of Joyce's pun in *Ulysses* on Balfe's opera *The Rose of Castile* (rows of cast steel) but of the brand of pure white soap with the same name as the province, namely *Castile*. Later that evening there was a dramatic contrast when two flamboyant gays, dressed in deliberately outlandish gear and topped off with fedoras, strolled into the bar to order a drink. I thought they might have been set upon by the locals but they provoked barely a ripple of interest.

Not far beneath so much proper behaviour in Spain at that time there was a raging storm of emotions. On our trip to Córdoba we witnessed passionate displays of controlled emotion with the famous Holy Week processions when religious statues would be carried through the narrow streets on *pasos* or floats. From an upstairs window a woman launched into singing a *saeta*, an ancient form of religious song with links to flamenco. The float with a statue of Jesus carrying his cross momentarily stopped, the crowd stilled, and the woman with outstretched arms sang what seemed to be extempore, making up the melody and impassioned lyrics as she went along. So vivid was the performance and indeed the whole scene that the statue itself seemed to come to life, and it could have been Mary Magdalene addressing Jesus all over again two thousand years ago on his way to Golgotha and the place of the skull. Those carrying the heavy float then exchanged places with others in the group and, with a jolt to remind everyone that it was only a statue, the procession continued.

The Maundy Thursday processions in Seville were on a grander scale and we decided to follow the famous exit of *La Macarena* from her basilica to the Cathedral. I think it was close to midnight when she made her appearance. The crowds were expectant and gave her a welcome as if the statue of Our Lady of Hope was a modern celebrity. Protecting her as she emerged was a group of *Nazarenos*, or Nazarenes, young men in tunics who were determined to show whose team that night was best. '*La Macarena!*' shouted the crowd, which was answered by the *Nazarenos*, '*Guapa!*' '*Guapa*' is what you'd hear young men saying about a pretty young woman as they passed her in the street. 'What a cracker!' 'My, what a beauty!' '*La Macarena!*' '*Guapa! Guapa! Guapa!*' If Córdoba was marked by intense religiosity, the procession we followed in Seville was something other, a kind of pagan ritual that had gathered into it a reverence for the ideal of virginity together with a hope that the marked-out virgin might make herself available to me alone. *La Macarena* was after all a woman of hope.

Later that night, after the crowds had retired, we dropped into the Cathedral. There in the pews toward the back of the Cathedral was a stylishly-dressed young woman still wearing a mantilla passionately kissing with her boyfriend or it could have been a casual pickup. Here, too, the Spanish labyrinth was at work, inviting me to make sense of it all if I could. One minute you believed you were embarked on this kind of evening or this kind of discourse, only to discover it was something else or something other. No wonder surrealism took hold in modern Spain. One minute at the cinema you are watching a party gathering in a bourgeois setting, the next minute Buñuel is sending in the sheep and the exterminating angel.

After about five months I began to have dreams where I spoke in Spanish. '¡*Cállete, niño!*' I heard myself shouting as the class began to get out of control, and at the same time I would search for the plural of 'you' because I knew '*te*' was only used in the singular. '¡*Dígame!*' I imagined saying picking up the phone (which I never used in Spain). '*Hay nata,*' which was a sign in the window of a restaurant indicating it had an artificial, sweetened, double cream. There's nata here, always a good sign for those, like me, who perused a menu in reverse order. '*Es nada mas que una tontería,*' (it's nothing more than a piece of nonsense) would also find its way into my night-time reveries. *Tontería* was a word I heard all the time when I was in Madrid. I'm told it's still in common use, but even my students, who were more articulate than the average person in the street, would resort to it. In fact, the impression created to me as a foreigner was that everything in the world could have *tontería* attached to it.

*Claro*, everything was potentially an example of trivia. Nothing was serious. He or she or they were not just *tonto* or *tonta* or *tontos* but examples of a *tontería*, as was a television soap or a novel. It was such a silly word that I couldn't get it out of my head.

I wonder if the streets still echo to words and phrases such as *los domingeros*, Sunday afternoon drivers, that is anyone who drove slowly, or making a *puente* or bridge between a Thursday feast day such as Corpus Christi and the weekend, a reference that is to taking a mini-holiday. And I wonder if with the coming of democracy there has been a decline in the use of *enchufe*, a word I heard all the time to describe favouritism or unfair influence in the conduct of business and social life.

But even as I was making some inroads into the language I never overcame my sense (or at times my fear) that no matter how long I stayed abroad I would never get inside the culture. As Christopher Isherwood also discovered in pre-war Berlin, the foreign language teacher is positioned thus. I was essentially an observer or a camera, confined to the terraces, enjoying things by proxy, once again called on but not chosen. It was a lonely sort of existence, more than I have conveyed here. Jangling a set of heavy keys and hurrying down the empty street when he heard me clapping my hands, a thick-set, small Galician porter, who took refuge against the cold inside a doorway or shelter, would let me into my block of flats after dark.

As I strolled aimlessly of an evening through the Glorieta de Bilbao consuming a *bocadillo de calamares*, I would notice headlines in the newspapers referring to events in Latin America, for Madrid was like a gateway to a vast southern continent, a continent which I judged would become increasingly important as the future of the world unfolded. While in Spain, I entertained the idea of teaching in Cuba and even went so far as to contact someone behind closed doors at the Cuban Embassy, who told me to apply in London. There was something romantic after dark coming across bands of students wearing ponchos bringing the music of the Andes to the streets of a European capital. But there was nothing romantic when I learned that some of the children in my classes in the evening, who would arrive in chauffeur-driven cars, were the offspring of deposed Latin-American dictators.

My sojourn in Spain was part of a continuing period of adjustment, and I returned to England with a stronger commitment to politics and to changing the world. The first Director of the British Institute in Madrid was Yeats's friend, Walter Starkie, and under his guidance from 1940 to 1954 the Library had been well-stocked with modern Irish writing. This deepened my interest in the subject, and on heading home I began research under David Craig at Lancaster on Anglo-Irish literature from 1800 to 1940. 'Anglo-Irish' was then the preferred term for Irish writing in English. I was keen to show the connections between literature and society and to make a contribution to understanding why Ireland has produced so many great writers in the modern period. I should have spent more time reflecting on my choice of university but I had no contacts with academics in recognised centres for the study of Irish writing such as Dublin or Cambridge, and, moreover, a three-month postal strike in Britain had also cut me off from the world. Had I not returned to Lancaster, I would never have met my lifelong partner.

## Apprenticeship

If in 1971 you wanted to pursue almost any topic in Irish Studies, you were heading for trouble. August 1971 marked the beginning of Internment in Northern Ireland and an upsurge in violence across the region. Thereafter the Troubles only became more intense, the mood more sombre, and for those bent on quiet reading it grew increasingly difficult to keep politics at a distance. This was the background to those early years of my research into Irish writing. As I drove down into Irish history, there was a constant interruption from the present. Indeed, it was quite a struggle to identify what was background and what was foreground. The political situation was providing a resurgence in the colonial encounter between Britain and Ireland, but my research concerned quieter, more literary questions, at first into writers from County Clare and the province of Munster but then into the relation between fiction and society beginning in the first half of the nineteenth century with Maria Edgeworth and William Carleton. How would I connect what was happening in the present with what happened in the past, or should I have addressed the dilemma in a much more direct fashion and undertaken work on contemporary writers from Ulster? Perhaps I should have applied what I had learnt about the Spanish labyrinth to the Irish situation, for in many ways that is what I was absorbing at this time, that there was an Irish labyrinth which embraced history and the present, politics and literature.

This is what can happen when politics is so intrusive, it threatens to monopolise all the space. Writers in the North took the lead in distinguishing their writing from what was happening on the streets. It was their way of responding to events and marked a refusal to retreat behind the traditional lines of their tribe as it were. Writing should act not as the expression of tribal beliefs or prejudices but as a gesture toward utopia, a world free from sectarianism. There was a certain irony about such a response and yet it was not without a history. Yeats, at the height of the Irish Civil War in 1922-3, pacing the battlements at the top of his tower at Ballylee on the Clare-Galway border, reflected on the little room that was Ireland: brothers, dressed in one kind of uniform, killing brothers, dressed in another. With its play on Killaloe, a monastic settlement in County Clare, 'Killallwho' is how Joyce the exile puts it in *Finnegans Wake*, a book that bears the scars of the Civil War, the period when he began his last great work. Kill all who are different, or, given that we're referring to a civil war or civil strife, kill all who are the same as you, farmers, labourers, members of the working class, or from the same family or who have the same surnames. Only rarely it seems to me have writers taken to the barricades as Liberty does in the famous painting by Delacroix, leading the people. In times of heightened political agitation, as was the case in Northern Ireland in the 1970s, writers did well to carry any sort of torch. That seems to be the political lesson to have come out of those bleak years.

I was no different to anyone else. I was observing a tragic story unfolding and I felt I should do something about it. But how would a cross-channel perspective help when lines were so sharply drawn? I continued with my reading, all the time agitated about something else. Left-wing groups in Britain tended to be pro-republican and some of them interpreted what was happening in the North as parallel to Vietnam in the 1960s. If the IRA could defeat the British Army then this would have repercussions internationally. But that would mean backing a movement whose social policies at that time had little to recommend them. And, besides, what would you do with the million Protestants who didn't want to live in a united Ireland? In retrospect, the early 1970s was a period that had 'cul-de-sac' written all over it. The hopes of the Civil Rights movement in 1967 had turned sour and had forced people back into their traditional allegiances. It would take a generation, and another generation, to begin to rediscover politics anew. The Left in Britain were also found wanting. As the early 1970s confirmed, interest in Irish politics has for the most part only ever been fitful, half-hearted, instrumental, or romantic. I kept up my research extending my reading and auditing the MA in modern literature.

When Williams published *The English Novel from Dickens to Lawrence* in 1970, it followed closely Leavis's *The Great Tradition: George Eliot, Henry James, Joseph Conrad* (1948). Williams selects a different set of authors and enlarges the historical frame, but he, too, like Leavis, is interested in a cultural tradition and in the idea of succession and continuity. The two accounts belong together as striking examples of critical compression and distillation, each critic conscious of how a novelist comes to represent a particular line or shift in the culture. Their approaches differ. Williams sought to extend the work of Leavis to allow for materialist or social contexts, whereas Leavis has in his sights the upholding of a distinctive set of values in writing. When I was at work on Irish writers there was very little by way of an equivalent body of criticism on which to draw. As was only proper, modern Irish history tended to be dominated by political history or church history. There were the beginnings of an interest in economic history, particularly around the Famine of the 1840s, and in social history. Literary history was distinguished by its attention to single authors. Irish cultural history was still in its infancy.

I should have begun with a conventional survey of the field and addressed the issue of my potential contribution, but I was devoting all my time to reading round the topic and not enough to reading through the topic. With the Anglo-Irish novelist Maria Edgeworth I became interested in her position vis-à-vis Irish writing compared with Jane Austen and her influence on English writing. I was intrigued by Edgeworth's sharply articulated political themes versus Austen's concern with manners and less overt or buried political themes. With William Carleton, the pre-Famine writer who came from a family of small farmers in Ulster, I was drawn into a comparison with Dickens, and always the Irish writer came off the worse. How to integrate material became a concern for me. There was social commentary, gothic elements, bits and pieces from an oral tradition, plot contrivances, larger than life characters, representative types, clichéd romantic scenes, authorial comment – how could I see a way of handling all this or grounding it? Moreover, the Irish novelist was always looking over his or her shoulder at the 'sister kingdom' whereas the English novelist just got on with the task in hand. In the wake of the Act of Union in 1801, the issue of Irish identity did not subside but intensified. For a young researcher in the early 1970s I needed a body of critical work to take me forward, and I also needed not always to see limitations as limitations but to understand them in a wider, more enabling framework.

In February 1972 I spent a fortnight in Belfast with a colleague and friend I had taught with at the British Institute in Madrid. Shivaun, who came from a large Catholic family, would frequently confess she was a rebel without a cause, but when she returned home in 1971 she discovered a cause. A week after Bloody Sunday we took part in a march in Newry to protest against those murders in Derry. When we arrived we parked in the centre of town and were given tissues or face-cloths to protect us against teargas and little cards in the shape of a coffin emblazoned with the number 13. Trouble was expected, but the size of the crowd made that unlikely. We were buzzed by an army helicopter and someone in a suitably imperious voice informed us that the march was illegal and that we should make our way home. The march proceeded peacefully, though no one was certain there wouldn't be a repetition of the previous week. It was dark when we came to retrieve the car, by which time the centre of Newry had been cordoned off. Crouching in every doorway was a soldier with blackened face and automatic rifle at the ready.

Belfast at that time was a war-torn city, or perhaps it's better to say it was a city turned in on itself. One evening one of Shivaun's sisters took us to the Markets area in Belfast to visit a friend who lived in a terraced street at the end of which stood an obtrusive and smelly gasometer, glowering. The house was about the size of my childhood home on Newland Road with an outside toilet. The family, minus the father, were all there in the front room, and we spoke about the situation, how the Army would regularly enter the area and 'lift' people, and how Catholics in the North had been abandoned by the Dublin Government and by people living south of the border. The house abutted onto the pavement, so you could hear every passing murmur and agitated footstep outside. It was apparent that these people enjoyed almost no protection from their immediate environment or from the wider social and political forces at work. All of us then made our way to an upstairs social club nearby, which was full of women but no men for they had all been 'lifted' in the autumn as part of the Internment process. Here I thought was Yeats's little room, except that whereas the poet imagined it full of hate what I encountered was a warm welcome for someone who could protest his family hailed from County Clare but who spoke with an English accent.

Let me come at this again. If you were engaged on an apprenticeship in Irish Studies in the early 1970s, you could do worse than spending time in

Belfast. As you stepped outside to go for a drink in the evening, you would catch the sound of gun-shots coming from some part of the city. Returning indoors you would phone the security services to ascertain the location, and then drive to a different part of the city. You never sat against the outside wall of a pub or restaurant and you found comfort in bars which had a wire-mesh round the outside of the building. That much was certain, but one evening listening to a group playing traditional Irish music we got into conversation with them only to discover something unexpected. Shivaun mentioned she was teaching in a Catholic secondary school in Downpatrick, and the conversation ended awkwardly when one of the musicians retorted: 'You only have to teach them, we have to fight them.' That was a bit of shock, for Shivaun and I considered we had a fairly sure touch when it came to distinguishing Catholics from Protestants, but we then realised afterward that traditional music in the North cuts across tribal boundaries, or, rather, it could cut across such boundaries, for this was a Protestant group playing traditional music.

*At the top of Yeats's tower at Ballylee on the borders of County Clare and County Galway. Taken around 1977 on a day when there was a break in the clouds. The view of the surrounding countryside today is much as it was in the 1920s when Yeats lived here.*

There were prejudices, then, on all sides, and communities, whether they wanted it or not, were in the process of returning to their own. At that time Shivaun's family lived in a mixed street, and in a house opposite there was an elderly Protestant woman I enjoyed talking to. She would refer to her son Earl (or he might have been Errol), who lived away, as a 'Markist'. This took me some time to work out and I didn't have the heart to ask her. No, he wasn't employed at Marks and Spencer but was in fact a Marxist. On another occasion we drove to visit a friend who lived on a mixed estate on the outskirts of the city. On approaching the estate we glimpsed ahead of us one of the many paramilitary checkpoints which had sprung up across the North, this time manned by a Protestant group. 'Have you any rosary beads on you?' Shivaun's sister turned to me anxiously before we pulled up. 'If you have, throw them out of the window immediately or hide them.'

Repeatedly, throughout this strange period, a sense of one's common humanity was being trampled on or squeezed. Under pressure, indeed more so under pressure, fellow-feeling was something you wanted to hang onto. People you met gave the impression they knew something they shouldn't know or had seen something they shouldn't have seen. In Shivaun's family when the death of a British soldier was announced on the radio, her parents stopped what they were doing, bowed their heads, and said a prayer for the soldier and his family. On the landing above the stairs hung a framed portrait of Robert Emmet, the leader of a failed rising in 1802 against the British connection, and Shivaun's elderly father would speak of the 'Imperial Parliament', meaning Westminster. But their political allegiance refused to countenance killing people. For them no amount of injustice could justify that. Their attitude wasn't a form of stoicism but more like tolerance learnt from the crucible of a troubled history, and it issued from a more noble tradition which understood how a wound took time to heal, for at some point the talking would have to begin again. I admired this attitude, especially as my pro-nationalist and pro-republican feelings were at their most intense. It cautioned me to think again about what I was coming increasingly to recognise in the light of my experience in Spain as the Irish labyrinth.

I understood why Shivaun in Spain had felt she was a rebel without a cause, for, like many of us who went to university in the 1960s as first generation, identity was linked too closely to the issue of one's family and class or religious background, from which we were hoping to escape. Identity was not something you wanted necessarily to wear as a label pinned to your lapel, but that was what was happening in the North. You were being forced back, co-opted, enlisted. 'Oh, so you went to such and such a school. You must be a Catholic.' 'Oh, you worked in the shipyards or in this particular hospital or brewery. You must be a Protestant.' I'm sure it was true for others as it was for me that identity veered too close to claustrophobia for comfort. In spite of left-wing and republican sympathies, I was not a fully signed-up member of anything. At the same time I was not a rebel without a cause. As I began to rethink the nature of identity and engagement in an era increasingly defined as post-Civil Rights and post-1968, I felt things on hold.

Little by little the months I spent in Ireland during the spring of 1972 changed me. When I arrived at my aunt's cottage in County Clare after the unsettling few weeks in Belfast, I found it difficult to express my feelings on the North. It was like being in a different country, which, of course, given the border, it, legally, was. I had heard the cock crowing again in the North, but nothing could wake the sleepy West from its slumbers. As a child, I rather took to the slow pace of life west of the River Shannon, but now that seemed like an obstacle blocking the road to rationality and the future. Two generations before, in the aftermath of the Easter Rising, the electorate in County Clare voted in Eamon de Valera in a famous landslide election, and throughout the nineteenth century the so-called Banner County could be relied on to rally their banners behind nationalist candidates and land reformers. Indeed, in 1831, a celebrated, advanced social experiment took place at Ralahine when a co-operative society was established on the estate of John Vandeleur in Newmarket-on-Fergus. I had been through something intense and imagined it might be of interest to share that with those who lived in the same country south of the border, but the traveller to foreign lands was in for an even greater shock on his return.

One evening, some elderly neighbours, on their way home from a drinking session in Liscannor, arrived at my aunt's cottage, and, propped up against the dresser, began singing together 'The West's Asleep', a song written in the 1840s for *The Nation* by Thomas Davis. Gaining confidence from each other, they moved steadily toward the final stanza when they eventually found the lift of the 'Hurrah!' they were waiting for:

And if, when all a vigil keep,
The West's asleep! the West's asleep!
Alas! and well may Erin weep
That Connacht lies in slumber deep.

But, hark! a voice like thunder spake,
'The West's awake! the West's awake!'
'Sing oh! hurrah! let England quake,
We'll watch till death for Erin's sake!'

We all cheered the successful execution of what is quite a difficult, ruminative song to sing. 'Good man, Peter! Fair play to you, Timmy! And you, Jimmy! You've still got it in you.' I should have responded more enthusiastically, but, somewhere deep inside, out of reach of my conscious mind, I was hearing not the strains of an heroic past, merely its echo. I was in an agricultural labourer's cottage, cottages which had been built after the Land War in the 1880s in part to defuse the continuing unrest in the countryside and to separate out the nationalist from the social question, and I was observing some of the locals giving voice to a rallying cry against the old enemy, and this at a time when the British Army was intimidating and interning Catholics in the North and the singers themselves largely indifferent to, or ignorant of, their plight. There was something depressingly ironic about all that. The armoured vehicles I had witnessed swaggering almost through the Victorian streets of Belfast only weeks before showed little sign the enemy was quaking. On the contrary, 'well may Erin weep,' I heard myself repeating.

The songs about the West, which I, too, throughout my teenage years enjoyed singing, were defiant, and spoke of revenge and resentment among the families of hill-siders, of making way for the bold Fenian men, and of taking the fight to the Saxon stranger. Several people independently told me, with the Black and Tans in mind, the old blood coursing again through their veins, how they would resist any future invasion if one were to be attempted. But this kind of talk or bravado was as far as the connection with the present, or the contemporary relevance of the songs, would go or allow. In the second half of the twentieth century, Clare people, the gentlest of people, had been increasingly confined to the role of passive spectators rather than active participants in events. I would have been surprised if any of those I knew had journeyed to Dublin to burn down the British Embassy in the weeks following the shooting dead of the thirteen people in Derry that year. In some ways that's not so remarkable. Each year, the Tolpuddle Martyrs are venerated for their role in the beginnings of trade unionism in Britain, but the pretty Dorset village today, with its picture-postcard, thatched cottages, betrays almost no sign of wanting to overthrow the status quo.

Repeatedly, then, news bulletins on Irish television carried reports of violence from the North, but there was a certain ambivalence in the South. One or two politicians advocated some sort of military intervention or covert supply of weapons to the IRA. At the other extreme, some (possibly the majority) hoped it would all go away. One of my close friends in the Irish Labour Party considered – perhaps not unwisely in retrospect – that you shouldn't have a policy on the North. On a prominent wall on the road to Ennistymon on the outskirts of Ennis, someone had scrawled the slogan 'Up the IRA'. It was dismissed at the time as the work of corner boys and not a reflection of those who were serious about politics, and in time it faded. Through it all, I was beginning to discern, firstly, how the chains with a radical tradition in the past had been broken or were no longer visible as such, and, secondly, how complex was the Irish labyrinth when you were in the middle of it.

Most days, the clouds queued up and the winds from the Atlantic drove in without respite, but nothing could shake the claustrophobia which was all around me. Indeed, few people showed any real interest in learning about what a city is like when the bombs are exploding. It felt as though I was speaking out of turn and being accused of something, of whipping up emotions for example, or, worse, of being an agitator. 'Let the cock crow' seemed to be the attitude. 'We have our own lives to lead down here, and, besides, we're now looking to join the Common Market. The North will only bring trouble to this island.' One of my favourite uncles, who belonged to the period of ancient myth and showed little appreciation of the thing we call history, would tell me with utter conviction in his voice: 'Those troubles will only end when they reach Loop Head and drown in the sea.'

I was reminded again of the frog with the amputated leg wriggling in the palm of my hand, which as a child I had brought in from the newly-mown meadow in Caherbarna to show to our elderly neighbour, Denny Guerin, and how he rounded on me: 'Take that thing out of the house, and leave it where you found it.' Without my realising it, perhaps it was the case that everyone was trying to protect me from myself, calling me back to the protection offered by the family, tribe, or parish. Could history, I began to ask myself, repair itself like nature without too much outside intervention or interference, and was history in the North now taking its natural, if bloody, course? Leave it where you found it.

In retrospect, I now see that what informed my thinking throughout these years was an attempt to redraw the map of literature and history to take account of the periphery and the margins. Today, we might define such an approach under the general heading 'localism', but it would be misleading to conclude that was my direction of travel. A dominant ideology can make use of localism to advance its cause and to forward its own ends. It suited a Whig-influenced historian such as George Cornewall Lewis in 1836 to call his study of agrarian agitation in the eighteenth century *On Local Disturbances in Ireland*. For, as every Head Teacher knows, it is convenient to claim that only a handful of unruly pupils are disrupting the work of the school as a whole. Not unlike Sean O'Faolain and Kate O'Brien in their novels in the 1930s, what I sought was some kind of shift in how the regional and the local were conceived. Occasionally, when reading Ascendancy writers such as Yeats and Lady Gregory on rural Ireland, I felt a certain resentment that they claimed ownership over the people I came from, treating them as examples in a larger argument against English influence in Ireland. At the time I found it difficult to articulate, but what I sought was the overthrow of such models of thinking in favour of a world where everyone could speak for themselves.

I could have been undone by so much youthful confusion and contradiction and talk of Irish identity, but, ironically, it's important to witness things close up to acquire some kind of perspective. Equally, I had observed enough to convince me that it would take me years to make any sensible contribution to Irish Studies. I felt that was part of my apprenticeship as a researcher, and I don't regret these early years not having a neatly defined programme nor being allowed by my tutor to find my own feet. Some kinds of encounters or passages of history take decades before they are absorbed by the mind or bear fruit.

People I come into contact with sometimes assume because I don't wear my heart on my sleeve that I'm not political, but all my training has been in the art of discerning a way through to a different kind of politics, a politics of hope which is impatient with the present and with much of what passes for politics. You don't always have to shout to be heard. Many people in Britain and elsewhere seem content to accept the view, repeated *ad nauseam* by my tutor when I was doing 'A' Level British Constitution in 1966, that 'politics is the art of the possible', but to my mind the 'possible' is never a given but always in need of unpacking or deconstructing.

A politics of hope not infrequently throws things up in the air and forces its adherents to reconsider past, present and future. In May 1986, a month after Chernobyl, at the invitation of Dorothea Siegmund-Schultze, I gave a paper at an Irish conference in Halle in the German Democratic Republic (GDR), and I happened to quote in passing a phrase about aesthetics being the ethics of the future. Two of the participants found this a genuinely insightful observation, and they joined me afterward in a small group discussion. They would have been active members of the Communist Party whose thinking would have followed fairly conventional lines of inquiry. Suddenly, there was something new in their lives, a comment that intrigued them and I could see them working with it.

I was more interested in why there was no premium on beauty in the culture or their lives, in why, for example, William Morris was missing from their pantheon of the great and the good. Halle, which was Handel's birthplace, had not been destroyed in the War, and it would have been an attractive city if the facades of the buildings had been cleaned up and if the Coketown-like pollution issuing from the huge chemical works on the edge of the city had been choked off. 'Never mind about the future,' I said. 'What about the present?' 'Oh, we don't have the money for that kind of thing. We have a team of six workers currently attending to buildings in Berlin. Halle is next in line.' In the GDR, beauty belonged not to Marx's economic base but to its ideological superstructure, determined but not determining, closer to a facade than to an informing structure. To my two listeners, the subsequent question I posed was a simple one, 'Do you not think Morris has something to contribute to our continuing understanding of Marx?' After the fall of the Berlin Wall in 1989, the question was put on hold but to my mind it hasn't gone away.

When I travelled to the GDR for conferences in the 1980s, I would rely on a politics of hope to see me through. I realised how difficult it was for academics there to get hold of material, so I would bring over with me a bag filled with modern literature books. I was told about a group of lecturers at the Humboldt University in Berlin who hatched a plan to buy a photocopier in West Berlin, undertake a one-day course while there in repairing the machine, then trundle it back through the border crossing. That way they could copy chapters of books borrowed from the UK's Inter-Library Loan service at Boston Spa. It struck me as a fairly hopeless venture, for photocopiers at that time kept breaking down, sometimes on a daily basis, and I came to see it as further proof, even though it was only a tiny example, that the system as a whole was at breaking point. However, I had to admire the resourcefulness of academics in tight circumstances, and I might have done the same. I could just imagine them returning the machine for its annual service across Check Point Charlie and reporting back on the conversation with East German officials (some of whom had once subjected me to a menacing, full-scale search and interrogation at Friedrichstrasse).

My visits to the GDR began with an invitation from Horst Höhne, who was a leading academic and critic. He wrote extensively on Shelley and Keats, and invited me on several occasions to what was then known as the Wilhelm-Pieck-Universiteit in Rostock. I stayed in his large, well-proportioned, first-floor flat, which had been built in the 1950s, when hope for a better future was in the air. As soon as I was ushered in out of the cold and the damp of an autumn evening, I recall noticing the handsome, wooden parquet flooring and the secondary glazing. One day he showed me a folio edition of Luther's Bible, dating from the 1530s, which had come down through the family of his wife, Barbara. After placing it on the dining table beside the light-filled window, he began reading verses from the Sermon on the Mount. Somehow, he made Luther's German, with its use of Saxon dialect, sound like its linguistic cousin, English.

On another occasion, we were surrounded by a group of middle-aged academics from all over what used to be called the 'socialist countries' of Eastern Europe. They were discussing the past and the difficulties of the present, when, suddenly, Horst produced the sword that accompanied him as a boy of sixteen when he rode into battle on horseback against the Russian Army. He told me afterward how he had participated in one of Hitler's last, desperate measures towards the end of the War, and how his unit had encountered a Panzer division in retreat, but nothing the tank commanders said would prevent the boys from fighting in the Fuhrer's cause. When he was captured, he was surprised to discover that the Russian peasantry farmed the land, for they had been told the enemy were just primitive people, without agriculture. He was then marched back into Germany and passed through his home village, where he caught sight of his mother for the last time. After the War came another momentous change in his life when he joined the Communist Party.

My first introduction to Horst, which took place at York Station, was, appropriately, like something out of a John le Carré novel. For at least thirty minutes we paced up and down on one of the platforms under the vaulted, Victorian canopy, suspiciously eyeing each other, before I approached a person in a pale blue suit to ascertain if he was the East German Professor I was supposed to be meeting. Thereafter, I got to know him well, and his knowledge of English literature and western culture rarely failed to impress me. When commenting on Keats's line 'A thing of beauty is a joy for ever', he focussed on the one word 'thing', a word that to him was, really, the German word *Ding*, and then proceeded to invoke Luther's project in using plain language and, more widely, the line in German philosophical thinking from Hegel to Marx on externalisation and reification. In that one move, taking his cue from the cockney poet, Keats, he launched into a discussion about aesthetics and politics from a historical and materialist perspective, at the same time reminding his audience of the positive gloss that could be given to the 'thinginess' of things. Horst was a compelling speaker and unbelievably responsive to the tenderness in Keats's later correspondence, but, with my long-standing interest in words rather than things, I found myself drifting off. At the outset, Keats must have had the opening line to *Endymion* (1818), for you couldn't imagine him beginning with 'An item of beauty' or 'Something that is beautiful'. That tentative phase in his poetic career was behind him.

After 1989, we corresponded occasionally, but we never managed to meet up again. I would try and encourage him to compile a memoir of his life, for that would have been quite something. Our paths seemed to cross at the wrong time, for in the 1980s I was increasingly looking to hope and the future and Horst to making history in a more practical way. Coming from Thatcher's Britain, where the very idea of society had been called into question, all his talk about 'our hospital' and 'our school' and even 'our working-class housing estates' would surprise me as he took me on a tour of the Baltic capital in his noisy, three-gear Trabant, a car which, he delighted in informing me, never broke down.

Horst's insistence on 'our' provoked several responses inside me. I didn't find it reassuring or indeed a sign of hope, but, rather, cloying and premature. After all, flying by night across the dark skies of East Germany and then hitting a wall of light on coming into land in West Berlin was a reminder that socialism had some way to go to compete with the dynamism of capitalism, and it looked increasingly unlikely that it would be given the chance to continue in such a form in the 'socialist countries'. When the Wall did come down in 1989, just over forty years after the country's birth as a democratic republic, there was surprisingly little resistance. It was as if the older generation had been unable to pass on the flame to the next. Of course, if capitalism fails in the century to come or loses its appeal, people might revert to development along socialist lines.

I think the appearance of the sword and Horst's story about the cavalry unit was designed to turn the discussion away from the awful past which had engulfed that whole generation. Anything which he couldn't pull along from the past, which he couldn't integrate or in some way own, Horst was given to dismissing. The sword had become an empty signifier, poetry a thing of beauty. However, joining the Left Opposition in western Europe after 1989 was, I suspect, temperamentally a step too far. I never did discover how he came to lose the sight in one eye.

Returning to the early 1970s, this was a particularly bleak period across the world. Along with many others I was deeply affected by the CIA-backed coup against Salvador Allende in September 1973, a coup which was the quickest in modern history and in many ways the most poignant. But today it is also apparent that the tender songs of the Chilean folk-singer, Victor Jara, for example, will outlast those who attempted to silence him. As his signature song, 'Manifiesto', reminds us, he didn't sing for singing's sake but to be heard. His *guitarra trabajadora*, his worker's guitar, carried in its heart a message, and part of that message is now from the other side of the grave, and even more poignant therefore. Appropriately, the phrase that stands over his grave in the cemetery in Santiago is '*Hasta la victoria*', towards victory. Chile and Ireland. Loss and struggle. As I learnt from my Irish grandmother: 'Never give in. Never give up.' *Siempre será canción nueva*. Always there will be a new song, a reference both to the Chilean folk-song movement associated with Allende and *Unida Popular* or the Popular Unity Party, and also, more generally, to the idea of rebirth in struggle. The accent on *siempre* reverberates long after the song has finished, but perhaps only those whose lives are surrounded by suffering can vouch for the truth of that final line.

I often return in my mind to the 1970s and 1980s and to what those years taught me about the movement of history and about the importance not so much of 'the pleasures of hope' in Thomas Campbell's comforting phrase from the Romantic period and 'the boundless fields of rapture yet to be' as of never abandoning hope. When defeat threatens, regroup and bide your time, and give the next generation something to do. Three decades later, the theme of loss and struggle surfaced as an extended argument in *Light, Freedom and Song*, my cultural history of modern Irish writing. As it happens, I took the title from Tom Moore's 'Dear Harp of My Country', a highly-charged, sentimental song of hope, which in turn issued from the long period of repression in Ireland before and after the Act of Union in 1801. Not infrequently, as I reflect on history and literature I find myself dwelling on the movement back and forth, on chords, and, then, on the music of all those who share a destiny obscure.

In the summer of 1973 we moved down to the pretty village of Meldreth, south of Cambridge, where, behind a high wall opposite, one of our neighbours, an elderly couple, dressed for candle-lit dinner attended by maids and servants. My partner began teaching at a comprehensive school in Letchworth and I found some part-time teaching at a language school in Cambridge. At the same time I continued reading in Cambridge University Library. I pored over material in the Bradshaw collection of Irish ballads, all the time trying to discern how they might be incorporated into my research on Irish writing. My interest in the oral tradition stemmed from an apprenticeship in my grandmother's cottage in Caherbarna, and I knew at some stage all that knowledge would pay off and I would find a way of bringing it back into my life. When I read Bob Dylan's autobiography *Chronicles* (2004), the sentence that leaps out at me is 'Folk songs were the underground story'. The 'invisible republic' is how Greil Marcus describes Dylan's lifelong quest, a phrase quoted with approval by the singer. I was reminded of the proximity of the adjectives 'underground' and 'invisible' to some of the guiding principles which inform my own memoir.

I could have done something with such insights if they had been available to me, for I too had been involved in a similar search or driven by the same belief. But it took me years and my Yale cultural history before I hit upon the Irish dark as an overriding theme governing modern Irish writing. The early 1970s was also a period when, in search of the absent, Irish Turgenev and of voices like Miguel Hernández, European writers who impressed me as having an integral connection with the people or whose sympathies were particularly engaged by their continuing plight, I read the work of the political activist Peadar O'Donnell and Liam O'Flaherty, the 'elemental' novelist from the Aran Islands, whose short stories I particularly admired at that time. However, nothing would distract me from the more ambitious task, encouraged by my tutor, of providing a reading of modern Irish writing as a whole.

The reading was progressing but the thesis wasn't, and at the end of that second year I came to the conclusion that I would need to go into secondary teaching to fund any future research. Without the necessary qualifications I couldn't guarantee that I would obtain an academic appointment, and, financially, I felt I was a drain on my partner. There is nothing more embarrassing than being asked in a busy bank in front of other customers to hand over your cheque book. That is what happened to me in the centre of Cambridge at this time. 'No, your branch at Lancaster are not prepared to lend you any more money, and, moreover, they want us to collect your cheque book.' Red-faced, a penniless Pierce exited that branch, cursing the system that had so reduced me to the status of an apprentice in financial matters. 'Be sure your sins will find you out,' my mother would regularly quote at us as children. Now, I could add to that proverb one of my own: 'Be sure your finances will find you out.'

In September 1973 I began a twelve-month postgraduate course in secondary school training at Balls Park College in Hertford, a college accredited by the University of Cambridge. It was a new venture, but I believed I might eventually secure an appointment in higher education, perhaps at a teacher-training college, at which point I might continue with my research in earnest. And I might then be able to open a new account, but I vowed it would be with a more sympathetic bank.


## School again

After a year's training, during which time I taught several local classes for the Workers' Educational Association, I spent eighteen months teaching in Stevenage, followed by a spell of two-and-a-half years in a Lancashire Catholic comprehensive. Both were called comprehensives but they were in effect secondary modern schools. In neither school did I come across any children from middle-class homes. At that time Stevenage boasted some seventeen secondary schools, and the school I taught at was near the bottom in terms of a pecking order with a high number of children in the care of the local social services. In my first-year tutor group there were several children from what used to be called broken homes, and one boy would follow me round the school when the world got too much for him. 'Pull up a chair beside me and sit quietly until you feel OK,' I would tell him as he opened the door to the room where I was teaching. I think his name was Jeremy and I must have been to him like the father he never had. I don't know if it was the right thing to do but I never chased him away or remonstrated with him. When I met his mother she was grateful for my kindness and hoped Jeremy would one day begin to stand on his own two feet.

That school was a good introduction to teaching. Many of the children came from families who had themselves relocated from the East End of London, and at weekends they would return to their grandparents to watch West Ham or whichever team the family traditionally supported. The issue of loyalty or identity among the pupils was invariably interesting as a topic to discuss, but things were still a little too recent to allow for more settled views. My loyalties, too, were divided. Stevenage was a New Town which had expanded in the post-war era. With its green spaces, dedicated bicycle tracks and an impressive mix of new housing, it was an attractive town especially for those brought up in slums or cramped conditions elsewhere. If there was a complaint it was that, with its colour coding for the various areas of the town, the planning was a little insistent, even severe. I preferred the look of Stevenage Old Town, which had grown up over centuries, but the high street that E.M.Forster would have known had been effectively consigned to the slipstream of history by the huge expansion on its doorstep.

'Only connect' is the epigraph to *Howards End* (1910), Forster's Edwardian, 'Hertfordshire' novel. Whether consciously or unconsciously, many people new to teaching adopt that motto as an invisible label, and I was no exception. I was keen to connect with all the children in my classes and went about my business with enthusiasm and commitment. In all kinds of ways but especially in terms of politics, industrial relations and the continuing oil crisis, 1974 was not the best of the times, but I felt I could do good work in a neglected spot helping those not best placed to succeed in life. 'Only connect' I kept repeating to myself, occasionally with gritted teeth, as I arrived at the school gates in the morning. Establish the right pitch and alight on something that will interest the class. And don't smile until half-way through the second term. I put up a range of friendly posters round the walls of my classroom, hoping to interest the pupils or allay their boredom when they were with me. A valuable *Biba* poster disappeared almost as soon as it was put up. In terms of classroom management, I brought in extra biros and pencils in case any of the class had forgotten or mislaid theirs. I didn't want to be distracted by things that could be avoided. So I was thinking ahead, hoping all the time I was accumulating brownie points with my charges. After all, even if my education was characterised in an earlier chapter by 'away', I came from the same social class as most of them.

I did a lot of reading out loud in the belief that there was value in involving their imagination directly and together as a class. At times the tension in a story was so acute that some of the children would hate it if I interrupted the reading to ask them what they imagined was going to happen next. The third and fourth years would enjoy having the stories of Alan Sillitoe read to them. I remember one such story involved a house burglary. 'No, you couldn't do it like that, sir,' one boy inadvertently let slip half way into the story, and several others concurred. 'Oh,' I said innocently, 'and why's that?' I was then treated to an advanced introduction in the art of breaking and entering.

I was never quite sure about these moments, not so much on account of masculine bravado or the truthfulness of their stories but really on account of what it meant to say 'only connect'. Was I with them in these moments of shared intimacy or against them or standing looking at them? Or did I think 'What exactly, David, do you mean by "only connect"? Change that to "only reflect", and when you've done that do some more reflecting. Do you honestly think you have any connection with their lives? Go home and sort yourself out and when you return take a more realistic view of what you understand by intervention.'

This was brought home to me on another occasion when I had forgotten the keys to the classroom cupboard where I kept their exercise books. With my back to the class I set about searching in the pockets of my flared denim suit. The class could appreciate my predicament and what was happening. I hate losing things or mislaying them and my agitation communicated itself to them, especially as I was keen to hand back their marked work and I had prepared nothing else for them. 'Sir, sir,' several boys shouted out, 'I can do that for you. I'm good at picking locks.' 'Right, Jason, let's see if you can put your knowledge to practical use.' Without a jemmy and within two minutes the lock was picked. In his proscribed Doc Martens and a number 4 haircut, both of which at that time signified defiance, the locksmith then turned round and gave us all a broad smile as if he'd just scored a penalty at Upton Park. The cupboard stood open, gaping at the class, its integrity breached.

Unless it was to give the boys some practice before they disappeared into the so-called real world, what, I concluded, was the use of keys and locking things away in a school full of expert petty thieves and happy pilferers? I sometimes felt that it was only in such moments that our parallel lives, outside the system that is, touched and lit up. For some pupils, school was the least of their problems; they had more serious things to turn their minds to.

Meanwhile, at home in our top-floor council flat overlooking the Great North Road, with the wine like a chemical experiment fermenting in bell-jars on the floor, and our neighbour's huge, lazy Pyrenean Mountain dog called 'Snowy' stretched out on the balcony above the stairwell 'guarding' the estate, I was trying to get some perspective on modern poverty by reading Arthur Morrison's *Tales of Mean Streets* (1894) and *A Child of the Jago* (1896). However, although several of them were beginning a life of crime, the pupils in my care were far removed from Morrison's imagined abyss.

A young teacher's first appointment is a time for making mistakes. If you're lucky, within a few years, you move on to a new school and leave your mistakes behind. At my first parents' evening in early November 1974, I met with the parents of a girl named Andrea in the fifth year. 'Andrea's attendance has been poor,' I remarked, running my finger down the list of names on the register. I then consulted Andrea's exercise book on the floor by my desk, but again there was little evidence that she had undertaken any written work. I explained I had only been teaching Andrea since September but I was anxious to do what I could for her. The parents looked at me slightly perplexed. That wasn't what they had come to talk about.

Their daughter had been along to the local further education college hoping to do a hairdressing course when she left school the following Easter. She undertook various tests including one to ascertain her reading age. 'What we'd like to know from you, Mr Whatever-your-name-is,' and I could feel there was a punch-line coming from the parents, 'is how come her reading age was 7.5 when she first came to this school and it is now 7.1?' That was below the belt I felt, four decimal points below, but I had to admit that it was a good question, and I don't believe I managed to reassure the parents of Andrea. I couldn't tell them that the system had failed her, for they were, rightly, only interested in their daughter. Evidently, something had gone wrong and I was now her English teacher and responsible for her progress. Subsequently, I went out of my way to set up meetings outside of class with Andrea, but she must have had a busy schedule for she never found time to attend. At that late stage in her academic career, I felt there was only so much a new teacher could do.

The day after the parents' evening, when I relayed this story to other teachers, something else emerged about Andrea. She may not have been attending school but she was gainfully employed. 'Oh, that girl spends all her time on her back,' was how one cynic on the other side of the staff-room helpfully chipped in. I assume he was coming to my rescue but it wasn't something I could relay to her parents by way of an excuse. Two years before, Andrea could have left school at fifteen but the school-leaving age had been raised to sixteen in 1972. She was therefore a ROSLA pupil, a pupil in those years identified by the acronym, the raising of the school-leaving age.

The ROSLA group proved quite a test for a new teacher. They didn't want to stay on at school and many of them struggled with academic subjects like English. The ROSLA group was often assigned to a temporary classroom, called a 'shed' at my Lancashire school. At Stevenage I taught my ROSLA class in a mobile classroom and not in my form room. The mobile was behind the main building and physically removed from the rest of the school. 'Do what you like with them,' I was told by my Head of Department. 'We're not entering them for public examinations and, besides, they'll be gone by Easter.' Such cynicism I considered offensive, and I resolved to ensure a proper scheme of work and to encourage them to strive to do their best. After all, I wasn't hired as a babysitter or a caretaker.

The most dispiriting moment at that school occurred on a Wednesday afternoon when fifth-formers from other classes, including that of my Head of Department, suddenly appeared at the window pulling faces to disrupt the class. That afternoon Wales were playing rugby and the three Welsh heads of department had adjourned to watch the match on television, leaving their classes to wander round the school. At the end of the afternoon I stayed behind to voice a complaint to the Headmaster. No disciplinary action was taken and there was no reprimand. Indeed, I discovered I had let the side down by complaining, and the following day when I walked into the staff-room I could feel rows of hostile eyes trained on me. It was clear I had outstayed my welcome.

I left that school fairly dissatisfied and my confidence dented. It was as if I had come away from an unfinished argument without having made my point or clarified my position. Some classes had gone well, others less so. I had entered teaching believing the curriculum was the key thing. If the syllabus was sufficiently interesting, the pupils would progress and the world would become a better place. At that time material from the Humanities Curriculum Project was finding its way into schools, and its interdisciplinary approach and loose-leaf handouts found favour with many of those new to teaching. If you wanted to do a project, say, on the 1930s, there would be a bank of relevant and stimulating material to discover among the HCP kit. By the time I waved goodbye to that Hertfordshire school I was more inclined to believe that pupils were influenced not by the official but by the hidden curriculum.

I still believed in the motto 'only connect' but, and it seems like heresy to admit as much, I was less concerned thereafter by what was taught and more by what such teaching contained or implied. Inside texts and poems and plays, I was fixated by their underlying ideology. Was the message essentially reactionary or designed to serve the status quo? Such an upside-down way of thinking or suspicion chimed with something else I absorbed at that school. Watching the way my Head of Department got pupils to write creatively – for he could teach when he wanted to – was quite something. It struck me that if the idea of handing down the curriculum was a concern, then perhaps giving pupils an opportunity to express themselves in writing might be the way to proceed. However, I was never fully convinced by such a move, for the hidden curriculum could just as easily emerge unchecked and pupils themselves could be deceived into imagining that articulation meant liberation.

In January 1975 my partner was appointed to head up Bolton's Adult Literacy Campaign, and, with renewed energy and purpose, we travelled north once again. I had been appointed to a fairly impoverished school on the brow of a steep hill on the edge of an industrial town now in decline. The brow of a hill in Sussex where I played football as a teenager was now nothing but a dim memory. When the cold winds from the north blew, the windows shook, as did the concentration of the weaker pupils. Dogs would stray into the school grounds from the town below or from nearby estates. Walking along corridors proved quite hazardous because of the holes and divets left by the high alumina cement used when the school was built in the 1960s. However, although physically it may have been crumbling and exposed to the elements, it was an ambitious school run by an ex-Salesian Brother, who, not unlike a drill sergeant, was keen to insist that we didn't teach children, we *instructed* them.

My kindly Head of Department acted as a mentor to me and was one of many dedicated teachers in that school. When considering the performance of another teacher, all Tom would seek to ascertain was whether or not the work of the children had been marked. 'I mean marked.' By which he meant not if there was a mark out of ten but if the work had been commented on throughout by the teacher and corrections to be done indicated. That was a measure of the school. It was in more ways than one down-to-earth. The children were instructed and their work marked and quite a few went on to university or college.

I was quickly promoted to Head of Department and took to running things quietly and efficiently. The staff in the Department, most of whom had been there since its foundation, were always supportive, and I cannot remember any occasion when I suffered an altercation. When I drew up the timetable, one senior colleague asked me not to give her an examination class for she felt she wasn't up to that. That surprised me, for in general staff enjoyed the challenge. Helah, the drama teacher, and Marion, the librarian, who also did some English teaching, were exceptional, always looking to see how to broaden the educational experience for the children. Elsewhere, someone with a Cambridge doctorate was in charge of Science. Whenever we passed in the corridor, Larry would humorously quip, 'Pushing back the boundaries of knowledge, that's what we're doing today.' A quietly-spoken Dominican priest, who reminded me of my old pal, Peter de Ath, at Wonersh, took RE and was always to be observed in quiet conversation with pupils and members of staff. In his white habit, he was like a still centre of a turning world, a sign or a hope of better things to come.

Every day there was something of interest going on especially among the staff, and it's now evident to me on reflection that I was happier there than I imagined at the time. The Geography teacher, who had worked on the railways for most of his life before entering the profession, was a model of unassuming decency and we would talk at length about the culture of the railways in Britain, picking up on a line of discussion where I had left off with my father. By way of contrast, the chirpy Business and Commerce teacher took great delight in voicing reactionary sentiments. 'I see the pound's taken another hammering on the foreign exchanges today. I wonder if it's got anything to do with the Labour government.' The rough-and-ready, slightly uncouth Head of PE was a law unto himself, and you only entered the changing rooms if you were obliged to and your immune system was not compromised. One day he went AWOL. A search party was dispatched to his home and to the various places round town he was known to frequent, but he couldn't be found. He had vanished. Then one day, two months later, like one of the stray dogs we were plagued with, he wandered into the staff-room as if nothing had happened. The only comment made was something to the effect that he was wearing the same unwashed track suit. I don't think anyone discovered where he had been loitering for so long.

I liked that about the school. It was an improbable collection of very different individuals who all shared a certain scepticism about what we were doing or what could be achieved but who all expressed a degree of tolerance toward each other. In any other school the Head of PE's contract would have been terminated, but it wasn't, and I am sure part of the therapy that enabled him to return was not filling out sick notes and the like. The Catholic ethos – if that's what it was – ensured a common purpose, something I never experienced at Stevenage, where I felt the knives sharpening when differences were aired. The discipline could be off-putting, with children being regularly bawled out in assemblies and along corridors, but the bark of the small group of disciplinarians was worse than their bite. At my previous school the Deputy Head, who had returned to Britain after a lifetime teaching in Egypt, would lock himself in his office at lunchtime to avoid patrol duty, but even that couldn't protect the 'Med man', as he liked to call himself, from children who would take delight in banging on his door and then scampering off by a nearby flight of stairs. In Lancashire, it was accepted that the children would misbehave if given half a chance, so their movements were always restricted. They were never for example allowed near the staff car park. That was the cardinal rule above all others, which amused me. Teachers looked after their cars first, thus ensuring that no matter what else happened during the day they could get away by 4 o'clock, secure in the knowledge that their tyres had not been slashed or their cars tampered with.

There were few pupils from ethnic minorities, or I should say few children from ethnic minorities gained admission to that school, and the racist attitudes of the children were rarely tackled. There were limits, then, to the amount of tolerance in circulation. Asian communities were well-established in most towns in that part of East Lancashire, but Asian pupils either didn't apply to the Catholic comprehensive or were refused entry. I should have spoken out more while I was there, but my Catholicism wasn't strong enough to carry me through what would have been an ensuing onslaught, and, besides, I was repaying a longstanding debt to the Church for my education and discerned this was one battle I couldn't face at this time. Just getting through the day was enough for the day.

What, then, had I learnt from my four years teaching English in comprehensive schools? I had gone into school teaching imagining I could identify with those from the same social class and intervene in their lives. I ended that period of my life in the realisation that the system wasn't much interested either in my radical ideas or, indeed, in what I had to say for myself. It could get by perfectly well with me or without me. I still had a tongue inside my head but it wasn't functioning as it once did. Teaching English as a foreign language I found at first interesting but in the end quite tedious. 'Does it matter that one more person speaks English in a world where half the globe speaks it?' When that thought came to me unannounced, I formed the view that my career lay elsewhere. Teaching in schools was different. It was not unlike missionary work, at least the teaching I had undertaken. It would have been different again at Winchester or Eton, where I might have been openly or more pointedly subversive or challenging to the status quo. Teaching in comprehensive schools at the sharp end seemed closer to a civilizing mission among those disadvantaged and less privileged in society, and I entered the profession believing I could shape the future. Education or capitalism – that was how the alternatives were often mapped out by my generation. However, I had been taught a hard lesson, that identity was not the same as being on the same wave length. In turn I had become slightly tongue-tied and less articulate. I never imagined I would ever say that.

Such teaching wasn't for me and it wasn't me. After four years, it felt as though I had been in a scrap in a playground and I was now being summoned inside. After a day's teaching I would arrive home drained, my nerves on edge, my time given over to something which I can only describe, following D.H.Lawrence's depiction of Ursula Brangwen's plight in *The Rainbow* (1915), as a machine. My quiet was being systematically destroyed and with it my thinking and my writing. 'Only connect' was now beyond me. If I hadn't obtained an appointment at a teacher training college in York in the summer of 1978, I would have gone the way of many new entrants to the profession, namely to undertake anything but what I had been trained for. It wasn't that I couldn't hack it as the saying has it, because I could; I was probably the youngest head of English in a Lancashire comprehensive at the time. That wasn't it. Like most of my pupils, I had other things on my mind and I wanted to attend to those.

The following year the book on fiction and social class, *Attitudes to Class in the English Novel*, which I had written with my partner and which had been originally suggested to the publisher by our tutor, David Craig, was published. It was composed entirely in those years when my partner was establishing an adult literacy programme and I was running a big department in a comprehensive school with a five-form entry and a small sixth form. You can undertake those kinds of things only once in your life. I didn't realise it then but the period of adjustment covering the years from 1970 to 1978 was over. When we crossed the Pennines that summer and exchanged a red for a white rose, my partner was five months pregnant and the boy from Sussex had just turned thirty one.

*In October 2000, the Irish edition of the* Sunday Times *ran a piece on my Cork* Reader *concerning the injunction taken out in the High Court in Dublin by the Joyce Estate preventing its publication. A similar photo to this one by Bob Collier accompanied the article. Before the photographer arrived at my house in York, I quickly arranged my desk to bring out how my book was in good company with other books which had been dragged through the courts - including* Ulysses. *My right hand is resting on the page where a notice says 'Pages 323-346 have been removed due to a dispute in relation to copyright'. I have the look of someone who identified with the people in history who wouldn't lie down.*

Chapter Ten

# Spring Time in York

### Yaark

When I was being interviewed in May 1978 for a lectureship in English at the
College of Ripon and York St John, the bells of York Minster tolled so loudly
that my interviewer was obliged to get up and shut the sash window. 'That's
one of the hazards of the job here, the sound of Great Peter on the hour,' he
humorously quipped. 'Oh, I can cope with that after where I've come from,' I
replied, and we then spoke about my research interests. 'Yes,' he reflected,
'Sean O'Casey's autobiographies. Wonderful the way he moves between
himself as author and himself as subject. Something very Irish about that,
don't you think?'

I established an immediate rapport with Brian Sourbut, and until his
untimely death in the early nineties there was hardly a day when we didn't
have something to say to each other. 'Have you ever thought,' he would
wonder, looking round him in the staff-room over lunch, 'that most of us were
appointed by the present or the previous Principal?' Some days he meant 'Do
you think we've anything in common with our colleagues?' Other days he
meant 'Isn't it amazing how someone can put you in the same group as this
lot?' Here was a person to converse with quietly and freely and funnily. Most
things you didn't need to say to him; you just knew what the one-time
member of the Boys' Brigade and former student at Oxford was thinking – or,
rather, not thinking.

So that's how I began around twenty happy years teaching in Gray's Court,
the former home of the Minster's Treasurer and the building with the longest
continuous occupancy in York, dating back to the twelfth century. I had a room
on the second floor overlooking the Medieval walls of the city and the gardens

and grounds occupied by various clerics at York Minster including the Dean. In the stately Long Gallery, the Duke of Cumberland, on his way south after defeating the Highlanders at the Battle of Culloden in 1746, was officially welcomed into the city with a banquet. The building was pretty-pretty and very private, one-time home of Laurence Sterne's uncle, Jaques Sterne. Only rarely was I disturbed in my room by something slightly disdainful. In the weeks leading up to Christmas, geese were kept in the long, narrow garden below me. Their undersides would become so distended that, when the butcher with his sack came to collect them, the poor creatures couldn't take off, and they would squawk for their lives, flapping hopelessly as they ran down the runway of the garden. It reminded me of a scene from a novel by Trollope, but it was a travesty in its own way, with fat clerics determined to make the most of the twelve days of Christmas, hell-bent on becoming fatter and their faces even oilier than before.

If there is a ghost in Gray's Court it wouldn't surprise me if it turned out to be that of William Chisholm, the Highlanders' standard-bearer and the subject of the beautiful Gaelic lament composed by his widow and entitled 'Mo rùn geal òg' (my fair, young love). I tried on many occasions but without success to raise his spirit by singing Jacobite songs as I climbed the stairs or walked down the corridor to my room. 'This one's for you, Butcher Cumberland,' I would find myself muttering. I shouldn't be critical, for the Anglican College paid only a peppercorn rent to the Minster for the use of Gray's Court, and outside of Oxbridge there couldn't have been a more conducive, physical environment in which to teach. But, with my once Catholic eyes, I was always in two minds about the justification for the Reformation, especially when so much of the activity of the Minster had precious little to do with things spiritual. With tongue-in-cheek, one of my Methodist colleagues constantly sighed for the Minster to be burnt down and Jesus come again, but that I judged was going a little far and I was never much in favour of direct action. Besides, I developed an affection for the 10.8 tons of Great Peter, who was utterly indifferent as to whom he was interrupting or calling to prayer. If the Minster had burned down in 1984 when the south transept caught fire after apparently being struck by lightning, the city would never have recovered its sense of itself.

I had been appointed initially to oversee the final years of the B.Ed, teacher-training, English programme. Subsequently, I taught only courses in literature on the B.A programme. I was the first appointment in English for ten years and offered the choice of Ripon or York as my preferred location. If I envisaged doing a lot of walking or if I wanted to live in the Yorkshire Dales, Ripon would have been ideal, but York was livelier and had more going for it. It proved the right choice, not least because throughout the time I was at College a doubt hung over the future of the campus at Ripon, which finally closed in 1999. Indeed, when Gordon McGregor was appointed Principal in June 1979, the question everyone wanted to know was 'Had he asked the right question at interview?' That is, what was he going to do about the twenty-five mile corridor connecting the two campuses? The merger, then, in 1974 between the teacher training college for women at Ripon and the equivalent for men in York was never entirely successful. I was always in two minds. Whenever I went across to Ripon for departmental or staff meetings, I would tread warily on highly polished corridors, and in the staff-room I would try and avoid sitting on chairs traditionally occupied by members of the staff at Ripon. I never got used to the oppressive, grammar-school ethos. At the same time, whenever the issue arose, I argued against its closure, for the kind of student it attracted, many of whom were a delight to teach, would not have gone elsewhere, not even to a small city such as York.

The Department of Language and Literature had around fifteen members of staff, with some three in French, two in Language Studies, and the rest in English. As had happened at Lancaster twenty years before, Language Studies eventually split off from English. They felt they could thrive independently of a subject in which they had little interest. The talented Dennis Freeman began life in English but grew increasingly frustrated with its rationale. 'What's the point of using dating exercises when you need to know the context to understand a passage?' 'Does anyone any longer believe all that Leavis stuff?' When the Cambridge English crisis emerged in the early 1980s around Colin MacCabe, he felt he had been justified in moving away from the subject. Interpretation he would leave to others; he was only interested in description. As Head of Language Studies, Freeman got on with appointing his team, which included someone with a doctorate in the art of turn-taking in conversation and another person whose specialism was forensic linguistics. I never heard either of them express the slightest curiosity about literature.

The seminar groups, which rarely exceeded fifteen, were small enough to permit me to teach in my room. Attendance was never a concern and neither was getting students to do the reading or preparing seminar topics. Each semester, B.A. students would undertake two modules, one in their major and one in their minor subject. Wednesday morning was devoted to careers work with mock interviews and mock applications and so on. It took four years for students to obtain an honours degree, but some left after three with an ordinary degree. Our lives were governed by a leisurely pace, with students having time to explore what was in their minds and time to prepare for work after graduating. Outside of term teaching, we ran three-week courses in the inter-semester break in January, and after exams in June we would enjoy literary walks along the banks of the river Ouse.

Throughout their undergraduate career, students could select from a range of course offerings, including American Literature, the English Novel, Hardy and Lawrence, Modernism, Writers and Politics, Satire, Literature and Society, and Women and Writing, a course my partner pioneered. Soon after I arrived, I introduced a course in Modern Irish Writing, which I taught every year thereafter. If students majored in English, they would study some ninety set texts in total, with most modules requiring them to read at least ten. By way of contrast, when I retired in 2007, students could do a single honours in English in three years, having studied in class around thirty five texts in total. Such a reduction in the exposure to a subject, which has been replicated across higher education, is essentially a form of betrayal whereby students have been short-changed and tutors compromised. I said as much at the time, courting unpopularity among my colleagues, and nothing has altered my opinion.

Until the early 1990s there was no reason for me not to enjoy my time at College. Students were very pleasant and responsive and to my mind well-prepared to face the challenges ahead of them. We were also fortunate in attracting very able American students each semester, some from prestigious colleges such as Smith and Bryn Mawr. One student came from Spelman College, a black liberal arts college in Atlanta, Georgia, where Alice Walker was educated. She enjoyed her time with us but then came the rub when I asked her about the city. 'Oh,' she replied, 'York is the only place I've ever lived in where I was taunted in the street for my colour.' Not surprisingly, we didn't get any more students from that College. One or two students returned to undertake graduate work in Britain and for some I was happy to write references. Many of the American students used us as a base for exploring Britain and Europe, but that never bothered me and they always had something to say for themselves when they returned. We also had long-established exchanges with Union College in upstate New York and with the Free University in Amsterdam, and the contacts I made with members of staff in those two institutions proved especially valuable over the years.

Inevitably, it is the exceptional students who stand out in the memory, and not always the brightest students. One woman surprised me in the early 1980s by going to work in Ethiopia among the poorest people on earth. When she was a student there was nothing to suggest she would undertake such selfless work. As far as I recall she was not a member of the Christian Union and there was nothing prissy or preachy about her. She was lively and outward-going, enjoying herself, much like anyone else at her age. I've often reflected on her decision since. I wonder how it turned out and if she ever recalled her student days in York. Such selflessness was impressive, to dedicate your life not to the accumulation of things or to fattening geese but to the pursuit of an ideal. Another student, Jayne Dunfield, transferred into training to become a nurse, but this was easier to understand, for nursing was similar to teaching, a public service, and she gave every appearance she would make a fine nurse. But the student who went to work in the vineyards abroad and whose name now escapes me raised a doubt in my own mind: what exactly was my vocation and was I indeed following it without realising it? It was only the exceptional student who could pose such a question for me. After my time teaching in secondary schools among the poor and disadvantaged, I had retreated indoors away from the noisy world of the playground, and perhaps life had become too comfortable for me – but not so comfortable that I didn't appreciate what must have been going on inside her throughout her time as a student.

The brightest student I taught was the daughter of an editor at a leading publisher. She had turned down a place at Oxbridge to read English at a college far from the madding crowd, where she presumably hoped she would be free of family pressures and pressures she brought on herself. The one essay she produced for me shocked me by its brilliance. There was nothing to suggest in the handwritten script that she had altered anything she had written. The transmission from head to hand looked effortless, and this in the days before word-processing has obscured that process. Unfortunately, her time with us was short and within three months or so she had departed, without bidding farewell. I wondered afterward if in praising her so highly I had contributed to her withdrawal. What I do know is that when I learnt she had left College I felt slightly abandoned, as if her feeling of abandonment had communicated itself to me.

Another student with psychological problems I remember was a diagnosed schizophrenic. Rick was an Art student who took several of my courses. For most of the year he was stable but then, often as it happened in autumn, there would come a time when he fell apart. During one of my Modernism seminars, he put a square-shaped object on the table in front of the class. 'Modernism,' he declared, 'what is it? Look at that object in front of you.' Then he swivelled it round. 'Now, look at it again,' and with that he moved it again. 'No object can be seen in the one light or from a single perspective. That's Modernism.' He had an immediacy about him, which owed much to a troubled, thinking mind. I enjoyed his company and, without interruption, I would listen to him talking about his art work and the painters he admired. He took several added years to complete his degree and nearly didn't do so since he refused to hand in his dissertation. As a last resort, one morning I went round to his house and physically removed it from him and handed it over to his examiners. 'No, it's not complete, and, besides, it's rubbish.' I dug in. 'Rick, help me. Without this, no degree. With it, completion.' Afterward, he appreciated what I had done. I still see him on my travels round York, and he always pitches in with something on his mind about art or literature or memories of the trip to Dublin I had arranged for his group. 'Beckett and Joyce,' he would chuckle, as much to himself as to his auditor. 'Where on earth did they come out of?'

Every year I could rely on a group of students to make life very pleasant for me. Normally this was because their interest in a writer or a topic had been sparked and they wanted to communicate that to me. A friend at Leeds would speak of sucking blood out of his students as if he were like Dracula. I could understand that image because without such enthusiasm my time at College would have been fairly dull I suspect. One of my History colleagues, Margaret Butcher, who died of lymphoma a couple of years after my arrival, would regularly complain about the art of resistance among her students. 'I cannot do anything to get them to respond,' she would observe about her Italian Renaissance class. 'What could be more enjoyable than studying this great period in western art and culture. And yet nothing.' Her face would strain and the Oxford graduate looked to her colleagues for understanding and sympathy.

Margaret was hoping her students would follow her into the space marked intellectual excitement, but a college in a cathedral city didn't tend to attract too many intellectually ambitious people. In her early forties, Margaret died before her time and I still miss her company. She was always expecting more from life, and it was appropriate that her chosen field of study was to do with rebirth. In her last months, she insisted on returning to Florence to receive what for her was like the viaticum on her final journey into the unknown, away from the colleagues who listened patiently to her complaints and away from her devoted elderly parents, who had come up from the hop-picking fields of Kent to be with their only child in her last illness. She reminded me, if indeed I needed reminding, that College was one situation where not giving all the heart, or, rather, not having excessive expectations, would enable you to survive inside the institution for longer than otherwise might be the case.

As ever, the good times came to end. The College couldn't afford the new rent for Gray's Court imposed by York Minster and we were relocated to the main building on Lord Mayor's Walk. Before that occurred, there came a moment when I realised the world was turning. It must have been around the early 1990s, and outside my office I overheard two students checking on their overall marks from the previous semester. 'Oh,' said one student to his companion, 'I've failed one module.' 'So what?' came the reply. 'You can carry one fail into your next year.' That was the first time I'd heard a student expressing such an attitude. Prior to that, our students would have been devastated to have failed a course. Now I began to look at my groups with more suspicious eyes, that they weren't as determined to succeed as their predecessors. It was only a fleeting moment and yet in retrospect that overheard exchange seemed to herald a changing of the guards.

When I was in my thirties I should have sought an appointment elsewhere, but York was a graveyard of ambition. I loved the city and, as background noise, it provided me with an opportunity to get on with my work quietly. Its special character stems from it being a place where people have lived since before the Romans arrived. Wherever you dig in York you discover something of interest. Five years ago, the skeleton of a Roman soldier who lived in the third century and who would have been a member of the Sixth Legion was uncovered on Bootham within a hundred metres of my house. As I write this in 2010, the remains of eighty Roman gladiators, one with the teeth marks of a lion, have been unearthed in Holgate, not far from where I live on the other side of the river. In the architecture of the city you can read a whole history of different phases of civilisation from the Romans and Vikings to the Normans and Elizabethans, and then all the way through the town houses of the gentry in the eighteenth century to the nineteenth-century city that emerged with the railways. Along the river that flows through the city came the stones that built the Roman headquarters that underlie the Minster. Every day I walk round the city delighting not only in its ever-changing sounds and lively improvised theatre but also in its varied domestic architecture and street furniture. The Roman soldier discovered on Bootham would have looked up at the same sky and noticed the same subtle changes of light as I do now. Like me, he would have observed the river in flood and walked along the same road as I do into the city from the north.

In York you sometimes hear people speaking English as if they hadn't refined anything of their Viking vowels, as with their place-name 'Yaark' for 'York', a city which began life under the more refined and civilised Roman name of 'Eboracum'. Eboracum, Eoforwic, Jorvik, modern York, or 'Yaark', as it is rendered in the mouths of some of its denizens, a word whose sound occupies a vacant lot in the mouth somewhere between 'yak' and 'yoke'. In a reversal of its history, as if it wanted to set down a marker against the prettification that would accompany its heritage status, there occurred a shortening of its place-name. It took a long time to shake off the juddering, initial 'J' sound in favour of the less judgemental and more inquisitive 'Y', the penultimate letter of the alphabet. Assume nothing about York. It's a city to be heard and listened to as much as read about in guide books.

Depending on the person and the context, 'Yaark' can be a term of endearment, a chip off the old block, something old, a partner for life, movement off the seam, a thick edge, a happy find, last year's bark, what yackers yoked together do, an entry at once magnificent, ornate and formal, Noah's reported backup, a good place to dig or to drown, a ghost town, a hardy annual, like nowhere else, depends on its ings, dances to the tune bully for you, a hole in the wall, a complete and utter shambles, nothing shire about it, a conundrum, a gateway to nowhere, an old tart, a close call, a scream in a dark ginnel, a pregnant pause, an exclamation mark, the inevitable q at Bettys, a substitute for a word or phrase, unknown blogger's shorthand for he's got the hump, a Viking compliment, site of struggles now rehearsed without bitterness, Lancastrians take guard, southpaws submit, the dismay of Minstermen seeking promotion, an unexpected discharge, fecal incontinence, suitably loose reflections on a Roman sewer, an unbelievable shock to the system, a wake-up call, a narcoleptic fit, a nose put permanently out of joint, an attempted yerk, an open blade, a weapon close to the heart, an almost tactile form of abuse, a raw throat, the morning after, something dredged up from the pit of the stomach or the bottom of a river, a complaint, a riposte, something to get off your chest, a chirpy bird, a cry for help. Three yaks for olde York. Clean bowled by a Yorker. Get the sandbags out.

In recent years, the Jorvik Viking Museum has recreated a whole Viking street and has filled it with snippets of Viking speech to evoke the city when it was known by its Scandinavian name. At times, as you emerge onto modern-day Coppergate, the street of the joiners, you could be forgiven for thinking it's the contemporary speech of locals you hear in the Museum. If it was ever possible, it would be quite something to trace the evolution of how people spoke in this city and how they lived through all the ages that constitute an official history. It would be a history full of linguistic distortion and corruption, of compressions and misunderstanding, not unlike the peculiar layout of the city itself with its absence of straight lines or North American grids or Paris boulevards, for York is not a city for driving a tank through or, indeed, for getting anywhere fast. How could it be otherwise when a street near the remains of St Leonard's Hospital was once known as Footless Lane?

In his letters Laurence Sterne spells the main river running through the city 'Owse', not Ouse, and I wonder if that's how the Shandean cleric pronounced it. Ow, say, with an 's', not ooze, as most people pronounce it today. The late-eighteenth-century grammarian Lindley Murray lived in Holgate, and the early editions of his grammar, beginning in 1795, were printed in York. There are over a hundred editions of his grammar available in book form in York Minster Library, and it is appropriate that among the collection there is also an anonymous skit on the grammarian (signed I suspect by the author) entitled *The Comic Lindley Murray; Or The Grammar of Grammars with Illustrative Sketches*, which was published in Dublin in 1871, Dublin also being a 'word city' or a city of words. You feel that anywhere which names its shortest street 'Whip-ma-whop-ma-gate' must have a special interest in language.

As soon as I arrived in York, one of my colleagues, the Medieval historian Alan Young, would delight in telling me that Grape Lane was once part of the red light area of the city and known as Grope Lane. He would then recite for me one of the many riddles about the city: 'A pub is a bar, a bar is a gate, and a gate is a street.' It was like something invented by the Vikings, a people who sowed confusion wherever they went and forced those who succeeded them into a never-ending, daily cycle of translating what they meant. Micklegate Bar is the most ornate entry gate into the city, but there is no gate in the actual street of Micklegate, *gata* being the Viking word for street. Someone must have enjoyed naming two adjacent roads in the city Gillygate and Goodramgate, similar-sounding names seemingly designed to confuse residents and visitors alike. And does anyone know for sure the derivation of Hungate, which might or might not be the 'street of the hounds'?

For well over thirty years I have lived in the city in a house dating back to around 1840. So I have occupied the house for a sixth of its lifetime. Of the two thousand years since the arrival of the Romans, my time in the city has been around a seventieth. I love all this about York. Time present and time past, and all together, you as part of something with a much longer history, including a house once owned by a shop assistant and a railway clerk, a house that in turn dates back to the years when the railways, courtesy of George Hudson, first arrived in the city. Unlike Coventry, it was not destroyed in the Second World War, and if the East Coast rail line hadn't come through York in the nineteenth century the city might have become a quiet market town like Ripon. None of that happened, and, with ears attuned to roads of iron since my childhood, I take comfort waking in the early hours from the metallic sounds of rolling stock getting ready for the day to come. However, it must be admitted that there is a certain inertia that can be off-putting, especially if you're young.

'But there's no culture here,' a friend from Rome who works in the catering industry in York remarks. 'Is there anything going on?' To some extent that's true, and I have to acknowledge that the fountain outside the City Art Gallery is more often than not out of action. Like a mouth full of teeth whose fillings have dropped out, the former churchgoing city is now populated with deconsecrated churches. If 'deconsecrated' is too close to 'desecrated' for comfort, or if the image of a paralysed, open mouth is profane and troubling, then I should add that such churches have been requisitioned by voluntary groups to serve not the bread of heaven to the faithful but homely mugs of tea and sponge cake to weary shoppers and day-trippers from Scarborough counting their pennies. The Benedictines, the Cistercians, the Franciscans, the Augustinians, the Carmelites have all gone, together with their distinctive habits, ancient liturgies and communities of silence. The harmonious bells on the parish churches, which Thomas Gent insisted on noticing in his noisy *History of York* (1730), are now also for the most part silent. Today, people who live here cannot but be conscious of a world that is gone, and for that reason develop a keen historical sense or construct their own take on things. Whatever the case, with the right kind of care, John Thornton's remarkably expressive face of St John on the stained glass Apocalypse window in the Minster, now six hundred years old, will outlast us all.

People are also less given to rituals when it comes to asserting their common identity, but when they do so the ancient city often comes sharply into view. One of the best recent examples of a spontaneous coming-together was the fireworks display held at Clifford's Tower on 5 November. What residents sought was an old-fashioned, communal experience, akin to older forms of ritual, and one which their children would long remember. The crowds that gathered to listen to the almighty boom from inside the medieval Norman Tower knew what they wanted, and it had nothing to do with York being the birthplace of Guy Fawkes or with the Tower being the awful place where the Jews from Coney Street were burnt to death on the night of 16 March 1190. To my mind, the occasion was a reminder of York as host to spectacle and as a once-proud city of spectacle for the people. It proved so popular that it was discontinued by the city fathers on the grounds of health and safety, and Bonfire Night in the city has never been the same since.

In a whimsical, Shandean sort of way, even when things are out of action or when pleasure is denied, I find the city endearing and never alien. Apart from altercations with his uncle, I'm sure that was true for Sterne, the Anglican cleric who loved attending the races in summer on the Knavesmire or flirting on some sentimental journey, gliding in and out of the Corinthian columns at dances in the Assembly Rooms. As far as I can see, no one today owns the city, though some have managed to get their feet under the table or think they have, but you will search in vain for a millionaire's row or for widespread examples of gentrification. If the name of Seebohm Rowntree were not enough, the number of almshouses for the poor is a reminder that the exercise of charity has a long history of concern in York.

In the York Mystery Plays, dating from the late fourteenth century, it is fitting that 'The Entry into Jerusalem', which commemorates Jesus's 'triumphal' entry on an ass into the place sacred to the Jews, should include an interpolated scene between a poor man and a blind man. As the pageant-wagon is hauled through the central streets of York, the blind man shouts at Jesus, 'To me give good eye,' and like the original audiences we find ourselves lingering between the Biblical story and its meaning or context for later generations. Every year on the feast of Corpus Christi, the crowds must have found comfort in a religion that seemed to speak to them directly about healing the lame, feeding the poor and giving good eye to the blind. As if to confirm it is a people's city, the York plays carried the forceful, local, north country dialect, and they were informed by an imagination that could absorb the sacred into the secular and in a single word or telling phrase bring Jerusalem and the Church's salvation history directly onto the streets of York.

The Protestant Reformation in the sixteenth century put paid to the spectacle, but nothing was going to hold back the voice of the people or, indeed, the poor who accompanied the people.

Except for the name, there is nothing royal about The King's Manor, which Charles I occupied when rallying his forces against the Parliamentarians in the 1640s. The building began life as the residence of the Abbot of St Mary's Abbey, and since 1963 it has been owned by the University of York. We are all in that sense, whether we are residents, commuters, students, or tourists, positioned as spectators or witnesses, on our way elsewhere, passing through, with everything in trust but not quite fully owned. The Minster was built by people who, every Sunday at Mass, confessed allegiance to the Pope. As its under-croft reveals, it was erected on the headquarters of a people who worshipped deities and dreamed of the sun-drenched shores of the Mediterranean.

Throughout the city, interest groups spring up to protect their neighbourhood and not infrequently win out against unscrupulous developers. At the same time, York is a university city but it's quite unlike a university city. In early March, without embarrassment, the people form long, orderly queues outside the Theatre Royal for tickets for the following year's Christmas pantomime. They are over-awed by nothing, not the prestigious university at Heslington, not antiquity, not history, not the past, and not the future. They know that eventually the whole world will come to visit them. As it happens, the city bathes in northern climes and northern attitudes, but to the question 'When is a university in the north not a northern university?' the answer is 'When it's at York'.

San Francisco is a city that prides itself on knowing how. If it possessed a little more self-consciousness, York would realise it is an impertinent city, and pride itself on being so described. Nothing in York quite fits into place or functions as it should. Subversive gargoyles, some no doubt designed to mock leading local figures, adorn the Minster; this year (2011) a colony of bats, not people protest, prevented the erection of a Big Wheel behind the City Art Gallery; in spite of repeated attempts by the authorities, traffic congestion outside the Railway Station has never been resolved and it is arguably worse now that it has ever been in the past three decades; in the busy, newly refurbished Central Library, I need a password to search the catalogue.

Those who write about the city also occasionally betray signs of impertinence, and let me illustrate this by reference to the extreme example of

Thomas Gent, who was a key player in the establishment of newspapers in the city in the 1720s and 1730s and who, incidentally, was inspired to compose his historical guide book on an afternoon walk with friends to Heslington. Here is Gent, an Irish printer by trade, waxing lyrical about his adopted city in his *History of York*, arguably one of the ugliest printed books in English:

> So great has been the Fame of this antient City (and I hope will ever be) as to employ the Pens of learned Foreigners, as of others: And it is with Pleasure we find their Unanimity in its Praise: That its Situation is on a beautiful Plain, adorned by the Intercourse of a fine River, strengthen'd with noble Walls near three Miles in Circumference, on which have been lofty Towers or Watch Houses: that the Gates and Posterns of York were so many Additions to the Lustre thereof; which flourish'd under all its Revolutions of Saxons, Danes and Normans, is at present a County and City within itself, govern'd by a Lord Mayor, 12 Aldermen, and 2 Sheriffs, habited in Scarlet Gowns; also a Recorder, Deputy Recorder, 8 Chamberlains, 72 of the Common Council, Town Clerk, Sword and Mace Bearers, Common Serjeant, and other Officers. So that on the whole, if we consider it in its present condition, we find it plentiful, splendid and noble, giving Title of Duke to the King's second Son: And if we look back to its antient Glory, how reverential, how awful has it appear'd; and consequently, in such a State of Opulency, how great and powerful, when so highly honour'd, as to be the Habitation of Emperors and Kings!

As the 'Eumaeus' episode of Joyce's *Ulysses* reminds us, there is something refreshing about writing that is over the top, which I take to be a form of impertinence. As you read Gent's passage, you cannot anticipate what is coming next. The use of a tagged-on, unconsciously deflating phrase such as 'as of others', or mixed metaphors such as 'adorned' and 'Intercourse', or a missing verb between 'have been' and 'lofty Towers', or inappropriate vocabulary such as 'Lustre', 'awful', and 'Habitation', or the uncertain order in a sequence of adjectives as with 'plentiful, splendid and noble', or examples of linguistic contamination as with 'habited', which seems to trigger 'Habitation' – the passage is a delight for the student of bad writing. The author is clearly wanting to tell the world that York is the greatest city on earth; the reader is left gasping for breath or weeping that anyone can write so poorly.

My advice to anyone seeking to praise the city is not to overdo it and to avoid words like 'Opulency'. If you cannot discover the most pertinent tone, under-statement is better than over-statement, and don't forget or ignore the sceptical and not always approving eye. That it's a friendly city will emerge only after long acquaintance; it can take up to twenty years of passing someone every day in the street before a token of acknowledgement is exchanged. It's only some five or six generations ago that the 'antient' city stopped executing wrong-doers on the Knavesmire (the blood of knaves), and – shock, horror – our splendid predecessors dangled the heads of traitors from Micklegate Bar, no doubt attended by Sheriffs 'habited in Scarlet Gowns'. In April 1739 and the night before he was paraded through the streets of York and hanged, Dick Turpin, in a dungeon that is now part of the Castle Museum, probably didn't sleep a wink.

Apart from one year spent in California, a period I recall in the next section, I have lived in York since 1978. Over half my life. The College has changed in those years more than the city. I had no trouble adjusting to the background noise of the city but discovered I couldn't do the same with the College. A memoir is not a place for a diagnosis of what went wrong in higher education, but perhaps some observations are worth recording. In the 1990s, teacher training colleges were encouraged to become universities and to compete with them on the same playing field. My College, which had been undergoing change since its merger with Ripon College, found this a step too far. When a leading academic was appointed in 1995 as the new Principal with the remit from the Bishop of Ripon as Chair of Governors to transform the institution, he encountered little support among the staff, and within three years he had left. As a writer and a keen researcher, I felt my position also under threat from that point on. What had been a very pleasant time for me became in my last ten years increasingly unpleasant.

At an interview when reapplying for my job around 2000, I was facetiously asked by a senior manager, 'What's it like having an international reputation?' What he meant was either 'We don't need people like you in an institution like ours' or 'Writing books doesn't make you special. So why should we rehire you?' In my reply I began to say something about cultural capital and the reputation that would accrue to the College on the basis of my reputation, especially as it was seeking university status, but invoking the work of Pierre Bourdieu was just hopeless. Any common language we should have shared was in the process of being overhauled by that generation of managers in higher education. Some of them believed they marched under the banner of progress and modernisation, but when it came to dealing with staff in their care they exhibited precious little care.

I had been brought up in a religion which had been persecuted for centuries in Britain. My hackles were aroused. I recalled the fate of the poor Irish who emigrated to York in the years after the Great Famine, who lived in dire poverty in Walmgate, and who subsequently disappeared without trace from the city. Whenever line managers referred to 'internal management systems', I couldn't help hearing 'infernal management systems'. An 'f' for a 't'. A comforting slip inside the remnants of my recusant mind. But the phrase above all that kept returning to me was *sin verguenza*, an accusation which my Catholic students in Madrid in 1970-1 used all the time about Americans, largely in response to US foreign policy and on account of their military bases in Spain. Without shame, guilt-free, the new generation had arrived to occupy rooms without books or mirrors. They then set about championing the cause of 'massification' and mistaking quality for elitism.

'God help us,' as my Irish grandmother, drawing in her breath, would never stop repeating, and she was right. 'Yaark,' I felt like replying. The world owed me a little something but largely nothing. Instead of invoking Bourdieu, I should have referred to the Medieval rubbish dump which lay directly beneath the building where I was being interviewed and how we would do well not to draw neat lines under the past. As in my thirties I should have moved on, but this didn't happen, in part because after a serious operation on my spine in 2002 I couldn't in truth have contemplated an appointment elsewhere. In 2001, my partner secured promotion to a Readership elsewhere and thus escaped the worst of the deluge. I managed to hang on until 2007 and my sixtieth birthday.

As a last act of defiance in my final weeks before departing, on as many display boards as I could locate around the campus, I pinned up copies of James Schevill's exquisite, little poem 'Colleagues'. The American poet, whom I had met at a conference in Rostock in the 1980s, is haunted by 'the communal Latin root / *Collega*, one chosen / At the same time as another.' It's a love poem to the colleagues he was most attached to, but to me I was lamenting the terrible loss of collegiality and of the 'transforming power' of attachment. I might as well have inserted the poem into a historic, coloured, glass bottle, driven to the Humber Bridge, and pitched it into the great river of forgetfulness a hundred feet below. With some phrase about being called but not chosen reverberating somewhere in the back of my mind, I could then have waited until the tide carried it downstream past the once-busy port of Hull, on past the lonely, sandy tip of the appropriately named Spurn Point, and out into Shelley's unfathomable sea.

This particular phase in the decline of the College is not something I want to return to in my memory, but let me just say this. The loss of charm and decency was something I witnessed every day. My case, while painful for me, was really as nothing by comparison with what happened to others, some of whom were made redundant in their forties with little prospect of work. When I retired, the only letter of thanks I received after nearly thirty years' service to a 'Christian' College was from Ed Balls, the then Secretary of State for Education. That was one of many ironies I experienced at the time, the juxtaposition of a government which came to power in 1997 on the slogan 'education, education, education' and me leaving my place of education ten years later with 'murder' in my ears. I had played a key role in the development of Access provision in the 1980s, had pioneered the first MA to be validated by the University of Leeds in one of their affiliated colleges, and had established a venue for visiting writers at the local City Screen under the Wakean title *riverlines*. What I struggle with is that few can agree on the narrative of what went wrong inside the College during that period. That must be true of many traumatic periods and massacres in human history, that there is no agreed version as to what took place. We are all in that regard victims of both the events and the later narrative. Needless to say, in the corridors of my mind I know what happened and it's not a pleasant story. Bitterness, however, is not me, but I do regret losing the College that I knew and liked.


## California excursion

Somehow I realised almost the moment I was appointed in 1978 that if I were to stay for any length of time at College I would need a year away in the first few years. If the College could remain a background noise, I would be fine. After all, I had a history I could draw on of being semi-detached from places, dating back to my primary school and my early experience of being 'away' from home. If not, the stuffiness of the College atmosphere and its narrow experience of life would get to me. Fortunately, two of my colleagues in English had established a tradition of staff exchanges with Cabrillo College in northern California, and my fourth year in College, 1981-2, was spent in sleepy hollow, away from the madding crowd, beside the Pacific Ocean in Santa Cruz County.

I had little idea what to expect, or, rather, I had a head full of images of what to expect but no reality against which to test them. We landed late one afternoon in early August at San Francisco airport and I went to get a trolley. Our son, Matt, who was then aged two-and-a-half, lay down on the crowded concourse to catch up on some sleep. He'd done well on the long flight and I couldn't blame him for succumbing. As I was crossing the concourse, a beautifully dressed, young, black woman brushed up against me. 'Have you somewhere to go for the night?' I think that's what I caught as we were crossing. If she was Irish she might have said, 'Have you nowhere to go for the night?' Well, that was an interesting introduction to America, I reflected. Not so much a welcome as a barely disguised proposition. It woke me up. I hadn't any such thoughts on my mind, for I was part of a group of exchange teachers from Britain on my way to an induction programme in the care of the Fulbright people. Once outside the terminal the first sight to greet me were blacked-out limousines, parked, or waiting. Yes, the movies were right. It was a lawless country and I was surrounded by hoods in parked cars, waiting. I looked round. I must be on my guard, ready to defend my family. Then we boarded the coach to San Francisco State University, and somehow my eye was drawn to a crack in the window pane where I was sitting.

A couple of days later, on the drive down to Santa Cruz along the coast road, Nick Roberts, who had come to collect us, pointed out where the gangsters in the 1930s took care of business. It seemed out of keeping, such a dramatic coastline to play host to foul murder, but that was California I discovered, where heaven and hell were brought into close alignment and its people, when not participants, reduced to spectators. In the end, after months in their company, I was impressed by the way my hosts handled what they witnessed. It didn't so much subvert as extend my idea of contemporary sensibility, for my immediate response was 'how awful' or 'how awful that so much beauty should play host to so much killing'. But here was something new. The attitude was either a pause somewhere between non-acceptance and acceptance, or a refusal to see the world in tragic terms.

The seventy-mile journey down to Santa Cruz took an age, or that was how it seemed to someone who was suffering fatigue or jet-lag. We passed some shacks in fields and then some more shacks in towns. Or they looked like shacks, wooden structures you might find at the bottom of a garden in England. I assumed they were for agricultural workers until I was gently disillusioned by Nick. 'Shacks? No, they're houses, that's where we live. In our climate, we don't need heavy structures as you have. And besides, you have to remember this is earthquake country.' Wood bends, I heard myself thinking, bricks collapse. My mind was slowing down. Better to be surrounded by wood than something that can kill you, I just managed to surmise.

There was something temporary about the whole landscape. In time the strip of land I was travelling through would end up where Alaska now is. That shapes the imagination and shapes the way you think about life. At the same time people had learned to adapt to their environment. 'At least we don't have hurricanes here,' Nick added, 'or snow storms, though we do have mudslides.' That was a theme that was to become familiar. Americans are convinced they live in places that aren't as bad as other places in America. It was the equivalent of British people confessing to strangers, 'The weather isn't normally this cold, or this wet, or this hot.'

The first fortnight was devoted to jet-lag. I spent my time reclining on a hard sofa in a ranch-style house near Aptos junior high school and across the road from a nasty-looking, steep-sided creek or gulch. In front of the house there grew a beautiful redwood tree, which had reached some forty feet in height in fifteen years. It was home to a million moths but these didn't seem to affect its vigour. During the day few people passed the house for it was a cul-de-sac. It was so quiet at times that I could have been in a short story by Raymond Carver. We had lunch sitting out in a large garden at the back of the house, overlooked by a shallow-rooted, acacia tree. Mornings tended to be overcast but by midday the sun had burnt off the coastal fog. Grass was for cutting but not for lying out on; only a harsh kind of grass would grow in that climate.

Jet-lag and the bright sunlight made it difficult for me to absorb what was happening. The phone would ring and then pause, ring again and then pause. I considered that courteous, as if the person at the other end was saying, 'Pick me up when you're ready.' I liked that too about the way people drove their cars and had huge spaces in which to park them. However, I was cautioned by Nick when I got behind the wheel of a car, 'Whatever you do, don't insist.' That was good advice, for you couldn't know what weapons were within reach of an angry person or whether those hoods hiding in their blacked-out cars I had observed at SFO had homes in Santa Cruz County.

It was evident from the crowded highway that there was a high density of people in the area of Santa Cruz County, but they seemed to live not in large conurbations but among the trees away from each other. Neighbourliness didn't mean living on top of each other, and in that regard you might say they were friendly from a distance. Some people were clearly involved in living out something, some dream or ideal, some pursuit perhaps of loneliness or solitude, and their house or plot, together with some vicious-looking dogs, acted as a bulwark against the world or prying neighbours. Trees did more than give added protection against the blazing hot sun, for, to my mind, they were the real neighbours or companions. The stately and independent sequoia and redwood were a reminder of the rewards of a simple life. They were never merely decorative but, like a church or mosque or temple, they inhabited the landscape and at the same time insisted on being noticed and set in dialogue, Buber-like, as a Thou, not an It. The eucalyptus tree, which had been imported from Australia, swayed in the ocean breeze and took root as if it were native to the area. To ease their consciences for having wiped out the native population, the early settlers along that coast must have concluded that if trees could take root so easily then so could they. Nearly everyone we met was from some other part of the United States, so establishing new lifestyle habits was like a theme-tune running through the year we spent in California.

As a footnote, when I returned to California in the summer of 2010 for a short visit I was determined to see the exhibition about Ishi at the Museum of Anthropology in Berkeley. I wanted to touch again the tragic strain that runs through California. In a building opposite the noisy corner of Bancroft and College, where stands a handy campus bus-stop, can be found in a low-lit display cabinet the effects of a man who was the last of his tribe, who, when he was discovered in 1911 in an area of central California thought to have been 'cleared' of native Americans, struggled to be understood for nobody spoke his language. His name means simply 'man', someone that is who is identical with his tribe. In this book I reflect on the idea of loss visiting the Coronation Room in the Castle Museum in York, on the loosening ties in my Irish family and on being deprived of my Jewish family, on the struggle to find myself growing up, but all this pales into insignificance beside the fate that befell Ishi. California, like Spain a land of contrasts, is a great antidote to those given to maudlin sentiments.

*Outside the Museum of Anthropology at Berkeley, California. August 2010. Amid the images, the face of Ishi stares out of the exhibition poster as if to remind us of his complex fate as a native American.*

I can't help thinking the long-expected 'big one' has already occurred, and it was the earthquake in the eighteenth and nineteenth centuries which wiped out whole peoples, tribes, languages, so much tenderness, a whole way of life, and astonishingly beautiful baskets. After that, after such knowledge, after such history, what forgiveness? And it's worse when you reflect on who you might turn to to apologise for the 'civilising' Spanish missions or for the series of massacres carried out by those generations of white settlers on the indigenous peoples. You find yourself rightly stumbling on those prepositions 'to to' and the interrogative pronoun. It is estimated that at the time of pre-Contact in 1769, when the first Mission was established in San Diego, there were some three hundred thousand to a million native Californians; by the end of the nineteenth century that number had dwindled to around twenty thousand. With some justification, 'California's holocaust' is the term Herbert Luthin uses to describe this period in his anthology of Indian writing, *Surviving Through The Days* (2002).

Thread some fifty beads on a string, one for every language lost out of the eighty to hundred languages, and say a rosary to them all. Start with 'Yana', the area where Ishi was discovered, and follow in your mind the long hot valley of the San Joaquin down through the San Francisco Bay Area of the 'Ohlonean' family of languages, through John Steinbeck's 'Salinan', down to 'Chumash' and 'Gabrielino', and end in the 'Mohave' Desert where aircraft land after their space missions. Such linguistic diversity, now irrecoverable, deserved to survive into the modern world. Yes, the 'big one' has already occurred.

In this context, by way of contrast, when we were there in 1981 everyone seemed to be in pursuit of loneliness, the title of an influential study by Philip Slater about American culture at breaking point and published ten years before in 1971. Ishi of course had been reduced to loneliness in dramatic fashion, but here, seven decades later, people, some of whom believed they had no history worth speaking of in comparison with Europe, were actively seeking solitude. Equally, while everyone was an individual they were in a sense doing the same thing. Such ironies brought out my instincts as a European, something I hadn't dwelt on before arriving in California. In Britain, unless you are wealthy, you tend to live in small houses and on top of each other. But here people could dream dreams of being an individual without limits. And for many, their dreams and their needs were satisfied, and for some their envy was quenched or assuaged.

Few people we came across really understood the idea of limits or what life would be like if every dream had been met or, better, found wanting. 'What then?' I would ask. That would normally take off in another direction, into a discussion about Eastern mysticism or the soul, but rarely back into the practical social dimension and the kind of society that was emerging or that you would want to see emerge. Few people we met in other words wanted to talk about circumstance, a topic that we never stopped talking about back home.

Perhaps they were right. Europe and the tyranny of social class were behind them, the future and opportunity for the individual were in front of them. After all, without realising it, at the local Safeway supermarket in Rancho del Mar, you could queue behind a millionaire in *Levi* jeans. The last best hope of earth, as Abraham Lincoln proclaimed and Ronald Reagan never stopped repeating. Bill Grant, who established the English Division at Cabrillo, lived on Pleasant Valley Road. To find him you took Highway 1 and turned off at Freedom Boulevard. Highway 1 to Freedom and then Pleasant Valley. That was a perfect way of defining the layout of Eden, and when you arrived at Bill's he would point out the apricot tree in the garden that grew from the discarded stone of an apricot he once ate several years before. On the deck on the side of the house facing south, humming birds would come to entertain him in the morning sunlight. When the moon was high in the night sky, in a big, wooden crypt of a room, which had been built for him by his colleague Dick Lundquist, Bill would listen to his favourite opera singers on his state-of-the-art, hi-fi system. When he retired from teaching, he made himself an expert in roses and would take groups all over the world on rose trips.

There was so much energy in the environment, and there did seem to be more hours in the day. We were repeatedly asked by colleagues what we did. At first we couldn't understand the question. 'What do you mean "what we did or what we do"? We teach. Isn't that enough?' 'Yes, I know that, but what outside of teaching do you do?' And then it all came out, in the same way it did when you discovered all the other cars that they had in their garages at home. Among my immediate colleagues, there were people who built houses, others like Dan Harper had become expert photographers, or had taken up hang-gliding for a hobby which took them to Mexico and Spain. Hiking in the Santa Cruz mountains or in the foothills of the Sierra was another favourite. If you took up something, you became expert at it. There was no room for dilettantes or for people like myself who just enjoyed curling up on the sofa with a book. Almost no one watched live television. They would rent movies from local stores but had accepted that an evening watching broadcast programmes, constantly interrupted by adverts, was not for them.

Of all the groups of people I taught with in my career, those at Cabrillo in 1981-2 were the ones I enjoyed being with the most. Ironically, the happiest year at my college in York was the year I spent in Santa Cruz. It was a blessed time, 'the golden years' as Dan Harper's wife, Alice, told me when we met up again after thirty years. My partner and I came in at the end of the drug phase, but even that had its comic side. One of my afflicted students decided to write about Santa Cruz after studying Joyce's *Dubliners* in class. 'You must have wondered coming here to California from England,' he addressed me in his formal essay, 'what to make of it all. Well, Joyce has given us an insight into his native city, and if I was to give you an insight into my native county I would say it was artsy, fartsy, and full of dope. That's a good impression to take away with you, but it wouldn't of course be enough. And Joyce wanted to convey more about his city.' Yes, he was right about that, for there was more to Santa Cruz, but I never forgot what he imagined was a helpful introduction. Artsy, fartsy, and full of dope. I can just see him now sitting down to write that essay and putting himself in my shoes. Taking drugs and reading Joyce had done something for his sympathetic imagination.

Among the staff there was also a small number of delightful 'flakes'. One of my colleagues had been in the San Francisco police department in the 1960s but had then undergone a conversion and he ended up teaching creative writing at Cabrillo in a tepee. Perhaps he judged that furniture and a solid building were just some kind of capitalist ploy and that to get the right kind of vibes you needed to be physically reminded of native American culture. But for the most part, tutors, or 'instructors' as they were called, were quite simply exceptional. You could tell they had been through something together and that they were now waiting for the second half of the performance to begin. Patterns of behaviour were well-established, so they were tolerant of each other, but there was still room for things to happen.

I was also blessed in following in the footsteps of my exchange partner, Mel Tuohey. In pursuit of another life, Mel had himself spent a year in County Clare not far from my family's people and was spoken of in hushed tones by his colleagues. 'What would Mel do in these circumstances?' would be invoked when facing a particularly hard decision. Linda Kitz, who lived in the 'city' (that is San Francisco) and who was my Head of Department, would take me to lunch and talk about her hopes or, rather, her fears for the future especially over the impending cuts in Cabrillo's budget. Don Young, who wrote a memoir of his experiences as a wire man in the Second World War, was one of the funniest people I have ever met. Fred Levy and John Morgan had read everything worth reading, or that was the impression they gave me. It was an extremely cultured department and at the same time at ease with itself. When he wasn't chopping down wood to supplement his income, Nick would spend his time at UCSC library reading Greek classics in the original.

Creative writing was one of the great strengths of the department, and several people were published poets such as Mort Marcus, Anita Wilkins and Joe Stroud, or novelists such as Kirby Wilkins. In the academy, Derrida and Deconstruction were in the ascendancy. I once attended a high-level seminar among the redwoods at UCSC where someone was cheered for punning on 'historical' and 'hysterical', but down at the local community college they were getting on with their teaching and writing and, when that was over, they turned to their hobbies. It was the best form of adult education. There were regular public readings in Santa Cruz and Capitola, and I would have an opportunity of hearing my colleagues perform in front of large gatherings. I also enjoyed more private discussions with these seasoned practitioners in the art of writing. There was no one sharper than Anita Wilkins at highlighting redundant phrases or images in a line of verse.

My colleagues taught students of all ages and from all walks of life in large classes of around twenty five, and they managed to involve them all. Teaching English at Cabrillo consisted largely of what was called composition class, where students learnt how to improve their command of the language and their skills at writing. The first two years of a degree were also catered for, so there were also some classes in Literature. In a newly-established Writing Center, staffed by English colleagues, students could drop in for remedial or just basic work. It was a community college both in name and practice, and at that time in California tuition was free.

I found the teaching quite challenging, with some classes starting at eight o'clock in the morning. The word 'quite' I am using here in its English sense as a qualifier, not in its American sense as an intensifier. Quite challenging, not very challenging. Mention of 'quite' triggers another memory for me. Listening was frequently challenging, not so much in the differences in the use of particular words, which is a common enough talking-point when people from Britain and the United States get together, but in the attitude to language and to the speaker's insertion in language. Some colleagues spoke as if they were actors in a play, addressing both me and the world and the language they were using. I could see they enjoyed the way I too relished the language that simultaneously joined us and separated us. There is something appropriate about the concept of 'the auditory imagination' being first propounded by T.S.Eliot, an American poet and critic. The alignment between ordinary conversation and fluent dialogue in modern American drama is often noticed, but, if I hadn't spent a year in California, I might never have attended to how the voice as much as the mouth distinguishes the whole culture. Several colleagues, independently, pointed out to me that what was missing from contemporary English poetry, in contrast to Irish verse, was the voice. They could hear Seamus Heaney's voice but only rarely the voice of his contemporaries writing in England. I think what they meant was the person behind the voice, but it was always couched in terms of the voice.

Class size was also an issue, with some as many as thirty seven. In a letter to Brian Sourbut, written in February 1982, a copy of which I kept, I observed with a mixture of prescience and hollow optimism: 'If we have to up our ratio to 1:15 at York, it'll just look more like school teaching. When the cuts come in earnest with the colleges next year, there won't be a bleep from the universities. Here in California they are in general about 6-18 months behind the UK.' Students, though, were lively and responsive, and some were very bright. When the surf was up, some wouldn't attend, which was fine by me. Some young men in their late twenties would want to show me their new mountain bikes. Again, fine by me. 'Just stop by at my office,' I would say. Twenty-eight going on eighteen, the new generation had arrived.

One elderly, immature student in his seventies objected to studying Lawrence's sensuous poem 'Gloire de Dijon' in class. It must have been on account of the reference to the poet looking at his partner's breasts swaying as she washed herself in the morning. I discovered afterward that his son in the 1960s was found guilty of murdering joggers in the Santa Cruz mountains, and he blamed libertarian counterculture for leading him astray. Until he withdrew from my class, he would love taunting the younger students in the class: 'Shape up or ship out'. I should have called him aside after the first class and told him in no uncertain terms to 'butt out'. I did think of doing so but was held back because of my status as a visiting instructor.

I particularly enjoyed the opening session when I would go round the class asking each student in turn something about themselves. 'My name's Thelma and I'm a poet.' 'I'm Chuck and I'm a novelist.' At school I was called facetious so I had to restrain myself from commenting on what the students were telling me, but I always enjoyed entertaining in my mind the 'dare'. Such students genuinely believed that if they were writing verse they were a poet and could legitimately describe themselves thus. I realise that 'genuinely' is not the best word, but then I sometimes couldn't decide what was the real thing in America. It took me quite a while before I gave straight answers to my colleagues. 'What do you think about living here?' Bill Grant would inquire. 'Oh, it's fine.' Later, when he asked again, I would find myself replying, 'Do you believe all that stuff that's out there in the ether and on the airwaves? And another thing, Bill. Why do they shout at you on television? Are you all hard of hearing or what?'

I had in mind Wendy Tokuda, an Asian American news anchor on a Bay Area channel, and the occasion during a five-day storm when she shouted across the airwaves that a particular district had seen so much rain that it was now 'flooded with water'. As she hit the 'd' in 'flooded' and flapped the 't' in 'water', in a phrase that rhythmically echoed her own name, I felt I had been drowned (with water) just listening to her. Bill was always keen to protect me from the worst excesses in the culture, but that was a forlorn task for, like the bulging, brown bags at supermarket check-outs, excess was pretty much in evidence everywhere. For the sake of balance, however, there were enough

273

students to force me to rethink my ideas and to learn that there were necessary distinctions to be drawn. 'My name's Colleen and I'm a refugee from Southern California.'

What I did learn quite forcibly was to take care when generalising about the culture. It was as if an indigenous counter-movement had grown inside me, and I date it to a time when Kirby Wilkins took us on a trip to the White Mountains on the other side of the Sierra. We were with my brother, John, and had camped at eight thousand feet. A mini-whirlwind greeted us when we arrived to pitch tent. The following day, looking down toward Nevada you could see a road which ran for some twenty-five miles into the distance. That would be equivalent to seeing Leeds from York. Turning round you could then trace the line from north to south of snow-capped peaks of the mountain range that forms part of the Sierra. If distance didn't cause you to pause, then antiquity would, for the White Mountains are home to the bristlecone pine, some of which have been growing in the dry and sheltered environment on the leeward side of the Sierra for eight thousand years. In the face of such immensity there's something to be said for just keeping your mouth shut or singing to yourself a hymn to silence. When I returned to York, I found it increasingly difficult to teach American Literature, and would wince when I heard the familiar clichés about American life and culture being rehearsed by students and tutors alike.

*Bristlecone pine tree growing in an arid part of the White Mountains. Much of the tree can die but new life emerges elsewhere. In this way it can live for eight thousand years.*

One morning we caught our son in front of the television, his hand on his heart, reciting the pledge of allegiance. We decided it was time to return home. It had been a memorable year. During the Christmas vacation, we visited Mexico, the country which, quite legitimately, lays claim to being at the centre of the earth, where all points north and south, east and west, past and present, finally come together in an extraordinary embrace. Not for nothing did I find myself surmising that if you wanted the *echt* Spanish experience or, indeed, one of the primary California experiences, go west or south to Mexico. We were there to spend a fortnight in Cuernavaca, the city of eternal spring, a city made famous by Malcolm Lowry in one of my favourite novels, *Under the Volcano* (1947). In the fields the farmers were harvesting, while on noisy, heavy, heaving buses dating back to the 1930s live chickens were being transported by the rural poor. At the entrance to the market, young boys of seven or eight would volunteer to help with the shopping while on the street outside older women would sit all day with a neat pile of oranges arranged in the shape of a pyramid, hoping, seemingly with little hope, to sell one or two to passers-by. You would need to be born to it to know how to survive such poverty. And yet the bougainvillea was all around us in bloom, lizards were climbing the walls of gated houses and communities, and murals by the revolutionary artist Diego Rivera on the stairs in the Palacio Cortés were as striking as the day they were painted in 1929-30. In the distance, in all its snow-clad majesty, watching and patiently waiting on for its next eruption, rose Popocatapetl, the smoking mountain.

On our return from Mexico we witnessed one of the worst floods to hit Santa Cruz. If the 'big one' had struck that January, when the power lines were down and whole hillsides washed away and bridges under threat from piled-up fallen trees and the rescue services at full stretch, well, that doesn't bear thinking about. In all kinds of ways it was a topsy-turvy time. In May 1982 I penned a polemical piece against the Falklands War in the Cabrillo newspaper, which was accompanied by a piece attacking her government by a colleague from Argentina. But our California excursion was over and it was right to return home and pick up where we had left off in York. We said goodbye for a final time to Yosemite and to my favourite bookstores and restaurants, closed my account with *Wells Fargo*, the bank that was always being robbed in westerns, and after a brief detour to see the sights in Boston, New York, and Washington DC, we landed home twelve months after our departure. Margaret Thatcher was still in power.

## Writing

The year in California was a fallow period in my life, but it did allow me time to extend my reading and to reflect on the next stage in my academic career. It also alerted me to the value of computers not only in the new world of information retrieval but also in the future of writing or 'word-processing'. I returned home anxious to get going on a doctorate on Yeats and Joyce under Graham Martin at the Open University and Timothy Webb at the University of York. My earlier attempt at a survey of Irish writing had resulted in an M.Litt., but I was keen now to focus more sharply on two of the leading Irish writers. I hadn't lost the appetite for undertaking ambitious projects and I eventually found a way of handling it, beginning with chapters on Yeats and the oral tradition and Joyce and the literary tradition and focussing in central chapters on their attitudes toward modernity. Throughout, I had at the back of my mind a concern with getting the two writers to face each other. I began to hear my voice again.

The year in the States had convinced me of the need to counter idealism with something more rooted in circumstance. Initially, I surmised there was mileage in calling it something like 'Irish Modernism and Cultural Materialism'. But eventually I settled on something less polemical with a focus on modernity: 'Towers of Accommodation: Yeats and Joyce as Irish Writers'. Somehow the issue of modernity, which had sparked into life at Wonersh in the 1960s, continued to preoccupy me. It was now linked with the Durkheimian idea of the homeless mind and with Peter Berger's subtitle to the book with that title, 'Modernization and Consciousness'. In the image of the Martello Tower at Sandycove, where *Ulysses* begins, and of Yeats's tower at Ballylee, Joyce and Yeats offered me a way of discussing competing responses to modernity. In the final paragraph of my thesis I reflected:

> The towers provide us with two primary responses to modernity, one which learnt through exile to accept the heterogeneity of experience and the dispersed subject, and the other, in its fear of modernity, continued to assert its separateness and its belief in a return to a pre-modern civilisation. These two positions continue to inform the modern world.

My two supervisors pushed me hard and let nothing slip. I have kept all their notes on my work and am astonished by the closeness of their close readings. Webb taught me to work with words and phrases and to spend time on delay, while Martin always queried my use of words such as 'typical' or 'characteristic'. I never believed I could satisfy them either separately or together. They expected so much from me. That must be a common experience among doctoral students, a mixture of pressure from supervisors and self-doubt as to outcome. Even when I submitted the thesis to the Open University in 1987, I wasn't sure it was finished. A joint-study of this kind was essentially always going to be unfinished, but I didn't realise that at the time. I kept imagining it was like a mathematical theorem where you ended it with 'Q.E.D'. But what had I demonstrated? That question haunted me and continued to do so even though I had satisfied my examiners that it did merit the university's highest award.

In time, what my doctorate gave me was not only stamina but also confidence. It had been a long apprenticeship getting to this point, but I felt I could now get on with tackling things without having constantly to seek approval, and I also had a bank of material, a storehouse, on which the apprentice could draw for years to come. The first big project came in 1989 with a guide to Yeats criticism for students. Graham Martin had put forward my name to Bristol Classical Press and that is how that book came about. I was familiar with much of the criticism for that contributed to the basis of the first chapter of the thesis. The difficulty lay in organising the material into appropriate chapters. Once I had settled on an outline of chapters for the most part by genre, the book wrote itself. My editor inserted 'State-of-the-Art' into the title, which I found slightly odd since most of the books and ideas I was discussing were written long before 1989, when the book was published. Being up-to-date or keeping up-to-date has never seriously bothered me. How could it when I was brought up on Aquinas and neo-scholasticism? However, I did include a final chapter on Yeats and contemporary criticism and that seemed to satisfy everyone.

The most ironic aspect about my first book on Yeats is that I received not a penny for all my troubles. Soon after it appeared, my publisher went bankrupt, or rather the catering business it was attached to in Bristol went bankrupt and dragged down the publisher with it. When it was subsequently taken over by Duckworth, I was informed that no royalties were forthcoming. So a comprehensive guide to Yeats criticism, published fifty years after Yeats's death, which is listed in some eighteen libraries in COPAC, the catalogue of the UK's leading research libraries, and over a hundred and ninety libraries on

Worldcat.org, produced absolutely nothing for its author. It was my first introduction to difficulties with publishers. No trips to the Bahamas, then, materialised with this publication, and I was left with Samuel Johnson's famous remark ringing in my ears: 'No man but a blockhead ever wrote, except for money.'

My involvement in international Joyce conferences began in 1987 and 1988 with a conference at the University of Leeds on *Finnegans Wake*, followed by the bi-annual International James Joyce Symposium in Venice. At both I gave papers on the politics of the *Wake*, which resulted in an article in *Textual Practice* at that time. The Venice Symposium, which was held on the island of San Giorgio opposite St Mark's, brought together the leading players in Joyce studies along with the heirs of Joyce, Pound, and Yeats. If that wasn't enough, I was staying at the Pensione Calcina, where John Ruskin had stayed in the spring of 1877. The Symposium attracted some of the best minds in Joyce studies, and in particular I had several enjoyable conversations with Bernard Benstock, who had just launched the *James Joyce Literary Supplement* with his move to the University of Miami. I discovered an immediate rapport with the boy from the Lower East Side in New York, who, like me, before entering Joyce studies had spent time reflecting on the work of Sean O'Casey and his significance for the Left. A massive heart attack cut short his life, but in his will, in a typical act of generosity towards his friend Rosa-Maria Bollettieri Bosinelli, he donated his library of books to the University of Bologna at Forli.

Fritz Senn I encountered for the first time in Leeds, and he was someone I got to know very well over the years. 'Venice was your first Symposium, wasn't it?' he would put to me as a question, knowing all the time it was the case. Whenever I gave a paper, the former Swiss printer would take me aside afterward and harangue me for reading it and not speaking from notes. He was consistently rude but I actually enjoyed this about him, for there was something both persistent and consistent about him as if the two adjectives were allied or in his case indistinguishable. At the Symposium in Monaco in 1990 I saw him in a room speaking and Joyce's grandson in front of him in the audience. Ironically, it was Fritz who most reminded me of Joyce, not in appearance, for Joyce dressed stylishly, but in attitude and mental outlook. On another occasion at the Joyce Summer School held in Newman House in Dublin, I recall Frank Delaney delivering a polished talk on the ubiquitous presence of *Hamlet* in *Ulysses*. Fritz, who was sitting close to the fireplace where in *A Portrait of the Artist as a Young Man* Stephen takes to task the Dean of Studies over the word 'tundish', was the first to rise in the audience. He didn't bother with the usual pleasantries about what a splendid talk he had listened to and so on, but merely observed that there were more references to buttons in *Ulysses* than to Shakespeare's play, and then he promptly sat down.

In 1990 at a Word and Image conference held at the University of Zurich, I delivered a paper on Sturge Moore's cover designs for the Macmillan editions of Yeats's poems. The visual dimension accompanying texts was a long-standing interest and I thought to combine it with my work on Yeats and Joyce. In 1991 I submitted to Robert Baldock at Yale University Press in London a proposal for an advanced introduction to Joyce which attended to his Irish contexts. The production values at Yale are among the best in the world, and fortunately the proposal was accepted. Baldock didn't have much to go on but he had seen something he liked, and I was lucky to have someone to support me. *James Joyce's Ireland*, which appeared in 1992, was printed in mainland China. It had a print run of some seven thousand copies, which were divided roughly equally between New Haven and London. Throughout the production of the book I was consulted, including being asked about the page layout, the cover design, and marketing. Catherine Carver, who had worked on Ellmann's famous biography of Joyce, was my copy editor for part of the time. With her neat, pencil annotations to my manuscript, she managed to prevent quite a few howlers from getting into print and ruining my reputation for ever. Unfortunately she died half way through editing my book and I never got to meet her.

The Index was the one thing I didn't see until it was published, and that was a mistake, for there are over sixty errors, which I would have been able to pick up within an hour or so. One of those mistakes still makes me laugh out loud. The person responsible for the Index was an American who either wasn't terribly familiar with *Ulysses* or who had an off-day. In the first episode of that novel, the Jesuit-educated Stephen Dedalus is taunted by his friend Mulligan to 'Chuck Loyola and come on down' to join him for a morning swim. In the Index there is a reference to 'Ignatius of Loyola, Saint' in connection with his *Spiritual Exercises*, and then later on there is a reference to 'Loyola, Chuck'. If a subsequent edition is ever contemplated, that was one error I vowed never to correct.

I was then asked to consider writing another book for Yale and this time I wanted to produce a portrait of Yeats which combined biography, history, and criticism and which attended to his English contexts. This was a more scholarly venture and involved me in visits to research libraries in the United States. I enjoy ferreting around, and in the Beinecke Library at Yale I discovered a previously unknown letter written by T.S.Eliot under his pseudonym, 'Possum', and addressed to 'Rabbit' (Ezra Pound), an amusing letter on the reception of *For Lancelot Andrews* (1928), which neither the Library nor Valerie Eliot knew anything about. Other finds proved more significant. The State University of New York at Stony Brook held at that time photocopies of a huge bank of Yeats material including his correspondence with his wife, George Yeats. One afternoon while researching there I came across a letter written in February 1923 at the height of the Civil War in Ireland, in which his English wife urged him not to abandon his country, for this might have a negative impact on his future reputation. What surprised me was that no one had made anything of the significance of this letter and yet it had been available for many years. However, when it came to publishing I could not get permission to quote the passage verbatim and had to resort to paraphrase, which was irritating. This is why I end that book with a hope that George's life might be told in her own words.

Scholars working in the field of modern literature not infrequently come up against the restrictive practices of those in charge of literary estates. In 1994 when I sought permission to cite unpublished Yeats material, I had to elicit the agreement of Michael Yeats for the family, Roy Foster, the official biographer, John Kelly, the editor of the letters, and Ann Saddlemyer, who was writing the biography of George Yeats. Rejections and put-downs were tiresome, and after my *Yeats's Worlds* was published in 1995 I put a time limit on my involvement in Yeats studies. I made an exception, however, for the four-volume edition of Yeats criticism published in 1999 by Amanda Helm, because I knew that would not involve unpublished material, and, besides, Amanda lived in my native county and was very persuasive.

The years between 1994 and 2000 were a busy time for me. An original study of Yeats and an anthology of Yeats criticism, a collection of essays on Sterne arising from an international conference in York which I helped my Dutch friend, Peter de Voogd, to edit, and then the large-scale undertaking for Cork University Press of *Irish Writing in the Twentieth Century: A Reader.* Each of the two anthologies came to a million words. The head-notes and footnotes for the Cork *Reader* took me over a year to compile, and that was before the proofs arrived. All that was too much and came on top of a full timetable at my College. The problems I had with the Joyce estate over the Cork *Reader* have been well-documented. Here is what I wrote in a letter in June 2008 to the *Times Higher Education:*

As the editor of *Irish Writing in the Twentieth Century: A Reader* and someone mentioned by name in Alistair McCleery's 'Dead Hands Keep a Closed Book' (5 June), let me add a brief comment. Like Joyce's *Ulysses*, my book was dragged through the courts, but, whatever edition of *Ulysses* you choose to buy, you will never see one with 23 pages excised and a page stitched in carrying a single sentence like some graffiti on a newly-painted white wall: 'Pages 323-346 have been removed due to a dispute in relation to copyright'. The case was high-profile, more so in Ireland than in the UK. It was also personally damaging. I was in New York in September 2000 with the only copy of the book then in the USA when my editor, Sara Wilbourne, rang to say that under no circumstances could I show anyone the book since a worldwide injunction had been imposed in the High Court in Dublin. For an academic it was the worst of times. Footnotes and head notes alone had taken me a year to research, and with 10,000 copies in a publisher's warehouse there was little prospect they would be pulped and a new edition set. Fortunately, the book of a million words did get published on World Book Day in March 2001 and it has been well-received in spite of its difficult birth.

I never got to appear in court but if I had I would have suggested the forum was inappropriate for settling such a dispute. The fee requested by the Estate of James Joyce for 'The Dead' was raised from £7000 to £7500 simply because I was tardy in my reply. For three weeks I was away from home attending the International James Joyce Symposium at Goldsmiths College in London, and I then went on to lecture at the James Joyce Summer School in Trieste. It was at that stage that I deleted 'The Dead' from the edition and advised the publisher to run the book without Joyce. My publisher took soundings in Ireland and concluded we could use extracts from Danis Rose's edition of *Ulysses*, a book which was then available in the bookshops. As I look at my book today I cannot believe anyone will think justice has been served. Does it significantly matter that 'catholic', 'christian' or 'jew' are in lower case or that someone sat 'crosslegged' or 'cross-legged'? Could that ever justify vandalising a book and reducing a university press to near penury?

My case is a visible one. What about all the other cases of books and editions which were never published in the years since European harmonisation and the extension of copyright to 70 years or which were abandoned at the last minute? Elsewhere, in North America, there is Michael Groden's remarkable hypertext edition of *Ulysses* that is still waiting to be loaded onto the net. McCleery is right to insist on academics and publishers, in the interests of the reading public, tackling copyright owners when they are unreasonable. The move on the part of the Irish Government in 2004 to protect its leading writer shows what can be done when we have states and governments on our side. In my new book *Reading Joyce*, I'm more philosophical but I had in mind my Cork *Reader* and a whole slew of books that have been silently dropped: 'It's not only in what he has to say but also in the legacy he has bequeathed us that Joyce remains our contemporary. In turn, for those involved in his recuperation and his continuing reception therefore, the struggle to spread the word of Joyce has a certain heroic quality which will be best appreciated perhaps by those who come after us.'

I can still feel the pain. All that autumn I feared the *Reader* might never see the light of day and that ten thousand copies might be pulped and two years and more of intensive work come to nothing. One of my Irish friends told me to forget about it for the time being, otherwise I would end up in a hospital. It was good advice for I wasn't sleeping. The book, without the offending extract by a certain Mr Joyce, was eventually published the following spring. Sara Wilbourne, my publisher, kindly arranged a launch at the National Film Institute in Dublin, where Fintan O'Toole spoke about the book to a gathering that included Medb Ruane, John Montague, Brendan Kennelly, and Terence Brown, as well as my brother-in-law, Terry Eagleton, and members of my family from County Clare. Kennelly let it be known that a copy should be in the library of every secondary school in Ireland. John Bowman devoted three of his radio programmes on Raidió Teilifís Éireann to the *Reader*, and there were kind reviews in the Irish newspapers. Nothing, however, made up for the physical attack on the book itself.

Then came a dramatic interlude. In May 2002 I was diagnosed with a very rare tumour inside the cervical part of my spine. My GP, Robert Ruston, rang me up one Friday lunchtime and told me to wait by the phone for a call from Hull Royal Infirmary. The MRI scan at York District Hospital had shown up something nasty and I would need to see a specialist immediately. That was the longest weekend of my life. I knew that a tumour inside the spinal cord was often fatal and didn't leave you a lot of time to set your house in order. In my mind I decided where all the books in my library should go to and prepared for a quick exit. I kept hearing the sentence about 'History is your own heartbeat', which the African-American poet, Michael S.Harper, uses for one of his early volumes of verse, but the beautifully composed observation, full of meaning, had now taken on a menacing aspect.

On the Monday, when I arrived in Mr Gerry O'Reilly's room at Hull, the first thing I wanted from the keen-eyed consultant as I sat down was to know if the tumour was going to kill me or not. 'No,' he reassured me, 'but it could do serious damage if not removed.' 'Oh, in that case, I have all the time in the world. Let's talk.' The scans revealed an intramedullary tumour the size of the top of my index finger down to the knuckle, extending from C4 to C6. My surgeon couldn't determine if it was an ependymoma or an astrocytoma; that would only become apparent when the spine had been opened up. As its name implies, an astrocytoma is star-shaped and more difficult to remove because it will almost certainly be entangled in neural tissue. 'Let's hope it's the other one,' I said.

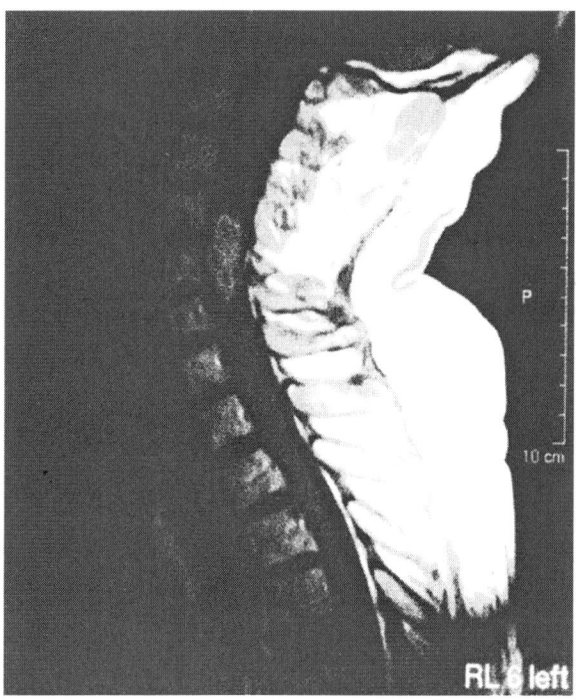

*MRI scan showing tumour trying to fill the empty space below C6.*

Before the operation, I had imagined modern medicine had devised some keyhole surgery for this kind of procedure. Simply inject some fine, flexible, piece of steel through a small hole and suck out or zap what shouldn't be there. That would be painless I figured, a little incision, a few stitches, and then home. The reality came as a bit of a shock or, rather, a series of shocks. No, there was no alternative to opening the spine, cutting above and below where the tumour had grown, prising back a whole lot of grey and white matter, and then if possible using an instrument called a CUSA, an ultrasonic surgical aspirator, to vaporize most of the tumour and then with a scalpel scraping away the rest. 'I wonder how long this will take?' I asked, trying to sound as detached as possible. 'Well, that depends on how much of it we can remove with the CUSA.' I kept scanning his hands to see if there was the faintest hint of a tremble. He was from Northern Ireland and had trained in Dublin at University College. In his early forties, although he hadn't performed this particular operation before, he gave every appearance of knowing what he was doing. 'Look, I can get a second opinion down in London,' and mentioned a name given to me by Chris Oliver, a friend who is an orthopaedic surgeon in Edinburgh. 'Oh, no,' said Gerry confidently, 'that chap is good at brains but this is spine. This is my territory.'

An operation was arranged for early September 2002 and I undertook some more reading round the subject. The night before the operation was the only night in my life I have not managed to get any sleep. The mind was racing. In my reading I had encountered the phrase 'sensory deficits'. 'What exactly were they?' I wanted to know from Gerry. 'Oh, you might come away from the operation with numbness, or the numbness you now have in your fingers and left hand might continue.' But supposing it was worse. After the operation, when the anaesthetist came round to the ward, he casually remarked, 'Of course, you were lucky. You could have ended up as a tetraplegic, lost not only your voice box but also control of your bladder and bowels.' 'Would you have trusted your fate to him?' I wanted to know. 'Certainly. I was with him for the whole eight hours. A real professional. Took no break but survived on wine gums.'

When I was coming round in the recovery ward, from afar I could hear someone asking me, 'David, can you wiggle it? Wiggle it, can you?' I don't know why but I replied, 'I can't, it has a mind of its own.' And then I realised it was a nurse asking me about my feet and toes. I had come through, the old facetiousness still intact. Yes, there was movement, enough for her to report back to the operating team. I was then taken up to a high intensity ward and nursed back into life. It surprised me how quickly the body heals itself. Within forty-eight hours I was walking up stairs and receiving visitors, and within a week, on the first anniversary of 9/11, I was home.

I was signed off work for five months. About the fourth month, I imagined I heard someone calling to me from the shoreline, 'You can come in now.' I had been out at sea in a dinghy on my own. Around six months after the operation, I reached a plateau in my recovery. At that point I realised that whatever deficits I had would be permanent. Damage to the central nervous system is unlike damage to the peripheral nervous system; you almost never get back what you've lost. I had read that if you go into these operations fit and well you will emerge fit and well. To some extent that was true. But the first thing I noticed was that my proprioception, or the awareness of the self in space, had been affected. One morning after returning home from my operation, I went to pick up the post behind the front door only to discover I fell over and couldn't get up. My balance has not been brilliant since the operation. I tend not to have baths because I can't get up to get out. Showers can be a challenge if I don't concentrate when turning round. In small gatherings at parties I tend to sit down rather than chat with people standing up. You watch a child learning to walk, one foot placed down in front of the other, deliberately but not always certainly, and you realise the child is learning about its position in space. At night my body doesn't tell me to turn over from one side to the other, so I momentarily wake when the pain gets to my ear on the pillow. Again, a baby has to be turned in a process whereby the skill at turning over is learned. Unfortunately, as an adult, the nerves, once they are damaged, don't seem capable of relearning some things or discovering other routes back to the brain.

I write all this using my laptop. After the operation I found craning quite painful and still do. So within a short time I bought an *Aeron Miller* chair, which has been nothing short of miraculous. I can angle the chair back and angle the screen on my lap. My body is damaged goods but the chair has been a great source of comfort. The desktop in my study I use only rarely. In my last years at College, marking student work was a struggle because it meant bending my neck. My hands continue to give me trouble. Four years before the operation I had tingling in the fingers of my left hand and surmised it might be neuropathy on account of diabetes. The tingling was diagnosed at York District Hospital by the Neuroscience Unit as mild carpal tunnel syndrome. The only reason I didn't make an official complaint against the Hospital was because the normal time for presentation of symptoms to diagnosis of my condition is four years. Equally, the surgeons at Hull might not have operated until the tumour had grown in size.

After the operation, both hands, but especially my left one, have been a problem, as has my whole body from the neck down. The symptoms are not easy to describe but it's a little like a water-tap that is always on. You can't turn it off or, indeed, moderate its intensity. In the middle of the night the pain or the burning or the numbness or the tightness are with me as soon as the brain flickers into consciousness. The only relief is unconsciousness. I have tried acupuncture, creams, heat patches, tens machines, but all they seem to do is to exacerbate the pain or burning or numbness. 'Keep typing,' Gerry, my surgeon, would say. 'Use it or lose it as the saying goes.' In winter I enjoy wearing gloves, that's if I can get my fingers into them, but I never use the left-hand pockets of my trousers or jacket since I can't distinguish a key from a tissue or a coin or notes. The only watch I can wear is a lightweight one made of titanium. I have no sensitivity but plenty of strength, so driving is not a concern. Of course, typing is full of errors. Most sentences I have to correct, so this tends to slow me down, but nothing frustrates me anymore. I was fortunate in that the tumour didn't come calling in my forties.

Liz Thompson, a nurse at my GP's surgery, was the first person to suggest there might be a connection between my tingling fingers and my back pain. After the operation she offered me a piece of advice which I adhere to every day, 'Always seek out the funny side to things.' In the United States the operation I had is sometimes known colloquially as 'numb butt syndrome', and some of the 'victims' are on heavy-duty drugs such as neurontin or gabapentin. I can cycle for up to fifteen minutes but then the ten-ton weight in my buttocks forces me to stop. I enjoy no true sensation from the neck down and find the only positive relief comes from a sports massage once a month with Liz Catterick, after which I feel 'grounded' for the only time in the month as if the muscles and the nerves are brought back into temporary alignment. Pilates exercises, which were developed for soldiers with back injuries in the Great War, are also a comfort. I take no medication. My legs feel unbelievably heavy as if they are wrapped in an astronaut's suit. Some days I walk better than on other days. I don't enjoy stopping and starting, so find walking round art galleries trying. The slightest incline along a pavement or corridor, which would have been unnoticeable before the operation, now forces me to change gears as if I was climbing a hill. Equally, while walking in a straight line is fine, avoiding people coming against me in the street is more of a struggle than you might imagine. With its wide pavements and flat paving stones, Chicago is the best city in the world for someone with my condition.

The thinking part of my brain, as if it was above the fray, has been unaffected by the operation. In *The Anatomy Lesson* (1983), a comic novel that in part explores the relationship between the mind that creates and the body that suffers, Philip Roth's protagonist Nathan Zuckerman wears an orthopaedic collar to ease the pain in his neck. On the first page we learn that 'Just having a neck, arms and shoulders was like carrying another person around.' Zuckerman has a pain in the neck; his rival and critic, Milton Appel, is to Zuckerman a pain in the neck. You can see how that phrase 'a pain in the neck', which is in turn associated with being Jewish, has enormous potential for humour and maudlin sentiment. After the operation, my body below the head has never been quite right and there are days when I like to imagine my left hand has been amputated, taking with it most of my pain. As a result of cutting and pulling back the muscles during the operation, my neck is weaker than it was and sometimes aches, but the acute pain is gone, and as long as I rest my head during the middle of the day I function without too much difficulty. At the end of a massage sometimes a masseuse will pull the head to stretch the spine. The first time that happened after the operation I thought my head might come away from the body, but was reassured when I stood up to discover I was still in one piece.

Roth has composed a witty novel about someone with a pain in the neck, but I don't believe he is describing a person who has had a tumour removed from inside the cervical part of the spine. Equally, if I had undergone heart surgery or suffered from lung disease, I might well have imagined, as Sterne does in *Tristram Shandy*, how 'Rumple the one, you rumple the other'. That for Sterne is a measure of the interdependence of the body and mind. But for me I look down at my body and think: 'This is my body. It is suffering now, but it is teaching me something, perhaps patience.' It hasn't yet been transformed into Yeats's 'dying animal'; that stage will come sooner or later. At the same time, my body says to me every day as if it registers I am a third child, 'Don't get above yourself or your station in life.' However, no matter how much my body has been rumpled it never rumples my mind. Patience knows how to triumph over agitation. If Thomas Willis, the pioneering seventeenth-century scientist and anatomist who is responsible for introducing the word 'neurology' into the English language, were ever to return, I would be surprised if he didn't seek me out as an interesting case-study.

Living with illness or with physical impairment is something I now have to face every day. Until I was fifty my body gave me no concern. Like most men I suspect, I just got on with life forgetting about it. Then, at fifty, everything changed. I developed Type II Diabetes and have been on tablets ever since. In due course I will have to go onto insulin. But as I walk down Coney Street in York or Grafton Street in Dublin, it occurs to me that most people above a certain age are probably taking tablets to keep them alive or in good health. I still have to undergo MRI scans on my spine; that should end in December 2011, nine years or so after the operation. I never complain. I lost a dear friend, Chris Weston, in 2010 to mesothelioma. He was my age and had worked for a time in the 1960s at York Carriage Works stripping out railway carriages. When he told me of his condition eighteen months before he died, Chris, who played the organ at his local Methodist church in Bishopthorpe, said in his droll way, 'Well, it was a good job I didn't develop the symptoms ten years ago.'

Even as I was recovering I was working on a third book for Yale, which was published in 2005 under the title *Light Freedom and Song*. The title obscured what was in fact a cultural history of modern Irish writing. I wanted it to be called 'The Harp without the Crown', but that did not meet with anyone's approval at Yale. It was the book I had been hoping to write all the way back to the early 1970s when I was at work on 'Anglo-Irish Literature and Society'. In terms of sales it hasn't proved the success that I was hoping for and, with all permission and reproduction fees counting against royalties as well as the Index, it will never earn me any money. It is, however, the book that fills me with the most pride, a book about the Irish dark and its afterlife. It was a struggle to write and is all about struggle, loss and struggle, and how this twin theme connects with the colonial encounter between the harp and the crown. In time perhaps it will attract to itself a readership; the reviews suggest this might happen. Now, as I write this in June 2011 after the collapse of the Irish economy, seems to be a singularly appropriate moment for a book about the responses by Irish writers in the past to the twin themes of loss and struggle, a book which shelters under an optimistic triplet for a title. Equally, I remind myself that when it was first published Richard Jefferies's *The Story of My Heart* was not read. My book, too, as I suggested in the section 'The loosening ties' in Chapter 4, is about the heart in ways that most of my other books are not.

*Reading Joyce*, which was published at the end of 2007, is a book about delay, and a tribute in its own to Tim Webb, my doctoral supervisor, but I wrote it very quickly in my last year of teaching. It came out soon after a collection of essays, *Joyce and Company*, was published by Continuum in 2006 (which included an essay on Willis, Sterne and Joyce). Philip Langeskov at Longman wanted a book on Joyce that would make the great writer more available to the general reader. This was the most fruitful exchange I had with an editor. I would send him down chapters and he would add copious notes, all of them designed to broaden the book's appeal. He urged me to make the book more personal by including anecdotes, personal reminiscences, and experiences from the classroom. I think drilling down into my reflections laid the foundations for the memoir you now have in your hands. I wrote *Reading Joyce* under Philip's eyes and I am for ever grateful to him, for it has proved very successful. The book design should have won awards, and the marketing of the book has been excellent. I was lucky to have such supportive people at Pearson Longman. It was my tenth book and I wrote it as a kind of farewell to teaching and to writing.

It wasn't quite the final farewell for I still had three more years acting as literary reviews editor for *estudiosirlandeses*, a Spanish internet Irish Studies journal edited by Rosa Gonzalez at the University of Barcelona. In February 2010 for Issue 5, at the end of my Introduction to the various reviews I had commissioned, I wrote:

This is an appropriate moment to thank all the reviewers for their contributions to this issue and all the previous five issues. It has been a pleasure and a privilege to work with so many different people from around the world who have given so generously of their time. This is also the place to thank Rosa Gonzalez for allowing me the space to carry out the reviews section for this journal over the last five years. That *estudiosirlandeses.org* is now a flourishing journal is down to Rosa. This is her achievement and her legacy, to have got something off the ground on behalf of the Spanish Association for Irish Studies (AEDEI) and to make the journal available without subscription to students and scholars across the globe. Indeed, wherever Irish Studies is taught, the name of this journal will be known. I told Rosa some time ago when I retired that I would be relinquishing my editorship. This is largely because I am no longer in sufficient contact with people in the field. I see new books in Irish Studies appearing almost every week, and I think to myself, 'I cannot do justice to the field now opening up. It's time to hand over the reins to someone who can.' So this is what I am now doing. As a footnote, you always know it's time to go when you start writing memoirs, and this is what I've been doing since October 2009.

What, then, have I learned about writing? Many things, and even as I complete these memoirs I am still learning, especially when reading the memoirs of others. In an entertaining account of a varied life, *Burning the Days* (1997), the American novelist James Salter returns at one point to the promissory note among his father's papers and casually observes, 'Despite all one knows, something clings to paper that once had value.' It is the use of 'clings' alongside 'paper' in the singular that resonates for me. 'Clings' is a word I use on only one occasion in my own account when my mother wouldn't let go of me in the reception hall of the John Fisher School. Salter puts the word to better use for 'clings' is a fairly obvious choice in that mothers invariably cling to their offspring. This ability to trigger things for the reader is particularly impressive in Salter's prose especially as such moments often arise suddenly out of descriptive passages which are fairly low-key. When you compile your own memoirs, you are for those months no longer a passive reader but somehow actively involved in the work of others, alighting on words and phrases that can be pressed into service in your own account. Thus, Salter reminds me how, on every page in what I've written here, there is something that clings to me and to my past. As for value, that too has an intriguing life of its own, moving between what happened in the past and what is recalled through the art of the memorialist, between the moment in time and the moment outside of time.

With a hint of something in his voice, Jacques Berthoud, a friend in York who used to run the English Department at the University, would say to me, 'O, you write easily, David'. If only he knew how much of a struggle it has been gaining admission to the school of eloquence, at least at first. Only now do I realise, or, rather, appreciate, the observation made by one of my teachers in an end-of-year report about my writing when I had just turned eight: 'Has an individual style'. For years I assumed that was a straightforward accolade and not something that could count against me. That teacher probably had the measure of me, as did Mr Bumptious in his report at the end of 1959: 'He has plenty to say and continued effort should bring fluency of style.'

However, I needed something else, and it had nothing to do with effort and everything to do with technology. That came in the shape of a second-hand *Apple* II Europlus, which I first laid my hands on in 1982 in my mid-thirties and which I had to use with the top off and a fan on because it was always overheating. It didn't take me long to learn to save every sentence – in both meanings of that phrase. Word-processing has been the making of me, for now I could set out a paragraph on a screen, scroll up and down, and rearrange sentences at will. The computer helped in this regard, for it broke what I imagined was the authentic link between hand and head. In the process it helped me to think straight, allowing me time to reflect and unhurriedly compose. I felt again the wind in my sail as, with renewed energy, I set about tacking and veering, revising and overcoming difficulty.

All of us make characteristic mistakes. I tend to drop a thought and then return to it, so the sequence in a paragraph would always need looking at. Equally, I would sometimes find it difficult to round off a paragraph, so I would move a sentence further up or add a more reasonable and less striking sentence by way of conclusion. Revising is one of the keys to good writing. That was something I learned from my year teaching in California, and especially from Roger Garrison's short introduction *How A Writer Works* (1981), which was recommended to me by Kirby Wilkins. Avoid overstating things. It's but a matter of courtesy to leave space for readers to respond in their own time and in their own way. Also, try reversing the claims made, for the opposite might be what you want to argue. Extremists remind us of something we all share: the mind often cannot distinguish truth from falsity or reality from fantasy. As my own memoir confirms, the mind needs checking or encouragement or just living with to discover its mooring or point of embarcation, and at times this may turn out to be nothing more than clarifying difficulties, or laying the groundwork for others, or settling on an appropriate metaphor. As ever, like church bells at night idly recording the passage of time, it is the movement back and forth that calls to me across the city of words.

You can never do enough, as Joyce constantly reminds us, but sometimes it takes the passage of time and a period of neglect to come to a decision about a word or phrase. For over six months my grandmother 'forced' the priest out of the house when he interrupted her house dance. But then in October 2010 it came to me that 'hunted', a word I frequently heard among my family in County Clare meaning to chase away, was a better choice. In Hiberno-English you will hear a sentence such as this: 'I was hunted out of the house by my father whenever I was late in the morning for school.' In Joyce's *Dubliners*,

Eveline's father used to hunt her in out of a nearby field with his blackthorn stick. The phrase 'sent packing' is more colloquial and inappropriate here, but it is the phrase I deliberately employ in a later chapter when I imagine people telling me to drop the idea of a vocation and where I recall the image of my grandmother grabbing hold of the priest's collar. The word 'forced' is neutral and more widely available to an international audience. However, 'hunted', with its threatening associations, hits the right note for what my grandmother did on that evening and on the earlier occasion with the Black and Tans. In revising a manuscript there is often a process of enrichment, and I particularly enjoy those little moments when I can add value and, hopefully, take my reader with me.

The final sentence I composed, my last act of settlement as it were, didn't come to me until the book was being typeset. It concerned my favourite aunt, Mary, the inhaler beside her, and how she would wonder aloud to me, 'How did we end up like this?' It was as if she was also saying, 'Was there nothing we could have done to prevent the conversation from ending? We've only just got going. How did we not see it coming?' I was struck as much by the rhetorical question as by her use of 'we', not 'I'. The remark took me back forty years and to chats we used to have together late into the night at Loughloon. With the embers of the turf fire slowly dying out on the floor-level hearth, she would recall a passage in the history of the family or parish. Our attention was periodically interrupted by manic runs across the flagstones of impossible-to-catch *ciarogs*, those night-time beetles who were also asserting their claims to tenancy. While she didn't know it, in that quietly engaging comment on her condition at the end, I like to imagine she was summing up the passing of a whole generation, my own included, overtaken now by the forces of history. With so much optimism behind us, augmented by so much hope in my case, how, indeed, did we end up like this?

In the last week of October 2010, twelve months after writing the first sentence about my wife, my mother died. It had been expected ever since we learnt from a cardiologist in early September that the aorta valve to the heart had badly calcified. She was seven weeks short of her eighty-ninth birthday. I decided to change nothing about the tenses of the verbs here and have left as they are all the references to her being alive in various places in this memoir. *Stet*. I wrote the book in her shadow but I didn't write it for her. The faith she acquired all those years ago in Caherbarna sustained her throughout her life. She lived an exemplary life and she died peacefully in her sleep. In her final year she resisted all our attempts at persuading her to go into a care home. 'Yes, I will do at some stage, but not yet,' she would say. If my father was perverse, my mother was obstinate, more so in her last years. I loved that about both of them, and I loved them equally.

As children we were 'thrown into existence', as I suggest in chapter 2, but there the Heideggerian anxiety ends, for we were thrown into existence 'in sequence', with my elder brother in winter, my sister in spring, me in high summer and my younger brother in autumn. In this way our lives were spread out like the seasons but also held together in a continuing and sometimes lively and competitive embrace. I wish, however, my parents had accompanied me into my own old age if only to hear their chuckle on the end of the telephone line in reply to one of my openers such as 'Still there, then?' or 'Got your teeth in?'

This is how I end the eulogy I wrote for her funeral on 12 November 2010:

> In common with her surviving siblings, Bridie was a survivor. She was the fourth in a line that began with Patrick, born in 1912, Margaret Spratt, born in 1917, John, born in 1919, Bridie herself, born in 1921, and Mary Haugh, born in 1923. And she was the last of that generation to survive. As we bid her a fond and a last formal farewell, she would want us to recall that line, that family, that house in that village we sometimes used to call 'the back of beyond'. She came to England at the tender age of fifteen and she lived nearly all her life in Worthing, but there wouldn't have been a day when Caherbarna, a word which means in English something like the townland of the gap, was missing from her thoughts. The music of that place and the liveliness, energy and caring of its people were with her throughout her life. May you, Bridie, together with your beloved husband and your dear brothers and sisters and all the faithful departed, live for ever! May there never be a day when you are not in our thoughts!

I know a book is complete when every sentence, every thought that is, is in its rightful place, its claimed spot, and, with the death of my mother, it is just that. The catch is down, the house shut behind me for the last time. She clings to me as she did when I first went away to school at the age of eleven, only now it's me with outstretched arms.

The first draft of the book you are reading was completed in under twelve months. Over a hundred thousand words composed in around fifty two weeks. That's around two thousand words a week, or two hundred and fifty words a day. And that doesn't take into account holidays, weekends away, or illness. It was followed by another twelve months spent on revisions and adding a further thirty five thousand words. I am speaking to you now, an author to his or her reader, but I can't hear you, and all this silence is getting to me. It's time I finished. But before I do so I want to reflect in a final postscript on what I wanted to say all along.

Postscript

# What I Meant to Say All Along

History tells us only so much. Some questions it cannot address or answer. Here in this memoir I have sought to broaden the idea of what happens in time to include moments frozen or outside of time, moments in time which seem to envelop us and which contain us. I am pushing my teddy along a road into the sun. No one is with me and I feel no anxiety about being lost. It's a moment that will always live in a haze of sunshine at the hinterland of consciousness and almost entirely without a supporting cast. The only chronology it belongs to is one that is retrospectively activated by me. Or consider the photo taken when I was eleven at the John Fisher School. It's a moment in time activated in this case by a photo. I want it desperately to speak to me. Without this photo there would be no moment for me. I have no idea what I was thinking, but it's one of my favourite photos. I seem to be at ease with myself, rooted, conscious of being photographed, as if the moment would capture something of me for posterity or the afterlife. The river we know as history flows on but that moment in time in a peculiar way lives for me. I wonder where that boy went to when he abandoned me. Whenever I take that photo down to look at I feel a dreadful ache or wrench inside, an ache which I acknowledge exists for me alone and for no one else.

From my earliest memories to writing my last book I have a trodden a path through time. Memoirs have a habit of staying close to a chronology even if they occasionally skirt over things or betray a false memory. The self lives through time, but at some points in my life I stepped outside the self and doubled back on time. I am held in time or rather I hold time still for enough time for it to become timeless. There are occasions in these memoirs such as pushing my teddy when I am caught between the experience and its decontextualisation, as if I was fated to follow, in the words of Philip Larkin, the 'blind impress' on the cover of a book, unsure of either origin or destination or meaning. At other times as with my John Fisher photo I am unable to access what I was thinking and yet I know that boy went away and vanished into thin air and that I regret his passing.

As I write this postscript, I discover that some things are easier to understand. You look back on your life and you can say not only this happened but this is me, this is my character and personality. It doesn't lie in the future. It's no longer 'unguessable'. It's all here in the past, the distinction between purpose and result, which I had struggled with in Latin classes at school, now idle or largely irrelevant. Whatever I've done or achieved, this is me. This the path, the apprenticeship, I took. There is no hiding, at least in one respect. If, following Newman, I could provide the 'true key to my whole life', it would be buried somewhere here in what I've written. In this sense, my life, a life set within a context of writing, resembles a text awaiting interpretation, or, looked at from another perspective, it shapes itself as a piece of writing within a certain genre, an exercise in life writing as well as an example of such writing, given over now to others.

On the positive side in my defence, like a good Pierce I ploughed my own furrow, lived for most of my life in a 'State of Opulency', took what I needed by way of intellectual nourishment, and came to my own conclusions. I never went to war, never made anyone redundant in my place of work, and never trampled on anyone to advance my career. However, like my father, I was never very good at joining in and I have a tendency to walk away from things. I believe this is connected with something else. Although I have written over ten scholarly books, I have lived and breathed for the most part outside the academy. I refused, that is, to pursue an academic career which would take me to the top. Without sounding too dramatic, and it must be pretty obvious from all that I have written here, I can honestly say that I don't really belong, preferring the status of outsider.

If I was a biographer of my own life, I could have made more of the class nature of such an attitude, disposition, and, indeed, way of being. The outsider theme, for example, is there from the beginning and it recurs throughout this memoir. There was never a time when I did not know my place. In the deepest reaches of my soul, seemingly the moment I was born in that tenement house on Newland Road, I had absorbed that I owed the world everything and at the same time nothing. On the other hand, I owe it to my mother that exclusion didn't destroy me. I share her emotional attachment to Ireland and the house of music, and it is through her that I developed a strong sense of a sympathetic imagination, a form of belonging that is. It clearly wasn't enough. Indeed, as this memoir underscores, belonging has its own drawbacks, and it partly accounts for my being a slow learner and why my apprenticeship has been longer than should have been the case. If the truth be known, I didn't prefer the status of outsider; it was assigned to me.

Thomas Hardy expressed the hope that he could escape from life with integrity. The poems to his first wife written in 1912-13 convey the angst he felt for her. 'Woman much missed,' he writes after her death, the woman he left forty years before, 'how you call to me, call to me'. The years in between must have made him reflect seriously on the self through time and on how he had behaved toward those once dearest to him. The path not taken, when I abandoned what I imagined was a vocation to the priesthood, haunted me in the early part of my life, but I got over it and recovered my sense of purpose and equanimity. In contrast with Hardy and the call of his first wife, my former life in the seminary, while it has commanded my attention here, never calls to me.

Hardy's sense of guilt and therefore loss is draped in the cerements of the nineteenth century. Integrity for me took a different form and largely focused on the self through time, the underground stream that is. What I meant to say in these memoirs is that in my twenties the self lost its intensity when I started teaching. On reflection, this is what my memoirs are telling me, and it defines itself as a question. What happened to the tension between the self and the soul when my teaching career began in earnest after 1974? The tension within seemed to be a luxury I couldn't afford in the classroom. This must be a common experience, how the self is partially dissolved when the world of work arrives and less authentic behaviour takes over. I say 'less authentic' but I'm not sure if that's right, for that implies the authentic self is the self when young and at its most intense. But supposing the self gives way to equanimity and supposing equanimity is what the young self is struggling to find? Then the outline and direction deserve to be re-imagined not in terms of the romantic self but in terms of the mature self that of necessity had to struggle before it could come into its own.

I could make more of the theme of happenstance or paths not taken, but writing about my life and times has reminded me of something else. Most of this book is taken up with the first third of my life. At the end of *Reveries Over Childhood and Youth* (1916), the first volume of his autobiography, Yeats entertains the idea that life is a preparation for something that never happens. It must be confessed that there is something disproportionate about the time it takes to grow up, and Yeats, like me, was a slow learner. But all that prelude and apprenticeship stuff is so important to allow us scope to judge properly who we are and where we came from. Seemingly, we need time as human beings to understand the world. The mind in particular needs educating and so too does the heart. What is bewildering for many of us who are above a certain age is that no sooner do we obtain an uncluttered view ahead of us than we have to pass the baton to the next generation. That is one of nature's tricks, like milk teeth, and in its own way, because so late in the day, quite unexpected, and for that reason it feels not unlike a form of betrayal. Elegies provide some kind of support, but we rarely seem prepared for the afterlife – and yet the afterlife is all around us, waiting to catch us out or strike us down.

A memoir, then, is a postscript to a prelude. After all that has been written there's something else to add, at times merely informative, at other times touching and profound. PS I've left the key next door. PS I love you. As we invoke the retrospective faculty, we discover that life is not unlike a postscript to a prelude. It started so full of promise, in a hinterland of consciousness, followed by a blaze of sunshine. Or to alter the metaphor, it begins like a prelude with music and ends with some final words penned at the end of a note or letter. PS Think of me when I'm gone. Or, taking our cue from the title to a popular song, PS Please don't talk of me when I'm gone. But even as I write this, for nothing is ever quite concluded, there is something else that intrigues me. Who can tell the moment when the prelude ended and the postscript began?

I have spent a long time on me in these memoirs, so let me return at the end to my immediate family. Nearly forty of my sixty odd years I have been married to Mary. Two-thirds of my life with one person, and when our son, Matthew, was born in 1978 he came to occupy a half of my life. Modern marriage has worked for me, and without my lifetime partner and son I would have cut a sorry figure, drifting in and out of relationships, many of which would I am sure have left me with a sense of guilt. Without her I would have had to face the fell demons which seemed to inhabit my underlying self. Without her there would have been no memoir. The stability and equanimity

I feel nearly all the time is due to the person I first caught sight of in an anonymous classroom on a university campus in the north of England in the autumn of 1971. It was but a chance encounter because I might never have returned to Lancaster after my Spanish interlude. Much else in my life has come and gone but she has remained a constant figure and presence, and if she doesn't feature much in the pages of this memoir that's because she asked me not to include her. But everything I've written here constitutes a tribute to her for sharing so much with me.

# Acknowledgements

In writing this memoir I have incurred debts to a number of people, some of whom read and commented on parts of the manuscript, some of whom supplied me with missing information or put me right on a particular memory, and some of whom gave me general encouragement. Let me thank them all: my sister, Christine, and brother, John, my Australian cousins, Kathryn Warren and Pat Daryan, my Irish cousin, Margaret Davis, Robert and Kay Dunleavy, who added important pieces to the story about Caherbarna, Claire Hobbs, Jörg Rademacher, Pauline Hall, Philip Langeskov, Robert Baldock, Robin Butlin, Rosa Gonzalez in Barcelona and Constanza del Rio Álvar in Zaragoza, Peter Beirne, Local Studies Librarian at Clare County Library, Dan and Alice Harper, Bill Grant, Carole Kealiher, Jo Hilton, Helen Sinar, Chris Barker, Harry Marten, Jim McCord, Eileen O'Carroll and Rina Giulivi. James McGrath kindly read and commented on an early draft of the whole manuscript. Alistair Stead, who has been like a mentor to me over the years, also gave me valuable advice and encouragement. As ever, my greatest debt is to my wife, Mary, and my son, Matt. For eighteen months and more they have patiently watched another book take shape in their sitting room, its author seemingly engaged in retreating even further from the world. I hope their patience has not been in vain. An extract from chapter 9 appeared in the 2012 issue of *www.estudiosirlandeses.org*, the Spanish internet journal devoted to Irish Studies. Finally, thanks also to Jeremy Thompson and all his team at Matador.

# Select Bibliography

## Titles by David Pierce

*Attitudes to Class in the English Novel* (with Mary Eagleton) (London: Thames and Hudson, 1979).

*W. B. Yeats: A Guide Through the Critical Maze* (Bristol: Bristol Classical Press, 1989).

*James Joyce's Ireland* (London and New Haven: Yale University Press, 1992).

*James Joyces Irland* (trans Jörg Rademacher and Cristoforo Sweeger) (Köln and Basel: Bruckner and Thünker, 1996).

*Yeats's Worlds: Ireland, England and the Poetic Imagination* (London and New Haven: Yale University Press, 1995).

*Sterne in Modernism/Postmodernism* (co-editor with Peter de Voogd) (Amsterdam: Rodopi, 1996).

*W.B.Yeats: Critical Assessments* 4 Vols (Robertsbridge: Helm Information, 2000).

*The House of Music and the Cupboard Under the Stairs* (Privately Printed, 2000).

*Irish Writing in the Twentieth Century: A Reader* (Cork: Cork University Press, 2001).

*Light, Freedom and Song: A Cultural History of Modern Irish Writing* (London and New Haven: Yale University Press, 2005).

*Joyce and Company* (London: Continuum, 2006).

*Reading Joyce* (Harlow: Pearson Longman, 2007).

## Books and Audio Cited

Aaron, Richard, *The Theory of Universals* (Oxford: Clarendon, 1952).

Allen, Thomas, *History of the Counties of Surrey and Sussex* 2 vols (London: I.T. Hinton, Holdworth and Ball, 1829).

Anon., *The Comic Lindley Murray; Or The Grammar of Grammars, With Illustrative Sketches* (Dublin: A. Murray, 1871).

Aquinas, Thomas, *Truth*, vol. 3: 21-29 (trans Robert W. Mulligan, James V. McGlynn, Robert W. Schmidt) (Chicago: H.Regnery, 1952-1954).

Auden, W.H., *Spain* (London: Faber and Faber, 1937).

Bacon, G.W., *New Large Scale Atlas of the British Isles* (London, 1881).

Beauvoir, Simone de, *Memoirs of a Dutiful Daughter* (trans James Kirkup) (1958; London: Penguin Classics, 2006).

Berger, Peter L, Brigitte Berger, and Hansfried Kellner, *The Homeless Mind: Modernization and Consciousness* (Harmondsworth: Penguin, 1974).

*Blue Guide England* 10th edition (ed Ian Ousby) (London: A & C Black; New York: WW Norton, 1989).

Brenan, Gerald, *The Spanish Labyrinth: The Social and Political Background of the Spanish Civil War* (1943; Cambridge: Cambridge University Press, 1962).

Bronte, Emily, *Wuthering Heights* (1847; London: Penguin Classics, 2003).

Browning, Robert, *Selected Poems* (ed Daniel Karlin) (London: Penguin Modern Classics, 2004).

Buber, Martin, *I and Thou* (trans Ronald Gregor Smith) (1923; London: Continuum, 2008).

Bunyan, John, *Grace Abounding to the Chief of Sinners* (1666; London: Penguin, 2006).

Bunyan, John, *The Pilgrim's Progress* (1678; London: Faber, 1947).

Burns, Emile, ed., *A Handbook of Marxism* (London: Gollancz, 1935).

Burns, Robert, *Poems Chiefly in the Scottish Dialect* (Glasgow: Cameron, 1804).

Campbell, Thomas, *The Pleasures of Hope; With other Poems* (Edinburgh: Mundell, 1799).

Carter, Angela, *The Bloody Chamber* (London: Vintage, 1979).

Carver, Raymond, *Will You Please Be Quiet, Please?* (1976; London: Vintage, 2003).

*The Catholic Directory of England and Wales 2007* (Manchester: Gabriel Communications, 2007).

Cervantes, Miguel de, *Don Quixote* (trans John Rutherford) (1604-5, 1615; London: Penguin, 2003).

Cluysenaar, Anne, *Introduction to Literary Stylistics* (London: Batsford, 1976).

Cooper, James Fenimore, *The Last of the Mohicans* (Introduction Donald Ringe) (1823; London: Penguin Classics, 2006).

Coplestone, Frederick, *A History of Philosophy* (London: Burns and Oates, 1946-1975).

Copley, Gordon J, ed., *Camden's Britannia: Surrey and Sussex From the Edition of 1789 by Richard Gough* (London: Hutchinson, 1977).

Copper, Bob, *A Song for Every Season* (London: William Heinemann, 1971).

Corbett, Jim, *Man-Eaters of Kumaon* (London: Oxford University Press, 1944).

Davis, Thomas, *National and Historical Ballads, Songs, and Poems* (Dublin: James Duffy, 1846).

Dean, Stephen, *Laudate* (Brandon, Suffolk: Decani, 1999).

Dickens, Charles, *Nicholas Nickleby* (Introduction Mark Ford) (1839; London: Penguin Classics, 2003).

Dickens, Charles, *David Copperfield* (1850; London: Penguin, 2007).

Dickens, Charles, *Great Expectations* (ed Margaret Cardwell (1860-1; Oxford: World's Classics, 2008)).

Dillard, Annie, *The Writing Life* (New York: Harper & Row, 1989).

Donne, John, *The Complete English Poems* (London: Penguin Classics, 2004).

Dreiser, Theodore, *Sister Carrie* (1900; London: Penguin, 1995).

Dubay, Thomas, *The Seminary Rule* (Cork: The Mercier Press, 1953).

Dutton, Hely, *Statistical Survey of the County of Clare* (Dublin: Dublin Society, 1808).

Dylan, Bob, *Chronicles Volume One* (London: Simon & Schuster, 2004).

Eliot, T.S., *Complete Poems and Plays* (London: Faber and Faber, 2004).

Eliot, T.S., *Selected Prose of T.S.Eliot* (ed Frank Kermode) (London: Faber and Faber, 1975).

Evans, E. Estyn, *Irish Folk Ways* (London and Boston, Mass: Routledge and Kegan Paul, 1957).

Forster, E.M., *Howards End* (Introduction David Lodge) (1910: London: Penguin Classics, 2000).

Friel, Brian, *Dancing at Lughnasa* (London: Faber, 1990).

Galbraith, J.K., *The Affluent Society* (London: Hamish Hamilton, 1958).

Garrison, Roger, *How A Writer Works* (New York: Harper and Row, 1981).

Gaughan, Dick, *Handful of Earth* LP record (London: Topic, 1989).

Gent, Thomas, *The Ancient and Modern History of the Famous City of York; and in a Particular Manner of its Magnificent Cathedral, Commonly Called York Minster* (York: 1730).

Gibbon, Lewis Grassic, *A Scots Quair* (Introduction Tom Crawford) (1932-4; Edinburgh: Canongate, 2008).

Golding, William, *Lord of the Flies* (London: Faber and Faber, 1954).

Goldmann, Lucien, *The Hidden God* (trans Philip Thody) (London: Routledge and Kegan Paul, 1964).

Graver, Brian, *Advanced English Practice* (Oxford: Oxford University Press, 1963).

Gray, Thomas, *Elegy in a Country Churchyard and Other Poems* (1751; London: Penguin, 2009).

Gregory, Lady Augusta, *Visions and Beliefs in the West of Ireland* (London: John Murray, 1920).

Hardy, Thomas, *Selected Poetry* (ed Samuel Hynes) (Oxford: Oxford World's Classics, 2009).

Harper, Michael S., *History Is Your Own Heartbeat* (Urbana, Chicago, London: University of Illinois Press, 1971).

Harrison, Tony, *Selected Poems* (London: Penguin, 2006).

Hazard, Paul, *The European Mind 1680-1715* (trans J. Lewis May) (Harmondsworth: Penguin, 1964).

Heller, Joseph, *Catch-22* (1961; London: Corgi, 1964).

Hemingway, Ernest, *Fiesta: The Sun Also Rises* (1924; London: Vintage, 2005).

Hobbes, Thomas, *Leviathan* (Introduction C.B. MacPherson) (1651; London: Penguin, 2002).

Höhne, Horst, *Ein Ding von Schönheit ist ein Glück auf immer: Gedichte der englischen und schottischen Romantik* (Leipzig: Reclam, 1983).

Hooley, Thomas, *A Seminary in the Making: Being a History of the Foundation and Early Years of St John's Diocesan Seminary, Wonersh* (London: Longmans, Green, 1927).

Hopkins, Gerard Manley, *The Major Works* (ed Catherine Phillips) (Oxford: Oxford University Press, 2009).

Hudson, W.H., *Nature in Downland* (London: Longmans, 1900).

Huxley, Aldous, *Brave New World* (1932; Harmondsworth: Penguin Modern Classics, 1969).

Ibañez, Paco, *La Poesia Española de Ahora y de Siempre* LP record (Madrid: MosheNaim, 1968).

Isherwood, Christopher, *Goodbye to Berlin* (1939; London: Vintage, 1989).

Jara, Victor, *Manifiesto; Chile September 1973* (Transatlantic Records, 1974).

Jefferries, Richard, *Wild Life in a Southern County* (1879; London: Jonathan Cape, 1940).

Jefferries, Richard, *The Story of My Heart: My Autobiography* (1883; London: Quartet Books, 1979).

Jefferries, Richard, *Field and Hedgerow: Being the Last Essays of Richard Jefferies* (collected by his widow) (London: Longmans, 1888).

Joyce, James, *Dubliners* (1914; London: Penguin Modern Classics, 2000).

Joyce, James, *A Portrait of the Artist as a Young Man* (1916; London: Penguin Modern Classics, 2000).

Joyce, James, *Ulysses: The 1922 Text* (ed Jeri Johnson) (1922; Oxford: Oxford University Press, 2008).

Joyce, James, *Finnegans Wake* (1939; London: Faber and Faber, 1964).

Keats, John, *The Complete Poems* (ed John Barnard) (London: Penguin Classics, 2003).

*Kelly's Directory of Worthing* (London, 1912).

*Kelly's Directory of Worthing* (London, 1962).

*Kelly's Sussex Directory* (1909).

Kempis, Thomas à, *The Imitation of Christ* (ca 1418; London: Dent, 1960).

Kierkegaard, Soren, *Concluding Unscientific Postscript* (1845; Cambridge: Cambridge University Press, 2009).

Kipling, Rudyard, *The Five Nations* (London: Methuen, 1903).

Kroeber, Theodora, *Ishi in Two Worlds: A Biography of the Last Wild Indian in North America* (Berkeley: University of California Press, 1961).

Langland, William, *Piers Plowman: A New Translation of the B-Text* (trans A.V.C Schmidt) (Oxford: World's Classics, 2009).

Larkin, Philip, *Collected Poems* (London: Faber, 2003).

Lawrence, D.H., *The Rainbow* (Introduction James Wood) (1915; London: Penguin Classics, 2007).

Lawrence, D.H., *Selected Poems* (ed James Fenton) (London: Penguin Classics, 2008).

Leech, Geoffrey, *English in Advertising* (London: Longman, 1966).

Leavis, F.R., *The Great Tradition: George Eliot, Henry James, Joseph Conrad* (London: Chatto and Windus, 1948).

Lewis, George Cornewall, *On Local Disturbances in Ireland: and On the Irish Church Question* (London: B.Fellowes, 1836).

Lonergan, Bernard, *Insight: A Study of Human Understanding* (London: Longman, Green, 1958).

Lowry, Malcolm, *Under the Volcano* (1947; London: Penguin, 2000).

Luthin, Herbert W., ed., *Surviving Through The Days: A California Indian Reader* (Berkeley and Los Angeles: University of California Press, 2002).

Maritain, Jacques, *The Degrees of Knowledge* (London: G. Bles, Centenary Press, 1937).

Marten, Harry, *But That Didn't Happen to You* (Gambier, Ohio: Xoxox, 2006).

Melville, Herman, *Moby Dick: Or, The Whale* (Introduction Andrew Delbanco) (1851; London: Penguin, 2003).

Mill, John Stuart, *Autobiography* (1873; London: Penguin, 2006).

Moore, Thomas, *A Selection of Irish Melodies with Symphonies and Accompaniments by Sir John Stevenson*, 6th Number (London and Dublin: J. Power's, 1815).

Morrison, Arthur, *Tales of Mean Streets* (1894; London: Faber, 2008).

Morrison, Arthur, *A Child of the Jago* (1896; London: Faber, 2008).

Morrison, Toni, *Beloved* (London: Chatto and Windus, 1987).

Moustaki, Georges, *Bobino* LP record (Polydor, 1970).

Murray, Lindley, *English Grammar, Adapted to the Different Classes of Learners* (York: Printed and Sold by Wilson, Spence, and Mawman, 1795).

Nabokov, Vladimir, *Speak, Memory: An Autobiography Revisited* (1951; New York: Vintage, 1989).

Nashe, Thomas, *The Unfortunate Traveller and Other Works* (London: Penguin Classics, 2006).

Newman, John Henry, *Apologia Pro Vita Sua* (1864; Harmondsworth: Penguin, 1994).

O'Casey, Sean, *Autobiographies* (London: Macmillan, 1963).

O'Neill, Joseph, *Netherland* (London: Fourth Estate, 2008).

Otto, Rudolf, *The Idea of the Holy : An Inquiry Into the Non-Rational Factor in the Idea of the Divine and its Relation to the Rational* (trans John W.Harvey) (London: Oxford University Press, 1923).

*Patrick Kelly from Cree Fiddle Music* cd (Published by Patrick Kelly's family, 2004).

Petre, M.D., *Autobiography and Life of George Tyrrell* 2 Volumes (London: Edward Arnold, 1912).

*Post Office London Directory* (1902).

Quevedo, Francisco de, *Selected Poetry of Francisco de Quevedo: A Bilingual Edition* (ed and trans Christopher Johnson) (Chicago: Chicago University Press, 2009).

Renan, Ernest, *La Vie de Jésus: Histoire des Origines du Christianisme. Livre premier* (Paris: Michel Lévy Frères, 1863).

Renan, Ernest, *Souvenirs d'enfance et de jeunesse* (1883; Paris: Gallimard, 2007).

Roth, Philip, *The Anatomy Lesson* (1983; London: Jonathan Cape, 1984).

Rowntree, Seebohm, *Poverty: A Study of Town Life* (London: Macmillan, 1901).

Russell, Micho, *Traditional Country Music of County Clare* cd (Free Reed, 2008).

Sallinger, J.D., *Catcher in the Rye* (1951; London: Penguin, 2010).

Salter, James, *Burning the Days: Recollection* (1997; London: Picador, 2007).

Schevill, James, *The Complete American Fantasies* (Athens, Ohio: Ohio University Press, 1996).

Shelley, Percy Bysshe, *The Necessity of Atheism* (Worthing: C. and W. Phillips, 1811).

Sinclair, Upton, *The Jungle* (1906; London: Penguin, 1986).

Slater, Philip, *The Pursuit of Loneliness* (London: Allen Lane, 1971).

Smith, Carole, *The Almshouses of York* (York: Quacks Books, 2011).

Steedman, Carolyn, *Landscape for a Good Woman: A Story of Two Lives* (London: Virago, 1986).

Sterne, Laurence, *The Life and Opinions of Tristram Shandy, Gentleman* (eds Melvyn New and Joan New) (1759-68; Gainesville, Florida: The University Presses of Florida, 1978).

Sterne, Laurence, *A Sentimental Journey* (ed Paul Goring) (1768; London: Penguin Classics, 2005).

*The Florida Edition of the Works of Laurence Sterne Volume VII The Letters Part I 1739-1764 and Volume VIII The Letters 1765-1768* (eds Melvyn New and Peter de Voogd) (Gainesville, Florida: University Press of Florida, 2009).

Thomas, Dylan, *Under Milk Wood* (1954; London: Penguin Classics, 2000).

Thomas, Edward, *The South Country* (1906; London: J.M. Dent, 1993).

Updike, John, *Endpoint and Other Poems* (London: Hamish Hamilton, 2009).

Urquhart, Jane, *Away* (London: Bloomsbury, 1994).

Webb, Beatrice, *My Apprenticeship* (1926; London: Penguin Classics, 1971).

Wilde, Oscar, *The Importance of Being Earnest* (1895; London: Penguin, 2007).

Williams, Raymond, *The English Novel from Dickens to Lawrence* (London: Chatto and Windus, 1970).

Willis, N.P. and J.S.Coyne (illustrations by W.H.Bartlett), *The Scenery and Antiquities of Ireland* 2 vols (London: George Virtue, 1844).

Willis, Thomas, *Cerebri Anatome Cui Accessit Nervorum Descriptio Et Usus Studio* (Amsterdam: Gerbrandum Schagen, 1666).

Wordsworth, William, *The Prelude* (1805; London: Penguin, 2004).

*York's Mystery Plays* (eds Richard Beadle and Pamela M.King) (Oxford: Oxford World's Classics, 1999).

Yeats, William Butler, *Reveries Over Childhood and Youth* (London: Macmillan, 1916).

Yeats, William Butler, *Selected Poems* (ed Timothy Webb) (London: Penguin Modern Classics, 2000).

Young, Don, *Wire as a Weapon* (Paducah, Kentucky: Turner, 1996).

Yourcenar, Marguerite, *How Many Years* (trans Maria Louise Ascher and Aidan Ellis) (1977; London: Virago, 1995).

# Index